THE GUINNESS BOOK OF

500 NUMBER ONE HITS

JO & TIM RICE
PAUL GAMBACCINI
MIKE READ

GRRR BOOKS
EDITORIAL ASSOCIATE: STEVE SMITH

GUINNESS SUPERLATIVES LIMITED
2 CECIL COURT, LONDON ROAD, ENFIELD,
MIDDLESEX

ACKNOWLEDGEMENTS

The four authors would like to thank many of the artists featured in this book for their interest and co-operation. We have referred from time to time to other rock publications, as well as the British Museum Library for original sources of information on many of the number ones in the early years. Among the authors whose works we have consulted are Paul Flattery, Simon Frith, Charlie Gillett, John Goldrosen, Phil Hardy, Jerry Hopkins, Derek Jewell, Dave Laing, Chris May, Joseph Murrells, Norm N Nite, Tim Phillips, Melvin Shestack, Joel Whitburn and Ian Whitcomb. However, any mistakes in the book are ours not theirs.

The copyright and archive sections of CBS, PRT, RCA, EMI, Red Bus and Decca have also in particular been helpful, and as usual the BBC allowed at least two of our number to burrow unmolested through their record library, for which we are grateful. We are also grateful for the help of Bob Altschuler, Karen Everly, Milt Gabler, Steve Hoffman, Peter Robinson, and Alan Warner.

Finally, we wish to acknowledge the work of Eileen Heinink, and the vast typing efforts of Jan Rice, without whom this book would still be in longhand.

Editor: *Alex E Reid*
Designer: *David Roberts*

Second impression 1982

Published in Great Britain by
Guinness Superlatives Ltd,
2 Cecil Court, London Road, Enfield, Middlesex

British Library Cataloguing in Publication Data
The Guinness book of 500 number one hits.
1. Music, Popular (Songs, etc.)—Great
Britain—Discography
I. Rice, Jo
016.7899 1245 ML156.4.P6

ISBN 0-85112-250-7

Typeset by Sprint, Beckenham, Kent
Printed and bound in Great Britain by Hazell Watson and Viney Ltd, Aylesbury, Bucks.

CONTENTS

Acknowledgements 2

Introduction 5

THE FIVE HUNDRED NUMBER ONES:

PART ONE: Listed Chronologically .6
The 500 number one hits listed chronologically, with full details of artist, catalogue number, writer, producer, the date it reached the top and the number of weeks at number one. Plus a few words about each record.

PART TWO: Alphabetically by Artist 227
The 319 artists listed alphabetically, with their number one hits listed for ease of cross reference with Parts One and Three.

PART THREE: Alphabetically by Title 245
The 500+ titles that make up the 500 number one hit records, listed alphabetically by title with the artists' names and year of reaching the top. Different versions of the same song, and different songs with the same title, are indicated.

PART FOUR: Facts and Feats 251
Including all the statistics you could wish to know about the records, artists, writers, producers and record labels that have been at number one.

THE HITS
Most Number One Hits 252 *Most Weeks at Number One* 252 *Most consecutive Number Ones* 252-3 *Most Weeks at Number One in One Calendar Year* 253 *Longest stay at Number One by One Record* 253 *First two hits at Number One* 254 *First three hits at Number One* 254 *Straight in at Number One* 254 *One Hit Wonders* 254 *Fastest Number One Hit* 256 *Slowest Number One Hit: Artist* 256 *Slowest Number One Hit: Disc* 256 *Gap between Number One Hits* 256 *Last hit at Number One* 257 *Most weeks on Chart by a Number One Disc* 257 *Fewest Weeks on Chart by a Number One Disc* 257 *Double sided Number One Hits* 257 *Records that returned to Number One* 258 *Records that have been top equal* 259 *Longest titles of Number One Hits* 259 *Shortest titles of Number One Hits* 259

THE RECORD LABELS
Most Number One Hits 260 *Most weeks at Number One* 260 *Consecutive Label Catalogue Numbers at Number One* 260

THE WRITERS
Most Successful Writers 261 *Writers of Consecutive Number One Hits* 261 *Most Versatile Writers* 262

THE PRODUCERS
Most Number Ones 262 *Most Number Ones with Different Acts* 262 *Consecutive Number Ones* 263

INTRODUCTION

It has been almost thirty years since the first British record sales chart was published, by the New Musical Express on 14 November 1952. In those thirty years, the chart has grown from a Top 12 to a Top 75, over 8000 recordings have become hit singles and almost 2000 different recording acts have been able to claim at least one week's glory as a chart act. But of those 8000 recordings over 30 years, only 500 have made it all the way to number one, and only a few more than 300 of the 2000 chart acts can accurately claim to be 'number one hit recording stars', although over the years many more than 300 have made that claim.

In this book, we are not putting forward theories or solving the problem of how to create a number one hit. The facts — and for the first time as far as GRRR Books is concerned, some opinions—in this book do not explain, for example, why **Up Town Top Ranking** reached number one, while **Let It Be** did not. It does not explain why Georgie Fame had three solo number one hits, but never had another hit in the Top 10. It does not try to tell the Who, Rick Nelson or Billy Fury where they went wrong in failing to come up with a number one hit. It does not explain why Norrie Paramor produced so many chart-toppers, nor why Jonathan King has not produced a single one.

All we are doing is celebrating 500 British Number One Hits. From Al Martino to Nicole, they are all here. The history of British pop follows no clear path, and that is why the Temperance Seven and Benny Hill can reach the top just as often as the Hollies or Eddie Cochran. The list of artistes includes male vocalists, female vocalists, male vocal groups, female vocal groups, mixed vocal groups, instrumentalists both male and female, instrumental groups, military bands, comedians, session musicians, cartoon characters and film stars. It includes the English, Scots, Welsh and Irish, Americans, Swedes, Greeks, West Indians, Spaniards, Australians, French, Israelis and Canadians. The list of writers of the number ones includes Rodgers and Hammerstein, Lerner and Loewe, Pomus and Shuman, Lieber and Stoller, Lennon and McCartney, Rice and Lloyd Webber, Jagger and Richard, Andersson and Ulvaeus, Gamble and Huff, Crewe and Gaudio, deKnight and Freedman, Bacharach and David, Martin and Coulter, Cook and Greenaway, Chapman and Chinn, Gibb, Gibb and Gibb and trad. Some records have reached number one in the week of release, some have taken years. Some have been over 5 minutes long, some last less than 2 minutes. There is no pattern, no formula, no similarity linking them all. The only thing they have in common is that for some time, whether it was 1 week or 18 weeks, they were the biggest selling record in the nation.

We hope that this book will add a little more information to the catalogues of chart success that we have produced in the past. Further editions of the *Guinness Book of British Hit Singles* will chart the progress of records which will make the number one spot in years to come, and also of those which fail to make the very top and have to be satisfied with a lower rung of the ladder. About the year 2012, we hope to be bringing out the *Guinness Book Of One Thousand Number One Hits*, and by then even Cliff Richard will be in his seventies.

JO RICE
TIM RICE
PAUL GAMBACCINI
MIKE READ

PART 1

The Five Hundred Number Ones: Listed Chronologically.

1 Al Martino

This section includes full details of every record that has reached number one on the British singles charts since their inception on 14 November 1952. Information given includes the title, the artist, the writer, the producer, the label and catalogue number, when the record reached number one and how many weeks it stayed on top. There are also a few lines about each hit, pinpointing some particular aspect of every number one.

Although details of many of the performers' careers do incidentally crop up in this section, we have not attempted to compile an encyclopaedia of pop and we make no apologies if, for example, you cannot find out from this book that Denny Laine's real middle name is Arthur or that Earl Palmer played drums on The Righteous Brothers' **You've Lost That Lovin' Feeling**.

The information that has been included has been cross-checked and is, we believe, accurate, but there are many areas still open to doubt. However, the attributions we have made are based on the fullest available information at the time of going to press.

— 1 —

HERE IN MY HEART

14 November 1952, for nine weeks

Al Martino *Capitol CL 13779*

Writers: Pat Genaro, Lou Levinson and Bill Borelli
Producer: Voyle Gilmore

Al Martino's career was at its height when the *New Musical Express* established the first ever record sales chart on 14 November 1952. **Here In My Heart** was the song at the top for the first 9 weeks of the new chart, setting up a record for longest continuous run at number one which even after almost 30 years has only been beaten twice. By staying at number one until 1953, Martino secured for himself for all time the record of being the only performer to have a number one hit in the entire year of 1952. Needless to say, no subsequent act has ever dominated the top spot so entirely in any later year.

Al Martino, born Alfred Cini in Philadelphia on 7 October 1927, faded from the charts after his version of **The Man From Laramie** made the Top 20 briefly late in 1955. After many fallow years, he came back with a strong performance as the Mafia-owned night club singer in *The Godfather*, and had a top five hit in 1973 with **Spanish Eyes**. He is thus one of only 14 acts whose chart career has stretched over 20 years.

On 25 November 1952, 11 days after the British singles chart was instituted, another British cultural phenomenon began. *The Mousetrap* opened in London.

— 2 —

YOU BELONG TO ME

16 January 1953, for one week

Jo Stafford *Columbia DB 3152*

Writers: PeeWee King, Red Stewart and Chilton Price
Producer: Paul Weston

You Belong to Me came on the chart on 14 November 1952, and made number one in its tenth week on the chart. This is not the slowest climb to the top, but in 30 years only 16 other records have taken over 2 months to climb to the number one spot. As the chart at that time was only a Top 12, **You Belong to Me** certainly took its time up the final few rungs of the ladder.

In her 1 week on top, Jo Stafford claimed for herself for all time the title of first female performer at number one. Thirty-eight solo female vocalists and one female instrumentalist (Winifred Atwell, see nos. 26 and 45) have followed Miss Stafford to number one, not counting female members of groups such as Stargazers, Abba, Blondie and Honeycombs. **You Belong To Me** was also the first case where the artist and producer of a number one were husband and wife.

Jo Stafford's chart career after **You Belong To Me** was undistinguished. She had only three more hits, of which one made the Top 10 in mid 1954 (**Make Love To Me**), and on 3 February 1956, she enjoyed her final chart placing. But by being the first girl at number one, her place in British chart history is secure.

— 3 —

COMES A-LONG A-LOVE

23 January 1953, for one week

Kay Starr *Capitol CL 13876*

Writer: Al Sherman
Producer: Mitch Miller

Kay Starr shares with Marvin Rainwater (see no. 70) the distinction of being the only full-blooded Red Indians to have reached number one in Britain. Johnnie Ray and Cher both have Indian blood, but not as many pints of it as Kay or Marvin. Miss Starr also shares with John Travolta and Olivia Newton-John the more doubtful honour of reaching number one with both their first and their last chart discs.

Kay Starr was born on 21 July 1922 in Oklahoma and began her career as a singer with the Glenn Miller and Bob Crosby bands, among others. She moved away from the big band sound and towards a more countrified approach by recording a few titles with Tennessee Ernie Ford in the early fifties. One of their duets, **I'll Never Be Free**, reached number four on the American country charts, but that was in 1950, before the British charts began. Her music had by 1953 become very middle of the road, in the style of Mitch Miller. Before her final hit (see no. 44) in 1956, Kay Starr's other British chart entries were two standards, **Side By Side** and **Changing Partners**, and a real country tune, **Am I A Toy Or A Treasure**.

4

OUTSIDE OF HEAVEN

30 January 1953, for one week

Eddie Fisher *HMV B 10362*

Writers: Sammy Gallop and Chester Conn
Producer: Hugo Winterhalter

The chart was just getting into its stride as January moved to a close, and after Al Martino's 9 weeks run at the top, Eddie Fisher's first number one became the third consecutive chart-topper to stay only 1 week on top. In all subsequent chart history, this has never happened again.

Eddie Fisher, perhaps better known in the 1980's as an ex-husband of Elizabeth Taylor, was at this time married to Debbie Reynolds. Their daughter, Carrie Fisher, has now earned her own riches and fame as a star of the box office smashes, *Star Wars* and *The Empire Strikes Back*. The grammatically incorrect **Outside Of Heaven** was the first British hit for Eddie Fisher, who had been discovered on an American TV amateur talent show in the 1940's. By the early fifties he had so thoroughly forsaken his amateur status that he was able to sign what was at that time the biggest TV contract ever.

5

DON'T LET THE STARS GET IN YOUR EYES

6 February 1953, for five weeks

Perry Como *HMV B 10400*

Writer: Slim Willet
Producer: Eli Oberstein

Born on 18 May, 1912 in Pennsylvania, 'The singing barber', as Perry Como became known, is one of the most long-lasting of all performers on the British charts. He began his singing career in the 1930's with the Freddie Carlone Band, and moved later to the better known Ted Weems Orchestra. After the war, he began to come up with big hits, the first of which on the British charts was also the first of seven 'Eyes' hits to reach number one. **Don't Let The Stars Get In Your Eyes** had originally been a country hit in America for the composer, Slim Willet, as well as for Pat Boone's father-in-law Red Foley, Skeets McDonald and Ray Price. It was Ray Price who many years later had the big American hit version of one of Perry Como's Top 10 hits of the 1970's, **For The Good Times**.

Como hit a blank chart period in Britain for over a year after his first hit dropped off the charts in April, but three more hits in the latter half of 1954 re-established him as a chart star. By the time of his second number one hit, **Magic Moments**, (see no. 69) he had become the world's highest paid television star, in succession to Eddie Fisher.

6

SHE WEARS RED FEATHERS

13 March 1953, for four weeks

Guy Mitchell *Columbia DB 3238*

Writer: Bob Merrill
Producer: Mitch Miller

The inexhaustibly successful early fifties team of Bob Merrill, Mitch Miller and Guy Mitchell came up with an astonishing run of successes in the first years of the chart. **She Wears Red Feathers** was their first number one. Of Guy Mitchell's first eight hits, between November 1952 and April 1954, six were written by Bob Merrill and all were produced by Mitch Miller and his production team at Columbia (CBS) in America.

Guy Mitchell was born on 27 February 1927, his real name being Al Cernik. His parents had emigrated to America from Yugoslavia and Mitchell made a name for himself as a child actor before the war. By the 1950's he had given up acting for singing, and was hugely popular all over the world. **She Wears Red Feathers** was his second success in the UK, following the number two hit **Feet Up**, which set the pattern of bouncy sentimentality for which Merrill, Miller and Mitchell became rich and famous. **She Wears Red Feathers** was a bizarre tale of an English banker's love for a hula-hula girl. The formula was repeated with less success in a later song, **Chick-A-Boom**, which extolled the virtues of a rich Eskimo lady and which Mitchell took to number four early in 1954.

7

BROKEN WINGS

10 April 1953, for one week

The Stargazers *Decca F 10047*

Writers: John Jerome and Bernard Grun
Producer: Dick Rowe

Twenty-one weeks after the chart was established, a British act hit the number one position for the first time. This

British weakness does not compare with the dominance of American acts from July 1957 to November 1958, when only 2 weeks of Michael Holliday (see no. 68) interrupted 70 weeks of American number ones, but it was long enough to make the emergence of the first British number one an important day in chart history. The group in question was The Stargazers, in the early fifties Britain's most popular – indeed almost our only – vocal group.

Three versions of **Broken Wings** made the charts, the original by the American duo Art and Dotty Todd, a cover by Dickie Valentine and the Stargazers' version, the first cover version to hit the top spot. Art and Dotty Todd suffered from cover versions just as badly as Ray Peterson, the original recorder of **Tell Laura I Love Her** and **The Wonder Of You**. Art and Dotty were first with **Broken Wings** and with another song that they took into the Top 20 of both the soul and pop charts in America – **Chanson D'Amour**.

8

(HOW MUCH IS) THAT DOGGIE IN THE WINDOW

17 April 1953, for one week

Lita Roza *Decca F 10070*

Writer: Bob Merrill
Producer: Dick Rowe

The first question to be asked from the number one spot was also probably the silliest. Nineteen other questions have been asked over the years by number ones, deep philosophical questions like **Da Ya Think I'm Sexy?** and **Are 'Friends' Electric?** (the answer to both questions being not unless turned on), but nobody else has asked how much anything is. For an industry in which money is the Holy Grail, it is surprising how unsuccessful money songs have been. Abba and the Bay City Rollers both failed to hit number one with money songs when they were at the peaks of their careers, and apart from this burning question, only a handful of songs, like **Can't Buy Me Love** and **Sixteen Tons** have dealt with money in any way, and still made it to the top. There must be a moral there somewhere.

For Lita Roza, whose record was a cover of Patti Page's original, this was the peak of her career. Cover versions of **Hey There** and **Jimmy Unknown** gave her small hits in the mid-fifties, but her career as Ted Heath's vocalist was knocked hard by the onslaught of rock and roll a year or two later. Lita Roza became just another name from the past, but at least a name on a number one hit record.

9

I BELIEVE

24 April 1953, for nine weeks, and from 3 July 1953 for six weeks, and again from 21 August 1953 for three weeks

Frankie Laine *Philips PB 117*

Writers: Erwin Drake, Irvin Graham, Jimmy Shirl and Al Stillman
Producer: Mitch Miller

Frankie Laine's quasi-religious hit **I Believe** broke all number one records, and after 491 successors in the top slot, still holds the record for most weeks on top. Although two records subsequently stayed at number one for longer than 9 consecutive weeks, no record has approached the 18 weeks in total which this record stayed at number one. During its stay at number one, Queen Elizabeth was crowned, Mount Everest was climbed and England won back the Ashes after 19 years.

No disc has quite matched the record of **I Believe** in having three separate runs at number one, although Guy Mitchell's **Singing the Blues** (no. 53) almost did. No artist has matched Frankie Laine's 27 weeks at number one in 1953, a year in which his discs notched up a total of 66 weeks on the chart, more than any of his rivals. Laine's success was mainly responsible for a run from 24 April 1953 to 1 January 1954 during which time the Philips label retained the top position for 34 out of 37 weeks, a domination by a single label that has never been equalled.

The song was revived by David Whitfield in 1960 and by the Bachelors in 1964 to give the song a total of 54 weeks on the chart, the tenth most successful composition of all time.

10

I'M WALKING BEHIND YOU

26 June 1953, for one week

Eddie Fisher *HMV B 10489*

Writer: Billy Reid
Producer: Hugo Winterhalter

Eddie Fisher became the first act to achieve a second British number one hit when the frankly unexciting song **I'm**

Walking Behind You ousted Frankie Laine's **I Believe** for one week. This was to be Fisher's last number one hit, although he had four more Top 10 hits stretching to early 1957 when **Cindy Oh Cindy** dropped off the charts. By that time Tommy Steele had reached the top with **Singing the Blues** and British pop music was changing irreversibly.

The song gave Dorothy Squires one week of chart glory with her cover version, but it was 16 years before she was to reappear as a solo act in the charts.

It was written by an Englishman, Billy Reid, and Eddie Fisher's version reached number one in the States as well as in Britain. It was his fifth million-selling single, and represented the height of his popularity. He could persuade the fans to buy anything he recorded, even mediocre material like this.

11

MOULIN ROUGE

14 August 1953, for one week

Mantovani and his Orchestra *Decca F 10094*

Writer: Georges Auric
Producer: Frank Lee

The first instrumental to top the charts was the theme tune of the film *Moulin Rouge* by the legendary British orchestra of Mantovani. Only 25 more instrumentals have reached the number one spot in the history of the charts, scarcely 5 per cent of all number ones.

Annunzio Paulo Mantovani was born in Venice, Italy on 15 November 1905, and moved to England with his parents in 1921. By the 1930's he had his own orchestra which became known for its 'cascading strings' and in the 1940's he began recording with Decca. He immediately became immensely popular on record as he had long been on radio, and in 1951 recorded an LP aimed at the American market. It was a huge hit, and a single from the LP 'Charmaine', became a million seller.

Two years later, with no sign of his popularity dimming, Mantovani took the theme from *Moulin Rouge*, the film which starred José Ferrer on his knees as Toulouse Lautrec, to number one in Britain. Percy Faith had the big hit in America, and both versions sold over a million. Mantovani died on 31 March 1981.

12

LOOK AT THAT GIRL

11 September 1953, for six weeks

Guy Mitchell *Philips PB 162*

Writer: Bob Merrill
Producer: Mitch Miller

When Frankie Laine's **I Believe** finally relinquished the top spot, it let in Guy Mitchell for his second number one hit. Mitchell's first four chart singles produced two number two hits and two number ones, and his chart career rolled on with fabulous success from 14 November 1952 until July 1957 when for the first time a Guy Mitchell single failed to make the Top 20. By then he had scored four number ones and seven other top ten hits, a track record almost as good as his label-mate Frankie Laine.

Once again, it was the team of Merrill, Mitchell and Miller (say that three times quickly) that created the record, but this was to be the last chart topper for this particular team.

One girl that much of America was looking at at the time was Jacqueline Bouvier, who on 12 September 1953 became Mrs John Fitzgerald Kennedy.

13

HEY JOE

23 October 1953, for two weeks

Frankie Laine *Philips PB 172*

Writer: Boudleaux Bryant
Producer: Mitch Miller

Frankie Laine's second number one hit, in direct contrast to his massively longlasting **I Believe**, only stayed in the charts for 8 weeks, having reached the number one position in its second week on the chart. That week Frankie Laine had three singles in the charts, which was only a Top 12 at the time. **I Believe** was in its 31st week on the chart, **Where The Wind Blows** which peaked at number two, was in its 8th week, and **Hey Joe** was at the top of the heap. The following week, Frankie Laine's third number one hit, **Answer Me** (see no. 15) entered the chart, giving Laine one third of all records on the chart, a feat that is never likely to be equalled in these days of a Top 75.

Hey Joe is not of course the same song as the one that gave Jimi Hendrix his first hit in 1967. It was the first

5 **Perry Como**

Left **10 Eddie Fisher** *Above* **14 David Whitfield**

11 Mantovani

number one written by Boudleaux Bryant, whose main success was to come writing songs with his wife Felice for the Everly Brothers.

14

ANSWER ME

6 November 1953, for one week
and 11 December 1953, top equal for one week

David Whitfield *Decca F 10192*

Writers: Gerhard Winkler and Fred Rauch, English lyrics by Carl Sigman
Producer: Bunny Lewis

The late David Whitfield, the largest selling British vocalist of the mid-fifties, began his chart career at the beginning of October 1953 with a forgettable song called **Bridge Of Sighs**. Two weeks later, his version of **Answer Me** hit the chart, two weeks ahead of Frankie Laine's original, and within 3 weeks David Whitfield had his first number one. On 13 November, for the first but not the only time in chart history, one version of a song was knocked off the top by another version of the same song. Four weeks later, for the only time in British chart history, the two versions of the same song were at number one together. Only six songs have ever made number one in two different versions (**Answer Me, This Ole House, Cherry Pink and Apple Blossom White, Singing the Blues, Young Love** and **Mary's Boy Child**), but none of the other five have been on the chart in as many as four versions. Ray Peterson, this time covering an original rather than vice versa, hit the chart for the only time in his career with **Answer Me** in 1960, and Barbara Dickson gave the song its third Top 10 version in 1976.

15

ANSWER ME

13 November 1953, for eight weeks
(11 December 1953, top equal)

Frankie Laine *Philips PB 196*

Writers: Gerhard Winkler and Fred Rauch, English lyrics by Carl Sigman
Producer: Mitch Miller

Frankie Laine rounded off an astonishing year of undiluted chart success by becoming the first act to have three number one hits, the first act to hit number one with consecutive releases and a phenomenal total of 27 weeks of 1953 in the number one position. In the history of the British charts, only 34 acts have had three or more number one hits, and nobody else has ever managed more than 18 weeks at number one in a year, which Elvis achieved in 1961.

Frankie Laine was born Frank LoVecchio in Chicago on 30 March 1913. Early publicity handouts talk of his holding the all-time marathon dance record of 145 days, set in 1932. However, his hold on that record must have been much shorter than his stranglehold on the top of the British charts, as our sister publication the *Guinness Book of Records* lists the record for marathon dancing at 173 days, completed on 30 November 1932, by two dancers neither of whom were Frank LoVecchio. However, it may have been marathon-dancing that ruined his clothes. On one trip to Britain, a reviewer criticised his clothing, which led Laine to reply from the stage that 'they can criticise my voice, but not my tailor'.

16

OH MEIN PAPA

8 January 1954, for nine weeks

Eddie Calvert *Columbia DB 3337*

Writers: Paul Burkhard, English lyrics by John Turner and Geoffrey Parsons
Producer: Norrie Paramor

'The Man with the Golden Trumpet', British trumpeter, Eddie Calvert, scored his first and biggest hit with the sentimental German tune **Oh Mein Papa**, from which most of the lyrics had been excised. A girl chorus wistfully sang the title from time to time behind Calvert's vigorous trumpet style, but listeners who could not stomach the full schmaltzy horror of the lyrics in Eddie Fisher's vocal version could keep their emotions in check by buying the Calvert arrangement.

Instrumentals have tended towards foreign titles, and to follow Mantovani's French hit **Moulin Rouge**, the second instrumental number one had a German title. Number one hits have had French, Italian, German, Scottish, South Pacific, American Indian and gibberish titles, as well as English, but until Elvis Presley's **Wooden Heart** (no. 115) 7 years later, no words of German made the number one slot again.

This record has a further claim to fame as the first number one hit recorded at the most successful of all British studios, Abbey Road. At least 75 of the 500 number ones have been recorded there, over a quarter of a century of continuing artistic and technical excellence from the white building not a cricket ball's throw from Lord's Cricket Ground.

17

I SEE THE MOON

12 March 1954, for five weeks
and from 23 April 1954 for one week

The Stargazers *Decca F 10213*

Writer: Meredith Wilson
Producer: Dick Rowe

In taking **I See The Moon** to number one, the Stargazers became the first of ten acts in British chart history to reach number one with their first two chart hits. Like three others of those ten, the Stargazers' number ones were not with consecutive releases, but all the singles between **Broken Wings** and **I See The Moon** missed the charts.

The Stargazers were led by Cliff Adams, the man who a few years later had a small hit with the theme from the Strand cigarettes advertisement, **The Lonely Man Theme**. At the time, Cliff Adams became the top act alphabetically in British chart history, taking over from Alfi and Harry who had been the first on the list for 4 years. Cliff Adams retained the title of alphabetically first chart act for 14 years until the current champions, Abba, hit the chart with **Waterloo** (see no. 348). Cliff Adams is also famous for years of *Sing Something Simple* with his Cliff Adams Singers on BBC Radio. He is the owner of Olympic Studio in London where several rock era number one hits were recorded. The other Stargazers were Marie Benson, Fred Datchler, Bob Brown and Dave Carey.

18

SECRET LOVE

16 April 1954, for one week and from 7 May for eight weeks

Doris Day *Philips PB 230*

Writers: Paul Francis Webster and Sammy Fain
Producer: Ray Heindorf

Doris Day, born Doris von Kappelhoff on 3 April 1924, was by far the most successful female vocalist of the early 1950's. Her two number ones remain two of the best known songs of the pre-rock era (see also no. 49) although some of her sillier songs from the Mitch Miller production line, like **Ooh Bang Jiggilly Jang**, failed to prise open the purse strings of the record-buying public.

Secret Love was the Oscar-winning song from the film *Calamity Jane*, which starred Miss Day and Howard Keel. It was an enormous success, justifying Day's belief that the producers of *Annie Get Your Gun* were wrong not to cast her in the title role. The success of the film owed much to Howard Keel, who was then one of the very top Hollywood musical stars, but by the early 1980's was reduced to playing Sue Ellen's boyfriend's father in Terry Wogan's favourite TV show *Dallas*. Doris Day continued a recording and film career throughout the fifties and early sixties, which led her to vast popular success until she gave up playing hard to get with Rock Hudson.

19

SUCH A NIGHT

30 April 1954, for one week

Johnnie Ray *Philips PB 244*

Writer: Lincoln Chase
Producer: Mitch Miller

Johnny Ray, born in Dallas, Oregon on 10 January 1927, was partially deafened in an accident at the age of nine, but like Beethoven he did not allow deafness to interfere with a musical career. At 15 he appeared on a child talent radio show in nearby Portland, Oregon, and at 17 worked his way south to Los Angeles where he became a soda fountain assistant and movie extra. He became one of millions who failed to be discovered and at the age of 24 moved to Detroit to sing at the Flame Club. There he made his first records for Columbia. From Detroit he moved to Cleveland, and his first taste of local stardom, which grew rapidly with his next recordings, the self-penned **Little White Cloud That Cried** and the classic **Cry**. The Prince of Wails was on his way.

Such A Night was not a US hit for Johnnie Ray, although the Drifter's version reached number five on the Rhythm and Blues charts in 1954, and the song was a hit for Elvis Presley in 1964 both in UK (number 13) and US (number 16).

There was 'such a night' for world athletics that week. Roger Bannister completed four laps of the Iffley Road track at Oxford in 3 minutes 59.4 seconds, to become the first man to break 4 minutes for the mile.

20

CARA MIA

2 July 1954, for ten weeks

David Whitfield with chorus and Mantovani and his orchestra *Decca F 10327*

Writers: Lee Lange and Tulio Trapani
Producer: Bunny Lewis

David Whitfield's second number one was one of the biggest-selling British records in the pre-rock days. It sold well over a million copies worldwide and David Whitfield joined Vera Lynn in the ranks of British stars who had achieved a Top 10 hit in America. In Britain, the 10 week run at the top was then the longest ever run of consecutive weeks at the top, and 480 hits later, Whitfield still takes second place only to Slim Whitman (see no. 36)

The writers, Lee Lange and Tulio Trapani, were actually Whitfield's producer Bunny Lewis and his arranger Mantovani. On this record Mantovani's orchestra is given label credit, and there is no doubt that the lush strings of the Mantovani sound were a major contribution to the phenomenal success of the record.

Although David Whitfield (born 2 February 1926) never topped the charts again, his light operatic tenor tones were regular fixtures in the charts until the end of 1956, when he like many others was swept away by the tidal wave of rock and roll. He never managed to make the sort of money that his success would have brought him if it had happened ten years later, and when he died on 15 January 1980 he left only £3000, but was accorded a four-column obituary notice in *The Times*.

21

LITTLE THINGS MEAN A LOT

10 September 1954, for one week

Kitty Kallen *Brunswick 05287*

Writers: Carl Stutz and Edith Lindemann
Producers: Milt Gabler, musical arrangement by Jack Pleis

Kitty Kallen is the first of the one-hit wonders, the recording acts whose only chart hit has reached number one. Nobody would pretend that Kitty Kallen or the Floaters have made a greater contribution to British popular music than The Who, Elton John, Nat King Cole or Stevie Wonder, but whereas none of those last four acts has had solo number one hits in England, Kitty Kallen has done.

Kallen's career in America was not so instantaneous. She had been a singer with the Jimmy Dorsey Band and apart from **Little Things Mean A Lot**, her biggest hit on both sides of the Atlantic, she made sporadic chart entries in the States until early 1963, when her last hit, a Top 20 version of **My Coloring Book**, dropped off the charts. **Little Things Mean A Lot** was written by disc jockey Carl Stutz, from Richmond Virginia and the leisure editor of the *Richmond Times-Despatch*, Edith Lindemann. As far as is known, they are one-hit wonders as much as the performer, Kitty Kallen.

22

THREE COINS IN THE FOUNTAIN

17 September 1954, for three weeks

Frank Sinatra *Capitol CL 14120*

Writers: Sammy Cahn and Jule Styne
Producers: Voyle Gilmore, musical arrangement by Nelson Riddle

The Academy Award-winning 'Best Original Song of 1954' was Frank Sinatra's first number one hit. Written by the prolific Sammy Cahn and Jule Styne for a lightweight film of the same name, **Three Coins In The Fountain** was Sinatra's first major hit in Britain. It actually entered the charts one week after Sinatra's version of **Young At Heart** had given him his first hit in Britain, but that song lasted only one week and disappeared as **Three Coins In The Fountain** arrived.

Francis Albert Sinatra, possibly the most famous and probably the richest popular singer of all time, was born in Hoboken, New Jersey on 12 December 1915. By the early 1940's he was creating scenes of hysteria among 'bobby-soxers' which would only be equalled with the rise of Elvis Presley in 1956 and then the Beatles in 1963. In the 1980's, still performing (but now with a hairpiece and a solid midriff) and still selling records, Frank Sinatra is Ol' Blue Eyes to record company executives and his fans alike.

Sixteen numbers songs have reached the top, of which this was the first. Four of those fifteen songs have included the number three, which makes it the most commonly used number in a chart-topper. If Bobby Darin's **Mack The Knife** (Theme from the *Threepenny Opera*) is included, one per cent of all number ones can be said to concern the number three. This fascinating fact has not had a motivating effect on writers or performers of potential hit records.

23

HOLD MY HAND

8 October 1954, for four weeks
and from 19 November 1954 for one week

Don Cornell *Vogue Q 2013*

Writers: Jack Lawrence and Richard Myers
Producer: Bob Thiele

Don Cornell, one of the least known number one hitmakers of the fifties, had two coincidental links with the rock music which swept him into obscurity a year or two later. He recorded on the same label as Buddy Holly and the Crickets, who gave the label their only other British number ones, and he also put out a single of the song **Mailman, Bring Me No More Blues**, which Buddy Holly heard, liked and subsequently recorded.

Don Cornell was born in New York City, and first joined the Sammy Kaye band in 1942. He served briefly in the Army, but in 1946 was able to rejoin Sammy Kaye and by 1949 was recording solo. **Hold My Hand** was featured in the 1954 film starring Dick Powell and Debbie Reynolds (at that time Eddie Fisher's wife) called *Susan Slept Here*. In Britain his only other hit was his version of **Stranger In Paradise**. In America he continued to hit the Hot Hundred until 1957, but his big days ended with **Hold My Hand**.

24

MY SON MY SON

5 November 1954, for two weeks

Vera Lynn *Decca F 10372*

Writers: Bob Howard, Melville Farley and Eddie Calvert
Producer: Frank Lee

Dame Vera Lynn, born Vera Welsh on 20 March 1919 in East Ham, had sung a certain amount with Joe Loss and Charlie Kunz by the time she began her wartime radio series *Sincerely Yours*, which quickly earned her such popularity that she became known as 'the Forces Sweetheart'. She then spent the remaining war years touring and entertaining the troops to become, by the end of the war, one of the most famous voices in Europe. Her popularity was not limited to Europe, because the American troops had heard her and liked her too.

In 1951, her recording of **Auf Wiederseh'n Sweetheart** climbed to the very top of the American charts, a feat she no doubt would have repeated in Britain had there been a chart here at the time. As it was, she managed her only British number one with the sentimental ballad **My Son My Son** towards the end of her active recording career. Eddie Calvert, who co-wrote the song, joined Mantovani as the second number one hit recording star to write a number one hit for somebody else.

25

THIS OLE HOUSE

26 November 1954, for one week

Rosemary Clooney *Philips PB 336*

Writer: Stuart Hamblen
Producer: Mitch Miller

Stuart Hamblen was supposedly out on a hunting expedition when he and his fellow hunters came across a tumbledown hut in the mountains, many miles from civilisation. They went into the hut and there, lying amongst the rubbish and rubble of a crumbling building, was the body of an old man. Most of us would have thrown up or made our excuses and left, but not Mr Hamblen. He sat down and wrote this song, which Rosemary Clooney (and later Shakin' Stevens) treated as a bouncy novelty number rather than the epitaph for a mountain man that it was meant to be.

Rosemary Clooney, born on 23 May 1928, was married to José Ferrer, star of the film *Moulin Rouge*, which gave Mantovani his number one hit. Clooney's first really big hit was **'Come On-A My House'**, written by author William Saroyan and his cousin Ross Bagdasarian, but it preceded the British charts. Ross Bagdasarian is the man who scored hits as David Seville, as Alfi and Harry and as The Chipmunks, making him the only man to hit the charts as a soloist, both halves of a duo and all three of a trio. Miss Clooney was possibly less versatile but in British chart terms more successful.

18 Doris Day

30 Tennessee Ernie Ford

22 Frank Sinatra

32 Tony Bennett

Left **26 Winifred Atwell**
Right **29 Ruby Murray**

26

LET'S HAVE ANOTHER PARTY

Medley of the following songs: **Another Little Drink Wouldn't Do Us Any Harm** by Nat D Ayer and Clifford Grey, **Broken Doll** by James W Tate, **Bye Bye Blackbird** by Ray Henderson and Mort Dixon, **Honeysuckle and the Bee** by Albert Fitz and William Penn, **I Wonder Where My Baby Is Tonight** by Gus Cahn and Walter Donaldson, **Lily of Laguna** by Leslie Stuart, **Nellie Dean** by Harry Armstrong, **Sheik of Araby** by Ted Snyder, **Somebody Stole My Gal** by Leo Wood, **When the Red Red Robin (Comes Bob Bob Bobbin' Along)** by Harry Woods

3 December 1954, for five weeks

Winifred Atwell *Philips PB 268*

Producer: Johnny Franz

Despite the almost total blanketing of the upper reaches of the chart by medley discs in the summer of 1981, Winifred Atwell's Christmas 1954 hit remains the only medley of over two songs ever to reach the very top of the charts. Winifred Atwell, the vast West Indian with the smile and the 'other piano', was the first black person to have a number one hit in Britain, and still the only female instrumentalist to hit the top. Her hit, the third instrumental disc at number one, was the first piano instrumental to reach the top, and after 30 years only Russ Conway, Floyd Cramer, B.Bumble and Lieutenant Pigeon have matched Winifred Atwell's success.

27

FINGER OF SUSPICION

from 7 January 1955, for one week
and from 21 January 1955 for two weeks

Dickie Valentine *Decca F 10394*

Writers: Al Lewis and Paul Mann
Producer: Dick Rowe

Dickie Valentine, born Richard Bryce in London 20 years earlier, was given his big break by Ted Heath in 1951 when he invited him to become vocalist with his Band, the most successful of all British big bands. By 1952 Valentine was voted Britain's Most Popular Singer, a title he retained for years beyond his chart heyday, which began early in 1953. His first number one hit came only two months after his marriage at Caxton Hall to Elizabeth Flynn, which caused scenes of crowd hysteria and was reliably expected to sound the death knell to his career. In fact, 1955 was by far his best chart year, with two number ones and three other Top 10 hits. But even when the hits stopped coming, Valentine kept working. There was a publicity story that reported that Valentine had been a pageboy at the London Palladium, but had been sacked for some undisclosed reason. 'I'll be back', vowed the determined young Master Bryce, 'I'll be back at the top of the bill'. And so he was, time and again throughout the fifties.

28

MAMBO ITALIANO

from 14 January 1955, for one week
and from 4 February 1955 for two weeks

Rosemary Clooney *Philips PB 382*

Writer: Bob Merrill
Producer: Mitch Miller

Only eleven of the songs that have reached number one have had foreign language titles, and of these five were instrumentals. Rosemary Clooney's second consecutive number one hit was the fourth foreign language title to reach the top, although both **Oh Mein Papa** and **Cara Mia** had topped the charts in two versions. It was the last vocal chart-topper with a foreign title until Jane Birkin and Serge Gainsbourg's excessively vocal **Je T'Aime . . . Moi Non Plus** made the top 14 years 235 days and 249 number ones later.

There is a story that around this time a visitor came to dinner at the home of José Ferrer and Rosemary Clooney. On seeing a child or two scattered amongst the furniture, the guest enquired how many children the Ferrers had. 'Seven', was the reply. 'And what are their ages?' asked the polite guest. 'Seven, six, five, four, three, two and one,' said Miss Clooney. 'Oh, I do hope I'm not interrupting anything', replied the guest, tucking into the fish.

29

SOFTLY SOFTLY

18 February 1955, for three weeks

Ruby Murray *Columbia DB 3558*

Writers: Mark Paul and Pierre Dudan, English lyrics by Paddy Roberts
Producer: Norrie Paramor

Ruby Murray, the shy little 19 year old from Ireland, was easily the most successful singer on the British Charts in 1955. Her first chart entry had been on 3 December 1954 with the song **Heartbeat** which was destined to rise to number three. At the end of January, her second hit, **Softly Softly** entered the hit parade and within a month was number one. By the end of the year, Miss Murray had taken seven songs into the British Top 10, including both sides of her third hit single, **Happy Days and Lonely Nights** (which reached number six) backed by **Let Me Go Lover,** which climbed one rung higher to number five. Yet just as suddenly as it had begun, it all stopped again. **I'll Come When You Call,** her sixth Top 10 record, dropped off the chart at the end of November 1955, and no Ruby Murray record hit the chart after that until the end of August 1956, when **You Are My First Love** tottered up to number 16. In 1957 she was hitless and her last brief spell of chart success came when **Real Love** hit the Top 20 over Christmas 1958 and a few months later **Goodbye Jimmy Goodbye** gave Miss Murray her final Top 10 hit. Then it was goodbye, Ruby, goodbye.

30

GIVE ME YOUR WORD

11 March 1955, for seven weeks

Tennessee Ernie Ford *Capitol CL 14005*

Writers: George Wyle and Irving Taylor
Producer: Ken Nelson

Tennessee Ernie Ford was born Ernest Jennings Ford on a farm near Bristol Tennessee on 13 February 1919. At school he played trombone, but on graduation moved to Pasadena to become a disc jockey, rather than a performer, on the local radio station. In 1941 he joined the US Air Force and it was not until 1949, when once again Ford was working in Pasadena (this time as a singer) that he was signed by Capitol Records.

Give Me Your Word was Ford's first hit in Britain. He had already scored regularly on the American charts, not only alone but also in duet with Kay Starr, and was by the mid-fifties one of the biggest of Capitol's acts. His deep country-tinged voice was ideally suited to the songs he sang, at first mainly romantic, but he also featured more muscular songs like **Shotgun Boogie** and his biggest hit, **Sixteen Tons** (see no. 41).

31

CHERRY PINK AND APPLE BLOSSOM WHITE

29 April 1955, for two weeks

Perez Prado *HMV B 10833*

Writer: Louiguy
Producer: Herman Diaz

Originally a French tune (by a Spanish composer!), and not surprisingly called **Cerisier Rouge et Pommier Blanc, Cherry Pink** was used as the theme tune of the 1955 film *Underwater*, starring Jane Russell, the girl for whom Howard Hughes re-invented the bra. Perez Prado was born in Cuba on 23 November 1918 and began playing in those pre-Castro days in Havana with Orquestra Casino de la Playa. In 1951 he first recorded **Cherry Pink**, but when the producers of *Underwater* decided to use the tune as their theme, Prado was asked to re-record it. The new recording of **Cherry Pink and Apple Blossom White** spent 10 weeks at the top of the American charts, and although in Britain its success was less long-lived he helped establish two insignificant records. Firstly, the title of his number one hit was the longest number one title at the time, equalling the record set by Lita Roza's doggie two years earlier. Secondly, **Cherry Pink** joined **Answer Me** as the only songs which had hit the top in two different versions, when Eddie Calvert's recording took over the one slot at the end of May.

English lyrics to the song were written by Mack David, but as the lyrics were not used in either hit version, perhaps Mack's efforts went unappreciated. Perez Prado did not play trumpet on this record – the featured trumpeter is one Billy Regis.

32

STRANGER IN PARADISE

13 May 1955, for two weeks

Tony Bennett *Philips PB 420*

Writers: Robert Wright and George Forrest, based on a theme by Alexander Borodin
Producer: Mitch Miller

Anthony Dominick Benedetto was born on 3 August 1926 on Long Island New York. His first public appearance was at the age of 7 in a church minstrel show, but his climb from there to the top was interrupted by World War II, by the end of which Benedetto was an infantryman in Europe.

After the war, an appearance on Arthur Godfrey's Talent Show led to a TV contract and Tony Bennett's career was under way. **Stranger In Paradise** was a song from the show *Kismet*, and Bennett had originally recorded his version in 1953. It was not until 1955 that the show, and thus the songs from the show, came to London. The song was undoubtedly the hit of 1955, as no less than six versions of the song hit the charts that year, while more failed to register.

Stranger In Paradise was Bennett's first hit in Britain, and his only Top 10 success. He is now best known for his international hit **I Left My Heart In San Francisco.** Despite the song's popularity with every nightclub entertainer and every drunk in every bar from San Francisco to Auckland, the song never climbed higher than number 25 in the British charts. Bennett had further success in Britain with Sacha Distel's **The Good Life** and Harry Secombe's song from *Pickwick*, **If I Ruled The World**.

33

CHERRY PINK AND APPLE BLOSSOM WHITE

27 May 1955, for four weeks

Eddie Calvert *Columbia DB 3581*

Writer: Louiguy
Producer: Norrie Paramor

The day after Winston Churchill's victorious last General Election as leader of the Conservative Party, Eddie Calvert moved his version of **Cherry Pink** into the top position, making it the second song to reach number one in more than one version, and to date the only instrumental to do this.

Eddie Calvert was born in Preston, Lancashire on 15 March 1922. His father was an amateur musician in a brass band and it was he who taught Eddie to play the cornet. No wonder Eddie's first million-seller was **Oh Mein Papa**. During the war, Calvert was a despatch rider and played part-time with various bands graduating from Jimmy McMurray's Band at the Birmingham Casino, past Billy Ternent's Band at BBC Wales at Bangor and finally, fully professional by this time, touring Europe at the end of the war with Geraldo.

His chart career, which had begun with two widely spaced number one hits, then faded a little. He reached the Top 20 with an instrumental version of Tony Bennett's chart-topper **Stranger In Paradise**, and still had enough of a following in 1958 to score a Top 10 hit with **Mandy**. By mid-1958, his chart successes had finished, but his simple style lived on via later chartbound trumpeters such as Herb Alpert, Al Hirt and Nini Rosso. He died in South Africa on 8 August 1978.

34

UNCHAINED MELODY

24 June 1955, for three weeks

Jimmy Young *Decca F 10502*

Writers: Alex North and Hy Zaret
Producers: Dick Rowe, musical director Bob Sharples

A cheap and instantly forgettable American B-film called *Unchained* had one redeeming feature, its theme tune. Those who came to see the film could be forgiven for thinking that any film with a tune as strong as **Unchained Melody** behind the credits would be worth sitting through. In fact, anybody who walked out once he had heard the tune missed nothing else of any merit. The original version was by the American singer Todd Duncan, but Dick Rowe at Decca decided it was right for a singer they had recently signed, whose career was then as far down as it had been up when his **Too Young** had been a major hit on the tiny Polygon label in pre-chart days.

So Jimmy Young got the song and the mighty Decca publicity machine was rolled out behind it. Al Hibbler's version took off first and seemed to be winning the race, but as more versions flooded on to the market (Les Baxter and Liberace also charted with their versions) Jimmy Young started picking up the airplay. By the end of June he was at number one, and Hibbler had to be content with peaking at number two. Suddenly Young was an overnight sensation again.

Unchained Melody is one of four songs that have been a hit in six different versions. **Stranger in Paradise** (see no. 32) is another, **Mack the Knife** (Theme from *The Threepenny Opera* (see no. 91)) is the third and **White Christmas**, which never reached number one in Britain, is the fourth.

35

DREAMBOAT

15 July 1955, for two weeks

Alma Cogan *HMV B 10872*

Writer: Al Hoffman
Producer: Walter Ridley

Throughout the mid-fifties, the most consistently successful female singer in Britain was Alma Cogan. From March 1954, when her first hit **Bell Bottom Blues** came on to the chart, until 1959, she was rarely out of the charts. She never achieved the huge sales of Ruby Murray in 1955 or Shirley Bassey in 1959, but her 17 hit records up to **Cowboy Jimmy Joe**, a few years before her death, make a list longer than any other female star of the fifties can boast. Only four of those hits were Top 10 hits, but her versions of the big hits of the day always gave the original stars a run for their money. Apart from her own number one, she hit the charts with her versions of three other number ones, **Little Things Mean A Lot** (Alma reached no. 11), **Why Do Fools Fall In Love** (she reached no. 22) and **The Story Of My Life** (she reached no. 25).

Alma Cogan was known for her chuckle and her yards of tulle petticoat. Yet her musical image was not just a light happy-go-lucky one. Shortly before her death from cancer, she recorded a few titles with Andrew Loog Oldham, manager and producer of the Rolling Stones. The tracks were never released, but the mere fact that the Stones' mastermind wanted to record her shows that her range was far greater than **Dreamboat**.

36

ROSE MARIE

29 July 1955, for eleven weeks

Slim Whitman *London HL 8061*

Writers: Rudolf Friml, Otto Harbach and Oscar Hammerstein II
Producer: Lew Chudd

The song that was number one when James Dean died was by Otis Dewey Whitman Jr., who was born on 20 January 1924, the same year that the musical *Rose Marie* was first produced. Like other country singers before and since (of whom Charley Pride is the best example) Slim Whitman was an excellent baseball player, and it was only the intervention of the war and enlistment in the US Navy that turned him into a singer rather than a baseball player.

His recording career began to flourish at Imperial Records which was one of America's fastest growing independent labels thanks to the success of Fats Domino. His career hit the very peak when Slim recorded a 30 year old love song which proceeded to break all records for sustained chart success in Britain. It was actually the second song from the musical *Rose Marie* that Whitman had turned into a million-seller, as he had topped the American charts in 1951 with **Indian Love Call**.

After *Rose Marie* there were no more number ones for Slim Whitman. Nevertheless he came back so strongly in the early 1970's that his albums topped the British LP charts and a single **Happy Anniversary** reached number 14 at the end of 1974, almost 20 years since the success of *Rose Marie*.

37

THE MAN FROM LARAMIE

14 October 1955, for four weeks

Jimmy Young *Decca F 10597*

Writers: Lester Lee and Ned Washington
Producer: Dick Rowe, musical director Bob Sharples

On Harry Webb's 15th birthday, Jimmy Young established a new record which Cliff Richard equalled but never beat – he became the first English star to put two consecutive single releases at number one. It was the theme from another Hollywood film, this time a big budget western starring

James Stewart rather than a B-film prison drama like *Unchained* which had given Jimmy Young his first number one. There were six versions of the song released in England, and the *Daily Mirror*, in reviewing the records, wrote 'it might just as well be "The Man From The Coalboard" for all the fire some get into it'. Only two of the six versions hit the British charts, the Al Martino record which climbed to number 19, and Jimmy Young's triumphant single.

The main immediate result of the success of **The Man From Laramie** was that Jimmy Young won a starring role opposite Hylda Baker in the Christmas pantomime *Robinson Crusoe* at the Grand Theatre, Wolverhampton. Success doesn't come much bigger than that, but more was to follow for JY. The *New Musical Express* listed him as the second biggest selling artist of 1955 – after Ruby Murray of course — and in the NME annual, that latterday bible of pop orthodoxy, Young (born in September 1927) was described as 'the success of the year. One name above all others deserves to shine forth in letters of gold. The name of course is Jimmy Young'.

And, as we all know, nearly 30 years later, he is one of Britain's most famous broadcasting voices – and with an OBE to boot. B.F.N.

38

HERNANDO'S HIDEAWAY

11 November 1955, for two weeks

The Johnston Brothers *Decca F 10608*

Writers: Richard Adler and Jerry Ross
Producer: Hugh Mendl

The musical *Pajama Game* was the source of this much recorded song, which provided the British Johnston Brothers with their only number one hit. Sadly, it reached number one in Britain on the day that one of the composers Jerry Ross died in New York. It was the second big hit from the musical, after **Hey There** which had been a Top 20 hit in no less than four versions – by Rosemary Clooney (number 4), Johnnie Ray (number 5), Lita Roza (number 17) and Sammy Davis Jr. (number 19). Johnnie Ray's version included **Hernando's Hideaway** on the B-side, and that B-side climbed to number 11. The Johnston Brothers did exactly the same thing, and although their version of **Hey There** never had a chart listing, its presence on the other side of **Hernando's Hideaway** certainly helped the sales considerably.

The Johnston Brothers were very much in the Stargazers mould as a vocal group (although rather more male than the Stargazers). Two of their hits were forerunners of Starsound and Tight Fit in 1981 – medleys of songs called **Join In And Sing Again** and **Join In And Sing No. 3**. The original **Join In And Sing** failed to hit the charts, but the Johnston Brothers' ability to come up with hit-making versions of middle of the road tunes continued until May 1957, when their **Heart** lost the chart race to Max Bygraves.

39

ROCK AROUND THE CLOCK

25 November 1955, for three weeks
from 6 January 1956, for two weeks

Bill Haley and his Comets *Brunswick 05317*

Writers: Jimmy de Knight (James Myers) and Max C Freedman
Producer: Milt Gabler

On 12 April 1954, a 28 year old country and western band leader went into the studios to record, as a favour to his manager, James Myers, a song which had failed completely in 1952 when Sunny Dae (*sic!*) recorded it. The record was a small hit for Bill Haley (born William John Clifton Haley in Detroit on 6 July 1925), but the follow-up, a version of Joe Turner's **Shake, Rattle and Roll**, made the Top 10 in both Britain and America.

It was not until **Rock Around The Clock** was featured in a 1955 Glenn Ford film called *Blackboard Jungle* that the record suddenly became the most significant recording in popular music history. Nine months after the song had briefly entered the British charts, it reappeared and within 6 weeks was at number one. Eventually it sold over a million copies in Britain alone and changed popular music for ever. Not bad for a little song co-written by a man (Max Freedman) born in 1893! In 1956, Bill Haley had more chart success in 1 year than any other act in Britain before or since, but his tour of Britain early in 1957 destroyed his popularity. In the flesh, Haley was not a teenager's dream, and Elvis took over and built on Haley's amazing success.

It is impossible to analyse his success with **Rock Around The Clock**. It reached the Top 20 in Britain twice more, in 1968 and 1974, and in chart longevity terms is the most successful number one hit of all time. But what did this lively dance number have about it that transformed the musical heritage of Western youth? Bill Haley, who died on 9 February 1981, never knew.

Above **39 Bill Haley and his Comets**

Below **40 Dickie Valentine**

Below **35 Alma Cogan**

40

CHRISTMAS ALPHABET

16 December 1955, for three weeks

Dickie Valentine *Decca F 10628*

Writers: Buddy Kaye and Jules Loman
Producer: Dick Rowe

For three weeks at Christmas, Dickie Valentine played King Canute to Bill Haley's incoming tide of rock and roll. More than that, his record marked the first time that a song created for the Christmas market had hit number one, and it showed that his astute management had learnt from Winifred Atwell's singalong successes of previous Christmas seasons. **Christmas Alphabet** was the first of the Christmas hits (always excluding **White Christmas** which Mantovani had guided into the charts in December 1952) and its chart career was almost as brief as the season of goodwill itself. The single had only 7 weeks in the chart, 3 of which were at number one, and it remains to this day the shortest-lived number one hit.

Dickie Valentine himself had only one more Top 10 hit after **Christmas Alphabet** – a song called **Christmas Island** the following year. But even so, he remained year in, year out Britain's 'most popular male vocalist' until Cliff Richard appeared on the scene. Dickie Valentine never lost his popularity entirely. He was travelling from gig to gig when he was killed in a car crash in 1971.

41

SIXTEEN TONS

20 January 1956, for four weeks

Tennessee Ernie Ford *Capitol CL 14500*

Writer: Merle Travis
Producer: Ken Nelson

Country and western superstar Merle Travis wrote the coal-mining song **Sixteen Tons** and first recorded it in 1947. Travis' father was a coal-miner in Beech Creek, Kentucky and the chorus was based on a saying of his father, 'Another day older and deeper in debt'.

Sixteen Tons was the biggest hit of Ford's career. In America it was one of the fastest selling records in pop history, and stayed at number one for 7 weeks. In Britain, it was his second consecutive number one hit, although like Eddie Calvert and the Stargazers before him, he had released records between his number ones that had missed the chart altogether. His follow-up to **Sixteen Tons**, which reached the top in its third week on the chart, was **The Ballad of Davy Crockett**. This made number three in the charts, but was kept off the top spot not only by Bill Hayes' original version of the song, but also by **Sixteen Tons**.

42

MEMORIES ARE MADE OF THIS

17 February 1956, for four weeks

Dean Martin *Capitol CL 14523*

Writers: Terry Gilkyson, Richard Dehr and Frank Miller
Producer: Lee Gillette

Dean Martin, born Dino Paul Crocetti on 17 June 1917, has achieved so much in all branches of show-business that his one number one hit in Britain must rank fairly low on his list of what memories are made of. The song came from the the film *The Seven Hills of Rome* in which it was sung by Mario Lanza. Dean Martin's double act with Jerry Lewis made them the top box-office stars of 1952, and when they split up, he continued to sing and appear in films with tremendous success. **Memories are Made of This** was his second million-selling single, but his eighth UK hit. Co-writer Terry Gilkyson, by coincidence, was born on the same day as Martin, one year earlier.

Dean Martin's chart career in Britain extended until 1969, when his last hit **Gentle on My Mind** became his fourth number two hit. The previous year he had signed what is still the largest TV contract ever signed for a series of shows on NBC television, and in the early 1970's he was one of the stars of the film *Airport*. Dean Martin's notorious affection for the bottle made him an odd choice to be cast as the captain of the aeroplane, so it was perhaps no wonder it ran into disaster on screen if not at the box-office.

43

IT'S ALMOST TOMORROW

16 March 1956, for two weeks
and from 6 April 1956 for one week

The Dreamweavers *Brunswick 05515*

Writers: Wade Buff and Eugene Adkinson
Producers: Eugene Adkinson, Wade Buff and Milt Gabler

Gene Adkinson and Wade Buff wrote **It's Almost Tomorrow** but could find nobody to record it. So, being resourceful people, they formed their own group and made the record. Decca in America picked it up, and in November 1955 the session group hit the American Hot Hundred. It was released in Britain early in 1956, and in climbing to the very top it established two minor chart records. Firstly, the Dreamweavers became the first session group to hit the top, beginning a list that now includes the Archies, Edison Lighthouse, the Rubettes and others. Secondly, by having no more chart success at all, they joined the one-hit-wonder club which at the time included only Kitty Kallen (see no.21), and after 457 more chart-toppers remain the only one-hit wonders to have got back to number one after slipping from the top.

In America, they were slightly longer lasting. **It's Almost Tomorrow** only reached number 8 on the Billboard Hit Hundred, but it was followed by two more singles, both sides of which hit the chart. At the end of June 1956, they disappeared simultaneously from both the British and American charts, never to return. **It's Almost Tomorrow** returned though. David Whitfield sang the song on **All Star Hit Parade** which reached number two in July 1956 and Mark Wynter's version climbed to number 12 at the very end of 1963 to give him his last but one hit.

44

ROCK AND ROLL WALTZ

30 March 1956, for one week

Kay Starr, with the Hugo Winterhalter Orchestra *HMV POP 168*

Writers: Dick Ware and Shorty Allen
Producer: Hugo Winterhalter

Miss Katherine Starks joined Rosemary Clooney on the list of female performers with two number one hits to their credit, a list that was extended to three 2 weeks later when Winifred Atwell equalled their feat. It is now a very long list, but only one solo female performer has managed three number ones – Sandie Shaw.

Kay Starr also established a record that has since been equalled by ten other acts (apart from one-hit wonders) by having a number one hit with her last chart record. As she had also made number one with her first hit (see no.3) she established a weird record, which has only recently been equalled by John Travolta and Olivia Newton-John, of starting and finishing with a number one. In Kay Starr's case, it was easily explained. Her chart success had really ended late in 1954, and a change of label from Capitol to RCA (HMV in Britain) had done her no good at all, until she found a Dick Ware/Shorty Allen song that brilliantly combined modernity and the conservative sound of the 1940's and thus appealed to a wide range of tastes. It was a number one hit on both sides of the Atlantic, and in America at least Miss Starr was able to follow it up with four more small hits over the next 2½ years. But even a label change back to Capitol in the early sixties could not restore her chart career to its mid-fifties glories.

45

POOR PEOPLE OF PARIS

13 April 1956, for three weeks

Winifred Atwell *Decca F 10681*

Writer: Marguerite Monnot
Producer: Hugh Mendl

The second chart topper for the girl from Tunapuna, Trinidad was the second 'French' instrumental, after Mantovani's **Moulin Rouge**, to top the hit parade. Winifred Atwell, a qualified chemist, began playing for charity in Trinidad before going first to New York and then to London to study the piano. She hit the big time when she realised that boogie piano was more lucrative than classical piano, and by 1951 she had a recording contract. It was a happy birthday for her in 1956, for on that day, 27 April, she was at number one, and all in all the entire year was a good one for her. She followed up **Poor People of Paris** with two more French sounding tunes, **Port Au Prince** (which is of course in Haiti) and **Left Bank** (one of which there is in Paris). Her version of another European tune, **Theme From The Threepenny Opera** also featured on the **All Star Hit Parade** single which climbed to number two in July 1956. And all this on that 'other piano', which reportedly cost Miss Atwell 50 shillings in a Battersea junk shop.

The **Poor People of Paris** may have been referring to those Parisians not super-rich or super-chic enough to be invited to the wedding of the year in Monte Carlo, where Prince Rainier of Monaco married Grace Kelly on 19 April 1956. Actually, though, the title was a mistake. Originally called 'Pauvre Jean' (Poor John) in French, somebody misheard the title as 'Pauvre Gens' (Poor People), so Miss Atwell's version became **Poor People of Paris**.

46

NO OTHER LOVE

4 May 1956, for six weeks

Ronnie Hilton *HMV POP 198*

Writers: Richard Rodgers and Oscar Hammerstein II
Producer: Walter Ridley

From the comparatively unknown Rodgers and Hammerstein musical **Me and Juliet**, written in 1953, Ronnie Hilton took the hit tune **No Other Love** and scored his one and only number one hit. He fought off competition from the UK-based Canadian Edmund Hockridge and from the Johnston Brothers, but no American versions of this song ever reached the British charts. Perry Como had been successful with the song in America, but his version had been released in 1953, when *Me and Juliet* opened on Broadway.

Ronnie Hilton's light operatic style, in the tradition of David Whitfield, was already by mid-1956 being overtaken by events. Elvis Presley's British chart career began in the second week of Ronnie Hilton's six week run at the top, and by the time **No Other Love** dropped off the charts, Elvis had already racked up three hits. Nevertheless Ronnie Hilton continued to hit the charts regularly until the middle of 1959, when his last hit for 5 years was a song that Elvis was to take to number one in 1970, **The Wonder Of You**. In 1964 and 1965 Ronnie Hilton came back to the Top 30 with two novelty hits, and his total of 128 weeks on the chart places him equal with multi-chart-toppers Anthony Newley and the Searchers.

47

I'LL BE HOME

15 June 1956, for five weeks

Pat Boone *London HLD 8253*

Writers: Ferdinand Washington and Stan Lewis
Producer: Randy Wood

Pat Boone, born 1 June 1934, is the clean-cut All American boy of popular music. His real name is Charles Eugene Boone. Dean Martin once said, 'I shook hands with Pat Boone and my whole right side sobered up.' Boone refused to kiss his co-star in the film *April Love* on the grounds that it might jeopardise his marriage, and his ghost-written book *Twixt Twelve and Twenty* gave teenagers all the right advice, which they ignored in their millions.

Pat Boone's records, however, they did not ignore. **I'll Be Home** was his second hit in Britain, following up his version of the Fats Domino classic, **Ain't That A Shame**, which reached number seven. Domino's own version finally charted in Britain in 1957, but only reached number 23. By 1957, Boone was moving towards the ballads he knew best how to handle, and monster hits like **April Love, Love Letters In The Sand** and **It's Too Soon To Know** followed. His chart career continued until 1962, and in just over 7 years of chart life, Boone was so successful that he is still one of the 15 top chart performers of all time in Britain.

He is married to Country Hall Of Fame star Red Foley's daughter Shirley. The eldest of their four daughters, Debbie Boone, had the biggest US hit of the 1970's with her recording of **You Light Up My Life**.

48

WHY DO FOOLS FALL IN LOVE

20 July 1956, for three weeks

The Teenagers featuring Frankie Lymon *Columbia DB 3772*

Writers: Frankie Lymon and George Goldner
Producer: Richard Barrett

Rarely has a star shone brighter so soon and gone out so quickly than in the case of Frankie Lymon. Discovered singing gospel songs with friends on a New York street corner, Lymon and his group had an international hit with their very first attempt. **Why Do Fools Fall In Love** entered the American Top 100 the first week of February, 1956, ultimately reaching number seven. It got to the top of the rhythm and blues list in the first week of March, and remained there for 5 weeks. It spread to the United Kingdom in June, beginning a 3 week run at the summit in July. This was the first rhythm and blues side to go to number one in Britain. Frankie Lymon was only 13 years old when he wrote this standard with George Goldner and cut it with the Teenagers. He was the youngest artist to top the British chart and remained so until Little Jimmy Osmond chirped his way to the heights in 1972. Lymon was also the youngest star to top the bill at the London Palladium, achieving this

Left **50 Anne Shelton**

Below **46 Ronnie Hilton**

Above **49 Doris Day**

Left **47 Pat Boone**

in 1957 at the age of 14. In that year the group scored three more chart hits, including the immortal **I'm Not a Juvenile Delinquent** the Top 10 **Baby Baby** and the evergreen **Goody Goody**. Lymon's career went downhill from then on. Diana Ross took his song to the Top 10 a quarter of a century later, but Frankie was not alive to see it. He had died of a drug overdose in 1968, one of the very first rock drug casualties.

49

WHATEVER WILL BE WILL BE

10 August 1956, for six weeks

Doris Day *Philips PB 586*

Writers: Ray Evans and Jerry Livingston
Producer: Mitch Miller

Whatever Will Be Will Be (**Que Sera Sera**) was the Oscar-winning song from the 1956 film *The Man Who Knew Too Much*, directed by Alfred Hitchcock and starring James Stewart and Doris Day. It was the second time within a year that a song from a James Stewart movie had hit number one in Britain, coming only twelve hits after Jimmy Young's **Man From Laramie**. It was also the second time that Doris Day had taken an Oscar-winning song to number one in Britain.

By this time, Miss Day was moving rapidly away from recording and into movie-making, which explains why she had only two more small hits after her second number one, and then a long gap until her last Top 10 hit in 1964, the theme of her box-office smash film with Rock Hudson, *Move Over Darling*.

Whatever Will Be Will Be was Doris Day's last million-seller, and was to prove to be one of the few hits for one of the only two recording acts to have a number one written about them, Geno Washington. Washington and his Ram Jam Band took **Que Sera Sera** to number 43 at the end of 1966, 13½ years before Dexy's Midnight Runners took their tribute **Geno** to the very top (see no. 457). No prizes for working out who is the only other recording act to feature in the title of a number one hit – it is John Lennon (and Yoko Ono), who wrote his own tribute to himself, **The Ballad of John and Yoko** (see no. 272).

50

LAY DOWN YOUR ARMS

21 September 1956, for four weeks

Anne Shelton *Philips PB 616*

Writers: Leon Land and Ake Gerhard, English lyrics by Paddy Roberts
Producer: Johnny Franz

Paddy Roberts, the humorist and songwriter who had put English lyrics to Ruby Murray's **Softly Softly** (see no. 29), found a Swedish song called **Ann-Caroline** and turned it into a saga of a returning soldier, **Lay Down Your Arms**. He showed it to the popular band vocalist Anne Shelton, who liked it enough to record it. Miss Shelton had been vocalist with the Ambrose Orchestra since the age of 14 and was the only serious rival in popularity to Vera Lynn during the war years, so it was shrewd of Miss Shelton to record a song which harked back to her great years a decade earlier. Messrs. Land and Gerhard thus became the only Swedes until Andersson, Anderson and Ulvaeus to write a British number one hit. Miss Shelton's previous experience of singing a European song with English lyrics was Tommy Connor's adaptation of **Lilli Marlene**. Miss Shelton was the first to record it in English, and it gave her her biggest hit in the days when there was no record sales chart.

In America, the Chordettes recorded **Lay Down Your Arms** in a reverse of the usual route for cover versions and took it to number 16. Britain had its revenge when the Mudlarks covered their **Lollipop** and took it to number two in Britain, leaving the Chordettes a few places lower down at number six.

51

A WOMAN IN LOVE

19 October 1956, for four weeks

Frankie Laine *Philips PB 617*

Writer: Frank Loesser
Producer: Mitch Miller

A Woman in Love has been the title of two different songs that have reached number one. Frankie Laine's song and Barbra Streisand's song in 1980 (see no. 468) have nothing in common except the title. The same can be said for the only other title used twice by different number one hits,

Forever And Ever, by Demis Roussos (see no. 392) and by Slik (see no. 384). Frankie Laine's **A Woman in Love** was written by Frank Loesser, composer of many popular songs in the forties and fifties, including for example **Slow Boat to China**. With the towering tonsils of Frankie Laine behind it, it was almost inevitable that it would climb to the very top of the charts.

There is no doubt that sales of **A Woman in Love** were enormous, if not quite on the scale of **I Believe** or **Answer Me**. However, during the record's run at the top, most of the world had other matters on their minds. The Suez crisis culminated in the Anglo-French offensive between 31 October and 5 November 1956, which for some time caused a rift in the tight bonds of friendship between Britain and America, which not even the lungs of Mr Laine could repair. With what Sir Anthony Eden called 'very grave issues at stake', it is not surprising that most people concentrated less on **A Woman in Love** than on the future of the world.

52

JUST WALKIN' IN THE RAIN

16 November 1956, for seven weeks

Johnnie Ray *Philips PB 624*

Writers: Johnny Bragg and Robert S Riley
Producer: Mitch Miller

Two and a half years after his previous number one, at a time when the gathering tide of rock and roll was preparing to sweep the crooners into obscurity, Johnnie Ray scored with his second and third number one hits. By this time he was a show business institution, but many people considered him to be nothing more than a gimmick. The Sultan of Sob, the Cry Guy, the Tearleader, the Prince Of Wails were all nicknames given by the cynical critics who praised but scorned Ray's ability to play on the emotions of his audience. To that one can only reply in the words of the sleeve notes of one of his LPs : 'Johnnie's tears were always real, induced by the sadness of the songs he sang, and did not originate in some carefully concealed artificial tear duct devised by some James Bondian genius of refined gadgetry. He didn't hide his feelings, which meant he was the centre of controversy around the world, particularly here in Britain where our upper lips retain much of their traditional stiffness and we are often embarrassed by public displays of emotion.' Embarrassing maybe, but it sold.

53

SINGING THE BLUES

4 January 1957, for one week
and from 18 January 1957 for one week
and again from 1 February 1957 for one week
(top equal)

Guy Mitchell *Philips PB 650*

Writer: Melvin Endsley
Producer: Mitch Miller

Guy Mitchell's third number one, and the fourth song to hit number one in two different versions, was written in 1954 by Melvin Endsley, who had been paralysed since contracting polio at the age of 3, in 1937. It was number one in America late in 1956 and crossed the Atlantic in style, taking over the top spot in its fifth week on the chart and outlasting the heavily hyped local competition from Tommy Steele. The backing that the Ray Conniff Orchestra gave to Mitchell made it a very different arrangement from the slaphappy skiffle-rock of the Steelemen, who perversely may well have come closer to the sound that Melvin Endsley was looking for than the men under the technical precision of Mr Conniff's baton.

Singing The Blues all but equalled the record of **I Believe** in returning twice to the number one spot, the second time to share top spot with Frankie Vaughan, Guy Mitchell's run of 22 weeks on the chart with the song was the longest chart run of any of his 14 hits. Dave Edmunds revived the song in 1980, reaching number 28 and increasing the total number of weeks the song has spent on the chart to 45, one of the more successful songs in British chart history.

54

SINGING THE BLUES

11 January 1957, for one week

Tommy Steele *Decca F 10819*

Writer: Melvin Endsley
Producer: Hugh Mendl

The story of Tommy Hicks, the boy from Bermondsey, who became Tommy Steele – Britain's answer to Elvis Presley – is too well known to bear repetition here. Steele was never a rock'n'roller, but it is worth noticing that his number one hit came 6 months and a day before Elvis himself hit the top of the charts for the first time.

At the time, Steele was managed by an honest hustler called John Kennedy, with Larry Parnes (Mr Parnes, Shillings and Pence) also acquiring a share of the action about this time. Despite Larry Parnes' subsequent stableful of pop stars (Marty Wilde, Billy Fury, Duffy Power, Georgie Fame, Joe Brown and so on), Tommy Steele was the only Parnes act ever to have a number one hit. Marty Wilde, Billy Fury and Joe Brown all reached number two, but Georgie Fame's number ones came only after he left the Larry Parnes fold. Incidentally, Marty Wilde's daughter Kim followed her father in 1981 by reaching number two, the only case of two generations of a family reaching number two without making number one.

Lionel Bart was writing for Tommy Steele at this time, although both this song and the follow-up, **Knee Deep In The Blues** were Guy Mitchell covers written by Melvin Endsley. Two and a half years later, Lionel Bart wrote his first number one hit, this time for Britain's real answer to Elvis Presley, Cliff Richard.

55

GARDEN OF EDEN

25 January 1957, for four weeks (one week top equal)

Frankie Vaughan *Philips PB 660*

Writer: Dennise Norwood
Producer: Johnny Franz

Frankie Vaughan was the first Liverpool act to top the charts, but his style was far apart from his famous successors like Billy Fury or the Beatles. He was an extension of the music-hall tradition and his high-kicking top-hatted routine of 'Give Me The Moonlight, give me the girl, and leave the rest to me' is still instantly recognisable in the 1980's.

By 1958, Frankie Vaughan had taken over from Dickie Valentine as 'Britain's Most Popular Male Singer' in most of the music press annual polls, and one of the main pillars of his success was his recording of **Garden Of Eden**. At the end of 1956, Frankie Vaughan had scored his first Top 10 hit with his version of **Green Door**, revived by Shakin' Stevens in 1981, and **Garden Of Eden** was the follow-up. The original version, by American Joe Valino scoring his only chart success on either side of the Atlantic, was covered in Britain by Dick James, later to achieve fame and fortune as the Beatles' publisher, by Gary Miller and by Frankie Vaughan. Vaughan won the chart battle easily, and established himself over the next two years as one of Britain's most successful and popular male vocalists, with six Top 10 hits on his own and two more with the vocal trio, the Kaye Sisters.

56

YOUNG LOVE

22 February 1957, for seven weeks

Tab Hunter *London HLD 8380*

Writers: Carole Joyner and Ric Cartey
Producers: Billy Vaughn, executive producer Randy Wood

Tab Hunter was born on 11 July 1931 in New York. His real name is Arthur Gelien, which without doubt is a name to be discarded early on in the climb to the top. He made his film debut in 1948 in a film called *The Lawless* and when **Young Love** was recorded, he was an established box office attraction, if a rather undistinguished actor. In 1982, his name is still a box office attraction, as his 'Special Guest Appearance' billing in the film *Grease II* shows.

Young Love was originally recorded by country star Sonny James, 'The Southern Gentleman', who took the song to the top of the American country charts to give him the first of many country chart-toppers. His version sold a million and reached number two on the American Hot Hundred, kept out of the top slot by Tab Hunter. Sonny James also took his version to number 11 in Britain. The Tab Hunter version, on the other hand, was anything but country. It was one of the first examples of marketing the singer as much as the song. Hunter was no great vocalist but his face was right for selling a dreamy pop ballad to the teenagers of 1957. So his producers turned **Young Love** into a dreamy pop ballad.

When **Young Love** hit the top of the charts again in 1973 (see no. 336) it was again the singer as much as the song that lured the kids into the record shops. But at least Donny Osmond can sing, and he made sure that **Young Love** became one of the few songs to have sold a million in as many as three versions.

57 Lonnie Donegan,
Below left to right
55 Frankie Vaughan, 56 Tab Hunter,
59 Andy Williams

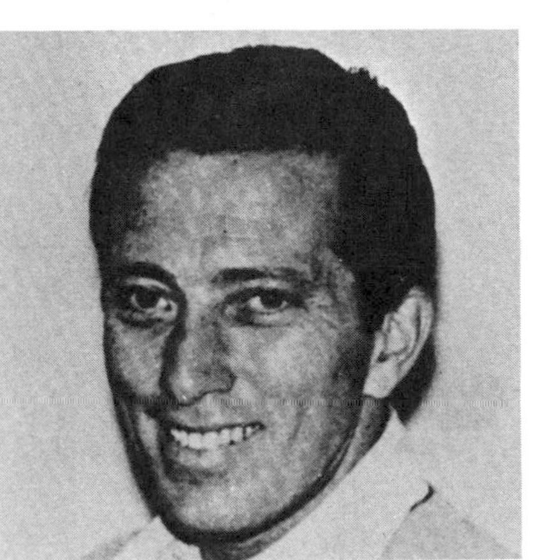

57

CUMBERLAND GAP

12 April 1957, for five weeks

Lonnie Donegan *Pye Nixa B 15087*

Writers: Traditional, arranged by Lonnie Donegan
Producer: Alan Freeman

Lonnie Donegan, born Anthony Donegan in Glasgow on 29 April 1931, was the most successful popular music star in Britain up to the arrival of Cliff Richard. He was the King of Skiffle, the craze that swept the world in the early fifties and which enabled anybody with a tea-chest, a broomhandle and a washboard to perform popular songs. After completing National Service in 1951 (note Donegan is only 2½ months older than teen idol Tab Hunter), Lonnie joined Ken Colyer's Jazzmen where he took the name 'Lonnie' after his hero Lonnie Johnson. He played guitar in Ken Colyer's skiffle group, along with Chris Barber. When Barber formed his own jazz band, Lonnie Donegan went with him as banjoist.

In 1954, Barber's band recorded **Rock Island Line** as a skiffle record, with Lonnie Donegan on vocals. Included originally on an album, it was not released as a single until the beginning of 1956 when it rose quickly into the British Top 10, and more amazingly into the American Top 10 as well. Donegan left Barber, somewhat reluctantly, and the hits rolled out with a consistency that had never before been achieved, even by the likes of Frankie Laine and Guy Mitchell. **Cumberland Gap** was Lonnie Donegan's fifth single. The previous four had all reached the Top 10. In fact he was so popular in 1956 that an EP, 'Skiffle Session' and an LP 'Lonnie Donegan Showcase' also reached the singles Top 30.

58

ROCK-A-BILLY

17 May 1957, for one week

Guy Mitchell *Philips PB 685*

Writers: Woody Harris and Eddie V Deane
Producer: Mitch Miller

Guy Mitchell's fourth and final number one was a pleasant little tune, as near as Mitch Miller would ever get to admitting the existence of rock'n'roll, skiffle or the blues. The title of the song became the name for a whole style of music, a cross between rock and hillbilly country music which bore only slight resemblance to the style of the song **Rock-A-Billy**. It pre-dates Rocky Burnette's claim that rockabilly was invented by his father Johnny Burnette and his uncle Dorsey, and that they named their music after Rocky and his cousin, Dorsey's son Billy.

Rock-A-Billy missed the Top 10 altogether in America, and cannot frankly be described as one of Mitchell's greatest records. It proved to be his last big hit for almost 3 years, during which time the rockers completed their conquest of the charts of the world and left the disciples of Mitch Miller out in the cold. Mitchell's comeback hit, his last hit in Britain, was called **Heartaches By The Number** and it reached number one in America. It climbed as high as number five over here, making it the most successful of the comeback hits of the three 1950's superstars who were all back briefly in the charts at the same time at the end of 1959. Frankie Laine's **Rawhide** reached number six, Johnnie Ray's **I'll Never Fall In Love Again** made number 26, and then the three cornerstones of Philips success faded into the sunset.

59

BUTTERFLY

24 May 1957, for two weeks

Andy Williams *London HLA 8399*

Writer: Anthony September
Producer: Archie Bleyer

Andy Williams (born in Iowa on 3 December 1928) has only ever had one number one record in Britain or America. **Butterfly** climbed to the top on both sides of the Atlantic and launched Andy Williams on a long chart career, but remains his only chart-topper. It was written by Anthony September, who turns out to be Kal Mann and Bernie Lowe, writers of **Teddy Bear** for Elvis and founders of the Cameo-Parkway label which gave us Chubby Checker, Bobby Rydell and the Orlons.

Butterfly is now one of Williams' rarest recordings. His hits of the sixties and seventies, like **Can't Get Used To Losing You**, **Almost There** and **Where Do I Begin** (**Love Story**) are the songs he is known for, while **Butterfly** remains cocooned in obscurity. As Andy Williams owns the masters of all his early recordings, one can assume he wants this cut to remain obscure, which is a pity.

Andy Williams is one of 14 Williamses to hit the chart, Britain's most common chart surname. His chartmaking nephew shares his name so the name Andy Williams, like the names Karen Young, Sylvia or Kenny, is one of the few names to have been used by more than one chart act. Nevertheless, few people doubt who will appear when Andy Williams is billed at Las Vegas or the London Palladium.

60

YES TONIGHT JOSEPHINE

7 June 1957, for three weeks

Johnnie Ray *Philips PB 686*

Writers: Winfield Scott and Dorothy Goodman
Producer: Mitch Miller

Johnnie Ray's third and final number one was one of the very few happy songs he recorded. It was an uptempo number, as near to rock'n'roll as Ray ever came, but more in the tradition of **Green Door** and **Rock and Roll Waltz** than **Hound Dog** or **Why Do Fools Fall In Love**. Producer Stuart Colman dug out the song in 1981 for the Jets, but it was not as successful as his revamping of **This Ole House** or **Green Door** for Shakin' Stevens.

By the middle of 1957, rock was finishing forever the popularity of Guy Mitchell, Frankie Laine and Johnnie Ray. From then on it was the nostalgia market that guaranteed record sales for the early fifties balladeers, and not the pop fans. For producer Mitch Miller, the mastermind of American Columbia's amazing successes in the early chart years, it was the end. He fought against rock, he condemned it and ignored it in his productions, but it wouldn't go away.

Nowadays, Ray is still performing, still bringing in the fans to hear the songs that 30 years ago made the bobby-soxers go crazy. He is a wealthy, contented professional whose years of experience and natural talent have kept his head well above the waves since the tide of rock'n'roll came in.

61

GAMBLIN' MAN/PUTTING ON THE STYLE

28 June 1957, for two weeks

Lonnie Donegan *Pye Nixa N 15093*

Writers: Gamblin' Man – Woody Guthrie and Lonnie Donegan
Putting On The Style – Traditional, arranged by Norman Cazden
Producers: Alan Freeman and Michael Barclay (recorded live at the London Palladium)

Lonnie Donegan's second consecutive number one, his sixth consecutive Top 10 hit, was also Britain's first double-sided number one hit. Of the first 500 number ones, only 18 have been listed as double-sided hits (apart from the two number one EPs) and few have been so genuinely split in sales between the two sides as this skiffle classic single.

Gamblin' Man was a Woody Guthrie tune, adapted by Lonnie Donegan. Guthrie, whose son Arlo still performs successfully in America, was the major influence on Bob Dylan, who in turn influenced very many of the biggest acts of the late sixties and seventies. By the time Lonnie Donegan was at number one with the only Woody Guthrie song that ever reached the top, Guthrie himself had already given up performing as he became increasingly disabled by a rare nerve disease, Huntington's chorea. It was to be 10 more years till he died, on 3 October 1967, by which time his name was synonymous with the best of American folk music, thanks to the performances of people like Bob Dylan and Lonnie Donegan.

62

ALL SHOOK UP

12 July 1957, for seven weeks

Elvis Presley *HMV POP 359*

Writers: Otis Blackwell and Elvis Presley
Producer: Steve Sholes

After two number two hits and seven other hits in the first year of his chart career, Elvis finally hit number one with his tenth British hit single, his only number one hit on HMV and the only one of his seventeen number ones on which he shares a writing credit.

All Shook Up was Presley's only number one on the HMV label because almost immediately after its success, RCA set up their own distribution network in UK. The deal to go independent of HMV allowed HMV to retain the 'Nipper the dog' trade mark which RCA originated and controls in virtually every country of the world, but this proved to be of little consolation for losing the rights to Elvis Presley.

Born in Tupelo, Mississippi on 8 January 1935, Elvis Aron Presley was to prove to be the King, the man who invented rock and created the mammoth music industry that surrounds rock'n'roll. He once said, 'Rhythm is something you either have or you don't have, but when you have it, you have it all over.' He had it so much they only dared televise him from the waist up.

63

DIANA

30 August 1957, for nine weeks

Paul Anka *Columbia DB 3980*

Writer: Paul Anka
Producer: Don Costa

Canadian-born Paul Anka was 16 years and 31 days old when his self-penned single became the shortest title to hit the top of the charts up to that time, and he was not much older by the time his paean to young love had become one of the biggest selling records of all time. Total record sales are as much a subject of obfuscation as Gary Glitter's age, but there is little doubt that **Diana** is, with Bing Crosby's **White Christmas** and Bill Haley's **Rock Around The Clock**, one of the biggest selling singles in the world in the pre-Beatles era.

Paul Anka never had another number one hit in Britain, although his chart successes lasted into the seventies with his US number one hit **(You're) Having My Baby** which reached number six in Britain at the end of 1974. Although his performing career may have been reduced to making Japanese whisky advertisements, his writing career has never flagged. He wrote **It Doesn't Matter Anymore** for Buddy Holly and thus became the first person ever to write a British chart-topper for himself and for somebody else. His **Puppy Love**, which gave Anka a number 33 hit in 1960, became a number one for Donny Osmond over 10 years later, while his main claim to composing fame must now be his English lyrics for British chart history's most successful song, **My Way**. Add the fact that he is happily married to a beautiful and rich wife, and it seems astonishing that he still needs to earn money by advertising Japanese whisky.

64

THAT'LL BE THE DAY

1 November 1957, for three weeks

The Crickets *Vogue Coral Q 72279*

Writers: Buddy Holly, Jerry Allison and Norman Petty
Producer: Norman Petty

That'll Be The Day was the phrase used by John Wayne in the 1956 film, *The Searchers* (which is also where the **Needles And Pins** group found their name). Buddy Holly turned the phrase into a song, co-written by Cricket drummer Jerry Allison and took it to Decca, who recorded the song. This version did not come out well and was not successful when released in the States, but Holly still had faith in the song. He took it to Norman Petty's studios at Clovis, New Mexico and re-recorded it with himself, Jerry Allison, Larry Welborn and Niki Sullivan comprising the Crickets. The result was excellent, but Holly's contract with Decca meant that they could not sell the song elsewhere. Eventually, Bob Thiele, A&R manager at the Decca subsidiary Coral Records, decided he wanted to release the track, and Decca released him from his contract with Decca and bound him to another with Coral.

The record was released in America in June 1957, but moved very slowly until New England regional breakouts boosted the record onto the national chart by the end of July. Buddy Holly and the Crickets had arrived.

65

MARY'S BOY CHILD

22 November 1957, for seven weeks

Harry Belafonte *RCA 1022*

Writer: Jester Hairston
Producer: René Farnon

Harry Belafonte, who like Elvis switched from HMV to RCA in the summer of 1957, gave his employers their first British number one with the most famous Christmas hit of all. It was the first record to sell a million copies in Britain alone, and reached the top over a month before Christmas. The record's 7 week run at number one is the longest by a song with a Christmas theme, and it has remained a Christmas favourite. Belafonte's version returned to the charts for each of the next two Christmases, Danish duo Nina and Frederick charted with it in 1959, and Boney M's version reached number one in 1978 (see no.430).

Harold George Belafonte was born in New York on 1 March 1927. He spent 3 years in the US Navy and then enrolled at the American Negro Theatre Workshop. His singing came to the attention of manager Monty Kaye, and eventually a recording contract with RCA Victor followed. He starred in a series of films such as *Carmen Jones, The World, The Flesh And The Devil* and *Island In The Sun.* It was this last film, together with his 1957 albums 'Calypso' and 'Belafonte Sings Of The Caribbean' which gave him the nickname 'King of Calypso' and hits like the self-penned **Banana Boat Song, Scarlet Ribbons** and **Mary's Boy Child.**

66

GREAT BALLS OF FIRE

10 January 1958, for two weeks

Jerry Lee Lewis *London HLS 8529*

Writers: Otis Blackwell and Jack Hammer
Producer: Sam Phillips

Jerry Lee Lewis, born in Ferriday, Louisiana, on 29 September 1935, was and remains one of the great originals of rock. He is one of the many great stars who began their career at Sam Phillips' sun label in Memphis (like Elvis Presley, Roy Orbison and Johnny Cash among others) and the only white rock and roller of real note to use a piano rather than a guitar as his main weapon.

Great Balls Of Fire, written by Otis Blackwell of **All Shook Up** fame and the aptly named Jack Hammer, is the wildest rock record ever to reach number one in Britain. Jerry Lee lived as wild a life as the music he played, and his first career came to an abrupt end when it was disclosed that he had married his 14 year old cousin. Three years later he was back with still the only version of the Ray Charles classic **What'd I Say** to reach the British charts. But by this time a move back to his country roots, coupled with further personal problems, pushed his career into obscurity as far as Britain was concerned.

By the early seventies, Jerry Lee was back yet again. Now he is an established and very successful US country star, with a string of hits to his name. Songs like **Thirty-Nine and Holding** (which sounds like a West Indian Test Match score) and his own inimitable version of **Me and Bobby McGhee** have been good to him, but in this period only his rendition of The Big Bopper's **Chantilly Lace** made the British charts, reaching number 33 in 1972.

Happily, he survived serious illness in 1981, after hovering between life and death for several days.

67

JAILHOUSE ROCK

24 January 1958, for three weeks

Elvis Presley *RCA 1028*

Writers: Jerry Lieber and Mike Stoller
Producer: Steve Sholes

For the first time since the chart began over 5 years earlier, a record entered the hit parade at number one. Needless to say, it was Elvis Presley who achieved this unthinkable feat with the title tune from his third film, *Jailhouse Rock*. Most Elvis fans would list *Jailhouse Rock* as his best movie: his four pre-Army films seem in hindsight to be in a completely different class from the increasingly insipid post-demobilisation efforts.

Written by Jerry Lieber and Mike Stoller, whose hit songs for the Drifters and others had made them one of the most successful of rock writing teams, the title tune of *Jailhouse Rock* showed off Elvis' talents at their very best. Elvis cut over 20 Lieber/Stoller songs during his career, after he had come across their work through a lounge group's version of Willie Mae Thornton's original R and B hit **Hound Dog**, but this was the only UK chart-topper written solely by these two songwriting giants. They were two-thirds of the team that wrote Elvis' twelfth number one **She's Not You**. The recording was made at MGM's studio in Culver City on 2 May 1957 with the following line-up: Elvis (vocals and guitar), Scotty Moore (guitar) Mike Stoller and Elvis Presley (piano) Bill Black (bass) D J Fontana (drums) and the Jordanaires (backing vocals). For 5 weeks one of the records selling in opposition to **Jailhouse Rock** in Britain was an EP containing five songs from the movie, including **Jailhouse Rock** itself. No other number one A-side has ever appeared in the Top 20 twice in the same week, but many fans were presumably buying both single and EP, needing both to get all six songs from the movie, as the flip of the single, **Treat Me Nice** (another Lieber/Stoller song) was not on the EP.

68

THE STORY OF MY LIFE

14 February 1958, for two weeks

Michael Holliday *Columbia DB 4058*

Writers: Burt Bacharach and Hal David
Producer: Norrie Paramor

The story of Michael Holliday's life was tragic. Born in Liverpool in the late 1920's, Michael Miller changed his name by deed poll to Michael Milne, but used his mother's maiden name for his singing career. By the beginning of 1956, he was beginning to break through the ranks of the British hopefuls and into the charts, basing his style on the casual phrasing and delivery of Perry Como and Bing Crosby. In 1956, he had three chart singles and soon found himself with his own TV show. However, Holliday was

64 Crickets

65 Harry Belafonte

68 Michael Holliday

69 Perry Como

extremely nervous and was unable to cope with the success he found. All the same, his popularity continued beyond the end of the decade and in 1960 he scored his second chart-topper, (see no. 95). Three years later he shot himself.

The Story Of My Life, was the first of six Bacharach/David number one hits and had been first recorded by Marty Robbins in America. Robbins, one of the biggest country stars in American musical history, issued it as the follow-up to his number three pop hit, **A White Sport Coat,** which had been covered and obliterated in England. His version of **Story Of My Life** also failed to make the charts in Britain, and it was not until the release of his four minute single **El Paso** that he made a small dent on the British charts. Burt Bacharach and Hal David have proved more successful in Britain than Robbins or Michael Holliday, and longer lasting.

69

MAGIC MOMENTS

28 February 1958, for eight weeks

Perry Como *RCA 1036*

Writers: Burt Bacharach and Hal David
Producer: Joe Reisman

For the first time in chart history, consecutive number ones were written by the same writers. Burt Bacharach and Hal David, the team that has written number one hits for more acts than any other pop partnership, came up with a second number one with this classic 'list song' for Perry Como. The flip side, **Catch A Falling Star** by Paul Vance and Lee Pockriss, was listed separately from **Magic Moments** but still reached the Top 10, making the record the biggest selling hit in Perry Como's career.

This was the singing barber's last number one in Britain, and it came at the peak of his fame when the Perry Como Show was the most popular variety show on British television. Como was now the highest paid TV star in the world, a title he took over from an earlier number one hitmaker, Eddie Fisher, and a guest appearance on his show could turn a flop into a hit. Throughout it all, Como remained relaxed both on stage and off, and a genuine Mr Nice Guy. Michael Holliday shared Como's taste in writers and his on-stage relaxed image. It was a pity his off-stage personality was so different.

70

WHOLE LOTTA WOMAN

25 April 1958, for three weeks

Marvin Rainwater *MGM 974*

Writer: Marvin Rainwater
Producer: Jim Vinneau

With a name like Marvin Rainwater, you either had to succeed outrageously or else sink without trace. He actually did both, in that order. Born on 2 July 1925 in Wichita, Kansas, full-blooded Cherokee Marvin Percy took his mother's maiden name to become a country singer.

He first scored on the national charts in America in the summer of 1957 with **Gonna Find Me A Bluebird.** That had reached number three on the American country charts, and number 22 on the pop charts, and the combination of Marvin Rainwater and the hot MGM label seemed certain to carry on succeeding. His follow-up was a duet with the girl destined to be MGM's hottest star of the late fifties, Connie Francis, which also sold a million. Then came **Whole Lotta Woman**, which for no apparent reason (it made only number 60 on the Billboard pop charts) was released in UK and started picking up airplay action, what little of it there was in 1958. In a year which featured **Great Balls Of Fire, Jailhouse Rock** and **It's Only Make Believe** at the top of the British Charts, **Whole Lotta Woman** stands comparison with those greats as a fine rock and roll record, typical of the era when country and rock were still blood brothers.

Marvin Rainwater's follow-up was a lesser hit, called **I Dig You Baby**. Thereafter, obscurity reclaimed him almost as quickly as he had found fame.

71

WHO'S SORRY NOW

16 May 1958, for six weeks

Connie Francis *MGM 975*

Writers: Ted Snyder, Bert Kalmar and Herman Ruby
Producer: Harry Myerson. Orchestra and chorus arranged by Joe Lippman

For one last attempt at a hit before her recording contract at MGM lapsed, pint-sized Concetta Franconero revived the 1920's standard **Who's Sorry Now?** The answer – nobody except the acts she kept away from the top of the charts for 6 weeks in the early summer of 1958.

Born on 12 December 1938, Connie Francis left university in New York before graduation to concentrate on her musical career. At first the decision seemed mistaken. Apart from a duet with Marvin Rainwater, **Majesty Of Love** in 1957, all her recordings failed totally. Then she was given a song from 1923 to record, and with a very straightforward arrangement, she took it to the top of the British charts. Contrary to popular legend, **Who's Sorry Now** did not make number one in the States, peaking at number four. Her other British number one, **Stupid Cupid** coupled with **Carolina Moon** (see no. 75), made only number 17 in America, while her three American number ones all failed to reach the very top in Britain. Generally speaking, her successful songs in Britain were the up-tempo numbers like **Stupid Cupid** and **Robot Man** and **Lipstick On Your Collar. Who's Sorry Now** was the exception that launched her career.

72

ON THE STREET WHERE YOU LIVE

27 June 1958, for two weeks
(one week top equal)
Vic Damone *Philips PB 819*

Writers: Alan Jay Lerner and Frederick Loewe
Producer: Mitch Miller

The musical *My Fair Lady* is probably the best known of all post-war musicals. It launched the career of Julie Andrews, while Rex Harrison gave non-singers new career prospects in the musical with his expert and much imitated style of talking to music. When the show opened on Broadway, the producers went to great lengths to ensure that the music was not exported, so that the show could open in markets like Britain before audiences to whom it would all be new. The formula worked.

Vic Damone was the lucky man with the hit version of the hit song, **On The Street Where You Live.** The only other chart version was by David Whitfield but Vic Damone had the advantage of having already had an American Top 10 hit with the song, even though it had been 2 years earlier in the spring of 1956. Thanks to the producers' international secrecy policy, by the time **On The Street Where You Live** reached number one in Britain, Damone's version of the title tune of Lerner and Loewe's next musical *Gigi* had been and gone from the American charts.

Vic Damone, who had begun his recording career at Mercury under the supervision of Mitch Miller, had little chart success after his one smash. The follow-up, **The Only Man On The Island**, was covered by Tommy Steele, and they both had small hits. Thereafter, nothing happened for him chartwise, although he still turns up on television from time to time. In 1981 he was seen singing a tribute to Bob Hope to the tune of **On The Street Where You Live.**

73

ALL I HAVE TO DO IS DREAM/CLAUDETTE

4 July 1958, for seven weeks
(one week top equal)
The Everly Brothers *London HLA 8618*

Writers: All I Have to Do Is Dream – Felice and Boudleaux Bryant
Claudette – Roy Orbison
Producers: Archie Bleyer. Arranged by Don Everly

Don (born 1 February 1937) and Phil (born 19 January 1939) Everly launched their careers as the most successful vocal group in the world before the Beatles, with the classic **Bye Bye Love.** That reached number six in UK, and the follow-up **Wake Up Little Susie** (which was covered by the Stargazers among others) reached number two. Their third single was the country ballad that became a standard – **All I Have To Do Is Dream.** Written by the husband and wife team of Felice and Boudleaux Bryant who have become closely associated with the early career of the Everlys, it has been covered many times, most successfully by Bobby Gentry and Glen Campbell, whose duet reached number three in 1969. But none of the covers quite match the plaintive harmonies of the Everly Brothers, with whom the song will always be associated. In 1981 Phil Everly appeared on stage with Cliff Richard to sing **All I Have To Do Is Dream**, the only version that ever got near the original.

The flip-side, which was listed with the A side for 20 of the record's 21 weeks on the chart, was a rocking tribute to his wife Claudette, written by the then unknown Roy Orbison. Orbison's chart career began in 1960, when his **Only The Lonely** made him only the second person after Paul Anka to write a number one for himself and for another act. It was the first of two number ones for the Everlys with a girl's name in the title – **Cathy's Clown** (see no. 101) was to follow. All in all, the Everlys charted with songs about

Left to right Above
73 Everly Brothers,
83 Russ Conway,
88 Cliff Richard and the Drifters
Centre
71 Connie Francis, 72 Vic Damone
Below
78 Conway Twitty, 74 Kalin Twins,
80 Elvis Presley

Susie, Claudette, Mary, Jenny, Cathy, Lucille and Ebony Eyes, who were only seven of the millions of girls who worshipped the Everlys when they were at their peak.

74

WHEN

22 August 1958, for five weeks

The Kalin Twins *Brunswick 05751*

Writers: Jack Reardon and Paul Evans
Producer: Jack Pleis

Harold and Herbie Kalin were born on 16 February 1939, making them one day older than John Leyton (see no.124). They were discovered by Clint Ballard Jr., the writer of many hits including **Good Timin'** for Jimmy Jones and **I'm Alive** for the Hollies. Harold and Herbie were the first set of twins to reach number one in Britain, and remain the only set to make it on their own. Twins Robin and Maurice Gibb of the Bee Gees, and Dervin and Lincoln Gordon of the Equals are probably the only other twins to reach number one, but the list is hard to finalise. There were no twins in the England World Cup Squad, but what about the St. Winifred's School Choir?

The Kalin Twins were the third one hit wonders. The plea of their follow up **Forget Me Not**, was not heeded and the fans quickly forgot them thoroughly. It is a useless but coincidental fact that three of the first four acts to be classified as one hit wonders had surnames beginning with K – Kitty Kallen, The Kalin Twins and Jerry Keller. Fern Kinney added herself to the list in 1980, and the only K's with number one hits who are not one hit wonders are Kraftwerk, Johnny Kidd, the Kinks and Eden Kane, who did manage to have a hit with a (different) song called **Forget Me Not.**

75

CAROLINA MOON/STUPID CUPID

26 September 1958, for six weeks

Connie Francis *MGM 985*

Writers: Carolina Moon – Benny Davis and Joe Burke, Stupid Cupid – Neil Sedaka and Howard Greenfield.
Producers: Connie Francis and Leroy Holmes. Arranged and conducted by Leroy Holmes.

The combination of a revival of a 1928 Guy Lombardo standard and brand-new teenybop rocker by Neil Sedaka and Howard Greenfield gave Connie Francis her second number one in three releases. It also meant that she spent 12 weeks of 1958 at number one, a domination of the top spot only beaten five times in 30 years. At the end of 1958, she was second only to Frankie Laine's unbeatable total of 27 weeks in 1953, although she has now been overtaken by Elvis Presley (in 1961 and 1962), the Beatles (in 1963) and John Travolta and Olivia Newton-John in 1978.

After 1958, Connie Francis never had another number one in the UK. Top 10 hits, eight more in all, continued until 1962, and she remains the second most successful female vocalist, behind Shirley Bassey, in British chart history. Connie Francis attempted acting in the movie *Where The Boys Are* in 1961, but even she admitted she was hardly a candidate for an Oscar. 'I can't understand why I can't act' she is reported as saying. 'I put so much emotion into my singing'. Her career reached its nadir when she was raped in a motel room in Westbury, Long Island, in 1974 and subsequently suffered a breakdown. However, by 1982 she had made one of the music business' bravest comebacks, making many highly acclaimed personal appearances in America.

76

IT'S ALL IN THE GAME

7 November 1958, for three weeks

Tommy Edwards *MGM 989*

Writers: Charles Gates Dawes and Carl Sigman
Producer: Harry Myerson

MGM's hot streak continued as Tommy Edwards revived a song based on a tune written by President Calvin Coolidge's Vice-President Dawes in 1912, to which words were added by Carl Sigman in 1951. Edwards was born on 17 February 1922, the year of Coolidge's election, and is exactly 17 years older than John Leyton, 19 years older than Gene Pitney and 25 years younger than Sir Anthony Eden, who had resigned as Britain's Prime Minister the year before.

Tommy Edwards originally recorded **It's All In The Game** in 1951, and reached number 18 on the American charts. Then nothing. In 1958 he re-recorded the song with a stronger rhythm section and found himself with his first hit on any chart since 1951. It was a number one R&B and pop hit in America, and quickly repeated the dose in Britain as well.

The song has been a Top 10 hit twice since 1958. Cliff

Richard took it to number 2 in 1963, when it also gave Cliff his biggest American hit (number 25) until the late seventies. The Four Tops version reached number five in Britain in 1970. By then Tommy Edwards was dead, dying at the age of 47 on 22 October 1969.

77

HOOTS MON

28 November 1958, for three weeks

Lord Rockingham's XI *Decca F 11059*

Writer: Harry Robinson
Producer: Harry Robinson

In 1756 it was recorded that 'my Lord Rockingham and my Lord Oxford have made a match of five hundred pounds between five turkeys and five geese to run from Norwich to London.' History does not record the outcome of that particular business venture by Lord Rockingham, but 202 years later, a claimant to his title succeeded spectacularly with a project that might have appeared even more risky than putting £500 to win on five turkeys. The Lord Rockingham of 1958 was Scottish bandleader Harry Robinson, and his XI recorded a rocking novelty instrumental interspersed by snatches of Scottish small talk in Robinson's artificially thick accent. Never before had a foreign language record reached the very top (if 'braw bricht moonlicht nicht' isn't a foreign language, we'd like to know what is). Never before or since has a Roman numeral appeared in the name of a chart-topping act. Indeed, only George Hamilton IV and Napoleon XIV besides Lord Rockingham's XI have brought Latin mathematics into the charts at any position. And never before had a peerage proved so effective a selling factor among pop's usually egalitarian fans. The Sir Douglas Quintet, Queen and the King Brothers are among those who have used noble titles to further their careers, but sadly in the case of Lord Rockingham, it held no long term magic. The next single, **Wee Tom**, flirted briefly with the lower reaches of the Top 20, and after that, oblivion. One of the XI's leading lights was author and music critic, often scathing about rock and roll, Benny Green. He keeps fairly quiet about his contribution on tenor sax to this piece of rock and roll history.

78

IT'S ONLY MAKE BELIEVE

19 December 1958, for five weeks

Conway Twitty *MGM 992*

Writers: Conway Twitty and Jack Nance
Producer: Jim Vinneau

Conway Twitty, born Harold Jenkins in Mariana, Arkansas on 1 September 1933, is reputed to have chosen his stage name from the names of two towns he passed through on one of his first tours. The name was certainly memorable, and it gave Peter Sellers the inspiration for his parody of a pop star, Twit Conway. It could have been worse. He might have passed through Chipping Sodbury and Fulking (Sussex) the night he needed a handle.

Twitty was signed to Mercury until 1957, making a stream of totally unsuccessful country singles and almost equally forgotten rock singles, based on his ability to sound like Elvis. The switch to MGM changed everything. Perhaps it was the knowledge that any record company which already had Marvin Rainwater on its books would not find anything odd about the name Conway Twitty, but whatever it was, Twitty came up with a massive worldwide hit with his first single for MGM.

It's Only Make Believe, a mournful rock ballad, was number one in America, number one in Britain and has gone on to become the only song to reach the British Top 10 on four separate occasions. After Twitty's original success, Billy Fury took the song to number ten in 1964, Glen Campbell reached number four in 1970 and teenybop group Child made number ten in 1978.

Since the early seventies, Conway has returned to country music, and by 1982 had had more number one country singles in America than any other performer.

79

THE DAY THE RAINS CAME

23 January 1959, for one week

Jane Morgan *London HLR 8751*

Writers: Gilbert Becaud, English lyrics by Carl Sigman
Producer: Vic Schoen

Jane Morgan, born Jane Currier in Boston Massachusetts, was trained as a lyric soprano at the Juillard School of Music in New York. To work her way through school, she sang blues in the night clubs and was there noticed by

French impresario Bernard Hilda, who offered her a contract to sing in Paris. What happened to her lyric soprano training is veiled in the mists of time, but within weeks of Miss Morgan's arrival in the French capital she had taken the city by storm. For the next few years she appeared all over Europe establishing a fine reputation and a growing following. In 1958, she recorded a song by Gilbert Becaud in French, called **Le Jour Où La Pluie Viendra** which she decided to record in English as well. It climbed only to number 21 in the States, but in Britain her European reputation helped to push this dramatic ballad to the very top. The French version, incidentally, was on the B-side of the British release.

She subsequently married Jerry Weintraub, the man who put Elvis back on the road in 1970, and who managed John Denver among others.

80

ONE NIGHT/I GOT STUNG

30 January 1959, for three weeks

Elvis Presley *RCA 1100*

Writers: One Night – Dave Bartholomew and Pearl King; I Got Stung – Aaron Schroeder and David Hill
Producers: Steve Sholes and Chet Atkins

Elvis' third UK number one was his first to get there after he went into the US Army in March 1958, and was his first double-sided British chart-topper. **One Night** was written by Dave Bartholomew, responsible for many of Fats Domino's hits, and Pearl King, and was recorded without great commercial success by Smiley Lewis in 1956. Elvis got to grips with it in Radio Recorders Studio, in Hollywood in February 1957, his vocal and guitar being supported by Scotty Moore (guitar), Dudley Brooks (piano) Bill Black (bass), D J Fontana (drums) and the backing vocals of the Jordanaires. It thus remained unissued for two years, to become one of many tracks that kept Elvis' name in the chart while he was a guest of Uncle Sam in Germany and unable to make any new recordings. **I Got Stung** was actually cut shortly after Elvis' induction into the Army, at RCA in Nashville in June 1958, his last sessions for nearly 2 years. It was written by Aaron Schroeder and David Hill. By this point in Elvis' career, his recording output was controlled by music publisher Freddy Bienstock who acted as a clearing house for all the enormous number of songs that were submitted for Elvis, together with Steve Sholes and Chet Atkins. Atkins played guitar on **I Got Stung**, the rest of the line-up being Floyd Cramer on piano, Bob Moore on bass, D J Fontana on drums, Murray Harmon bashing the bongoes, and the Jordanaires backing Elvis Presley's vocals.

81

AS I LOVE YOU

20 February 1959, for four weeks

Shirley Bassey *Philips PB 845*

Writers: Jay Livingston and Ray Evans
Producer: Johnny Franz

The most successful female vocalist on the British charts has been Shirley Veronica Bassey, born in Cardiff on 8 January 1937, Elvis Presley's second birthday. It was also the 44th birthday of Max Freedman, the writer of **Rock Around The Clock**. Shirley Bassey's chart career began a month after her 20th birthday, when her version of Harry Belafonte's **Banana Boat Song** entered the charts. Although beaten by the original version, she nevertheless scored her first top ten hit. Two more small hits followed, but 1958 was a blank year until TV exposure broke **As I Love You**, a single which had already been followed up when it started to move.

As I Love You reached number one 9 weeks after its first chart placing, and at the same time the follow-up, **Kiss Me Honey Honey Kiss Me** was racing into the Top 10, to peak at number three. The two songs were so different, one an emotional ballad and the other a bouncy singalong song, that Miss Bassey's versatility was there for all to hear, and she has never looked back.

Miss Bassey's greatest chart achievement is to have had a bigger hit with a song the Beatles put out as a single than the Beatles did themselves. Her version of **Something** reached number four, which is the same position that the Beatles climbed to, but Shirley Bassey's record stayed for 22 weeks on the chart, compared with only 12 weeks for the Beatles. There have been many other versions of songs the Beatles recorded as singles, but only Shirley Bassey has come up with a bigger hit than the original.

82

SMOKE GETS IN YOUR EYES

20 March 1959, for one week

The Platters *Mercury AMT 1016*

Writers: Jerome Kern and Otto Harbach
Producer: Buck Ram

The Platters were formed in 1953, and by the time **Smoke Gets In Your Eyes** hit number one, the line-up was Tony

Williams, lead vocalist, David Lynch, Herb Reed, Paul Robi and Zola Taylor. But the brains behind the group was their manager and producer, Buck Ram. At the end of 1955, the Platters kicked off their American chart career with a top 10 million-seller which has now hit the British chart in five versions, **Only You**. The follow-up in America was **The Great Pretender** which was a Stateside number one, but nothing was released in Britain until late 1956 shortly after the fourth Platters single in America had given them their second number one. Their first British single was possibly the greatest double-sided single ever released, at least until the Beatles' **Penny Lane/Strawberry Fields Forever**. It was **Only You/The Great Pretender**, which eventually climbed to number five.

The British public was a little unsure of the Platters, and their first four singles bobbed in and out of the charts no fewer than twelve times between them. In 1958, the Platters switched to recording oldies, and this the fans loved. **Twilight Time** written in 1944, climbed to number three, and the follow-up, **Smoke Gets in Your Eyes**, from the 1933 musical *Roberta*, hit the very top.

83

SIDE SADDLE

27 March 1959, for four weeks

Russ Conway *Columbia DB 4256*

Writer: Trevor Stanford
Producer: Norman Newell

Trevor Stanford was born in Bristol on 2 September 1927 and joined the Merchant Navy at the age of 15 in 1942. Two years later he joined the Royal Navy and almost immediately cut off the top of the third finger of his right hand in mortal combat with a bread slicer. It was not for this action that he won the Distinguished Service Medal, but by the time he left the Navy in 1955, he was Trevor Stanford DSM. The transformation into Russ Conway was rapid. Stanford had taught himself piano during his sea-going years and on demobilisation began playing in clubs. There he was heard by the dancer Irving Davies, who recommended him to Norman Newell.

Russ Conway's recording career began on the well-worn lines of Winifred Atwell, with a medley, **Party Pops**, at Christmas 1957 and **More Party Pops**, his first Top 10 hit, at Christmas 1958. Then he wrote and recorded **Side Saddle** which hit number one, sold a million and stayed on the chart for 30 consecutive weeks, a run which at the time was second only to Frankie Laine's **I Believe**. It remains the longest run by any instrumental to reach number one, but it pales into insignificance beside the 55 week run of Mr. Acker Bilk's **Stranger On The Shore**, which never climbed higher than number two.

84

IT DOESN'T MATTER ANY MORE

24 April 1959, for three weeks

Buddy Holly *Coral Q 72360*

Writer: Paul Anka
Producers: Norman Petty, with orchestra directed by Dick Jacobs

The death of Buddy Holly in an air crash on 3 February 1959 is one of the major events of rock history. Buddy Holly, already established as a major force in pop music through his work with the Crickets, was just beginning a solo career which, to judge from the tapes he made before he died, would have been even more spectacular than his time with the Crickets. He has been since his death probably the biggest single influence on British pop music. The Beatles and the Rolling Stones recorded his songs, the Hollies named themselves after him, Adam Faith copied his pizzicato strings, Mud reached number one with their version of **Oh Boy** and too many acts to mention have used the Holly hiccup on their hits. **It Doesn't Matter Anymore** was Holly's only solo number one, and the first posthumous number one in Britain. It was written by Paul Anka, who thus became the first person in British chart history to write a number one hit for himself and for somebody else. He was on the fateful tour with Buddy Holly and is reputed to be one of the many people who gave up their seats on the doomed plane to make room for Buddy Holly, Ritchie Valens and the Big Bopper.

The flip-side, the classic **Raining In My Heart**, was written by Felice and Boudleaux Bryant. It was the only single till then by either the Crickets or by Buddy Holly solo on which Holly had no hand in the writing of either side.

85

A FOOL SUCH AS I/I NEED YOUR LOVE TONIGHT

15 May 1959, for five weeks

Elvis Presley *RCA 1113*

Writers: A Fool Such As I – William Trader; I Need Your Love Tonight – Sid Wayne and Bix Reichner
Producers: Steve Sholes and Chet Atkins

Elvis' fourth number one in Britain not only put him level with Guy Mitchell and Frankie Laine in the list of most number one hits, but also provided him with his first instance of number ones with consecutive releases, this double-sider following on directly after **One Night/I Got Stung** (see no. 80). **A Fool Such As I** had been a favourite of Elvis' since 1953, when it had reached number four in the American country charts recorded by Hank Snow, an artist at one time handled by Colonel Tom Parker. The first number one ballad hit for Elvis, it had been written by Bill Trader in 1952 and also provided a fair-sized pop hit in the States for Jo Stafford in 1953.

I Need Your Love Tonight was a new song written by Sid Wayne and Bix Reichner, and both titles were recorded in Nashville at the same sessions that produced **I Got Stung**. Almost certainly none of Elvis' number ones featured all the legendary musicians who regularly backed Elvis – Chet Atkins, Floyd Cramer, D J Fontana and Bill Black. These tracks featured the first three, but not Bill Black or even Scotty Moore, who had both been on **One Night**.

86

ROULETTE

19 June 1959, for two weeks

Russ Conway *Columbia DB 4298*

Writer: Trevor Stanford
Producer: Norman Newell

The only solo instrumentalist ever to achieve consecutive number one hits is Russ Conway, which he achieved with ridiculous ease as his second self-penned composition glided easily to the number one spot 8 weeks after **Side Saddle** dropped off the top. **Roulette** was not as memorable a tune as **Side Saddle**, which is still earning Russ Conway a crust or two, but it was good enough to beat out the opposition in mid-1959.

After **Roulette**, Conway never topped the charts again, but racked up four more Top 10 hits and a succession of smaller chart entries up to 1963. **More and More Party Pops** and **Even More Party Pops** gave Conway two more Christmas medley hits, bringing his total up to four, which was still a long way short of Winifred Atwell's seven medley hits, the most by any act ever.

The hits stopped in the mid-sixties, and although Russ Conway went on working almost as busily as ever, he subsequently suffered a nervous breakdown and went into retirement. Now happily restored to health, the breezy smile and nine-and a half finger playing style of Russ Conway can be seen and heard with increasing frequency on radio and television.

87

DREAM LOVER

3 July 1959, for four weeks

Bobby Darin *London HLE 8867*

Writer: Bobby Darin
Producer: Ahmet Ertegun

The first record produced on Atlantic Records new eight-track machine was cut on 19 May 1958. The producer was Ahmet Ertegun, the song was **Splish Splash** and the singer was Bobby Darin. **Splish Splash** was his first hit (covered by Charlie Drake in Britain), his second climbed to number 24 in Britain but his third was another self-penned song which reached number one on both sides of the Atlantic, **Dream Lover**. Walden Robert Cassotto (born 14 May 1936) had made it. It was his last teeny-bopping single, though, for his next release turned him into a major jazz-orientated star, and thus began the odyssey through different styles which proved that Bobby Darin was a great singer looking for a style. If he had settled in one style, he would have had a far greater following. But **Dream Lover**, **Mack The Knife**, **Multiplication**, **Things** and **If I Were A Carpenter**, five of Darin's hits, were in five completely different styles, so as Darin picked up one set of followers he was continually losing others.

He suffered from heart problems for most of his career, which limited his output, and he died from a heart attack at the age of 37 on 20 December 1973. Two number ones and seven other top ten hits is not the achievement of an unsuccessful performer, but he was vastly under-rated, even at the peak of his popularity.

88

LIVING DOLL

31 July 1959, for six weeks

Cliff Richard and the Drifters *Columbia DB 4306*

Writer: Lionel Bart
Producer: Norrie Paramor

After Elvis Presley and the Beatles, Cliff Richard has had more number one singles in Britain than any other act.

Cliff was born Harry Roger Webb in Lucknow, India on 14 October 1940 and with his parents moved back to England, their native country, in 1948.

After playing with various local groups in Cheshunt, Hertfordshire, he eventually signed a long-term contract with Columbia on 9 August 1958, making his television debut on ABC TV's *Oh Boy* just 4 weeks later. The beginning of 1959 saw Cliff with his first permanent backing group the Drifters, who later that year changed their name to the Shadows. It was as the Drifters that they backed him on his first chart-topper **Living Doll**. The song was written by Lionel Bart for the film *Serious Charge* in which Cliff had a small part, and although initially conceived by the composer as an up-tempo rock'n'roll song, it was Drifters rhythm guitarist Bruce Welch who suggested the slower country feel which was eventually adopted. **Living Doll** won an Ivor Novello award and became Cliff Richard's first million seller, earning him his first of many gold discs.

89

ONLY SIXTEEN

11 September 1959, for four weeks

Craig Douglas *Top Rank JAR 159*

Writers: 'Barbara Campbell' (Lou Adler, Herb Alpert and Sam Cooke)
Producer: Bunny Lewis

Only Sixteen was Sam Cooke's eighth American hit, but like six of its seven predecessors, it peaked outside the Top 20. In Britain, Cooke also missed the Top 20, but that was mainly because of the local competition from an Isle of Wight milkman called Terence Perkins. Perkins had become Craig Douglas a few months earlier, and first brushed the charts with his rendering of Dion and the Belmonts' immortal piece of 50's punk, **Teenager In Love**. That song had taken Marty Wilde to number two, his biggest ever hit, but Craig Douglas was undaunted. Picking up another American hit, he and his cover version climbed to the summit, and gazed down on Sam Cooke's and Al Saxon's records far below.

Craig Douglas starred in the 1961 movie *It's Trad Dad*, with Helen Shapiro, which did not really boost either acting career. He also achieved the almost impossible feat of four consecutive number nine hits, which included probably his best record, **Our Favourite Melodies**. Shortly after his last hit, **Town Crier**, lost its voice in March 1963, Douglas was signed to do commercials for a well-known detergent. This was very lucrative for some years, and meant that he has never had to go back to his milk round.

90

HERE COMES SUMMER

9 October 1959, for one week

Jerry Keller *London HLR 8890*

Writer: Jerry Keller
Producer: Richard Wolf

Jerry Keller, born on 20 June 1937 in Arkansas, moved with his family to Tulsa at the age of 6. His first group, which went under the zippy name of The Lads Of Note was formed in Tulsa in the early fifties, and soon won a talent contest which led to a job with Jack Dalton's band in the mid-west. That was short-lived, and Keller then became a disc jockey back in Tulsa from mid-1955 for less than a year. In 1956, still only 19 years old, Keller went to New York to try to hit the big time as a singer.

Sometimes being good pays off, as it did with Jerry Keller. Another regular member of the congregation of Keller's church in New York was Pat Boone, and he gave Keller the introductions that led to his being signed by Kapp Records. His first single was **Here Comes Summer** which hit the British charts at the end of August. Either summer was even shorter than usual in 1959, or else Keller's timing was about as good as Wizzard's **Rock'n'Roll Winter**, released in April 1974. Not that it mattered, as **Here Comes Summer** became the ultimate high-school summer song and it soared to number one, his only hit in Britain and America.

91 **Bobby Darin**

89 **Craig Douglas**

92 **Cliff Richard and the Shadows**

That meant that three of the four one hit wonders of the 1950's had surnames beginning with K (Kallen, Kalin and Keller) and no K act really broke the jinx until the Kinks in 1965.

91

MACK THE KNIFE

16 October 1959, for two weeks

Bobby Darin *London HLE 8939*

Writers: Bertolt Brecht and Kurt Weill. English lyrics by Marc Blitzstein
Producer: Ahmet Ertegun

One of the biggest hits in history would never have been made had not the artist insisted. A teen rock and roll favourite, Bobby Darin longed to be a respectable mass audience artist. He recorded an album of adult-oriented material, including Brecht and Weill's **Moritat** from *The Threepenny Opera*, translated into English by Marc Blitzstein and called **Mack the Knife**. The inclusion of the song was not as odd as it may sound, since at one point in early 1956 there had been five versions in the American Top 40, the greatest cover duel in chart history. Even more confusingly, the competing artists included Dick Hyman and Richard Hayman.

It was Louis Armstrong's version that inspired Darin. The young rocker gave the song a hip, jazz-flavoured treatment. Bobby phoned television disc jockey Dick Clark, a personal friend, and informed him he would debut the record on Clark's Saturday night ABC network show. The host told him he was crazy, and the programme's producer said 'If he wants to turn his career into chopped liver, so be it.' It was Darin who was right. **Mack the Knife** was his second consecutive number one, America's list leader for 9 weeks, and Atlantic's best selling single to date. Bobby Darin had a new career, and never returned to rock and roll.

92

TRAVELLIN' LIGHT

30 October 1959, for five weeks

Cliff Richard and the Shadows *Columbia DB 4351*

Writers: Sid Tepper and Roy C Bennett
Producer: Norrie Paramor

Living Doll was the only record that ever topped the chart for Cliff Richard and the Drifters as the name was changed to Cliff Richard and the Shadows for the follow-up, **Travellin' Light**. The change was to avoid confusion with the American Drifters, as Cliff's singles began to be released in the States.

Cliff's first four singles had all been up-tempo, all in the fashionable rock'n'roll vein, and all sung with a hint of surliness in the voice, but it wasn't until the easy paced **Living Doll** that he had actually topped the charts. The same winning format was used for his sixth single, **Travellin' Light**, which topped the singles chart for 5 weeks from October to December 1959, and re-appeared in December 1960 on **Cliff's Silver Discs** EP. The B-side **Dynamite** was so popular that it charted for 4 weeks in its own right, reaching number 16.

Travellin' Light was an aptly titled song to be at the top when the first sections of the M1 were opened. The motorway system has done at least as much for live gigs as the invention of the synthesiser.

93

WHAT DO YOU WANT

4 December 1959, for three weeks
(one week top equal)

Adam Faith *Parlophone R 4591*

Writer: Les Vandyke
Producer: John Burgess, arranged by John Barry

Few people watching BBC-TV's *Drumbeat* in the summer of 1959 would have expected the blond, moody Adam Faith to become one of Britain's most successful acts of the early sixties. His first singles, including a version of Thurston Harris' **Runk Bunk**, deservedly failed to sell, and it was Adam Faith's good fortune that composer/arranger Johnny Worth decided Adam was the person to put over his songs, songs written under the name Les Vandyke. He took the name Vandyke from his telephone exchange in London. (His real name was not Worth, it was Yani Skordalides.) Adam Faith, born Terence Nelhams on 23 June 1940, was taken into the Parlophone studios and, despite his uninspiring track record, produced one of the pop classics of the pre-Beatles era. The last line, 'Wish you wanted my love bay-bee' gave Adam a catch phrase that lasted well beyond his first hit. It was also the first ever number one for Parlophone, Adam Faith being at the time the only pop act recording on Parlophone. Before George Martin signed the Beatles to Parlophone and turned it into the most successful record label of all time, Faith's stable mates were acts like the Temperance Seven, Mike Sarne (both of whom subsequently reached number one) and Peter Sellers. Long on talent, but short on rock and roll. Still, if Adam Faith hadn't recorded on Parlophone, it is quite possible that Brian Epstein would not even have tried to get the Beatles signed to the label. Then we might have missed the Liverpool sound altogether.

94

WHAT DO YOU WANT TO MAKE THOSE EYES AT ME FOR?

18 December 1959, for six weeks (one week top equal)

Emile Ford and the Checkmates *Pye 7N 15225*

Writers: Joseph McCarthy, Howard Johnson and Jimmy Monaco
Producer: Michael Barclay

Emile Ford was born Emile Sweetman in Nassau in the Bahamas on 16 October 1937, and moved to Britain with his family as a young boy. His first single was a resurrected version of a song which remains the longest question asked from number one. He was the first black man living in Britain to have a major hit, although Winifred Atwell and Shirley Bassey, two black girls in Britain, had already reached the top.

Not that he owed his success to his blackness. By the time he reached the top, blackness was neither a help nor a hindrance in reaching the charts. He owed his success to the arrangement and his totally unthreatening delivery of lyrics like 'I'll get you alone some night, and baby you'll find you're messing with dynamite'. It was a happy, friendly, singalong version of the old song, which made it perfect for the Christmas season.

His follow-up was Frank Loesser's **Slow Boat To China**, which reached number three early in 1960, but apart from the upbeat **Counting Teardrops** at the end of the year, there were no more Top 10 hits, and in March 1962, Ford disappeared from the charts for the last time. He then moved to Sweden where for many years he earned a respectable living from live appearances and record sales, returning occasionally but unsuccessfully to Britain.

95

STARRY EYED

29 January 1960, for one week

Michael Holliday *Columbia DB 4378*

Writers: Earl Shuman and Mort Garson
Producer: Norrie Paramor

Michael Holliday had been out of the charts for 18 months when he was given a song by Mort Garson and Earl Shuman (no relation to Mort Shuman) which an almost unknown American singer called Gary Stites had just released in the States. Holliday recorded the song, and although Gary Stites' single stopped at number 77 in America, the confidence of Holliday and his producer Norrie Paramor paid off.

It was not enough to give his career a real boost, though. After **Starry Eyed**, he had two further small hits, but his last chart single **Little Boy Lost** was aptly titled for Michael Holliday. **Starry Eyed** was about the only thing Holliday never was about his life in show business. The first Liverpudlian to achieve two number ones never coped with his yoyoing career, which went up and down.

96

WHY

5 February 1960, for four weeks

Anthony Newley *Decca F 11194*

Writers: Bob Marcucci and Peter de Angelis
Producer: Ray Horricks

Anthony Newley, like John Leyton and David Soul after him, was an actor who fell into being a pop star almost by accident. As a child star, he had appeared in such films as *Oliver Twist* in 1948, in which as a 17 year-old he played the part of The Artful Dodger, and Peter Ustinov's *Vice Versa*, in which one of his co-stars was another child star turned pop singer, Petula Clark (see no. 113).

The film *Idle on Parade*, a quickly thrown together movie about a pop star called up for National Service, inspired by the brief but highly publicised army career of Terry Dene, gave him his first chance to be a pop star, and the EP from the film reached number 13 in mid 1959. A single from the

Left **97 Adam Faith**
Below left **94 Emile Ford and the Checkmates**
Below **98 Johnny Preston**

film was also issued, **I've Waited So Long**, a pastiche of a hundred pounding 'rock-a-ballads' as they were known in those far off days of Tin Pan Alley pop. Despite the fact that the song was included on the **Idle On Parade** EP, it still reached number three. A profitable career as a pop singer awaited Anthony Newley if he cared to follow it up.

He did. His next single was a cover version of Frankie Avalon's American number one hit, **Why** and it became the seventh question to reach number one in England. It was also at that time the shortest song title ever to reach number one, a title it has subsequently surrendered to Telly Savalas' **If**. At the end of its four week run at the top, the *Record Retailer* magazine launched its Top 50, and the significance of the *New Musical Express* chart, the pioneer of English charts, was reduced. It did mean, however, that Newley's 4 week run at the top was in fact 4 weeks and 6 days thanks to the different date base of the two charts.

97

POOR ME

10 March 1960, for one week

Adam Faith *Parlophone R 4623*

Writer: Les Vandyke
Producers: John Burgess, arranged by John Barry

The first number one on the *Record Retailer* chart was Adam Faith's second consecutive number one, written, produced and arranged by the same team that had been responsible for **What Do You Want?** A very similar construction, with pizzicato strings and hiccuping delivery from Adam made it a formula number one, but all the same a number one. Suddenly Adam Faith was on a hat-trick, but like Cliff Richard a few weeks earlier, he failed in his attempt at a third number one in a row when the follow-up, **Someone Else's Baby**, stopped at number two. Unlike Cliff, Adam Faith never had another number one, although when his last chart hit – **Cheryl's Going Home**, a Tim Hardin song – dropped off the chart in November 1966, Faith had clocked up two number ones, nine other Top 10 hits and a total of 251 weeks on the chart. It was not until 1981 that he slipped out of the Top 20 all-time most successful chart acts, when Stevie Wonder overtook Adam Faith's total number of weeks on the chart.

A rare example of a pop singer who can really act, Adam's subsequent career in films and television has won him even more praise than his long string of record smashes. He remains delightfully (and wrongly) modest about his days in music to which he vows never to return.

98

RUNNING BEAR

17 March 1960, for two weeks

Johnny Preston *Mercury AMT 1079*

Writer: J P Richardson
Producer: J P Richardson

Texan Johnny Preston's only number one hit was the Romeo and Juliet saga of Running Bear and Little White Dove, whose tribes fought with each other, so their love could never be. Written by J P Richardson, the Big Bopper, it reached the top over a year after he had died in the plane crash that also killed Buddy Holly and Ritchie Valens. Johnny Preston, born 28 August 1939 in Port Arthur, Texas, managed one more Top 10 hit and a total of 45 weeks on the chart before disappearing back into obscurity. Like other white novelty hitmakers of the early sixties (Buzz Clifford of **Baby Sitting Boogie** fame immediately springs to mind), Johnny Preston was a poor performer on stage, which was the kiss of death in the age of package tours. He thus never lived up to the prediction of the teenaged Tim Rice who won a free LP for a letter to *DISC* headlined, 'I Tip Johnny Preston For Number One Hat Trick'. It was to be a year and a week before anybody managed the elusive hat-trick, and it was not to be Johnny Preston, but the rather better known Elvis Presley.

99

MY OLD MAN'S A DUSTMAN

31 March 1960, for four weeks

Lonnie Donegan *Pye 7N 15256*

Writers: Traditional, new lyrics by Lonnie Donegan, Peter Buchanan and Beverly Thorn
Producers: Alan Freeman and Michael Barclay (Recorded live at the Gaumont, Doncaster)

Lonnie Donegan's third number one, **My Old Man's A Dustman**, is the song everybody thinks came into the chart at number one. It didn't: it reached the top in its second week on the chart, which is still pretty good going but not all that unusual. It made Donegan the third act, after Michael Holliday and Adam Faith, to have a number one in two decades and it also changed his musical style for the rest of his chart career. Having had two number ones and eight Top 10 hits in his nasal bluesy style of skiffle, he switched his priorities to music-hall skiffle, which had already given him one other Top Tenner, **Does Your Chewing Gum Lose Its Flavour**, a year earlier. **Dustman**, complete with dreadful music-hall jokes ('My dustbin's full of lilies' – 'How d'you know they're lilies?' – 'Lily's wearing them') was a cleaned up version of the old pub song, **What Do You Think About That?**, and gave Donegan his biggest British hit of all. But his subsequent hits, like **Lively, Lumbered** and **Have A Drink On Me**, were increasingly weak attempts to repeat the success of **Dustman**. All were Top 10 hits, but sold on Donegan's name, not on their merits.

Lonnie Donegan last hit the charts at the end of 1962, but is still one of the ten most successful acts in British chart history. His appearance on the Royal Command Performance of 1981 shows he is still around, and popular. A return to the charts is not out of the question.

100

DO YOU MIND

28 April 1960, for one week

Anthony Newley *Decca F 11220*

Writer: Lionel Bart
Producer: Ray Horricks

The one hundredth number one hit in British chart history was the second number one for both the singer Anthony Newley and the composer Lionel Bart. Both went on to greater fame in the musical theatre, but for both it was their last touch of chart supremacy. After consecutive number ones with question songs, Newley's chart career faded gradually, although his personal fortune was assured by writing another question song, **What Kind Of Fool Am I?** with Leslie Bricusse, which became the hit of the show which he wrote and in which he starred, *Stop The World – I Want To Get Off*. It is not often remembered that before the success of *Stop The World*, Newley played the title role in the unusual TV series, *The World Of Gurney Slade*. The theme tune of the series, by Max Harris, reached number eleven at the beginning of 1961.

For Lionel Bart, *Oliver* was imminent. By the end of 1960 it was the most successful British musical in history, and was well set on a run in London that would not be eclipsed until *Jesus Christ Superstar* broke all box-office records in the late seventies. But the biggest hit from *Oliver*, Shirley Bassey's version of **As Long As He Needs Me**, reached only number two, despite a 30 week run on the charts. Bart's career has been down and up since *Oliver*, but nobody can deny his leading place among British popular composers of this century.

101

CATHY'S CLOWN

5 May 1960, for seven weeks

The Everly Brothers *Warner Brothers WB 1*

Writers: Don and Phil Everly
Producer: Wesley Rose

The day before Princess Margaret married Anthony Armstrong-Jones, Don and Phil Everly took over the number one spot, which they held on to until well after the **Caribbean Honeymoon** (a no. 42 hit for the Frank Weir Orchestra) was over.

The Everly Brothers had recently signed a lucrative contract with the newly-formed Warner Brothers record label, and the industry felt that taking Don and Phil away from Cadence, away from Archie Bleyer and away from Felice and Boudleaux Bryant, was a great risk. The Brothers replied with the biggest hit of their career as the first single on the Warner Brothers label. It sold in enormous quantities and if Warner Brothers had been able to ship enough copies in the week of release, it might well have entered the chart at number one. As it was, it took over at the top in its fourth chart week and stayed there for longer than any number one since their own **All I Have To Do Is Dream**, which had spent 7 weeks on top in July and August 1958. **Cathy's Clown** remains one of the greatest of all pop records, capturing in less than 3 minutes all the skill, excitement and emotion of the Everlys at their best. And the Everlys at their best were brilliant. They remain over 20 years later easily the most successful duo in British chart history.

102

THREE STEPS TO HEAVEN

23 June 1960, for two weeks

Eddie Cochran *London HLG 9115*

Writers: Bob and Eddie Cochran
Producers: Jerry Capehart and Eddie Cochran

Eddie Cochran, born 3 October 1938, was killed in a car crash at Chippenham, Wiltshire on his way from Bristol to

Top left **105 Johnny Kidd and the Pirates** *Above* **100 Anthony Newley** *Right* **102 Eddie Cochran** *Left* **108 Roy Orbison** *Below* **104 Cliff Richard and the Shadows**

London airport on 17 April 1960, shortly after recording the prophetically titled **Three Steps To Heaven**. It became his only number one hit single and the second posthumous number one on the British charts. Since his death at the age of 21, Cochran has become a legend for his astonishing guitar work and the songs he wrote, some of which can rank with the best of Chuck Berry and Buddy Holly as rock classics. **Three Steps To Heaven**, written with his brother Bob and revived with great success in the 1970's by Showaddywaddy, was not his greatest composition. **C'mon Everybody** and **Summertime Blues** remain the songs for which he is best remembered. His greatest influence on the people that followed him was not his writing, but his guitar style. Listen to his playing on **Hallelujah I Love Her So** or **Don't Ever Let Me Go** and you will hear the roots of the styles of many of the great rock guitarists of the sixties and seventies.

103

GOOD TIMIN'

7 July 1960, for three weeks

Jimmy Jones *MGM 1078*

Writers: Fred Tobias and Clint Ballard Jr.
Producer: Otis Blackwell

Jimmy Jones, born on 2 June 1937, began his career with an all-time classic single that failed to make number one. That song was **Handy Man**, a number three hit which introduced rock falsetto to the British charts, and subsequently gave hits to Del Shannon and James Taylor. Following that up ought to have been impossible, but Jones came up with a song as different as possible from **Handy Man** and reached the very top. **Good Timin'**, a simply structured verse/chorus/verse/chorus song about what Carl Jung called synchronicity was really nowhere as good as the free-running **Handy Man**. But it was **Good Timin'** that hit the top.

There it stopped. Jones' follow-up was the underrated **I Just Go For You/That's When I Cried**, which like Jones' next two singles hit the charts but failed to make the Top 30. **Good Timin'** was also the last in a long while for MGM. After four number ones on the yellow label in 1958, **Good Timin'** was their only chart-topper until the Osmonds between them gave MGM five more number ones and eighteen more weeks at the top between 1972 and 1974.

In 1982, **Good Timin'** was revived by who else but Showaddywaddy, proving it is still remembered by the rock fans.

104

PLEASE DON'T TEASE

28 July 1960, for one week
and from 11 August 1960 for two weeks

Cliff Richard and the Shadows *Columbia DB 4479*

Writers: Pete Chester and Bruce Welch
Producer: Norrie Paramor

Cliff's third chart-topper held the unique distinction of having been chosen by members of the public.

A cross-section of people were played a selection of songs and over tea and biscuits were asked to choose their favourite. The majority went for a song written by the Shadows' rhythm guitarist Bruce Welch and Pete Chester, son of Charlie Chester the comedian. The song was **Please Don't Tease**, which Cliff re-recorded in a slower vein in 1978. It was subsequently released on the B-side of **Please Remember Me** in July of that year.

After two consecutive number two hits, it was no doubt a great pleasure for Cliff to be back on top. Cliff Richard has never achieved a hat-trick of number one hits, despite the fact that all 19 single releases between **Living Doll** and **Don't Talk To Him** at the end of 1963 reached the top four. In that period, he had seven number ones, six number twos, four number threes and two number four hits, but never more than two consecutive number ones. Twice he issued five consecutive singles which gave him three number ones and two number twos, but he has not yet managed the hat-trick.

105

SHAKIN' ALL OVER

4 August 1960, for one week

Johnny Kidd and the Pirates *HMV POP 753*

Writers: Frederick Heath and Gus Robinson
Producer: Walter Ridley

Johnny Kidd was probably Britain's greatest rocker, probably Britain's only true rocker of the pre-Beatles era. Born Frederick Heath two days before Christmas 1939 in Willesden, North London, he released his first hit single, **Please Don't Touch** at the age of 19½ and immediately earned a reputation as a rocker who might follow the recent sensation

Cliff Richard. Cliff's **Move It** still stands as probably the best rock record ever made by an Englishman. But Cliff recorded **Living Doll** and abdicated his throne, while Johnny Kidd rocked on. **Shakin' All Over** was written by Johnny Kidd under his real name with his manager Gus Robinson, and represented the artistic and statistical peak of his career. The image he presented on stage, the jeans, the leather jacket, and the eye patch (originally worn one night on stage after a guitar string broke into his eye) was almost as stereotyped as the very different image later presented by his near-contemporary Gary Glitter. During his brief career, Kidd never quite reached the popularity his talent deserved, partly because for his first years, he was battling against the Elvis of **Wooden Heart** and **Return To Sender**, the Cliff of **Living Doll** and **Bachelor Boy** and a host of lesser mortals like Bobby Vee, Billy Fury and Frank Ifield. No rockers there. The last years of his life were spent competing with the Beatles and their followers. Despite another Top 10 hit **I'll Never Get Over You** in summer 1963, Kidd was out of fashion until well after his death in a car crash at Radcliffe, Lancashire on 7 October 1966.

106

APACHE

25 August 1960, for five weeks

The Shadows *Columbia DB 4484*

Writer: Jerry Lordan
Producer: Norrie Paramor

In 1960 the Shadows were Hank B Marvin on lead guitar, Bruce Welch on rhythm guitar, Jet Harris on bass and Tony Meehan on drums. As well as backing Cliff Richard, they had issued three records in their own right before the success of **Apache**. Two of these discs were issued under the name The Drifters, a name which they changed after the American Drifters (**Save The Last Dance For Me** etc.) had issued an injunction over the name duplication.

The group first heard **Apache** while they were on tour around Britain, when a fellow artiste on the bill, singer Jerry Lordan, played them the tune on his ukelele. Bert Weedon had already recorded the song, but seemingly had no plans to release it. The Shadows recorded the tune, released it and soon had knocked their boss (see no. 104) off the top. In America they were beaten out by a cover version by the Danish guitarist Jorgen Ingmann, who three years later won the Eurovision Song Contest with his sister Grethe.

The Shadows won many accolades in the polls of 1960, including being voted Britain's top instrumental group of the year, and **Apache** being voted Top Record of 1960 in the prestigious *New Musical Express* Readers' Poll.

107

TELL LAURA I LOVE HER

29 September 1960, for three weeks

Ricky Valance *Columbia DB 4493*

Writers: Jeff Barry and Ben Raleigh
Producer: Norrie Paramor

In the 1950's and early 1960's, death songs were almost always automatically refused airplay by the BBC. This ludicrous 'moral' attitude meant that records like Mark Dinning's **Teen Angel** sank without trace, while other American death records were not even released in Britain. Most of these songs were tasteless (**Tell Laura I Love Her** most certainly is), but they were not immoral nor likely to have a bad influence on the listener.

When Ray Peterson's original version of **Tell Laura I Love Her** was not originally even released in Britain, EMI found a Welsh singer called David Spencer, who had nothing to lose by covering a notorious and banned song. In a move as cynical as the decision to record the song in the first place, his name was changed to Ricky Valance, to remind the fans of Ritchie Valens, who died with Buddy Holly and the Big Bopper in the Iowa snow a year and a half earlier. The record was released, the BBC banned it and it climbed merrily to the very top of the charts. Great satisfaction for all at EMI, and total obscurity for Ricky Valance as soon as **Tell Laura I Love Her** dropped out of the charts.

108

ONLY THE LONELY

20 October 1960, for two weeks

Roy Orbison *London HLU 9149*

Writer: Roy Orbison
Producer: Fred Foster

Roy Kelton Orbison (born 23 April 1936 in Texas) had such talent that even if he had looked like Robert Redford (he doesn't) he could never have been described as just another pretty face. His credentials were impeccable: he was signed to the Sun label, home of Elvis Presley, Johnny Cash and Jerry Lee Lewis, he wrote **Claudette**, a number one hit for the Everly Brothers, and finally broke through in Britain with one of the best rock ballads of the sixties, the self-penned **Only The Lonely**.

Only The Lonely was released very early in the summer of 1960 and appeared to have sunk without trace. Then at the end of July it hit the chart, only to drop off again a week later. On 11 August it returned to the charts, but took more than two months to reach the top, the sixth slowest climb to the top in chart history. It established Roy Orbison as one of the great acts of the 1960's. In fact Orbison only ever hit the charts in the 1960's, his last hit **Penny Arcade** falling off the last chart of 1969, yet he remains tenth on the list of all time successful chart acts in Britain. He is the only act of the Top 30 chart acts to have had all his hits in the same decade, and with the Shadows is one of only two of the Top 10 acts to have started his chart career with a number one hit.

109

IT'S NOW OR NEVER

3 November 1960, for eight weeks

Elvis Presley *RCA 1207*

Writers: Eduardo di Capua, Aaron Schroeder and Wally Gold

Producerss: Steve Sholes and Chet Atkins

As soon as Elvis left the US Army in March 1960, he was rushed back into the recording studios at RCA in Nashville. Sessions there in March and April produced some of Presley's most famous and successful sides, including the entire **Elvis Is Back** album, **It's Now Or Never** and **Are You Lonesome Tonight. It's Now Or Never** was Elvis' fifth British single to reach number one but for quite some time it seemed possible that it would never be issued over here at all. Instead of being Elvis' second post-army single (**Stuck On You** which reached number three, was the first) it was delayed by copyright problems arising from the fact that the song was an adaptation from the 1901 Italian song **O Sole Mio** written by G Capurro (words) and Eduardo di Capua (music) by American writers Aaron Schroeder (who also co-wrote **I Got Stung** – see no. 80) and Wally Gold. No such problems existed in the States where the single became the biggest hit of even Elvis' career during the summer of 1960. To keep the UK fans happy, RCA released the US B-side, **A Mess Of Blues**, as an A-side and even that made number two, thanks in part to the enormously popular song put onto the British flip, **The Girl Of My Best Friend**. When **It's Now Or Never** was finally cleared for UK release in November, the interest had built up to such proportions that Elvis' second straight-in-at-number-one record was almost a formality. Recorded on 3/4 April 1960, **It's Now Or Never** gave Presley a whole new adult audience to add to his millions of younger fans and featured Scotty Moore (guitar), Hank Garland (guitar), Floyd Cramer (piano), Bob Moore (bass), Murray Harmon (drums) and the Jordanaires (vocals). No other Elvis single had as many as 8 weeks at the top of the UK charts.

Incidentally, **O Sole Mio** had been adapted once before for contemporary use in 1949, recorded by Tony Martin as **There's No Tomorrow**.

110

I LOVE YOU

29 December 1960, for two weeks

Cliff Richard and the Shadows *Columbia DB 4547*

Writer: Bruce Welch

Producer: Norrie Paramor

Cliff's fourth number one virtually reverted to the easy-paced style of his first two chart-toppers **Living Doll** and **Travellin' Light**. Written by Bruce Welch it stayed in the pole position for a fortnight, from the last few days of 1960 into January 1961.

It was now apparent that Cliff and his group were fast becoming capable of being a self-contained unit thanks to the song-writing talents of Shadows Bruce Welch and Hank Marvin. **I Love You** was Cliff's eleventh single in just over two years, and of those, only his third single, **Livin' Lovin' Doll** had failed to reach the Top 10. Cliff's 26 consecutive Top 10 hits, of which **I Love You** was the eighth, are a record that will probably remain unbeaten for all time.

I Love You must be the most unimaginative title of all the five hundred number ones. Nevertheless, it was the first song of that title to enter the British charts, and it was not until 1977 that a second song called **I Love You**, this time by disco queen Donna Summer, hit the UK charts.

111

POETRY IN MOTION

12 January 1961, for two weeks

Johnny Tillotson *London HLA 9231*

Writers: Paul Kauffman and Mike Anthony
Producer: Archie Bleyer

Johnny Tillotson was born on 20 April 1939 in Jacksonville, Florida, and before the age of 20, he had been signed to Cadence Records, the label that discovered the Everly Brothers, the Chordettes, and Andy Williams. Basically, a country singer, Tillotson's biggest UK hit had country influences but was nearer to Frankie Avalon and Bobby Vee than Ray Price or Hank Williams. His other singles were more countrified, which explains their relative lack of success in Britain, but in America he is still as well known for songs like **It Keeps Right On A-Hurtin** and **Talk Back Trembling Lips** as for his British number one.

When the Everly Brothers moved from Cadence to Warner Brothers in 1961, it was not long before Archie Bleyer wound up his record company, incidentally selling most of his masters to Andy Williams. Tillotson moved to MGM, where the country hits continued in the States for many years. Johnny Tillotson is still an active country singer, even though the hits have all but dried up.

112

ARE YOU LONESOME TONIGHT?

26 January 1961, for four weeks

Elvis Presley *RCA 1216*

Writers: Roy Turk and Lou Handman
Producers: Steve Sholes and Chet Atkins

For his sixth number one hit, Elvis revamped a song from 1926 and shot to number one mainly on the basis of a long spoken passage beginning with the immortal line based loosely on Jaques' speech in Act II Scene VII of Shakespeare's *As You Like It* – 'You know, someone said that all the world's a stage'. He hardly ever seemed to be able to remember this long recitation or to want to recite it accurately at his concerts in the seventies. RCA even released a live version of **Are You Lonesome Tonight?** in the UK in 1982 in which Elvis sings incorrect (and unfunny) lyrics and laughs all the way through the spoken word section of the number. Not a worthy release. The 1960, version, however was deservedly one of Elvis' most popular recordings of all. Recorded in Nashville at the **It's Now Or Never** sessions of April 1960 (see no. 109) the track did nearly as well as its predecessor on both sides of the Atlantic. By the beginning of 1961, Elvis was at his peak of popularity with the record-buying public. **Are You Lonesome Tonight?** was the second of a run of a dozen successive Presley single releases in the UK, of which ten made number one. From now until the emergence of the Beatles, Elvis had no challenger to his position as the most popular singer in the world.

113

SAILOR

23 February 1961, for one week

Petula Clark *Pye 7N 15324*

Writers: Fini Busch, Werner Scharfenburger, English lyrics by David West
Producer: Alan Freeman

Petula Clark first came to notice immediately after the war, in a radio series called *Meet The Huggets*, in which she played Jack Warner's daughter. She was born in Epsom on 15 November 1933, so she was only in her mid-teens when stardom struck. By the mid-fifties, she was well established as a bouncy singer, a British imitation of the all-conquering Mitch Miller style, and she managed four Top 10 hits before 1958.

Her first number one was a song written by two Austrians, Fini Busch and Werner Scharfenburger, and titled **Seemann**. A German girl called Lolita turned into a monster European smash. English lyrics were added by EMI A & R man Norman Newell, under the pen-name David West, and Lolita re-recorded the song in English. So did Petula Clark. Lolita's English version then took off in the States, where it reached number five in the Billboard charts, but on Petula Clark's home ground, she not only annihilated Lolita, who failed to make the Top 30, but also beat Anne Shelton (see no. 50) who was hoping for a second number one with a European song, but had to be content with just a Top 10 hit.

114

WALK RIGHT BACK

2 March 1961, for three weeks

The Everly Brothers *Warner Brothers WB 33*

Writer: Sonny Curtis
Producer: Wesley Rose

The Everly Brothers' third number one hit, and their second for the new Warner Brothers label, was a double-sided number one in all but chart listing. There have been only 18 double-sided number ones in the first 500, including four by Elvis and two by the Beatles, but only one officially by the Everly Brothers (see no. 73)

The most played side was written by Sonny Curtis of the Crickets. The other side was called **Ebony Eyes** and was less plugged because it was a death song, a classic to rank with **Tell Laura I Love Her** and **Leader Of The Pack**. The writer, John D Loudermilk, has over the years come up with a wide range of highly original songs, but **Ebony Eyes** is probably his best known. Songs like **Indian Reservation** for Don Fardon, **Tobacco Road** for the Nashville Teens and **Language of Love** which he performed himself are all Loudermilk compositions, and all Top 20 hits in Britain.

The sad saga of Flight 1203 ('They may have run into some turbulent weather, and had to alter their course'), made **Ebony Eyes** one of the most parodied songs in pop history.

115

WOODEN HEART

23 March 1961, for six weeks

Elvis Presley *RCA 1226*

Writers: Bert Kaempfert, Kay Twomey, Fred Wise and Ben Weisman
Producer: Steve Sholes

Elvis' seventh UK number one was unique in that it was not released as a single in the US at the time of its enormous success in Britain and Europe. The most popular song from Elvis' first post-Army movie, **GI Blues**, it made Elvis the first artist to score three number one hits with consecutive British releases (see also nos. 109 and 112). It was an adaptation of a German folk song, **Muss I Denn**, by Fred Wise, Kay Twomey, Ben Weisman and Bert Kaempfert, the latter being the German bandleader who recorded the Beatles in Hamburg in 1961 and had his own US number one that year with **Wonderland By Night**, which knocked Presley's **Are You Lonesome Tonight?** off the top! Bert Kaempfert also wrote **Strangers In The Night** for Frank Sinatra, and thus has close connections with three of the top four chart acts of all time.

RCA's baffling decision not to release **Wooden Heart** as an American single allowed unknown singer Joe Dowell to take his version to number one in America in the summer of 1961. The 27 weeks that Elvis Presley's **Wooden Heart** spent in the UK Top 50 was the longest consecutive run by any of Presley's 100-plus singles. During the record's 6 week run at number one, King Zog of Albania died (9 April) and Yuri Gagarin became the first man in space (12 April).

116

BLUE MOON

4 May 1961, for two weeks

The Marcels *Pye International 7N 25073*

Writers: Richard Rodgers and Lorenz Hart
Producer: Stu Phillips

One of the only songs that Rodgers and Hart wrote outside a musical, *Blue Moon* was published in 1934 as a 'slow fox-trot ballad'. It had survived most recorded versions over the next 27 years (including a straight version by Elvis Presley), but the Marcels brought a new meaning to the song with their astonishing arrangement, featuring vocals not in the original version, ending each chorus with the unanswerable 'dang-a-dang-dang, ding-a-dong-ding Blue Moon'.

There was a record issued in 1957 called **Zoom Zoom Zoom** by the Collegians on the obscure Wimley label. It failed to do anything on any chart, but it has been mentioned as an inspiration for the Marcels' **Blue Moon**. Listening to the two records clarifies the issue – **Blue Moon** was not so much inspired by **Zoom Zoom Zoom**, it was virtually a direct copy of the arrangement.

There is some confusion as to who the Marcels were on the record. The probable line-up of the lads from Philadelphia is Cornelius Hart (lead vocals), Ronald Mundy, Fred Johnson, Dick Knauss and Gene Bricker. Anyway five Marcels appeared in the Chubby Checker movie *Twist Around The Clock* which still holds the world record as the quickest-made feature film of all time – 28 days from the day producer Sam Katzman got the idea to release of the film. Not much shorter than the Marcels' career.

117

ON THE REBOUND

18 May 1961, for one week

Floyd Cramer *RCA 1231*

Writer: Floyd Cramer
Producer: Chet Atkins

Floyd Cramer, born in Shreveport Louisiana on 27 November 1933, was Elvis Presley's pianist on many of the early RCA hits. The Nashville sound of the late fifties and early sixties was built around the guitar style of Chet Atkins and Les Paul, the bass of Bill Black, the drums of D J Fontana and the piano of Floyd Cramer. Elvis was never a pure country singer, even though he regularly used many of these musicians on his sessions, but just as he influenced a thousand pure country singers, so his musicians were more versatile than the country styles their imitators created.

Floyd Cramer's biggest hit, a number two hit in America, demonstrates this perfectly. It was called **Last Date** and failed to register in Britain, but it was more than just country piano. It had traces of jazz, rock and rhythm and blues which crop up again in the records of people as diverse as Alan Price, Roger Williams and Elton John. If **Last Date** was Floyd Cramer's masterpiece, **On The Rebound** was not far behind. It climbed to number four in America as the follow up to **Last Date**, and in Britain it gave Cramer the first of three hits over the next 18 months.

118

YOU'RE DRIVING ME CRAZY

25 May 1961, for one week

The Temperance Seven *Parlophone R 4757*

Writer: Walter Donaldson
Producer: George Martin

The Temperance Seven was formed, so their publicity said, in 1906 for a season at the Pasadena Cocoa Rooms in the Balls Pond Road. The personnel were Captain Cephas Howard (trumpet and euphonium), leader of the gang, Sheikh Haroun Wadi el John R T Davies (trombone and alto sax), Frank Paverty (sousaphone), Mr Philip 'Fingers' Harrison (alto and baritone sax), Alan Swainston-Cooper (clarinet, soprano sax, phonofiddle, swanee whistle and pedal clarinet), Canon Colin Bowles (piano and harmonium), Brian Innes (drums), Dr John Gieves-Watson (banjo), with vocal refrain by Whispering Paul McDowell. **You're Driving Me Crazy** was written in 1930 by Walter Donaldson, whose **I Wonder Where My Baby Is Tonight** was one of the tunes on **Let's Have Another Party** (see no. 26). Perhaps their most important contribution to pop music history is the fact that **You're Driving Me Crazy** was producer George Martin's first number one hit single. There were 25 more of these to come in Britain.

The Temperance Seven, so named because they are always one over the eight, were a dance band rather than a jazz band in the style of Kenny Ball or Acker Bilk, and their brief spell of glory inspired acts like the Bonzo Dog Doo Dah Band and the New Vaudeville Band in the years that followed. They broke up not long after their hits ended less than a year later, although in the early 1970's Ted Wood, brother of Face and Stone Ron Wood, briefly reformed the band. Little success ensued.

119

SURRENDER

1 June 1961, for four weeks

Elvis Presley *RCA 1227*

Writers: Ernesto de Curtis, B G de Curtis, Doc Pomus and Mort Shuman
Producer: Steve Sholes

For his eighth British number one, Elvis chose another old Italian song and revamped it, using the **It's Now Or Never** formula with almost equal success. This time it was **Torna A Sorrento (Return to Sorrento)**, written in 1911 by Ernesto and B G de Curtis, who sound no more Italian than Doc Pomus and Mort Shuman who wrote the English lyric. The song gave Elvis his fifth US number one with successive releases, and his fourth on the trot in the UK. It was recorded in Nashville on 30 and 31 October 1960, the only non-spiritual song laid down at those sessions. Elvis recorded the entire **His Hand In Mine** LP, his highly successful gospel album, **Crying In The Chapel**, which was to become a British number one nearly five years later (see no. 197), and **Surrender**. The Jordanaires were present but there is no accurate record of the musicians who played on the tracks, which were all produced as usual by Steve Sholes.

120

RUNAWAY

29 June 1961, for three weeks

Del Shannon *London HLX 9317*

Writers: Del Shannon and Max Crook
Producers: Harry Balk and Irving Micahnik

Del Shannon, born Charles Westover on 30 December 1939, began his recording career with one of the most influential records in pop history, a disc that used both falsetto and the organ for the first time in a really commercial way. The organ was played by Max Crook, who co-wrote the song with Del Shannon, and his solo in the middle of the song has become one of the best known instrumental breaks in pop history. It was at the time an entirely original record, a strange new sound that was an inevitable number one from the day of release.

Del Shannon's subsequent chart career was very successful, even though he had no other number ones. He recorded a Roger Miller song, **Swiss Maid**, when Miller was still unknown. He also recorded **From Me To You** for the American market in 1963 when the Beatles were unheard of in the States, and with that record became the first man to take a Lennon/McCartney song into the US Hot Hundred. He produced Brian Hyland and gave the **Sealed With A Kiss** hitmaker a 1970's US hit with an interesting version of **Gypsy Woman**, which featured Max Crook again on organ. Del Shannon is still active, but even if he were to give up tomorrow, his reputation as a rock innovator is secure.

121

TEMPTATION

20 July 1961, for two weeks

The Everly Brothers *Warner Brothers WB 42*

Writers: Nacio Herb Brown and Arthur Freed
Producer: Wesley Rose

The Everly Brothers' fourth and final chart-topper was a drum dominated reworking of **Temptation**, a song originally performed by Bing Crosby in the 1933 film, *Going Hollywood.* Twenty-one records reached number one in 1961, of which five were old songs (**Are You Lonesome Tonight, Blue Moon, You're Driving Me Crazy, Temptation** and **Michael**) and a further two (**Wooden Heart** and **Surrender**) were old tunes with new lyrics. There have never been before or since such a dominance of the top of the charts by old songs, although 1981 ran it close. With hindsight it is clear that the world was ready for something new, something which emerged little more than a year later when **Love Me Do** entered the charts. The Beatles were of course destined to take over Don and Phil's title as the world's top vocal group, but in fact the decline in the Everlys' popularity was not connected with the Beatles' rise. The Everlys had only two more Top 10 hits after **Temptation** and their decline didn't get any faster when the Liverpool explosion came. Until the end of 1965, Don and Phil regularly reached the Top 40, but the days of glory ended in 1961.

122

WELL I ASK YOU

3 August 1961, for one week

Eden Kane *Decca F 11353*

Writer: Les Vandyke
Producer: Bunny Lewis

Almost two years after Johnny Worth/Les Vandyke wrote **What Do You Want** and **Poor Me** for Adam Faith (see nos. 93 and 97), he came up with his third and final number one song, for another newcomer with a name nicked from Genesis Chapter One, Eden Kane. Eden Kane began life on 29 March 1942 as Richard Sarstedt. Like Cliff Richard and Engelbert Humperdinck, he was born in India and returned to Britain as a child. He first created interest with an advertising jingle for Cadbury's called **Hot Chocolate Crazy**, which was played almost as often as Horace Batchelor's football pools advertisement on Radio Luxembourg. **Well I Ask You** followed, and then further Top 10 hits, **Get Lost, Forget Me Not** and **I Don't Know Why**.

A couple of flops, financial problems and a change in labels finished Eden Kane's career. One comeback hit, **Boys Cry** on Fontana in 1964, was just a hiccup on the downward spiral. The Sarstedt family was not finished, though. Brother Peter reached number one in 1969 (see no. 267) and brother Clive (who for some reason called himself Robin Sarstedt) reached number three in 1976 with his rendition of **My Resistance Is Low**. In the mid-seventies, the brothers all sang together briefly, but this did not create new chart action for Eden Kane.

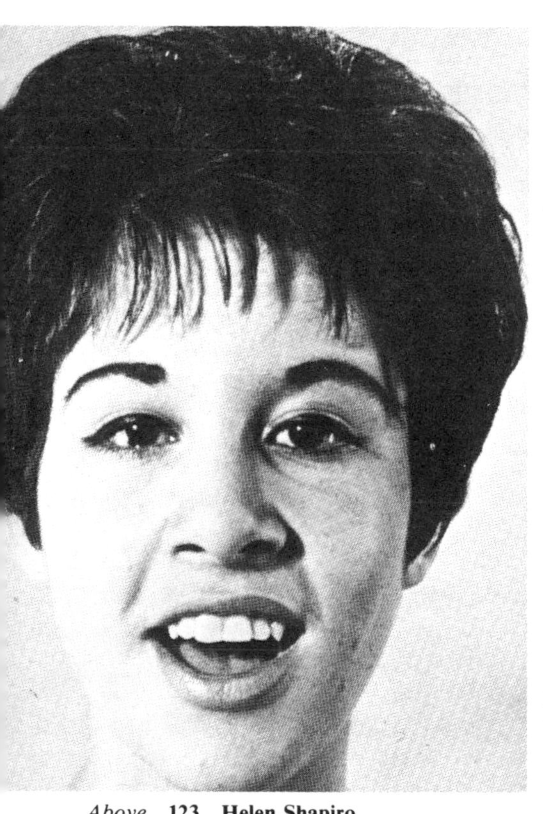

Above **123 Helen Shapiro**
Right **120 Del Shannon**

Above **113 Petula Clark**

123

YOU DON'T KNOW

10 August 1961, for three weeks

Helen Shapiro *Columbia DB 4670*

Writers: John Schroeder and Mike Hawker
Producer: Norrie Paramor

By reaching number one with her second single while still at school, Helen Shapiro became a national celebrity, the schoolgirl with the grown up voice. Helen was 14 years and 316 days old when she hit the top, thus becoming the youngest British artiste to get to number one. But she was still a year older than Frankie Lymon had been when **Why Do Fools Fall In Love** hit number one in 1956 (see no. 48).

Born in Bethnal Green on 28 September 1946, Helen Shapiro was a protégée of the well-known singing coach, Maurice Burman, who introduced her to John Schroeder, then an assistant to Norrie Paramor at Columbia. Her first single was a Schroeder song, **Please Don't Treat Me Like A Child** which cruised happily into the Top 10. For the follow-up, Schroeder and Mike Hawker wrote a ballad, and it took over the number one spot on 10 August 1961. Three days later, in a move apparently unconnected with Miss Shapiro's success, the East Germans began building the Berlin Wall.

124

JOHNNY REMEMBER ME

31 August 1961, for three weeks
and from 28 September 1961 for one week

John Leyton *Top Rank JAR 577*

Writer: Geoff Goddard
Producer: Joe Meek

John Leyton, born on 17 February 1939, was a TV actor known mostly for his portrayal of the part of Ginger in the BBC-TV children's serial, *Biggles*, when he landed the part of a pop singer called Johnny St Cyr in a weekly series called *Harpers West One*. His manager at the time was a young Australian on his way to his first million, called Robert Stigwood. Stigwood realised the importance of TV exposure and managed to arrange for Leyton to feature his latest single on the show. The song, written by early sixties weirdo Geoff Goddard and produced by the first great British independent producer, Joe Meek, was a minor-key agony-laden song about a dead love 'singing in the sighing of the wind, blowing in the treetops, Johnny remember me.' It couldn't miss and it didn't.

John Leyton followed Tab Hunter and Anthony Newley as an actor turned pop star by accident, and cashed in on his initial success with one more Top 10 hit and seven other chart hits over the next 2½ years. He also landed his biggest film part, in *The Great Escape* with Steve McQueen.

125

REACH FOR THE STARS/CLIMB EV'RY MOUNTAIN

21 September 1961, for one week

Shirley Bassey *Columbia DB 4685*

Writers: Reach For The Stars – Udo Jurgens, English lyrics by David West,
Climb Ev'ry Mountain – Richard Rodgers and Oscar Hammerstein II
Producer: Norman Newell

Shirley Bassey, the Queen Of Batley and the most successful solo female artiste in British chart history, is also the only solo female artiste to have had number one hits in two different decades. Her second number one was a double-sided success, one side a song by the man who won the 1966 Eurovision Song contest for Austria, translated by Miss Bassey's producer Norman Newell under the pseudonym David West. The other side was a song from probably the most successful musical of all time, *The Sound Of Music*, which despite its fabulous success as an LP and on stage and celluloid, has not supplied as many hits to the singles charts as some other less successful shows. The only other single hit of a song from the show was Vince Hill's **Edelweiss** which climbed to number 2 in 1967.

From 14 September to 19 October 1961, the British charts had a new number one each week. There were actually only five records involved in this 6 weeks of musical chairs, as **Johnny Remember Me** reached the top twice, but there has never in the history of the British charts been a longer run than this one, 6 weeks of new number ones. The record was equalled in 1968, when again one record (**Mony Mony** – no. 254) featured twice.

— 126 —

KON-TIKI

5 October 1961, for one week

The Shadows *Columbia DB 4698*

Writer: Michael Carr
Producer: Norrie Paramor

The Shadows' fifth hit was their second to top the chart. It was written by Michael Carr, who had also penned their follow-up to **Apache** (see no. 106), the number five hit **Man Of Mystery**, which also served as the theme for a series of black and white B-movies based on the stories of Edgar Wallace. Michael Carr was born in Leeds in 1904, but moved to Dublin at a tender age and took to the sea at the age of 18. He became a windjammer seaman, film stuntman, cowboy and globe-trotter, experiences which no doubt inspired him to write such hits as **South Of The Border, The Wheel Of The Wagon Is Broken** and **Hang Out The Washing On The Siegfried Line**.

The line-up for this record was still the original Shadows line-up, but by the time the tune was at number one, drummer Tony Meehan had left the Shadows and had been replaced by the drummer from Marty Wilde's Wildcats, Brian Bennett. For Bennett this was a wise move. Marty Wilde had scored his final Top 10 hit at the beginning of 1961, but the Shadows were still making Top 10 hits in 1979.

— 127 —

MICHAEL

12 October 1961, for one week

The Highwaymen *HMV POP 910*

Writer: Traditional, arranged by Dave Fisher
Producer: Dave Fisher

Lonnie Donegan covered four American hits in his chart heyday, but the only time he lost out to the original version was when he took on the Highwaymen and their version of the traditional spiritual, **Michael**. The Highwaymen were five students from the Wesleyan University, Middletown, Connecticut, who got together to put on a show for their fellow students in 1959, and were so well received that they decided to carry on performing together. A visit to New York late in 1960 resulted in a contract with United Artists and a first LP, from which the title track, **Michael**, was released as a single. By late summer it was number one in America, and it duly repeated the success in Britain, leaving Lonnie Donegan floundering at number six.

The Highwaymen were Dave Fisher, the lead tenor and arranger, Bob Burnett, Steve Butts, Chan Daniels and Steve Trott, but their career never got going after **Michael** because the lads wanted to complete their university studies and so turned down offers of tours and TV appearances. Nevertheless, they managed one more hit in Britain and three more in America before their boat ran aground.

— 128 —

WALKIN' BACK TO HAPPINESS

19 October 1961, for three weeks

Helen Shapiro *Columbia DB 4715*

Writers: John Schroeder and Mike Hawker
Producer: Norrie Paramor

Helen Shapiro was still at school when her third single became her second consecutive number one. Another hit from what were rapidly becoming the prolific pens of John Schroeder and Mike Hawker, **Walkin' Back To Happiness** was a lively song in the style of **Don't Treat Me Like A Child** and would have been perfect Eurovision material. It has always seemed odd that while singers like Lulu, Mary Hopkin and Sandie Shaw have all sung Britain's Song For Europe, Helen Shapiro never had the opportunity.

She did have the opportunity to make a film, though, and left school early at the end of 1961 to begin filming *It's Trad, Dad.* The film was successful, making good profits for the producers, but it was no help to the stars, Helen Shapiro and Craig Douglas. For both of them, the future just went downhill. At the beginning of 1963, she headlined a nationwide tour on which the Beatles were the main supporting act. Nobody could have coped with that, least of all a 16 year old girl. Her career never recovered from the impact of that tour, so successful for the Beatles and so disastrous for her. She is still active in showbusiness, but no chart comeback has materialised.

129

LITTLE SISTER/HIS LATEST FLAME

9 November 1961, for four weeks

Elvis Presley *RCA 1258*

Writers: Little Sister—Doc Pomus and Mort Shuman.
His Latest Flame—Doc Pomus and Mort Shuman
Producers: Steve Sholes and Chet Atkins

Elvis recorded both sides of his ninth UK number one at sessions in Nashville on 25 and 26 June 1961, while his eighth UK number one was still at the top of the charts. Both sides of the new single were by Doc Pomus and Mort Shuman, who had also written the English lyrics for that eighth number one, **Surrender** (see no. 119). Elvis had surprisingly missed number one honours with his previous single **Wild In The Country/I Feel So Bad**, possibly because **I Feel So Bad** was the first Elvis single to feature saxophone. **Little Sister/His Latest Flame** put him back on top again, proving to be the start of his longest stretch of successive chart-toppers (five). **His Latest Flame** is sometimes known as (**Marie's The Name) His Latest Flame. Little Sister** was Elvis' first genuine rock number one since **I Need Your Love Tonight** in 1959 (see no. 85).

130

TOWER OF STRENGTH

7 December 1961, for three weeks

Frankie Vaughan *Philips PB 1195*

Writers: Burt Bacharach and Bob Hilliard
Producer: Johnny Franz

A number five hit in America for Gene McDaniels was turned into a number one hit in Britain by Frankie Vaughan. It was yet another number one for Burt Bacharach, the only one not written with Hal David. Co-author of this one was Bob Hilliard who wrote various hits with other partners, like **Seven Little Girls Sitting In The Back Seat, Dear Hearts And Gentle People** and **In My Little Corner Of The World**. He died on 1 February 1971.

Frankie Vaughan's career had been in some considerable lull when he recorded **Tower Of Strength**. His previous hit had dropped off the charts almost a year earlier, and his previous Top 10 hit, **The Heart Of Man**, was a summer 1959 release. However, **Tower Of Strength** was perfect for Vaughan's vigorous style and he quickly cornered the airplay to find himself with the Christmas number one of 1961. After this hit, he was never to be a major chart force again, although he had further Top 10 hits in 1963 and 1967 to bring his total to nine. But as a cabaret performer, he retained his drawing power for very many years and has never had to wonder where the money to pay the gas bill was coming from.

Another cover version of this song that Frankie swamped was one by Paul Raven, who had to change his name to Gary Glitter a decade later to find Vaughan-type chart fame himself.

131

MOON RIVER

28 December 1961, for two weeks

Danny Williams *HMV POP 932*

Writers: Henry Mancini and Johnny Mercer
Producer: Norman Newell

The fourth Oscar-winning song to top the British charts, the theme from the Audrey Hepburn film, *Breakfast At Tiffany's*, gave Danny Williams his third chart hit, and his only chart-topper. The big hit version in America had been by Jerry Butler, who must be the most successful and most influential star never to have had a hit in Britain. Butler recorded the original of the Walker Brothers' first number one, **Make It Easy On Yourself** (see no. 203), and many of his other songs, like **For Your Precious Love, He Will Break Your Heart** and **Only The Strong Survive**, are now soul standards. In Britain, Danny Williams' only competition was composer Henry Mancini's instrumental version, which peaked at number 44.

Danny Williams was for a couple of years Britain's answer to Johnny Mathis, with a smooth as silk delivery and a choice of material that accentuated his talents. All the same, for 14 years after his seventh hit, **My Own True Love**, dropped off the charts, Danny Williams disappeared from the chartwatcher's view. He re-emerged in 1977 with **Dancing Easy**, a song that began life as an advertising jingle for a well-known alcholic beverage.

136 Elvis Presley

128 Helen Shapiro

Left 130 Frankie Vaughan
Below 131 Danny Williams

132

THE YOUNG ONES

11 January 1962, for six weeks

Cliff Richard and the Shadows *Columbia DB 4761*

Writers: Sid Tepper and Roy C Bennett
Producer: Norrie Paramor

The Young Ones was not only Cliff's second million-selling single, but it also became the fourth single in the history of the charts to enter at number one, the first by a British artist. By the day of release, **The Young Ones** had amassed an all-time record advance for a single to date of 524 000 copies. It was written by Sid Tepper and Roy Bennett, the Americans who had also written **Travellin' Light** (see no. 92) for Cliff, and was the title song for the film starring Cliff Richard, Robert Morley, Carole Gray, Grazina Frame and the Shadows, as well as featuring budding actors Melvyn Hayes and Richard O'Sullivan. In America the film was released as *It's Great To Be Young*, so the title tune became an ex-title tune, and flopped accordingly.

Cliff's fifth number one remained on the chart for 20 weeks, his second longest run with one single, **Living Doll** having been the most durable with 23 weeks in three separate runs. **The Young Ones** also gave Cliff his longest stay at number one, equal with **Living Doll**.

133

ROCK-A-HULA BABY/CAN'T HELP FALLING IN LOVE

22 February 1962, for four weeks

Elvis Presley *RCA 1270*

Writers: Rock-A-Hula Baby—Fred Wise, Ben Wiseman and Dolores Fuller,
Can't Help Falling In Love—George Weiss, Hugo Peretti and Luigi Creatore
Producer: Steve Sholes

The third consecutive number one hit to come from the movies was Elvis Presley's tenth number one and his fourth double-sided number one hit. The film in question was his eighth and most money-spinning film, *Blue Hawaii*. It was not one of the King's very best films but it has a very strong soundtrack and crops up on late night television with monotonous regularity. **Can't Help Falling In Love**, written by George Weiss and **Plume de Ma Tante** hitmakers Hugo and Luigi, was an integral part of the film from the outset and subsequently became one of Elvis' most popular recordings and the closing number in his Las Vegas stage act. **Rock-A-Hula Baby** on the other hand was inserted in the film after regular filming had been completed, to help the film cash in on the twist boom. The 'Blue Hawaii' Album recorded at Paramount in Hollywood in September 1961, became Presley's biggest ever soundtrack LP.

Can't Help Falling In Love, based on the old French tune, 'Plaisir d'Amour', has subsequently been a British hit for Andy Williams (number three in 1970) and the Stylistics (number four in 1976) – a rare instance of the same song providing three different Top 10 records at different times. The Stylistics' single was produced by Hugo Peretti and Luigi Creatore, who masterminded the career of the Stylistics during the heights of their popularity.

134

WONDERFUL LAND

22 March 1962, for eight weeks

The Shadows *Columbia DB 4790*

Writer: Jerry Lordan
Producer: Norrie Paramor

The Shadows' third number one was the second from the pen of Jerry Lordan, who has proved the most successful writer of instrumentals in the history of the British charts. Jerry Lordan had three hits as a singer in 1960, **I'll Stay Single** (which had the next line, 'not one thing'll/make me change my mind'), **Who Could Be Bluer** and **Sing Like An Angel**. But his voice was very lightweight, and his talents clearly lay in writing rather than performing.

Wonderful Land had a horn section added to the basic lead/rhythm/bass and drums line-up, an example of the adventurous production style of Norrie Paramor which brought him his 16th number one, to put him at that stage only one behind Mitch Miller's total. **Wonderful Land** stayed at the top for 8 weeks, a record for an instrumental second only to Eddie Calvert's **Oh Mein Papa** (see no. 16) which held the top for 9 weeks in 1954 and which was another Norrie Paramor production.

While the Shadows' third chart-topper was still riding high, bass guitarist Jet Harris left the group to concentrate on a solo career. He was replaced by another musician from the rapidly thinning ranks of Marty Wilde's Wildcats, Brian 'Licorice' Locking.

135

NUT ROCKER

17 May 1962, for one week

B Bumble and The Stingers *Top Rank JAR 611*

Writers: Tchaikovsky, arranged by Kim Fowley
Producer: Kim Fowley

For the first time in British chart history, an instrumental took over from another instrumental at number one. B Bumble and the Stingers – the first instrumental one-hit wonder – revamped Tchaikovsky's *Nutcracker Suite* and created a classic from a classic. Mastermind of this hit was Kim Fowley, born in Los Angeles on 27 July 1942 and who had already produced another one-hit wonder in America, the Hollywood Argyles' **Alley-Oop**. In Britain, **Nut Rocker** was the zenith of his achievement, but his influence on and involvement with chart acts like P J Proby, the Rockin' Berries, Emerson Lake and Palmer and REO Speedwagon has kept his name in the rock press and cash in his pocket.

His reputation is that of a rather weirder American version of Jonathan King, brillant at producing hit singles but incapable of creating a long-lasting successful chart act. But at least, unlike Jonathan King, he has one number one hit to his credit. Nut Rocker stayed on the charts for 15 weeks in 1962 and when re-issued on the Stateside label in 1972, spent another 11 weeks on the chart and reached number 19.

136

GOOD LUCK CHARM

24 May 1962, for five weeks

Elvis Presley *RCA 1280*

Writers: Aaron Schroeder and Wally Gold
Producers: Steve Sholes and Chet Atkins

Number eleven in the staggering list of Presley number ones was a gentle rock ballad, not from any movie, recorded in Nashville on 15/16 October 1961. The exact line-up is unknown but the Jordanaires were there and are in fact featured even more than usual on this particular cut. The song was written by Aaron Schroeder and Wally Gold who had already provided Elvis with a UK number one with **I Got Stung** in 1959 (see no. 80) and with their adaptation of **O Sole Mio (It's Now Or Never)** in 1960 (see no. 109). Everything Presley released on singles in 1962 went to the top of the charts – he was at number one for 15 weeks of the year, a record surpassed only by Frankie Laine (27 weeks in 1953), the Beatles (16 weeks in 1963), John Travolta and Olivia Newton-John (16 weeks in 1978) and by Elvis himself (18 weeks in the previous year, 1961, although that year not every one of his singles made number one).

Good Luck Charm also completed Elvis' second hat-trick of number ones, a unique achievement at the time, since matched only by the Beatles and Abba.

137

COME OUTSIDE

28 June 1962, for two weeks

Mike Sarne with Wendy Richard *Parlophone R 4902*

Writer: Charles Blackwell
Producer: Charles Blackwell

Mike Sarne was born Michael Scheur in 1939 of German extraction. Wendy Richard was just beginning as an actress specialising in the not-so-dumb blonde roles that were still coming her way almost 20 years later, especially after her success as Miss Brahms in the long running BBC television series *Are You Being Served?* **Come Outside** was one of the very few comedy records ever to make the very top of the charts. After **My Old Man's A Dustman** by Lonnie Donegan, it was only the second comedy disc at the top, and since 1962 comedy has done little better. Only **Lily The Pink, Grandad, Ernie, My Ding-A-Ling, D.I.V.O.R.C.E., Combine Harvester** and **Shaddup You Face** have reached the very top in the past 20 years.

Mike Sarne followed up **Come Outside** with **Will I What?** with Billie Davis, and other increasingly forgettable variations on the theme. When he turned his hand to film directing, he succeeded with *Myra Breckinridge* (starring Raquel Welch) in creating what many eminent critics consider the worst film of all time.

138

I CAN'T STOP LOVING YOU

12 July 1962, for two weeks

Ray Charles *HMV POP 1034*

Writer: Don Gibson
Producers: Sid Feller, orchestra and chorus conducted by Marty Paich

One of the most influential LP's of all time was Ray Charles' 1962 LP 'Modern Sounds In Country and Western Music'. For the first time there was an acknowledged crossover from rhythm and blues to country and western, meeting in the middle – in pop. The highlight of the album was Don Gibson's beautiful country ballad, completely reworked by Ray Charles to give him his biggest worldwide hit.

Ray Charles Robinson was born in Albany, Georgia on 23 September 1932. He was blinded by glaucoma at the age of 6, and orphaned at the age of 14. He found himself in Seattle, Washington in the early fifties where he formed a trio based on the successful Nat King Cole formula. He dropped his surname to avoid confusion with boxer Sugar Ray Robinson, and by 1952 had a recording contract with Atlantic. His career at Atlantic produced the blues standard **What'd I Say**, but it was not until he moved to ABC Paramount in 1960 that he started his string of hits in the States.

I Can't Stop Loving You has been his only number one in Britain, partly because a long but ultimately successful fight against drug addiction severely limited Ray Charles' career in the late sixties and early seventies. He is now recording again, and even acted a cameo role in the recent John Belushi–Dan Ackroyd comedy film *The Blues Brothers*.

139

I REMEMBER YOU

26 July 1962, for seven weeks

Frank Ifield *Columbia DB 4856*

Writers: Johnny Mercer and Victor Schertzinger
Producer: Norrie Paramor

Frank Ifield was born in Coventry on 30 November 1936, but emigrated from that much-bombed city to Australia with his parents shortly after the war. He began his singing career in Australia, and returned to Britain in 1959 to try to break through in his homeland. Almost immediately, he had a small hit with a song called **Lucky Devil**, covering the American hit by Carl Dobkins Jr. After that, the success which had seemed so near, drifted away and Ifield looked destined to join the ranks of not-quite-stars like Dickie Pride, Mike Preston and Nelson Keene.

Then, in the middle of 1962, Norrie Paramor and Frank Ifield decided on one more try. Like Connie Francis, four years earlier, they went through the box of old sheet music and came up with **I Remember You**, a song from the 1942 Dorothy Lamour movie *The Fleet's In*. What was different was the yodelling that Ifield put into '*I Remember Yoo-hoo*'. Suddenly he was a big star, with a record that stayed at number one for 7 weeks and which eventually sold a million copies in Britain alone.

140

SHE'S NOT YOU

13 September 1962, for three weeks

Elvis Presley *RCA 1303*

Writers: Doc Pomus, Jerry Lieber and Mike Stoller
Producers: Steve Sholes and Chet Atkins

Elvis completed a round dozen of UK number ones with his fourth chart-topper in as many releases (another first for Tupelo's favourite son). The song was not linked to any movie and was one of a dozen or so titles recorded in Nashville (RCA studios) on 19 March 1962. The majority of the titles recorded that day found their way onto the **Pot Luck** album (including **Suspicion** which, like **Wooden Heart**, was 'lost' by RCA as a possible single and became instead a huge hit for unknown Terry Stafford in 1964, at a time when Elvis was running short of strong material). 'Pot Luck' was a healthy album seller for Presley in the last half of 1962. Jerry Lieber and Mike Stoller had been asked by Elvis' publisher, Freddy Bienstock, to come up with some new country-flavoured material for this session, and they produced **She's Not You**, together with Doc Pomus, and the song that became its flip, **Just Tell Her Jim Said Hello**, on their own. **She's Not You** thus became the second Elvis number one for Lieber and Stoller and the fourth for Doc Pomus who had co-written both sides of Elvis' ninth number one **Little Sister/His Latest Flame** (see no. 129), and were partly responsible for his eighth, **Surrender** (see no. 119).

141

TELSTAR

4 October 1962, for five weeks

The Tornados *Decca F 11494*

Writer: Joe Meek
Producer: Joe Meek

The third instrumental number one of 1962 was one of the better and more significant records of the early sixties. It was written, produced and arranged by Joe Meek, the man who had earlier hit the top with John Leyton and who had used the five men who now made up the Tornados as session musicians since before Leyton's success. The Tornados (Alan Caddy, Heinz Burt, Roger Jackson, George Bellamy and Clem Cattini) were officially Billy Fury's backing group, but their relationship with Fury was short-lived. **Telstar**, named for the American communications satellite launched earlier in the year, was an organ-dominated instrumental that not only reached number one in England, but went right to the top of the American charts as well. This was the first major British hit in America for years, and apart from novelties like Lonnie Donegan's **Does Your Chewing Gum Lose Its Flavour**, and Laurie London's **He's Got The Whole World In His Hands** was about the only straight pop hit from Britain since the days of Vera Lynn and David Whitfield. It prepared the way for the Liverpool invasion a year later.

Adding accidentally to the significance of the record, it was during **Telstar's** weeks on top that the first Beatles hit, **Love Me Do**, entered the British charts, and the world of popular music was changed forever.

142

LOVESICK BLUES

8 November 1962, for five weeks

Frank Ifield *Columbia DB 4913*

Writers: Irving Mills and Cliff Friend
Producer: Norrie Paramor

Following up a monster hit like **I Remember You** is not easy. Frank Ifield, the man with the yodel gimmick, looked a racing certainty for obscurity as rapid as his fame. In the event, not so. Ifield and Paramor came up with the country and western standard **Lovesick Blues**, which had given Hank Williams one of his biggest successes over 10 years earlier. The song had originally been recorded by Emmett Miller in 1928, but despite the many hit versions that have been recorded since, nobody has sold as many copies of **Lovesick Blues** as Frank Ifield.

Ifield was now following in the well-worn footsteps of Cliff Richard, Adam Faith, the Shadows and others in achieving two consecutive number one hits. Only Elvis Presley had completed a hat-trick of number ones (see no. 115), and in retrospect it is amazing to think that the Aussie from Coventry could even have had a chance of completing the hat-trick, for the Liverpool bombshell was on the point of exploding.

143

RETURN TO SENDER

13 December 1962, for three weeks

Elvis Presley *RCA 1320*

Writers: Otis Blackwell and Winfield Scott
Producers: Steve Sholes and Chet Atkins

Return To Sender was Elvis Presley's fifth consecutive number one, a record for consecutive chart toppers that lasted only 1 year and 363 days, until 10 December 1964, when the Beatles' sixth consecutive number one, **I Feel Fine**, hit the top. **Return To Sender** was from Elvis' eleventh film, the uninspiring *Girls! Girls! Girls!*. The main interest in the film is the ineptness of the title as there were actually only two girls featured in the film, played by Stella Stevens and Laurel Goodwin, although in addition to this number one smash, the score included the attractive ballad **Because of Love** covered on a single by Billy Fury, himself perhaps the greatest British pop singer never to have a number one.

Otis Blackwell, author of such classics as **All Shook Up** and **Great Balls Of Fire**, did not extend himself in concocting, with Winfield Scott, this lightweight gentle rocker for the abdicating King to churn off the production line. Amazing to relate, **Return To Sender** was the first Elvis UK number one to feature saxophone. The track was recorded late in 1962 at Paramount Studios in Hollywood, but the line-up of musicians at the session, apart from the Jordanaires on backing vocals as usual, is not clear.

144

THE NEXT TIME/BACHELOR BOY

3 January 1963, for three weeks

Cliff Richard and the Shadows *Columbia DB 4950*

Writers: The Next Time – Buddy Kaye and Philip Springer; Bachelor Boy – Bruce Welch and Cliff Richard
Producer: Norrie Paramor

The first and only time that Cliff topped the charts with a double A side was with two songs from the film *Summer Holiday*. **The Next Time** was a slow romantic ballad, performed in Greece against the exotic setting of the Acropolis, with Cliff sporting a rather unflatteringly English string vest, whereas **Bachelor Boy** was an afterthought. It was written by Cliff – his only number one as a writer – and Bruce Welch after it was discovered that the film was a few minutes too short, and shot at Pinewood studios as a semi-dance routine with the Shadows rather than incur the extra cost of taking the film crew back out to the continent for just one sequence.

145

DANCE ON!

24 January 1963, for one week

The Shadows *Columbia DB 4948*

Writers: Valerie and Elaine Murtagh and Ray Adams
Producer: Norrie Paramor

Dance On! was a tune found by the manager of Cliff Richard and the Shadows, Peter Gormley, who was listening to the piles of tapes that were always being sent in to his office, and looking for a potential single. It had been written by the three members of the vocal group, the Avons, who had hit the Top 3 over Christmas 1959 with their cover version of Paul Evans and the Curls' American Top 10 hit, **Seven Little Girls Sitting In The Back Seat**. Their fourth and final hit had come early in 1961 with their version of Bobby Vee's American smash, **Rubber Ball**. The Avons only reached number 30 with that song, being thoroughly beaten by Bobby Vee, who reached number four, and by Marty Wilde who reached number nine. Playing on the Marty Wilde single had been then Wildcats Brian Bennett and Licorice Locking, so perhaps it was apt that the Avons' only connection with a number one hit should come with the help of two of the people whose **Rubber Ball** had bounced higher than theirs.

As well as being a chart-topping instrumental for the Shadows, Kathy Kirby reached number 11 with her vocal version in 1963. **Dance On!** thus just failed to join the ranks of songs that have been Top 10 hits in both vocal and instrumental versions – songs like **Oh Mein Papa**, **Annie's Song**, **Amazing Grace** and **Don't Cry For Me Argentina**.

146

DIAMONDS

31 January 1963, for three weeks

Jet Harris and Tony Meehan *Decca F 11563*

Writer: Jerry Lordan
Producer: Dick Rowe

Terence 'Jet' Harris was born on 6 July 1939, in Kingsbury Middlesex, and David Joseph Anthony Meehan was born in Hampstead on 2 March 1943. After both had played with assorted groups during 1958, Cliff Richard enlisted them on bass and drums respectively for his backing group The Drifters. They subsequently became The Shadows and had notched up five Top 10 hits by the time that Tony vacated the drumstool in October, 1961. Jet Harris remained with the group until March 1962, when he left to pursue a solo career.

After a couple of hits, **Besame Mucho** and **Main Title Theme From The Man With The Golden Arm**, Jet teamed up with Tony, who had since become involved in production work for Decca, and they released the six string bass dominated **Diamonds** at the tail end of 1962.

The tune had been written by singer/songwriter Jerry Lordan who had already supplied the Shadows with **Apache** and **Wonderful Land**. As **Diamonds** hit number one, ironically deposing the Shadows' **Dance On** from the top spot, Jet and Tony spoke out about each other. Jet said 'As a musician, Tony is one of the best: I have learned musical terms and ways that I never knew existed. He's a wizard and impresses me a great deal'. And Tony's thoughts on Jet – 'I have learned a great deal from Jet about stage-work, self-confidence and how to present myself!' After just two more big hits, both in 1963, **Scarlett O'Hara** and **Applejack**, the duo split up.

Neither of them hit the big time again, although Jet, who now lives in Gloucester, and Tony who is London based, have been contemplating going back into the studio together.

144 Cliff Richard and the Shadows

141 Tornados

150 Gerry and the Pacemakers

146 Jet Harris and Tony Meehan

151 Beatles

147

WAYWARD WIND

21 February 1963, for three weeks

Frank Ifield *Columbia DB 4960*

Writers: Stan Labowsky and Herb Newman
Producer: Norrie Paramor

On 21 February 1963, Frank Ifield succeeded in completing the first hat-trick of number one hits by a British born artist, when his version of the Tex Ritter/Gogi Grant hit of 1956, **Wayward Wind** reached the top. It was perhaps an unusual choice of a song to complete a hat-trick, but it was Ifield's third consecutive revival of a country hit, and it did the trick. Where Helen Shapiro, Anthony Newley and Jimmy Young (who coincidentally had a small hit with **Wayward Wind** in 1956) had failed to achieve a third chart-topper in a row; Frank Ifield succeeded. By the end of 1963 he had been joined by both Gerry and the Pacemakers and the Beatles, as British pop spread over the UK charts in preparation for its world-conquering achievements in 1964.

From 8 November 1962, when Ifield's previous number one **Lovesick Blues** hit the top, until 16 January 1964, only four of the 19 songs that reached number one were not recorded at EMI's Abbey Road Studios. From 21 February 1963, seven consecutive number ones over a period of 23 weeks all came from Abbey Road, by far the most successful run by any studio in the history of British pop music.

148

SUMMER HOLIDAY

14 March 1963, for two weeks
and from 4 April 1963 for one week

Cliff Richard and the Shadows *Columbia DB 4977*

Writers: Bruce Welch and Brian Bennett
Producer: Norrie Paramor

The title song from the film was written by Bruce Welch and the Shadows' drummer Brian Bennett, while they were on a tour of England. The idea came while they were rehearsing in the orchestra pit of an empty theatre, and Bruce just started singing 'we're all going on a summer holiday, no more working for a week or two' and Brian immediately came up with the 'middle-eight' 'we're going where the sun shines brightly – we're going where the sea is blue . . . '. Over the past 20 years it has almost become a traditional song to sing in coaches and cars on the way to the annual holiday.

Cliff Richard is the only act in British chart history to have had more than one chart-topper that has fallen from the top and then climbed back. **Please Don't Tease** (see no. 104) was the first, and **Summer Holiday** was the second.

149

FOOT TAPPER

28 March 1963, for one week

The Shadows *Columbia DB 4984*

Writers: Hank B. Marvin and Bruce Welch
Producer: Norrie Paramor

Norrie Paramor's third consecutive production at the top of the charts was probably the least memorable of the Shadows' five number ones. It was also Bruce Welch's second consecutive number one as a writer, as he co-wrote **Summer Holiday** (see no. 148) for Cliff Richard, on which the Shadows also played. Although Bruce had already written or co-written four of Cliff's number ones, this was the only one of his compositions that the Shadows took to the top.

Foot Tapper featured in the film *Summer Holiday* and so another chart record was established by consecutive number ones coming from the same film. Other films, like *Grease* and *Saturday Night Fever* have been more successful in total chart terms, but no other film has provided two number ones in a row. Two other tunes were featured by the Shadows in *Summer Holiday*. These were called **Round And Round** and **Les Girls**, but neither was released as an A-side of a single.

Foot Tapper was the Shadows' tenth consecutive Top 10 hit, of which five had been number one. This was to prove their last number one hit, although they hit the Top 10 six more times, twice more with their next two singles to give them a round dozen of consecutive Top 10 hits.

150

HOW DO YOU DO IT?

11 April 1963, for three weeks

Gerry and the Pacemakers *Columbia DB 4987*

Writer: Mitch Murray
Producer: George Martin

The last of four consecutive number ones on the Columbia label was also the first number one by a Liverpool group. The Beatles' second single, **Please Please Me**, had peaked at number two, and it was left to Gerry and the Pacemakers, also managed by Brian Epstein and produced by George Martin, to take the number one slot for Liverpool with a fairly un-Liverpool sound and a song written by non-Liverpudlian Mitch Murray for the Beatles. The Beatles did not want to record the song as a single, so it went to Gerry and the Pacemakers. **How Do You Do It?** has always sounded more like a Eurovision song than a Liverpool hit, and would have been a far stronger entry than the actual 1963 entry, Ronnie Carroll's **Say Wonderful Things**. Gerry Marsden, born 24 September 1942, had none of the white soul of the Beatles or the Searchers, or the plaintive little-boy-lost appeal of Billy J Kramer, and was always much more in the tradition of Tommy Steele and Lonnie Donegan than the first wave of the Liverpool sound. The Pacemakers were Gerry's elder brother Fred, born 23 November 1940, Les Maguire, born 27 December 1941, and Les Chadwick, born 11 May 1943.

151

FROM ME TO YOU

2 May 1963, for seven weeks

The Beatles *Parlophone R 5015*

Writers: John Lennon and Paul McCartney
Producer: George Martin

When the Beatles' first single, **Love Me Do**, crept into the Top 50 on 11 October 1962, few people could possibly have guessed that by the end of the next year these four strange people from somewhere north of Watford would have sold more records more quickly than anybody in the world before or since, including two singles which at the time were the two biggest selling singles in British history. But of course they did.

From Me To You, their third single, was the first of 11 consecutive number one hits. It was on top for 7 weeks, which was to be their longest run at the top, equalled only by **Hallo Goodbye** 4½ years later. The Beatles were, of course, John Lennon (9 October 1940 to 8 December 1980), Paul McCartney (born 18 June 1942), George Harrison (born 25 February 1943) and Ringo Starr (born Richard Starkey on 7 July 1940), who joined the group just weeks before the Beatles bonanza got under way.

Everything was ready for the Beatles. The mediocre quality of popular music in 1962 showed that something new had to come from somewhere, and the 7 year cycle was up. At the end of 1955, Bill Haley had introduced rock'n'roll. Late in 1962 the Beatles arrived, and in 1969 they broke up, consigning British pop to 7 lean years. In 1976, the Sex Pistols and the other punks rejuvenated British pop. In 1983 who knows?

152

I LIKE IT

20 June 1963, for four weeks

Gerry and the Pacemakers *Columbia DB 7041*

Writer: Mitch Murray
Producer: George Martin

Gerry and the Pacemakers' second single repeated the success of their first, but with one extra week at the top of the charts. Up until that time, no act had reached number one with their first two releases (although others had reached number one with each of their first two hits). The song repeated almost exactly the formula of the first song, using the same writer, producer and studio, and it repeated the success. It was therefore surprising that for the third single (see no. 159), George Martin took Gerry so very far away from the bouncy formula so successfully established by the first two hits.

The difference about Gerry and the Pacemakers was the piano. Instead of the standard line-up of lead, rhythm and bass guitars and drums, Les Maguire's piano was used as lead. He played very much in the tradition of Winifred Atwell and Russ Conway (though he was neither black nor had a finger missing), which fitted the bouncy voice of Gerry Marsden perfectly and set the group apart from all the other groups who were then crawling from every dark and noisy cellar in Liverpool towards the bulging wallets of the London record companies.

153

CONFESSIN'

18 July 1963, for two weeks

Frank Ifield *Columbia DB 7062*

Writers: Al J Neiburg, Marty Symes and Jerry Levison
Producer: Norrie Paramor

After **Wayward Wind**, Frank Ifield's attempt to score a fourth consecutive number one failed when **Nobody's Darlin' But Mine** peaked at number four. By then the grip of the Liverpool sound on Britain's charts was total, and the knowledgeable pundits wrote off Frank Ifield almost immediately as somebody who had better start working out his routine for singing his old hits in the clubs, for that was all the future held in store.

It was all a little too soon, and Frank Ifield refused to be written off immediately. Picking up a song written in 1930, and originally titled **Lookin' For Another Sweetie**, he yodelled his way back to the very top of the charts. But when Elvis eased him out on 1 August, it was indeed the end of the chart-toppers for Frank Ifield. More hits followed, but only one more record, a revival of **Don't Blame Me**, reached the Top 10. Ifield's career is unique in that he had four number one hits and two Top 10 hits in the space of seven releases in 18 months, but he never reached the Top 20 before or since despite another eight singles that reached the charts. His last hit **Call Her Your Sweetheart** dropped off the charts in February 1967, but his total of 158 weeks on the chart places him higher on the all-time list than, for example, Sandie Shaw, Gary Glitter or the Four Seasons.

154

(YOU'RE THE) DEVIL IN DISGUISE

1 August 1963, for one week

Elvis Presley *RCA 1355*

Writers: Bill Giant, Bernie Baum and Florence Kaye
Producers: Steve Sholes and Chet Atkins

At the end of February 1963, Elvis released what was probably his worst and definitely his shortest single at considerably less than 2 minutes. Despite the fact that **One Broken Heart For Sale** would not have sold more than ten copies if it had not had the magic Presley name on the label, there was a sensation in the charts industry when this atrocious single peaked at number twelve. Elvis had failed to reach the British Top 10 for the first time since the switch to RCA in 1957.

The follow-up to this disaster was eagerly anticipated, and the song that was chosen from those recorded at a Nashville session at the end of May 1963 had one important difference from **One Broken Heart For Sale**. The Jordanaires reappeared, having been usurped by the Mello-Men on the previous single. **(You're The) Devil In Disguise** did make number one, for 1 week, but it was already the end of an era. Never again would Elvis be able to claim the top spot as his by right. In fact, of the eight releases between **(You're The) Devil In Disguise** and his next number one **Crying In the Chapel** 2 years later, only one reached the Top 10.

Elvis was not the only American in decline. Such was the domination of the Liverpool groups and British pop at this time, that from 26 July 1962 to 25 June 1964, Elvis was the only non-British act to top our charts. Between 3 Jan 1963 and 25 June 1964, a period of 77 weeks, this 1 week from August 1963 was the only week when a British record was not on top of our charts.

155

SWEETS FOR MY SWEET

8 August 1963, for two weeks

The Searchers *Pye 7N 15533*

Writers: Doc Pomus and Mort Shuman
Producer: Tony Hatch

The day of the Great Train Robbery was also the day of the Searchers' first number one. The Searchers were the Beatles' favourite Liverpool group. They took their name from the same John Wayne movie that had inspired Buddy Holly to write **That'll Be The Day**. Mike Pender (born Michael Prendergast on 3 March 1942) and John McNally (born 30 August 1941) are the two founder members who were still with the group when they performed on the 1981 Royal Variety Show. The other two Searchers on **Sweets For My Sweet** were Tony Jackson (born 16 July 1940) and Chris Curtis (born Christopher Crummey on 16 August 1941). Unlike most of the successful groups in the first wave of Liverpool success, the Searchers were not managed by Brian Epstein nor produced by George Martin. Their manager was a well-established and highly astute show business entrepreneur, Tito Burns, and their producer a Pye staff producer who would later become a highly successful writer, performer and husband of Jackie Trent, Tony Hatch.

Sweets For My Sweet was a song written by the prolific Pomus-Shuman team, originally recorded by the Drifters. The Drifters version had completely failed in the UK, but it became one of the many rhythm and blues songs in the repertoire of the groups in the Liverpool clubs. What made the Searchers different was that they put out these songs as singles: the others just used them as fillers on LPs.

156

BAD TO ME

22 August 1963, for three weeks

Billy J Kramer and the Dakotas *Parlophone R 5049*

Writers: John Lennon and Paul McCartney
Producer: George Martin

Billy J Kramer (born William Ashton on 19 August 1943) was a British Railways employee who sang lead with a group called the Coasters until Brian Epstein saw him. He liked Kramer, but not the Coasters, so he teamed him with a Manchester group, the Dakotas, who thus became the first non-Liverpool group to hit the top on the crest of the Liverpool wave. The Dakotas were Mike Maxfield on lead guitar, Robin MacDonald on rhythm guitar, Ray Jones on bass guitar and on drums, Tony Mansfield, whose sister later achieved chart fame under the name Elkie Brooks.

Bad To Me was Billy J Kramer's second release. The first had been another Lennon/McCartney tune from the Beatles' **Please Please Me** album, **Do You Want To Know A Secret?** It became one of those singles which were better made and better known than the follow-up, but it was the follow-up that made number one. The careers of Jimmy Jones, the Troggs and Alvin Stardust feature similar discs. **Bad To Me** is one of only two Lennon/McCartney songs that reached number one by other acts, but were never recorded by the Beatles, the other being the Paul McCartney song for Peter and Gordon, **World Without Love**.

157

SHE LOVES YOU

12 September 1963, for four weeks
and from 28 November 1963 for two weeks

The Beatles *Parlophone R 5055*

Writers: John Lennon and Paul McCartney
Producer: George Martin

In chart terms, this was the Beatles' biggest hit, staying on the charts for 33 weeks. It sold over a million copies in Britain alone, and until the follow-up **I Want To Hold Your Hand** sold even more, it was the biggest seller in British musical history. It is also one of only two records to come back to the top of the charts after two other songs had reached number one, the other being Doris Day's **Secret Love**. Only 19 records have ever regained the top spot, mostly after only 1 week in a lower position. However, the 7 week period while Brian Poole's **Do You Love Me** and **You'll Never Walk Alone**, by Gerry and the Pacemakers were on top of the charts is the longest period ever between spells at number one by the same record.

She Loves You was the record that changed a generation. When **From Me To You** was number one for 7 weeks, Beatlemania was rising, but it was no greater than the fan worship that surrounded Cliff Richard earlier or the Bay City Rollers later. But **She Loves You** was something else – the trigger for the swinging sixties. 'She loves you, yeah, yeah, yeah' was the message and the lovable mop-tops were the medium. After almost 20 years, the record still sounds outstanding, with the driving rhythm section of John and Ringo, the simple lead of George and the hard-edged vocals of John and Paul. The message was happy, positive, upbeat. The doubts of **Help** and **We Can Work It Out** were yet to come. The despair of **Yesterday** and **Get Back** were years ahead. **She Loves You** and **I Want To Hold Your Hand** were the peak of the Beatles' achievements, the songs which most created their image. The only way should have been down from here, but somehow it never happened.

158

DO YOU LOVE ME

10 October 1963, for three weeks

Brian Poole and the Tremeloes *Decca F 11739*

Writer: Berry Gordy Jr.
Producer: Mike Smith

Brian Poole, the son of a Dagenham butcher, was a regular on the Light Programme's most popular show *Saturday Club*, introduced by Brian Matthew. The Tremeloes (spelling was never their strong point) were Ricky West on lead guitar, Alan Blakely on rhythm guitar, Alan Howard on bass and Dave Munden on drums. Like the Searchers, Poole had the audacity to record some of the rhythm and blues classics he performed regularly, and their first hit, the Isley

Brothers' classic **Twist And Shout**, reached number four in the charts. They were in competition with the Beatles, whose **Twist and Shout** EP sold enough to have made the top three, if the chart at that time had been counting EPs. Without the competition from the Beatles, Brian Poole would almost certainly have kicked off his chart career with a number one.

As it was, his next single did go all the way. Written by the founder of Tamla Motown, Berry Gordy, **Do You Love Me** had been an unsuccessful single for the Contours in Britain, despite reaching number three in the States in the late summer of 1962. After **Do You Love Me**, a terrible rip-off single called **I Can Dance** deservedly failed to make the Top 30, and Poole's career hiccuped. Two Top 10 hits followed in 1964, but the chart hits soon stopped and Poole and the Tremeloes split in 1966. The Tremeloes went on to greater chart success (see no. 233), but Brian Poole is now back at the family butcher shop in Dagenham.

159

YOU'LL NEVER WALK ALONE

31 October 1963, for four weeks

Gerry and the Pacemakers *Columbia DB 7126*

Writers: Richard Rodgers and Oscar Hammerstein II
Producer: George Martin

To follow two consecutive number ones with their first two singles, Gerry and the Pacemakers' producer George Martin came up with Shirley Jones' showstopper from *Carousel*. The gamble paid off, and Gerry and the Pacemakers set up the unique record of reaching number one with each of their first three releases. It was possibly not as much of a gamble as it appeared – George Martin had already recorded the Beatles' version of **Till There Was You** for the 'With The Beatles' album, and knew how popular a Liverpool version of a standard could be.

The success of **You'll Never Walk Alone** coincided with the rise of Liverpool Football Club, and the Kop crowd adopted the song and the arrangement so that it has now become the most widely sung song on the Saturday afternoon terraces of England. Not that Rodgers or Hammerstein earned many extra royalties from these public broadcasts of their work, but listen to the way the crowds all hiccup on "You'll ne – e – ever walk alone", just like Gerry Marsden.

The record was at number one on 22 November 1963 when Lee Harvey Oswald fired the shots from the Texas Book Depository building in Dallas that killed President John F Kennedy.

160

I WANT TO HOLD YOUR HAND

12 December 1963, for five weeks

The Beatles *Parlophone R 5084*

Writers: John Lennon and Paul McCartney
Producer: George Martin

When **I Want To Hold Your Hand** took over from **She Loves You** at number one, the Beatles completed a hat-trick of number one hits, to equal the achievements of Elvis, Frank Ifield and Gerry and the Pacemakers. **I Want To Hold Your Hand** also took over from **She Loves You** as the biggest selling single in British history, a record it kept until Paul McCartney's Wings sold over two million copies of **Mull Of Kintyre** (see no. 416). It was also the first time an act had succeeded itself at number one, a record the Beatles kept until John Lennon equalled the feat with **Imagine** and **Woman** in 1981 (see nos. 473 and 474).

The main significance of **I Want To Hold Your Hand** is that it is the record that conquered America. On 18 January 1964, 2 days after the record had dropped off the top of the British charts, it entered the Billboard Hot Hundred and soared quickly to the top. By the end of 1964, the Beatles had achieved six number one hits in America, five more Top 10 hits and no less than 19 other charted sides, on a total of six different labels. Even **Love Me Do** on the now defunct Tollie label, reached number one, while its B-side, **P.S. I Love You**, climbed as high as number ten. In later years, the Bee Gees have equalled the Beatles record of six consecutive number ones in America, and Christopher Cross has swept the Grammy Awards, but nobody has ever dominated world popular music like the Beatles did in 1964.

161

GLAD ALL OVER

16 January 1964, for two weeks

The Dave Clark Five *Columbia DB 7154*

Writers: Dave Clark and Mike Smith
Producer: Dave Clark

Ah, those long-lost innocent days of the Tottenham Sound! Dave Clark on drums owned, led and paid the salaries of the

Below **160 Beatles**

Above **158 Brian Poole and the Tremeloes**

Above **161 Dave Clark Five**

Below **163 Bachelors**

other four, and his driving beat gave the lads from the South Grove Youth Club a number one hit with their third chart single. Dave Clark himself was born on 14 December 1942, and his clean cut cheeky image was of as much value to his group as his drumming. Clark's co-writer and lead vocalist on **Glad All Over** was Mike Smith, born 12 December 1943. The other group members were saxophonist Denny Payton, born 1 August 1943, guitarist Lenny Davidson, born 30 May 1944, and on bass Rick Huxley, born 5 August 1942. Having missed out with their version of **Do You Love Me** which made number 30 while Brian Poole hit number one, **Glad All Over** (which was not about a young man with roving hands and a girlfriend called Gladys) set the DC5 off on the standard sixties group career route. American hits, a film – slightly better than most, called *Catch Us If You Can* – and break-up in the seventies followed as surely as night follows day. Dave himself however remains active in the fields of record production and artist management having been almost unique in being a sixties beat boom star with business sense and the ability to hang onto his earnings after the hits were over.

162

NEEDLES AND PINS

30 January 1964, for three weeks

The Searchers *Pye 7N 15594*

Writers: Sonny Bono and Jack Nitzsche
Producer: Tony Hatch

The Searchers' second number one came with their third single on Pye. It was another old song which, like **Sweets For My Sweet** had not made any dent on the British charts when originally recorded. In fact, Jackie de Shannon had only reached number 84 in America, so putting it out as a single was a bit of a risk for the Searchers. Their faith in the song was justified as it became their biggest hit and the song that even today people scream for at Searchers gigs.

Written by Jack Nitzsche and Sonny Bono, destined to achieve stardom 18 months later with his wife Cher (see no. 201), **Needles and Pins** was a perfect example of a supreme production that transformed a minor song into a brilliant record. Tony Hatch had incidentally written the Searchers' second single, **Sugar and Spice**, which only reached number two. Had it not been for the domination of the charts at the end of 1963 by the Beatles, the Searchers would have started their chart career with four consecutive number ones. Tony Hatch, thanks largely to his entertaining but blunt comments as a judge on TV talents shows, has come in for occasional ill-informed criticism during his career as a writer, producer and performer, but his production of records like this one, or **Downtown** by Petula Clark, show that he has been one of the most imaginative and influential producers in Britain.

163

DIANE

20 February 1964, for one week

The Bachelors *Decca F 11799*

Writers: Erno Rapee and Lew Pollack
Producer: Michael Barclay

Totally against the overwhelming Liverpool tidal wave, the Bachelors, three married men from Dublin, built up a highly lucrative career based on sweet harmony versions of old favourites. Starting with **Charmaine** in 1963, they had top ten hits with **Diane**, **I Believe**, **Ramona** and **Marie** among others. **Diane** was their only number one hit.

Originally formed as a novelty instrumental trio called the Harmonichords, the Bachelors were (and still are) Con Clusky (born 18 November 1941), his brother Declan (born 12 December 1942) and John Stokes (born Sean Stokes on 13 August 1940). Their clean smiling image and highly professional stage presence made them particular favourites with TV producers, and it seemed for a year or so that no variety show was complete without the thick Irish brogue of the Bachelors, or failing them, Val Doonican. They were only the second Irish act to top the British charts, after Ruby Murray. Since them, the only Irish group to top the British charts has been the Boomtown Rats (see nos. 428 & 440) with whom the Bachelors have only their Irishness in common.

164

ANYONE WHO HAD A HEART

27 February 1964, for three weeks

Cilla Black *Parlophone R 5101*

Writers: Burt Bacharach and Hal David
Producer: George Martin

Cilla Black was born Priscilla White on 27 May 1943, and used to be the hat-check girl at the Cavern in Liverpool.

Brian Epstein discovered her (what sort of hat he was checking at the time is unrecorded) and signed her up as his token female to complete his stable of stars. He probably did not realise that after the Beatles, this tall ginger-headed girl would be the most successful of all his signings.

Cilla's first record was a Lennon/McCartney ballad, **Love Of The Loved**, which was presumably churned out on a bad day for all concerned. It reached number 35 in late 1963. To follow up, she chose a Bacharach/David song recorded by Dionne Warwick in America, where it reached number eight. Cilla's version featured to full effect her astonishing voice which changes its tone entirely when she turns up the volume. She quickly became known as the girl with two voices, one soft, gentle and Scouse for the quiet bits, and one a real belter for the climax of her songs.

Anyone Who Had A Heart was the first number one by a female soloist since Helen Shapiro at the end of 1961. Cilla Black was on her way, and Brian Epstein's 25 per cent of the action was worth having.

165

LITTLE CHILDREN

19 March 1964, for two weeks

Billy J Kramer & the Dakotas *Parlophone R 5105*

Writers: Mort Shuman and John Leslie MacFarland
Producer: George Martin

As Jerry Reed so aptly remarked in his American smash of the early seventies, 'when you're hot, you're hot'. The Epstein stable, Parlophone, Liverpool and producer George Martin came up with yet another number one, this time in the form of an American song, by Mort Shuman in one of his rare songs without Doc Pomus, recorded by Billy J Kramer and the Dakotas.

It turned out to be Billy J's last number one, and indeed his whole career cascaded to a halt quickly afterwards, with only two more singles reaching the charts. Kramer's follow-up was **From A Window**, another Lennon/McCartney tune. It reached number ten. The next single was called **It's Gotta Last Forever**, but it didn't. It failed even to reach the charts. Suddenly Epstein had his first failure on his hands (the debacle of Tommy Quickly's career was later in the year). Kramer's last chart entry was the Bacharach/David song **Trains and Boats and Planes** in 1965, but Bacharach's own version easily outsold Billy J. A few more flop singles and then Billy J Kramer and the Dakotas split up. Billy J Kramer's first solo single, **Town of Tuxley Toymaker Part I** was a turntable hit, but it failed to chart. Today, Billy J still plays the variety club circuit recording now and then.

166

CAN'T BUY ME LOVE

2 April 1964, for three weeks

The Beatles *Parlophone R 5114*

Writers: John Lennon and Paul McCartney
Producer: George Martin

The Beatles' fourth number one was from their first film, *A Hard Day's Night*, and it gave George Martin the unique honour of having produced three consecutive number ones for the second time in 12 months.

Shooting on the film began in March 1964, after the Beatles got back from their first American visit, but much of the music had been recorded earlier. **Can't Buy Me Love** set an unbeaten record in Britain by having advance sales of over one million copies, and yet it still failed to reach the top in its week of release. It took 2 weeks to reach the top, as did every Beatles' number one from **I Want To Hold Your Hand** to **Hey Jude**. It was, in retrospect, a slight let down from the two previous releases, which had been the supreme achievements of the Beatlemania days. All the same, **Can't Buy Me Love** gave the Beatles yet more Gold Records and their third American number one.

The flip side was a John Lennon song, **You Can't Do That**. He described it as his attempt to be Wilson Pickett. Wilson Pickett's last British hit was **Hey Jude**, his attempt to be John Lennon.

167

A WORLD WITHOUT LOVE

23 April 1964, for two weeks

Peter and Gordon *Columbia DB 7225*

Writers: John Lennon and Paul McCartney
Producer: Norman Newell

Peter Asher's sister Jane was Paul McCartney's girlfriend in the early sixties. John and Paul had written **I Want To Hold Your Hand** (see no. 160) in the basement of her London house. This explains how the unknown duo Peter and Gordon (Peter Asher born 22 June 1944 and Gordon Waller born 4 June 1945) got access to a very strong Lennon/McCartney song, which shot them from obscurity to becoming the 100th act to top the British charts. Like Billy J Kramer's **Bad To Me** (see no. 156) and Cilla Black's **Love Of The Loved**, **A World Without Love** was one of those rare Lennon/McCartney songs which the Beatles never recorded.

When the hits stopped for Peter and Gordon in 1966, Peter Asher stayed in America, where the duo had been more successful than in Britain, to become a producer, masterminding the careers of James Taylor and Linda Ronstadt among others, two acts who were very successful in the States but never meant much in Asher's homeland. Gordon Waller, whose singing voice was far more commercial than Peter's, somehow never achieved much more than regular appearances as Pharaoh in *Joseph And His Amazing Technicolor Dreamcoat*, and sad to relate, has drifted out of the music business.

168

DON'T THROW YOUR LOVE AWAY

7 May 1964, for two weeks

The Searchers *Pye 7N 15630*

Writers: Jimmy Wisner and Billy Jackson
Producer: Tony Hatch

After recording **Needles and Pins**, Tony Jackson left the Searchers amidst a certain amount of ill-feeling, and formed his own group, the Vibrations. Mike Pender took over as lead vocalist and Frank Allen was brought in on bass from Cliff Bennett's Rebel Rousers. The next session produced their third number one hit, an old Orlons song called **Don't Throw Your Love Away**. The split had apparently left the Searchers' popularity intact.

At this stage, the Searchers were the second most popular of the 'beat boom' groups, with only the Beatles having a larger fan club. The Beatles themselves were reported as saying that the Searchers were their favourite group. However, their success had not much longer to run. After **Don't Throw Your Love Away**, their only major hits were **When You Walk In The Room** (with its incredible rhyme of 'nonchalant' with 'you I want') which reached number three at the end of 1964, and **Goodbye My Love** (number four early in 1965). In 1966 drummer Chris Curtis left the group. The occupant of the Searchers' drum stool for the past decade has been Billy Adamson. Curtis made one single which failed and the Searchers' singles also slipped into obscurity. The group is still performing superbly, though, and occasionally crops up on television to remind the fans of their great days in 1963 and 1964.

169

JULIET

21 May 1964, for one week

The Four Pennies *Philips BF 1322*

Writers: Mike Wilsh, Fritz Fryer and Lionel Morton
Producer: Johnny Franz

In October 1963, Marie Reidy of 'Reidy's Home Of Music' in Blackburn Lancashire (the place where they had to count all the four thousand rather small holes, according to the Beatles' **Day In The Life**) telephoned Johnny Franz to ask whether he might be interested in a local group, the Lionel Morton Four. 'Send a tape', replied Mr Franz, and according to his later recollections, 'the tape was so good they were immediately signed to a contract.' The first session produced **Do You Want Me To?**, the first single, which crept in to the charts at the beginning of 1964, and **Juliet**, the second, which climbed all the way to number one. It had originally been selected as the single's B-side.

Lead singer Lionel Morton had been in the choir at his local church in Blackburn for 7 years, and was married to Julia Foster, the actress. Co-writers of **Juliet** Fritz Fryer played guitar and Mike Wilsh was on keyboards. The fourth Penny was Alan Bush, who had drummed for both Joe Brown's Bruvvers and Johnny Kidd's Pirates before joining the Four Pennies. **Juliet** proved to be the group's only Top 10 hit, although the next three singles all reached the Top 20. One of those singles was **Until It's Time For You To Go**, a song that Elvis Presley took to number 5 in 1972.

170

YOU'RE MY WORLD

28 May 1964, for four weeks

Cilla Black *Parlophone R 5133*

Writers: Umberto Bindi, Gino Paoli, English lyrics by Carl Sigman
Producer: George Martin

Cilla Black's second consecutive number one was an Italian song by Gino Paoli and Umberto Bindi (whose **Il Nostro**

Above **172 Animals**

Below **169 Four Pennies**

Right **167 Peter and Gordon**

Concerto had hit number 47 in Britain late in 1962), translated by the ubiquitous Carl Sigman, whose earlier translations and adaptations had included **Answer Me, It's All In The Game** and **The Day The Rains Came**. It was George Martin's eleventh number one production out of the past 21 chart-toppers, and all Martin's records had been with Brian Epstein acts.

After **You're My World**, Cilla Black never hit the very top again, but the hits continued for some time. Her version of **You've Lost That Lovin' Feeling** looked as though it would hit number one until the Righteous Brothers version overtook Cilla to win the race. By the end of the sixties, Miss Black had become the most successful of the many female vocalists tried as Saturday night BBC-TV variety show hostesses, her personality proving entirely suitable for the TV cameras. Now happily married to her manager Bobby Willis, Cilla Black performs and records when she wants to, and certainly not because she needs the money.

171

IT'S OVER

25 June 1964, for two weeks

Roy Orbison *London HLU 9882*

Writers: Roy Orbison and Bill Dees
Producer: Wesley Rose

The first American number one hit for 47 weeks was Roy Orbison's second British chart-topper. As usual, it was a song of lost love, for Orbison never won the girl until **Oh Pretty Woman** (although he might have done in **Running Scared** – Orbison scholars differ on their interpretations of the lyrics). The Big O's popularity was considerably greater in Britain than in his homeland, and **It's Over** was his twelfth hit here in less than 4 years. He toured regularly in Britain, and despite his almost totally immobile stage act, he packed the theatres wherever he went. An Orbison concert was a great experience in those days. He could reproduce apparently with ease the sounds he created on record, and his soaring tenor was as soulful as any black voice of the time. He was always the loser, but never sentimental. His songs were based in country music, but upbeat enough to appeal to all tastes. He wrote a succession of classic hits after **Only The Lonely** (see no. 108) such as **Running Scared**, **Crying**, **Dream Baby**, **In Dreams** and **Blue Bayou**, all of which have attained the status of standards. **It's Over** was possibly not his best record, but it nevertheless gave him that magic number one hit, for the first time in almost 4 years.

172

THE HOUSE OF THE RISING SUN

9 July 1964, for one week

The Animals *Columbia DB 7301*

Writer: Traditional, arranged by Alan Price
Producer: Mickie Most

The Animals came from the North-East of England, and brought a harder, more bluesy sound to the charts than the Mersey beat of the Beatles or the rock and roll of the Rolling Stones. Their only number one hit was the blues standard, **House Of The Rising Sun**, arranged by organist Alan Price (born 19 April 1942), who had founded the group as the Alan Price Combo. The other members of the Animals were vocalist Eric Burdon (born 19 May 1941), drummer John Steel (born 4 February 1941), bass guitarist Chas Chandler (born 18 December 1938) and rhythm guitarist Hilton Valentine (born 2 May 1943). Alan Price left the Animals in May 1965 and later scored hits with his own band, the Alan Price Set, and also with Georgie Fame. He was replaced by Dave Rowberry, but the Animals broke up altogether in 1967, at which time Eric Burdon moved to the States. There he had hits as the lead vocalist with the New Animals and with his next band, War, who went on to greater chart success in America than their original boss. Chas Chandler moved into management when the group disbanded and as manager of Jimi Hendrix and then Slade, enjoyed massive success in the late sixties and early seventies. He now runs his own record label, Cheapskate.

Considering the importance of the Animals in 1960's pop history, and in particular the influence of this record, it is surprising to find that it only enjoyed one week at number one.

173

IT'S ALL OVER NOW

16 July 1964, for one week

The Rolling Stones *Decca F 11934*

Writers: Bobby Womack and Shirley Womack
Producer: Andrew Loog Oldham

The first number one by the only group that could ever stand comparison in popularity with the Beatles was a Bobby and Shirley Womack song that was at the same time a small

GEORGE V

American hit for the Valentinos. It only held the top spot for one week, but with their fourth single, the Stones had finally made the big time.

Their first single was Chuck Berry's **Come On** which gave them their first hit, and like the first single of many acts who were to become major chart powers, it hung around the lower reaches of the charts for some time without ever getting as high as the Top 10. That single was followed by a Lennon/McCartney tune which Ringo had sung on the 'With The Beatles' album, **I Wanna Be Your Man**. This was the first time that the Stones had to put up with the 'Beatles copiers' tag, which dogged them throughout their career and which John Lennon commented acidly on in his interviews with the magazine that took its name from Mick Jagger and Co – Rolling Stone. The group's third single was a magnificent version of the Crickets B-side, **Not Fade Away**, and to prove the title prophetic, they scored the first of five consecutive number ones with their fourth single, **It's All Over Now**. It wasn't, it was only just beginning.

174

A HARD DAY'S NIGHT

23 July 1964, for three weeks

The Beatles *Parlophone R 5160*

Writers: John Lennon and Paul McCartney
Producer: George Martin

The title song from the Beatles' first film was their fifth consecutive number one, equalling the record for toppers on the trot held by Elvis Presley. It was their second number one hit from the film, after **Can't Buy Me Love** which had not been written specifically for the film.

Dick Lester directed *A Hard Day's Night*, which starred Wilfred Brambell as Paul's Irish grandfather and featured Patti Boyd as a schoolgirl on the train. It has always been considered the best pop musical to come out of Britain, and was justifiably a huge success. The soundtrack was one of the strongest collections of Beatle songs ever put together. Only seven songs were actually in the film, but these included **And I Love Her** and **If I Fell** as well as the two number one hits. **A Hard Day's Night** was chosen as the title for the film after Ringo, at the end of one long session on the set, quoted from John Lennon's book, *In His Own Write* with the comment, 'That was a hard day's night, that was'. Fittingly, Lennon sang lead.

The late Peter Sellers took his version of the song, recorded as an imitation of Laurence Olivier playing Richard III, into the Top 20 a year later. It became the first version of a previous Beatle single to hit the British charts.

175

DO WAH DIDDY DIDDY

13 August 1964, for two weeks

Manfred Mann *HMV POP 1320*

Writers: Jeff Barry and Ellie Greenwich
Producer: John Burgess

A song by Ellie Greenwich and Jeff Barry, soon to come to the notice of the British record-buying public with his productions of **I'm A Believer** (see no. 228) and **Sugar Sugar** (see no. 279), gave Manfred Mann their first number one. Manfred himself (né Mike Liebowitz in South Africa on 21 October 1940) had played jazz keyboards in South Africa before coming to UK and forming the Mann-Hugg Blues Brothers with Mike Hugg (born 11 March 1940). Mike Vickers (born 18 April 1941) had also joined the band, along with one Dave Richmond, when their first single, an instrumental, was released in July 1963. It flopped.

The second single was the first to feature their newly recruited vocalist, Paul Jones (born Paul Pond on 24 February 1942), but like the first, it missed the charts. At this point Dave Richmond left and Tom McGuinness (born 2 December 1941), joined and this was the line-up that recorded their third single **5-4-3-2-1**. This record was used as the theme for the ITV teen show *Ready Steady Go!* and thus soared to number five. It was no real surprise when their third chart hit, **Do Wah Diddy Diddy** stormed to the top. Manfred Mann had arrived.

176

HAVE I THE RIGHT

27 August 1964, for two weeks

The Honeycombs *Pye 7N 15664*

Writers: Ken Howard and Alan Blaikley
Producer: Joe Meek

The Honeycombs had a girl on drums, so in 1964 they were news. There was nothing else very exciting about the group, except that they were the first act to be taken over and

Above **175 Manfred Mann**

Above
178 Herman's Hermits

Below **181 Supremes**

Right **183 Beatles**

marketed by Ken Howard and Alan Blaikley, who later achieved massive success with Dave Dee, Dozy, Beaky, Mick, and Tich (see no. 246) and even wrote **I've Lost You**, a number nine hit for Elvis Presley in 1970.

The Honeycombs were Dennis D'Ell (born Dennis Dalziel on 10 October 1943) on lead vocals, Martin Murray (born 7 October 1941) on lead guitar, Alan Ward (born 12 December 1945) on rhythm, John Lantree (born 20 August 1940) on bass and his sister, Ann 'Honey' Lantree (born 28 August 1943) bashing out a rhythm every bit as subtle as Dave Clark's on drums. Martin Murray owned a hairdressing salon where Honey Lantree worked, which was the way the group got together and the origin of the group's name. The fact that Miss Lantree boasted a beehive hairdo was probably coincidental.

As soon as **Have I The Right** was in the charts, the Honeycombs embarked on a long tour of Australia and New Zealand. The single was a hit in Britain, America (where it reached number five) and of course Australia, but the tour meant the group were not around to promote the follow-up. Success was short-lived and Martin Murray was able to go back to hairdressing.

177

YOU REALLY GOT ME

10 September 1964, for two weeks

The Kinks *Pye 7N 15673*

Writer: Ray Davies
Producer: Shel Talmy

Without any doubt, the Kinks were among the most exciting, most talented and most original groups in the mid-sixties. Their singles bear comparison with even the Rolling Stones and the Beatles; 11 of their first 12 hits were Top 10 smashes and they were all written by lead guitarist and vocalist Ray Davies (born 21 June 1944). His brother Dave (born 3 February 1947) played rhythm, Pete Quaife (born 23 December 1943) was on bass and Mick Avory (born 15 February 1944) was the drummer. Their first single was the only one with an A-side not written by Ray Davies. It was a version of **Long Tall Sally** and it flopped. Single number two, **You Still Want Me** also disappeared down the plughole, but single number three was a classic of mid-sixties rock, **You Really Got Me**.

Jimmy Page, of Yardbirds and Led Zeppelin, is persistently rumoured to have played lead guitar on both this single and Herman's Hermits' **I'm Into Something Good**. If the rumours are true, he would join Hank Marvin and George Harrison as the only people to play lead guitar on consecutive number ones. Even if the rumours are untrue, Page certainly played lead on Joe Cocker's **With A Little Help From My Friends** (see no. 260), so he got there in the end.

178

I'M INTO SOMETHING GOOD

24 September 1964, for two weeks

Herman's Hermits *Columbia DB 7338*

Writers: Carole King and Gerry Goffin
Producer: Mickie Most

Mickie Most, hot from his success with the Animals, saw the actor Peter Noone on Coronation Street in 1964 and decided he looked like John F Kennedy. Noone was leader of a group called the Heartbeats in Manchester when Most contacted him, and Herman's Hermits and 'Hermania' were born. Peter Noone was born on 5 November 1947. His Hermits were Derek 'Lek' Leckenby, born 14 May 1946, Keith Hopwood, born 26 October 1946, Karl Green, born 31 July 1946 and Barry Whitwarn on drums, born 21 July 1946.

Most came up with **I'm Into Something Good**, which is amazingly enough the only Goffin/King song ever to top the British charts. The Hermits recorded it (with a little help from session men), and the disc moved rapidly to the top of the charts. It also established them in America, where their bouncy unsophisticated style gave them many more hits than in their homeland. **Mrs. Brown You've Got A Lovely Daughter** (originally written for a TV play starring Tom Courtenay) and **I'm Henry VIII I Am** were the biggest of twelve consecutive American Top 20 hits, a far better track record than in Britain.

When the Hermits broke up in 1971, Herman had one hit under the name Peter Noone before disappearing from the charts. He emerged at the 1979 World Popular Song Festival in Tokyo, singing an Elton John discard called **I'll Stop Living If You Stop Loving Me**, and in 1982 released a solo album after a brief spell fronting a new wave group called the Tremblers.

179

OH PRETTY WOMAN

8 October 1964, for two weeks
and from 12 November 1964 for one week

Roy Orbison *London HLU 9919*

Writer: Roy Orbison
Producer: Wesley Rose

In the middle of the British domination of the number one position during 1963 and 1964, Roy Orbison managed two chart-toppers and was virtually the only American act whose records were guaranteed to sell in vast quantities at this time. It was a time of major upheaval in the real world – on 15 October Harold Wilson became Prime Minister for the first time and on the same day, Nikita Khrushchev was ousted by Messrs. Brezhnev and Kosygin. The next day, the Chinese exploded their first atom bomb. Despite all this, the big hits had optimistic titles like **I'm Into Something Good, Oh Pretty Woman** and **I Feel Fine**.

This was Roy Orbison's final chart-topper, although the hits continued throughout the sixties. His first hit was in 1960, his last at the end of 1969, and yet such was his success in that decade that he remains one of the top ten chart acts of all time. In the 1970's and 1980's the popularity of his songs continued, but his own records stopped selling. When Don McLean's version of **Crying** reached number one (see no. 460), Orbison's compositions had become chart-toppers in three decades, the 1950's – **Claudette,** the 1960's and the 1980's. In 1981, Orbison had a comeback country hit in America in partnership with Emmylou Harris called **That Loving You Feeling**. It missed out in Britain, but it is quite possible that the Big O could be back on the charts here in the 1980's, over 10 years since his previous hit.

180

(THERE'S) ALWAYS SOMETHING THERE TO REMIND ME

22 October 1964, for three weeks

Sandie Shaw *Pye 7N 15704*

Writers: Burt Bacharach and Hal David
Producer: Tony Hatch

Sandra Goodrich was born in Dagenham, Essex on 26 February 1947. Rather than become a Girl Piper or a Ford factory worker, young Miss Goodrich made her way to Adam Faith's dressing room and sang for the great man. He was impressed and the 17-year-old landed a recording contract. She changed her name to Sandie Shaw, and her second single was a cover version of a small Lou Johnson hit in USA, written by Burt Bacharach and Hal David. It gave her her first hit and her first number one in only her third week on the chart.

Sandie Shaw is now remembered mainly for the fact that she never wore shoes and that her fringe was always in danger of restricting even further her already imperfect sight. What is forgotten is that of all the female soloists who have appeared on the British charts over the past 30 years or so, Sandie Shaw is the only one who has achieved three number one hits. She would never claim to be a great singer, but she could put across a song magnificently. Her range was surprisingly wide, from the plaintive **(There's) Always Something There To Remind Me** to the bouncy singalong **Puppet On A String**, so she appealed to a wide public without ever being a cult figure to anybody.

181

BABY LOVE

19 November 1964, for two weeks

The Supremes *Stateside SS 350*

Writers: Brian Holland, Lamont Dozier and Eddie Holland
Producers: Brian Holland, Lamont Dozier and Eddie Holland

The Supremes were the first black act to top the UK singles list in nearly four years. **Baby Love** served notice that a new form of rhythm and blues had arrived, a pop-orientated music that was heavy on beat and strong on melody. It became known as 'The Motown Sound', after the label formed by Berry Gordy Jr, and it provided one of the lasting styles of the sixties.

Florence Ballard, Diana Ross and Mary Wilson were the Supremes who made the group's first successful recordings, though when they had started as the Primettes there had been five and Ross used her real name, Diane Earl. Ballard was the original leader of the group but was gradually phased out for the more glamorous and charismatic Ross, a personal favourite of Gordy. Both he and Smokey Robinson had tried fruitlessly to write and produce for the group. The trio of Holland-Dozier-Holland had better results, providing the Supremes with four years of hits.

The breakthrough came with **Where Did Our Love Go**, an American number one and a British number three. Holland-Dozier-Holland took notice of the attention-grabbing 'Baby, baby' intoned by Ross at the start of that single and incorporated it in the title of **Baby Love**, an international smash. This single was the second of five consecutive American number ones.

182

LITTLE RED ROOSTER

3 December 1964, for one week

The Rolling Stones *Decca F 12014*

Writer: Willie Dixon
Producer: Andrew Loog Oldham

Originally a US soul hit in 1951 for the Griffin Brothers featuring Margie Day, the Willie Dixon song **Little Red Rooster** was covered by Sam Cooke twelve years later. It was this recording, which reportedly featured Billy Preston on keyboards, that brought the song to the attention of the Stones

The Rolling Stones hold many all time chart records, and among the countless groups of the early and mid sixties, their consistency and longevity is second to none. They were formed in 1962 and played regularly at clubs like London's Marquee and Giorgio Gomelsky's Crawdaddy Club in Richmond. There they quickly acquired a following and a manager – Andrew Loog Oldham. He juggled the line-up so that by the time they signed with Decca and cut their first single, they were five Londoners – Mick Jagger (born on 16 July 1944) on vocals, lead guitarist Keith Richards (born on 18 December 1943), who dropped the 's' off his surname in imitation of Cliff Richard, drummer Charlie Watts (born 2 June 1941), Bill Wyman (born 24 October 1941) on bass and Brian Jones (born 26 February 1944, died 3 July 1969) on rhythm guitar. This was the line-up on all their number one hits except **Honky Tonk Women** (see no. 274).

183

I FEEL FINE

10 December 1964, for five weeks

The Beatles *Parlophone R 5200*

Writers: John Lennon and Paul McCartney
Producer: George Martin

Brian Epstein understood the importance of release dates. In the first five years of Beatlemania, from 1963 to 1967 inclusive, the only year the Beatles did not have the Christmas number one was 1966, when the Beatles were too involved in the making of *Sgt Pepper* to release a single. The second of these Christmas hits was **I Feel Fine**. This was the single that put the Beatles one ahead of Elvis in the successive number one stakes. **I Feel Fine** was six out of six for the moptops – Elvis' greatest run had been five.

The fourth Beatles album 'Beatles For Sale' was also released that Christmas and for the first time it was admitted that not all Lennon-McCartney tunes were co-operative efforts. In his liner notes, Beatles publicist Tony Barrow says that various tracks on the LP were considered as potential singles 'until John Lennon came up with **I Feel Fine**'. John Lennon also sang lead on the single, but perhaps the feature of it was his feed back guitar work. By the end of their second year as the biggest thing ever to hit British show-business, the Beatles were beginning to be recognized as musicians, and not just pretty faces. George Harrison was the first to attract approving remarks from the critics, and was always considered the best musician of the Beatles. Before long he was being called one of the best rock guitarists in the world.

184

YEH YEH

14 January 1965, for two weeks

Georgie Fame with the Blue Flames *Columbia DB 7428*

Writers: Rodgers Grant, Pat Patrick and Jon Hendricks
Producer: Tony Palmer

Georgie Fame began life as Clive Powell on 26 June 1943, at Leigh in Lancashire. He played at Butlin's Holiday Camp in Pwllheli in the summer of 1959, and as a result joined Rory Blackwell's band and came to London. By chance Lionel Bart, hot from the success of **Living Doll** for Cliff Richard, heard Powell play and recommended him to Larry Parnes, who had been a colleague of Bart's since the early days of Tommy Steele in 1956.

Larry Parnes turned Clive Powell into Georgie Fame to match his other acts, Billy Fury, Marty Wilde, Vince Eager, Dickie Pride and so on. But Fame was never any good as a rock'n'roller and in the early sixties he drifted away from

Parnes. He formed the five man Blue Flames, a rhythm and blues-cum-jazz group, to back him, and earned a residency at London's Flamingo Club, which Fame almost single-handed turned into a thriving centre for his kind of music. A live LP brought Fame a wider audience, but all the same the success of his first chart single was unexpected.

The Blue Flames were Speedy Acquaye from Ghana on conga, Pete Coe on saxophone, Bill Eyden on drums, Colin Green on guitar and Tony Makins on bass. Georgie Fame played keyboards.

185

GO NOW

28 January 1965, for one week

The Moody Blues *Decca F 12022*

Writers: Larry Banks and Milton Bennett
Producer: Denny Cordell

Denny Laine, born Brian Hines in a boat off Jersey on 29 October 1944, had been with the Diplomats, a Birmingham group which had also included Roy Wood and Bev Bevan who went on to Move and Electric Light Orchestra. The Diplomats were one of the most popular groups in the Midlands, so when Denny Laine formed a new group, it had a lot going for it from day one. The group he formed was the Moody Blues, and the other members were Graham Edge, born 30 March 1942, Mike Pinder, born 27 December 1942, Ray Thomas, born 29 December 1942, and Clint Warwick, born Clinton Eccles on 25 June 1939.

Go Now was their second single and it climbed quickly to number one. The next three singles all reached the chart, but as the hits slowed down, both Denny Laine and Clint Warwick left. Their replacements, Justin Hayward and John Lodge, turned the group around and the first sign of their new direction came in a single in late 1966, a turntable hit but a sales flop called **Boulevard de la Madeleine**. 1967 was the bottom commercially for the Moody Blues, but at the end of the year a new label, Deram, and an amazingly successful song called **Nights In White Satin**, put failure into the past. The only question is, whatever happened to Clint Warwick?

186

YOU'VE LOST THAT LOVIN' FEELIN'

4 February 1965, for two weeks

The Righteous Brothers *London HLU 9943*

Writers: Phil Spector, Barry Mann and Cynthia Weil
Producer: Phil Spector

Mickie Most's favourite record is one of the best known records of all time, and the best production of Phil Spector's long and successful career. The tiny California based Moonglow Records put out the first Righteous Brothers single in the spring of 1963, a song called **Little Latin Lupe Lu** which got to number 49 on the Hot Hundred, but it took luck as much as the soulful voices of the two white and unrelated brothers to bring them to Phil Spector.

Bill Medley, born 19 September 1940 in Los Angeles, and Bobby Hatfield, born 10 April 1940 in Beaver Dam, Wisconsin, are the Righteous Brothers. British TV producer Jack Good was the first to spot their national potential after two Hot Hundred singles in 1963 had given the pair something of a following in California. Good put them on his nationally networked TV show *Shindig* where Phil Spector saw them. The rest is history.

You've Lost That Lovin' Feelin' was also the first song that Jonathan King chose to re-issue when he became Sir Edward Lewis' sidekick at Decca in the late sixties. The success of the re-issue (it reached number 10 in the spring of 1969) encouraged other companies to re-issue past hits, setting a trend that has significantly increased the importance of researching catalogue material to create new chart hits.

187

TIRED OF WAITING FOR YOU

18 February 1965, for one week

The Kinks *Pye 7N 15759*

Writer: Ray Davies
Producer: Shel Talmy

The second number one for the Kinks was their third hit. The follow-up to **You Really Got Me** was **All Day And All Of The Night**, which reached number two at the end of 1964, while the group was beefing up its image as hardrockers by getting rid of the pink hunting jackets that manager

Below **187 Kinks**

Left **184 Georgie Fame**

Below **185 Moody Blues**

Below **188 Seekers**

Above **186 Righteous Brothers**

Robert Wace had originally suggested for them. Robert Wace had been the lead singer of a group called the Ravens, a group formed at the Croydon School of Art and consisting of Wace, Ray and Dave Davies, Pete Quaife and Mick Avory. It was Larry Page who suggested the name Kinks, at which time Wace decided to manage rather than sing.

Tired Of Waiting For You was a gentler single than the first two hits, and marked the first time that the lyrical quality of Ray Davies' songs was noticeable. Apart from one or two singles like the comparatively unsuccessful **Everybody's Gonna Be Happy** and **Till The End Of The Day**, Kinks singles became quieter, more subtle and lyrically outstanding from now on. Songs like **Well Respected Man** (never released as a single) and **Dedicated Follower Of Fashion** (number four in spring 1966) show the influence of Lonnie Donegan, of whom Ray Davies was a big fan. Lonnie Donegan influenced Ray Davies and Davies influenced Paul Weller of Jam. The line continues through 25 years of number ones, linking three acts all of whom have had three number one hits.

188

I'LL NEVER FIND ANOTHER YOU

25 February 1965, for two weeks

The Seekers *Columbia DB 7431*

Writer: Tom Springfield
Producer: Tom Springfield

I'll Never Find Another You (no relation to **I'd Never Find Another You** which gave Billy Fury a number five hit in 1964) was written and produced by Tom Springfield and launched the career of the group that took over the niche left empty when the Springfields broke up in 1963. The Seekers, four Australians, became far more successful than the Springfields, probably because Judith Durham's crystal clear voice was much more suited to folk-pop material than Dusty Springfield's smokier, more bluesy voice.

Judith Durham was born in Melbourne on 3 July 1943 and her fellow Seekers were Athol Guy, born near Melbourne on 5 January 1940, Keith Potger, born in Colombo, Sri Lanka, on 2 March 1941, and Bruce Woodley, born in Melbourne on 25 July 1942. Potger's family moved to Melbourne in 1947, so it is no surprise to learn that this city, with the largest Greek population of any city in the world apart from Athens, is where the Seekers found each other. In 1964 they worked their passage over to Britain, singing on an ocean liner, and within a very short time appeared on 'Sunday Night At The London Palladium'. Within a year of arriving in Britain, they were back in Australia, headlining a tour and picking up gold discs as easily as a cat picks up fleas.

189

IT'S NOT UNUSUAL

11 March 1965, for one week

Tom Jones *Decca F 12062*

Writers: Les Reed and Gordon Mills
Producer: Peter Sullivan

It's Not Unusual was originally intended for Sandie Shaw but she turned it down as unsuitable for her. So Gordon Mills offered it to an unknown Welshman, Tom Jones (born Thomas Jones Woodward on 7 June 1940). Jones' voice and the powerful orchestral arrangement made the song sound so unlike anything Sandie Shaw might have sung that it is hard to understand how it could have been written with her in mind. Still, her loss was Tom Jones' gain and a major career was launched. The song was played on Juke Box Jury with Tom Jones behind the screen listening to the comments of the jury. His appearance on that show probably made the difference – the all-male Welsh miner's son (if he wasn't a miner's son he ought to have been) with the tight trousers and the rabbit's foot swinging from the belt was what the female population of Britain from 8 to 80 had been waiting for. He became the most sophisticated, most sexy and most imitated British singer in pop history and his career was made. With the help of minor surgical alterations to the state of his nose and his tonsils, Tom Jones eventually conquered the whole world, to become the All-Round Entertainer that he remains to this day.

190

THE LAST TIME

18 March 1965, for three weeks

The Rolling Stones *Decca F 12104*

Writers: Mick Jagger and Keith Richard
Producer: Andrew Loog Oldham

The Last Time gave the Rolling Stones a hat-trick of number one hits, but more importantly it marked the first time a

Left top to bottom **191 Unit Four Plus Two, 198 Hollies, 199 Byrds**

Right **189 Tom Jones**

Rolling Stones A-side had been written by the duo that was to become one of the most creative in rock music, Mick Jagger and Keith Richard. At this stage the pair were still uncertain about their writing capabilities, and when every newspaper in the world was comparing the Stones and the Beatles, it is not surprising that Jagger and Richard were not confident of standing up to comparison with Lennon and McCartney. The B-side, **Play With Fire**, was credited to Nanker and Phelge, which was the pseudonym Mick and Keith used on many early sides, and was another, slower, classic Stones track.

The Last Time gave the Stones their second American Top 10 hit as the follow-up to **Time Is On My Side**. They had to wait for their first number one in America until the next single (see no. 202) which was recorded in the States.

191

CONCRETE AND CLAY

8 April 1965, for one week

Unit Four Plus Two *Decca F 12071*

Writers: Brian Parker and Tommy Moeller
Producer: John L. Barker

Unit Four Plus Two's brilliantly original number one hit **Concrete And Clay** was surprisingly one of the few big British hits of 1965 not to be an equal smash in America, climbing only to number 28 over there.

Unit Four Plus Two was a six man band, as the name suggests, which got its name from the very popular Alan Freeman radio show 'Pick Of The Pops' which he divided each week into four units, Unit Four being the Top 10. The group started out as Unit Four, but then added two more personnel, so adapted the name. The six members were Rod Garwood, Hugh Halliday, Howard Lubin, Buster Meikle, Tommy Moeller and Pete Moules. Russ Ballard, later to compose **So You Win Again** for Hot Chocolate (see no. 408) played on the record, but did not join the group until 1967 when its best days were past. In fact, their last chart hit, their fourth, was **Baby Never Say Goodbye** which lurched onto the chart for 1 week at number 49 from 17 March 1966, less than a year after **Concrete And Clay** had been at the top of the charts.

Lead singer Tommy Moeller was the brother of Billy Moeller, who became Whistling Jack Smith and took **I Was Kaiser Bill's Batman** to number five in 1967. It is said that the Whistlers on the record are actually the Mike Sammes Singers, which makes Billy Moeller possibly the only solo act not to have performed on his only hit record!

192

THE MINUTE YOU'RE GONE

15 April 1965, for one week

Cliff Richard *Columbia DB 7496*

Writer: Jimmy Gately
Producer: Norrie Paramor

The first Cliff Richard number one hit that did not feature the Shadows was Cliff's eighth number one. **The Minute You're Gone** was also the second British number one, after **Young Love** (see no. 56), to have been recorded earlier by American country superstar Sonny James. His version had reached number 9 on the American country charts in the summer of 1963. Cliff's version had been recorded in Nashville in the summer of 1964, but its release, as his 29th single, was delayed almost a year.

At the time of its eventual release, Cliff and the Shadows were coming to the end of their 3-month starring stint at the London Palladium in the pantomime *Aladdin*. Cliff took the title role, the Shadows were cast as Wishee, Washee, Noshee and Toshee, Una Stubbs was the romantic interest Princess Balroubadour, and evergreen comedian Arthur Askey played Widow Twankey.

The Minute You're Gone was Cliff's 26th consecutive Top 10 hit, and although it was the last in this record run of consecutive top tenners, he was still at the peak of his career. Nevertheless, Cliff was quoted in the daily papers as saying that he still drew just £10 a week pocket money, despite press insistence that he was a millionaire.

193

TICKET TO RIDE

22 April 1965, for three weeks

The Beatles *Parlophone R 5265*

Writers: John Lennon and Paul McCartney
Producer: George Martin

Track seven on side one of the Beatles fifth LP, the soundtrack of their second film *Help!* is **Ticket To Ride**, the seventh Beatles number one. By this time the statistics were unable to keep pace with their achievements. **Ticket To Ride** again featured John singing lead, but unusually the lead guitar was played by Paul, not George.

The tone of the Beatles singles was beginning to change. After the simple boy-meets-girl positiveness of the first number ones, the message was changing from 'I want to hold your hand' and 'I feel fine' to 'She's got a ticket to ride, and she don't care'. The title of the film was *Help* and the lyrics said 'I feel so insecure', an interesting change from the more lighthearted and positive original title for the film *Eight Arms To Hold You*. Still, whatever the Beatles sang about was a hit, and the meaning of **Ticket To Ride** was not its lyrical content; the message was 'Here's another superb 3 minutes of pop history.'

194

KING OF THE ROAD

13 May 1965, for one week

Roger Miller *Philips BF 1397*

Writer: Roger Miller
Producer: Jerry Kennedy

Roger Miller, born on 2 January 1936, was a country singer and composer whose songs weaved unsteadily between comedy and cloying sentimentality. He first hit the American charts as a composer in 1960 when Andy Williams took his song **You Don't Want My Love (In The Summertime)** to number 64. He then wrote Del Shannon's 1962 hit **The Swiss Maid** which also by coincidence reached number 64 in America, but climbed to number two in Britain.

In the summer of 1964, Roger Miller scored his first American pop hit with **Dang Me**, which reached number seven but disappeared without trace in Britain. The follow-up, **Chug-A-Lug**, reached number nine in America, but again nothing over here. It was his fourth single on the Smash label, a saga of a train-riding drifter, that introduced him to more British fans than just Peter and Gordon who had come back from their first American tour raving about him. **King Of The Road** was his biggest world-wide hit, but after that the country corn grew too thick for British fans to appreciate. Four more singles hit the charts, and the last of these, **Little Green Apples**, broke all records for schmaltz.

195

WHERE ARE YOU NOW (MY LOVE)

20 May 1965, for one week

Jackie Trent *Pye 7N 15776*

Writers: Tony Hatch and Jackie Trent
Producer: Tony Hatch

Tony Hatch and Jackie Trent are now Britain's 'Mr & Mrs Music'. In 1965 they were 'Just Good Friends Music'. Tony Hatch's career as a writer, producer and musician had not been properly rewarded in terms of his record sales as an artist. One week at number 50 on 4 October 1962 (the week before **Love Me Do** entered the charts) with a tune called **Out Of This World** certainly did not reflect the status and fame he had achieved in the popular music industry by the mid-sixties.

Jackie Trent did not even have one week at number 50 to boast about before the triumph of **Where Are You Now (My Love)**. Even though she was one of the busiest of female vocalists in Britain, regularly appearing on radio shows on the Light Programme, and to a lesser extent television appearances on both channels, she was considered by the record buying public to be a reproducer of other people's hits rather than creator of her own. **Where Are You Now (My Love)** disproved that theory, although Miss Trent failed to establish herself as a regular chart name after this one success. They should care, though, because through a continuous production of popular LPs, cabaret performances, TV shows and radio programmes, Tony Hatch and Jackie Trent know where they are now, my love. In the happy position of not needing hit singles.

196

LONG LIVE LOVE

27 May 1965, for three weeks

Sandie Shaw *Pye 7N 15841*

Writer: Chris Andrews
Producer: Chris Andrews

Most of Sandie Shaw's singles were written and produced by Chris Andrews, the man who wrote **The First Time** for Adam Faith, to give him his final Top 10 hit. He gave Sandie Shaw hits like **I'll Stop At Nothing**, **Message Understood**, **Nothing Comes Easy** and **How Can You Tell**. He also wrote **Yesterday Man**, which he sung and climbed to number three with at the end of 1965 but the only one of Sandie Shaw's three number ones that he wrote was **Long Live Love**, which has turned out to be the only Chris Andrews song to top the charts.

Sandie's underrated achievement in being the only solo girl to manage three number British hits is only partly explained by her voice, original and strong as it was (and is). Lulu, for example, recorded songs by Bowie, Neil Diamond and Marty Wilde, but her biggest chart success in England was her dire Eurovision song **Boom Bang-A-Bang** which reached number two. Sandie Shaw's choice of writers was always more conservative than Lulu's and over the years Lulu has had the benefit of far more TV exposure than Sandie. It must have been the bare feet.

197

CRYING IN THE CHAPEL

17 June 1965, for one week
and from 1 July 1965 for one week

Elvis Presley *RCA 1455*

Writer: Artie Glenn
Producer: Steve Sholes

The world of popular music had been turned upside down for the first time since the advent of Elvis himself between the King's 14th and 15th number one successes in the UK. The Beatles, of course, were responsible. Elvis' record sales, while still good by most artists' standards, had taken a major dive and no longer could he rely on his records hitting even the Top 10 every time out. The advent of the British groups was not solely responsible for Elvis' decline – his own career had been artistically off the rails anyway, consisting mainly of feeble movies and weak songs from undistinguished soundtracks which would have completely sunk any performer other than Elvis. But he still retained a devoted following despite his output and the fans rallied round in extremely healthy numbers to make **Crying In The Chapel** his first number one for 2 years. It was in fact recorded 5 years before, at the sessions that produced **Surrender** (see no. 119) and his sacred LP 'His Hand In Mine'. The song was written in 1952 by Artie Glenn, whose son Darrell and Rex Allen had separate country hits with it in 1953. The same year **Crying In The Chapel** was a R & B and pop hit in the US for the Orioles.

198

I'M ALIVE

24 June 1965, for one week
and from 8 July 1965 for two weeks

The Hollies *Parlophone R 5287*

Writer: Clint Ballard Jr.
Producer: Ron Richards

The Hollies have had more hit singles in Britain than any other vocal group in chart history, but only one of those hits topped the charts. That was **I'm Alive**, written by the man who wrote **Good Timin'** for Jimmy Jones and **The Game Of Love** for Wayne Fontana and the Mindbenders, Clint Ballard.

The Hollies' line-up on **I'm Alive** was Allan Clarke (born 5 April 1942), Tony Hicks (born 16 December 1943), Eric Haydock, Graham Nash (born 2 February 1942) and the permanently balding Bobby Elliott (born 8 December 1942) on drums. Bobby Elliott had been a Fentone, backing Shane Fenton who mutated into Alvin Stardust in the early seventies. Allan Clarke and Graham Nash had been together in several groups before forming the Hollies in 1962, naming the group after Buddy Holly.

The group has had more than its share of exits and entrances over the years, with Eric Haydock and Graham Nash leaving and being replaced by Terry Silvester and Bernie Calvert, and Allan Clarke leaving and then rejoining. All the same, the sound has remained very consistent and even in 1981 their rerecorded medley of their old hits (including **I'm Alive**), called **Holliedaze**, sounded almost identical to the sound of the originals 15 years before.

199

MR TAMBOURINE MAN

22 July 1965, for two weeks

The Byrds *CBS 201765*

Writer: Bob Dylan
Producer: Terry Melcher

In the summer of 1965, folk rock stormed the world. Producer Terry Melcher, the son of 1950's chart-topper Doris Day, took the Bob Dylan song, **Mr Tambourine Man** and electrified the jingle-jangle.

The Byrds were Roger McGuinn, a Chicagoan born on 14

July 1942, Gene Clark, David Crosby, Chris Hillman and Michael Clarke. However, on the **Mr Tambourine Man** single only Roger McGuinn actually performed, and the rest of the musicians were session men Leon Russell, Larry Knechtel and Hal Blaine. Blaine has drummed on so many major hits that he is arguably the most successful performer of all time. Hits like **Strangers In The Night**, **Bridge Over Troubled Water** and **You've Lost That Lovin' Feelin'** all feature Blaine's drumming, as do many of Elvis' later hits.

All the Byrds composed and played on their albums, but after a short while individual feelings replaced group harmonies and the Byrds began to disintegrate. David Crosby left to form Crosby, Stills and Nash. The late Gram Parsons, who became the major influence on Emmylou Harris and her pure country-rock style, joined the Byrds but left shortly with Chris Hillman to form the Flying Burrito Brothers. Soon McGuinn was the only Byrd left, just as he had been on **Mr Tambourine Man**.

200

HELP!

5 August 1965, for three weeks

The Beatles *Parlophone R 5305*

Writers: John Lennon and Paul McCartney
Producer: George Martin

The title song from their second film gave the Beatles their eighth number one, putting them at the time equal second with Cliff Richard on the list of most chart toppers in Britain. The Beatles eight were consecutive and achieved in a period of 2 years and 95 days, which is much quicker than any other act to have achieved so many number ones (Elvis, Cliff, Abba and the Rolling Stones).

The film *Help!* was originally to be called *Eight Arms To Hold You*, which would have made an interesting title for a love song, possibly breaking lyrical ground that was not actually achieved until **Je T'Aime** in 1969. The Beatles, however, did have another go at writing a song featuring a similar number of limbs when Ringo came up with **Octopus's Garden** on the Abbey Road LP.

Help! was not as successful a film as *A Hard Day's Night*. It was shot in colour, had a much larger budget, and made plenty of money, but the Beatles were not happy with it. They gave up films (apart from the self-produced *Magical Mystery Tour* TV film and the **Let It Be** documentary) and got back to what they knew best, performing and recording.

201

I GOT YOU, BABE

26 August 1965, for two weeks

Sonny and Cher *Atlantic AT 4035*

Writer: Sonny Bono
Producer: Sonny Bono

Sonny and Cher – she was the one with the deeper voice and the slightly longer hair – burst onto the British summer of 1965 with the ultimate hippie anthem, two years before hippiedom took over the youth of Europe and America. 'Don't let them say your hair's too long, I don't care, with you I can't go wrong' became the compulsive theme of all young lovers of the mid-sixties.

Not that Sonny, at least, was all that young. He was born on 16 February 1935 and had been writing and performing for some years. He wrote **Needles and Pins** with Jack Nitsche which became the 162nd British number one when recorded by the Searchers. He thus joined the select band who have written number ones for themselves and another act, at the same time proving convincingly that he was a better writer than a singer.

By 1971 Sonny had not 'got Cher, babe'. Cher (born Cherilyn LaPier on 20 May 1946), had many big solo hits in America in the early 70's and a successful TV series with her husband, but they divorced in 1974 and Cher began a hectic period as a gossip columnists' delight as her name was linked with many men, both eligible and ineligible. By 1981, she was to be found singing with Meatloaf on his Top 10 single **Dead Ringer for Love**.

202

(I CAN'T GET NO) SATISFACTION

9 September 1965, for two weeks

The Rolling Stones *Decca F 12220*

Writers: Mick Jagger and Keith Richard
Producer: Andrew Loog Oldham

1965 was the single most important year in the breakthrough of the Rolling Stones. They began writing their own hits with **The Last Time**, they passed the million mark in sales for the first time, achieving this with several discs, and they scaled the summit of the American chart for the first time with (**I Can't Get No**) **Satisfaction**. This latter title, recorded

201 Sonny and Cher

203 Walker Brothers

in Hollywood, remains their calling card. It stated eloquently and forcefully the Stones' unhappiness with the conventions of society, and in its power suggested the restrained violence that was part of the group's image at the time. Many American radio stations edited out the last verse, which they believed referred to menstruation.

Keith Richard composed the introductory riff. Though it became one of the most famous in rock history, Richard at one point thought it might have suited a horn section rather than a guitar. He was thus pleased when Otis Redding used brass to begin his version on **Otis Blue**.

Not only is **(I Can't Get No) Satisfaction** the definitive Rolling Stones track, it is one of only two songs to have been a hit in 5 different years, with charted cover versions by Redding (1966), Aretha Franklin (1967), Bubblerock (Jonathan King under a pseudonym, 1974) and Devo (1978). The other recurring title is **White Christmas**.

203

MAKE IT EASY ON YOURSELF

23 September 1965, for one week

The Walker Brothers *Philips BF 1428*

Writers: Burt Bacharach and Hal David
Producer: Johnny Franz

The Walker Brothers are not brothers, none of them is called Walker and they were not British even though based in Britain. They were Scott Walker (Scott Engel, born 9 January 1944), John Walker (John Maus, born 12 November 1943) and Gary Walker (Gary Leeds, born 3 September 1944).

Gary Leeds was not the world's greatest drummer, even though he drummed on one English tour with Jet Powers (who else but P J Proby alias James Marcus Smith) and through Proby had even once drummed for Elvis. By the time **Make It Easy On Yourself** was a number one, the magic factor in the Walker Brothers success was obviously the voice and looks of Scott Walker, backed by the voice and looks of John Walker, so it was easy to assume that Gary Walker was a pretty lucky guy to be included in the group. He even had another drummer on stage with him (in the shadows) on many gigs. But that criticism is unfair. It was Leeds who found the other two singing in a club called Gazzari's in Los Angeles and persuaded them that there was more money in being moody and Californian in England than in California. A Bacharach/David song as their third single fulfilled Gary's hopes and the Walker Brothers had arrived.

204

TEARS

30 September 1965, for five weeks

Ken Dodd *Columbia DB 7659*

Writers: Billy Uhr and Frank Capano
Producer: Norman Newell

Since 14 November 1952, only eight acts have had a number one hit and a chart career of over 20 years. These eight are Perry Como, Al Martino, Johnny Mathis, Elvis Presley, Cliff Richard, The Shadows, Frank Sinatra – and Ken Dodd, born 8 November 1932 in Liverpool.

The chief of the Diddymen had his first hit in the summer of 1960, when **Love Is Like A Violin** reached the Top 10. In 1981, he enjoyed a small Christmas Hit with **Hold My Hand**, his first hit for 6 years, and a few days later he joined the small list of number one hitmakers to have been honoured by the Queen when his OBE in the 1982 New Years Honours List was announced.

Ken Dodd's singing career has given him a completely different image from the wild-haired purveyor of the tickling stick that we all know and Mrs Thatcher loves. He has scored 19 hits, four of which reached the Top 10, including **Tears** which held the number one position for much of the autumn of 1965. But none of those hits has been a comedy record. Only **Happiness** (number 31 in 1964) and **Hold My Hand** were even cheerful. The Ken Dodd of the pop charts is a lugubrious soul, singing songs like the million selling **Tears, Let Me Cry On Your Shoulder, Tears Won't Wash Away My Heartache** and **Just Out Of Reach (Of My Two Empty Arms)**. As a comedian and singer he doesn't seem to know whether to laugh or cry – all the way to the bank.

205

GET OFF MY CLOUD

4 November 1965, for three weeks

The Rolling Stones *Decca F 12263*

Writers: Mick Jagger and Keith Richard
Producer: Andrew Loog Oldham

The fifth consecutive number one hit for the Stones was their second consecutive number one to be recorded in

Hollywood. It lasted at the top for one week more than **Satisfaction** even though global sales of **Get Off My Cloud** were lower.

By the end of 1965, the Rolling Stones were probably at their peak of popularity. They had achieved five number ones in a row, a total only previously achieved by Elvis and the Beatles, they had toured America, Australia and Scandinavia with massive success and they had not yet alienated any section of their fans through their problems with the laws of drug abuse. Certainly their image was non-conformist and anti-establishment, but at the end of 1965, the Rolling Stones were close to achieving conventional acceptance, something that they managed to avoid at the last minute by living up to the rebellious, orgiastic image they had been made to project. In this, Jagger, Richard and Brian Jones were the main protagonists. Nobody has ever been able to portray Charlie Watts or Bill Wyman, the two oldest members of the group, as anything but two nice guys who play drums and bass in the best rock band in the world.

206

THE CARNIVAL IS OVER

25 November 1965, for three weeks

The Seekers *Columbia DB 7711*

Writer: Tom Springfield
Producer: Tom Springfield

A Russian folk song is not the most obvious source for a British number one, but for Tom Springfield it proved a gold mine. Like Gene Raskin with **Those Were The Days** (see no. 259), Springfield found a Russian folk tune, adapted the melody, added English lyrics and the result was **The Carnival Is Over** – which gave the Seekers their second number one out of three singles. The single between **I'll Never Find Another You** (see no. 188) and **The Carnival Is Over** was another Tom Springfield song, **A World Of Our Own**, which climbed to number three.

The Seekers never had another number one, although their popularity and hits continued for some time. **Morningtown Ride** climbed to number two at Christmas 1966 but **Georgy Girl**, written by Tom Springfield and Jim Dale for the Lynn Redgrave film of the same name, was their biggest worldwide hit after **The Carnival Is Over**, reaching number three in 1967. In America, it reached number two.

When the Seekers broke up in 1967, Judith Durham went solo but apart from a small hit called **Olive Tree** that year, never achieved very much. Bruce Woodley and Athol Guy returned to Australia, where Guy is now a senator, and Keith Potger formed the New Seekers.

207

DAY TRIPPER/WE CAN WORK IT OUT

16 December 1965, for five weeks

The Beatles *Parlophone R 5389*

Writers (both sides): John Lennon and Paul McCartney
Producer: George Martin

The first of four Beatles singles to be officially released as a double A-side record duly became their ninth consecutive number one the week after it entered the charts, and gave them their third consecutive Christmas number one.

Both sides became immediate Beatle favourites, and attracted a lot of cover versions. **Day Tripper** hit the charts again in 1967, recorded by Otis Redding, and **We Can Work It Out** came back to chart life twice in the 1970's, once when Stevie Wonder took his version to number 27 in 1971, and again 5 years later when the Four Seasons followed up four consecutive Top 10 hits with their **We Can Work It Out** which stopped at number 34. A group called the Vontastics also took for themselves the title of Least Successful Chart Act in America when their recording of **Day Tripper** (a Top 10 soul hit) made number 100 for 1 week only, on 3 September 1966. It is a fairly great coincidence that the most successful and the least successful chart acts in America both hit with the same song.

208

KEEP ON RUNNING

20 January 1966, for one week

The Spencer Davis Group *Fontana TF 632*

Writer: Jackie Edwards
Producer: Chris Blackwell

The Spencer Davis Group were four men from Birmingham – Spencer Davis (born 17 July 1942), Pete York (born 15 August 1942) and brothers Muff Winwood (born 15 June 1945) and Stevie Winwood (born 12 May 1948). It was the 17-year-old Stevie Winwood's vocals that were the key to the success of the group, together with the reggae-blues style of Jamaican Jackie Edwards' songs.

A group had been formed by Spencer Davis some years before at Birmingham University. The two Winwoods and Pete York, who were playing semi-pro jazz in and around Birmingham, met Spencer Davis early in 1963 (when Stevie was only 14) and the four began playing together from that time, although they did not turn professional until Stevie was 16 and Chris Blackwell had found them and signed them to Fontana. Their first singles – the John Lee Hooker classic **Dimples** and other R & B standards like **Every Little Bit Hurts** and **I Can't Stand It** – failed to set the world on fire, but created a following. It only needed a really commercial song to catapult them to the top. That song was **Keep On Running**.

209

MICHELLE

27 January 1966, for three weeks

The Overlanders *Pye 7N 17034*

Writers: John Lennon and Paul McCartney
Producer: Tony Hatch

Track seven on side one of the Beatles' album 'Rubber Soul' was a song by Paul McCartney which featured the Beatles singing in French. It was the obvious song to cover on the album, and the Overlanders beat off the competition from David and Jonathan (in reality writers Roger Cook and Roger Greenaway) to take a cover version of a Beatles' LP track to number one for the first time.

The Overlanders were Paul Arnold, Laurie Mason, Pete Bartholomew, Terry Widlake and David Walsh. They are known as one-hit wonders in Britain, as **Michelle** was their only chart single, but in fact released eight singles before **Michelle**. One of these, their version of Chad and Jeremy's big American hit **Yesterday's Gone** even reached number 75 in America in mid-1964, but in Britain nothing worked. Skiffle tunes like **Freight Train**, old Coasters hits like **Along Came Jones**, quiet ballads like **The Leaves Are Falling** all fell on deaf ears. They were not particularly original and seemed to have no real musical policy, but all the same it is surprising that they failed to capitalise on the success of **Michelle**.

210

THESE BOOTS ARE MADE FOR WALKIN'

17 February 1966, for four weeks

Nancy Sinatra *Reprise R 20432*

Writer: Lee Hazelwood
Producer: Lee Hazelwood

Frank Sinatra's daughter, Nancy, was born on 8 June 1940 and like her father, in New Jersey. She was signed to her father's Reprise label from its beginnings in 1961, but for five years a succession of bland ballads and show tunes got her no further than being her father's daughter. Then in 1966, Lee Hazelwood, who had masterminded Duane Eddy's successful career in the fifties and early sixties, gave her the aggressive and beaty **Boots** to record, and the result was a number one hit on both sides of the Atlantic.

The London Zoo's panda, Chi Chi, had boots made for walking on 11 March 1966, when she flew to An An in Moscow. The follow-up to that event was less successful than Nancy Sinatra's next hit, which was aptly titled for the bashful panda pair, **How Does That Grab You Darlin'?** For the next year and a half, Nancy Sinatra was the hottest female vocalist in the world. She sang the title song for the James Bond film **You Only Live Twice**, she duetted with her father on another massive number one **Something Stupid** and she had her first hit in duet with Lee Hazelwood, a song called **Jackson**. Nowadays, she is back with the bland ballads and show tunes in her cabaret act, but as least people know her as something more than just her father's daughter.

211

THE SUN AIN'T GONNA SHINE ANYMORE

17 March 1966, for four weeks

The Walker Brothers *Philips BF 1473*

Writers: Bob Crewe and Bob Gaudio
Producers: Johnny Franz, music arranged by Ivor Raymonde

After **Make It Easy On Yourself** (see no. 203), the Walker Brothers put out another heavily emotional ballad, as the follow-up. They made the mistake, however, of choosing a basically optimistic song **My Ship is Coming In** which did not match the fragile and tortured image that Scott Walker had been moulded into, so it only climbed to number three.

Below **209 The Overlanders** *Right* **210 Nancy Sinatra**

Below **213 Dusty Springfield**

Below **215 Rolling Stones**

Below **208 Spencer Davis Group**

No such mistakes on the next single. A title as bleak as any that has reached number one, **The Sun Ain't Gonna Shine Anymore**, written by the Four Seasons' masterminds Bob Crewe and Bob Gaudio, gave the Walker Brothers a second number one. By the spring of 1966, Scott Walker was certainly the most popular male vocalist among the female teenage population of Britain and his looks and voice seemed destined to keep him at the top for as long as he wished. But signs of disintegration within the group were already beginning to appear by this time, and when the inevitable parting of the ways took place, not even Scott Walker found sustained success easy to achieve. Maybe he never wanted it, but after several powerful and big-selling albums, some TV shows and a couple of hit singles, he faded. Nothing of great import was heard from any Walker Bro. during the 70's until 1976 when they suddenly reunited out of nowhere, made an album and one excellent Top 10 single **No Regrets** before returning to mysterious inactivity.

212

SOMEBODY HELP ME

14 April 1966, for two weeks

The Spencer Davis Group *Fontana TF 679*

Writer: Jackie Edwards
Producer: Chris Blackwell

For their follow up to **Keep On Running** (see no. 208) Spencer Davis went for another Jackie Edwards song. It was a wise choice, and the Spencer Davis Group found themselves with another number one.

By this time, Stevie Winwood was clearly established as the star, and the seeds of the destruction of the group had been sown. The follow-up single, a weaker song called **When I Come Home** made number 12, but the next two singles were both Top 10 hits. The last single before Stevie Winwood left the group **I'm A Man** is often considered their best performance. The song provided Chicago with a hit 3 years later.

In the spring of 1967, Stevie Winwood quit to form his own group, Traffic. Muff Winwood left at the same time, to become a producer at Chris Blackwell's newly formed Island records, where he has enjoyed many years of success. Spencer Davis kept the group going, bringing in a variety of new members, including in 1968 Nigel Olsson, drummer with Plastic Penny and subsequently with Elton John. But by the end of the sixties the group was dead. Stevie Winwood has failed to achieve all that he promised, although his 1981 LP 'Arc Of A Diver' marked a comeback for a major talent.

213

YOU DON'T HAVE TO SAY YOU LOVE ME

28 April 1966, for one week

Dusty Springfield *Philips BF 1482*

Writers: Pino Donaggio, Vito Pallavicini, English lyrics by Vicki Wickham and Simon Napier-Bell
Producer: Johnny Franz

When the Springfields broke up in 1963, all three members of the group went on to considerable success. Mike Hurst produced, among many others, Manfred Mann's **Mighty Quinn** (see no. 244), Tom Springfield produced the Seekers (see nos. 188 and 206) and his sister embarked on a solo career that made her Britain's biggest female star, if not the most successful in chart terms.

Dusty Springfield was born Mary O'Brien in London on April 1939, but emphasised her Irishness. When the Springfields broke up, Dusty's solo career prospered from the beginning. **You Don't Have To Say You Love Me** was her ninth chart single in 2½ years and nine more were to follow. Ten of the eighteen were Top 10 hits, but only this one reached the very top. It was an Italian song, originally titled **Io Che No Vivo Senza Te**. Dusty's first single **I Only Want To Be With You** reached number four, and when the song was revived first by the Bay City Rollers in 1976 and then by the Tourists in 1979, both their versions also peaked at number four. **You Don't Have To Say You Love Me** was also a Top 10 hit for Elvis Presley in 1971, and a regular favourite at his Las Vegas concerts.

214

PRETTY FLAMINGO

5 May 1966, for three weeks

Manfred Mann *HMV POP 1523*

Writer: Mark Barkan
Producer: John Burgess

The second Manfred Mann chart-topper came five singles and nearly 2 years after their first, but in the meantime the group had been consolidating its position as one of the most popular in the country, behind only the Beatles and the Stones. Personnel changes were always a feature of Manfred Mann, and by the time **Pretty Flamingo** was recorded, Mike Vickers had left to be replaced by Jack Bruce (born 14 May 1943) who played bass, with Tom McGuinness switching to lead. It was the only occasion in the amazingly varied career of Jack Bruce (Cream, John Mayall, Graham Bond, even the Hollies) when he played on a number one hit single.

This was also the last big Manfred Mann hit featuring Paul Jones as lead singer. A single featuring Jones, **You Gave Me Somebody To Love** was released after he had left the group that summer, but it climbed no higher than number 36. It is remembered now only as the answer to the trick question, 'What was the last Manfred Mann hit to feature Paul Jones?'. The first single featuring the new lead singer hit the charts the weeks after **You Gave Me Somebody To Love** disappeared. The new singer was Mike d'Abo (born 1 March 1944) and the single was the second Bob Dylan composition that Manfred Mann released as a single, **Just Like A Woman**. The third Dylan-composed single was to give them their biggest hit of all.

215

PAINT IT BLACK

26 May 1966, for one week

The Rolling Stones *Decca F 12395*

Writers: Mick Jagger and Keith Richard
Producer: Andrew Loog Oldham

After **Get Off My Cloud** the Rolling Stones failed. Their next single, **Nineteenth Nervous Breakdown** was the first Stones single in 2 years not to hit number one. It still reached number two, as it did in America. The flip-side, **As Tears Go By**, provided a big hit for Mick Jagger's girlfriend, Marianne Faithfull, but still the follow-up single was crucial. The follow-up was **Paint It Black**, a song written during the Stones' tour of Australia, recorded in Hollywood and featuring for the first time on a single, Brian Jones on sitar. Once again, there was criticism of the Stones as mere copiers of the Beatles, whose 1965 album 'Rubber Soul' had first included George Harrison playing sitar, but the Beatles had never put out a death disc as a single. **Paint It Black** was a death disc.

After **Paint It Black** the Stones went off the boil a bit. Perhaps it was the use of drugs or just the prosecution of Jagger, Richard and Jones for the use of drugs that caused their standards to drop, but late 1966 and 1967 were not good years for the Stones, artistically or commercially. Mick Jagger sang on the Beatles number one, **All You Need Is Love** (see no. 235) but apart from that, singles like **We Love You** and **Let's Spend The Night Together** gave them Top 10 placings but nothing more.

216

STRANGERS IN THE NIGHT

2 June 1966, for three weeks

Frank Sinatra *Reprise RS 23052*

Writers: Bert Kaempfert, Charlie Singleton and Eddie Snyder
Producers: Jimmy Bowen, with orchestral arrangement by Ernie Freeman

Frank Sinatra's second number one hit came 11 years and 244 days after his first, the longest gap in British chart history between number one hits by the same artist. It came from the most unlikely source, an extremely forgettable James Garner spy film called *A Man Could Get Killed*. Bert Kaempfert, who had also been involved in Elvis Presley's **Wooden Heart** (see no. 115) wrote the complete score for the film, the first Hollywood score he had been asked to compose. The song, thanks to Ol' Blue Eyes impeccable performance, became far more successful than the film and won four Grammy Awards in 1966. 1966 was a very good year for the Sinatra family, as daughter Nancy had recently recorded her first number one (see no. 210), but by the end of the 1960's even more success was to be achieved by both generations of the family. Together they hit the top with **Something Stupid** (see no. 231) while Frank Sinatra broke all British chart records with his amazingly longlasting hit **My Way**. By the early 1970's it set up a record 122 weeks of chart life, selling over a million copies in Britain alone, and helping two other chart stars, Claude Francois and Paul Anka, keep the bills paid with the writing royalties.

217

PAPERBACK WRITER

23 June 1966, for two weeks

The Beatles *Parlophone R 5452*

Writers: John Lennon and Paul McCartney
Producer: George Martin

The tenth consecutive number one for the Beatles was a Paul McCartney song featuring Paul double-tracked singing lead.

Paperback Writer has become one of their best remembered singles, although at the time the press were wondering whether the record was up to the normal Beatle standard, or whether the downhill slide had begun. In retrospect, there is no reason why they should have started to doubt, except that the fall of the Beatles might have sold more newspapers than the continuing triumph of the Beatles.

Paperback Writer, like its seven immediate predecessors in the triumphant line of Beatles releases, reached number one in its second week on the chart. True, it only held the top for 2 weeks, which is the shortest run by any Beatles single at number one (equal with **Hey Jude**, see no. 258), but their best work was still to come. Two months later, the 'Revolver' album silenced the doubters. In 1967 the **Penny Lane/Strawberry Fields Forever** single and the Beatle masterpiece 'Sergeant Pepper's Lonely Hearts Club Band' turned the doubters into believers. The Beatles hadn't slipped.

The B-side of **Paperback Writer** was the John Lennon song **Rain**. Possibly no other Beatle single shows the difference between the styles of Lennon and McCartney as much as this, their twelfth single and tenth number one.

218

SUNNY AFTERNOON

7 July 1966, for two weeks

The Kinks *Pye 7N 17125*

Writer: Ray Davies
Producer: Shel Talmy

The final Kinks' number one, their third, was their ninth hit and eighth top-tenner. It marked a lyrical departure for Ray Davies from the very clever but basically destructive comment in **Dedicated Follower of Fashion** and **Well Respected Man** to the positive enjoyment of life as expressed by **Sunny Afternoon**. The song is all about the rich man with nothing left ('I can't sail my yacht/The taxman's taken all I've got') except a sunny afternoon, which is there to be enjoyed. The follow-up to **Sunny Afternoon** was **Dead End Street** (a number five hit) and then came the single that is generally reckoned to be the best song Ray Davies ever wrote – **Waterloo Sunset**, which gave the Kinks their second number two hit.

The Kinks have never quite gone away, despite fallow periods in their career. In 1969 John Dalton replaced Pete Quaife on bass, and shortly thereafter John Gosling was added on keyboards. Hits like **Lola** and **Apeman** happened in the early seventies, and 10 years later, the Kinks were back to being a major touring attraction and important album-sellers in the States. Ray Davies songs like **David Watts, Stop Your Sobbing** and **I Go To Sleep** continued to hit the British charts, and the Kinks themselves climbed to number 46 with **Better Things** in July 1981.

219

GET AWAY

21 July 1966, for one week

Georgie Fame with the Blue Flames *Columbia DB 7946*

Writer: Clive Powell
Producer: Tony Palmer

Originally written and performed by Georgie Fame as a commercial jingle for petrol, **Get Away** turned out to be so popular with all those who didn't leave the room to fix a sandwich during the advertisements that Fame decided to uncommercialise the song for general release. It gave him his second number one, and became the first jingle to hit the top – a pedigree that was shared by the New Seekers **I'd Like To Teach The World To Sing**. Numerous lesser hits like Cliff Adams **The Lonely Man Theme**, David Dundas' **Jeans On** and Danny Williams' **Dancin' Easy** also began life as advertising jingles.

After **Get Away**, Georgie Fame disbanded the Blue Flames, and his next single **Sunny** was the first to feature Fame on his own. He found himself in competition with the song's composer, Bobby Hebb, as well as a rather appalling version by Cher, but all the same he managed to climb to number 13, one place lower than Bobby Hebb. His next single, the last before he switched from Columbia to CBS, was the late Billy Stewart's **Sitting In The Park**. It reached number 12, his highest chart placing ever, apart from his three number ones.

220

OUT OF TIME

28 July 1966, for one week

Chris Farlowe and the Thunderbirds *Immediate IM 035*

Writers: Mick Jagger and Keith Richard
Producer: Mick Jagger

The week that England won the World Cup gave Chris Farlowe his only week at number one, and the Glimmer

Twins, Jagger and Richard, their only number one hit as writers for another act. Chris Farlowe began life as John Henry Deighton on 13 October 1940 in London, and at the age of 16 won the All-England Skiffle Championship as leader of the John Henry Skiffle Group. The John Henry Skiffle Group never recorded, but its leader landed a recording contract with Decca, moved rapidly towards R & B and formed the Thunderbirds. By the time they were playing regularly at Georgie Fame's haunt, the Flamingo, the Thunderbirds included Albert Lee on guitar and Carl Palmer on drums. In 1965, one of their Columbia releases, **Buzz With The Fuzz** became a highly popular record in the London clubs, but was deleted as soon as Columbia discovered what buzz and fuzz meant, and thus what Farlowe was singing about.

By this time, Farlowe was a cult figure among the leaders of the R & B boom and people like Eric Burdon and Mick Jagger rushed forward to boost his career. Farlowe's first Immediate single **The Fool**, was produced by Eric Burdon and the next two, **Think** and **Out Of Time**, were written by Mick Jagger and Keith Richard. Four more small hits followed, but somehow Chris Farlowe was out of time with the trends of success.

221

WITH A GIRL LIKE YOU

4 August 1966, for two weeks

The Troggs *Fontana TF 717*

Writer: Reg Presley
Producer: Larry Page

Reginald Maurice, born on 12 June 1943 in Andover, was a product of Andover Secondary Modern School. So was Ronald Bultis, born 4 May 1943 in Andover and so was Pete Staples, born 3 May 1944. Reg, Ron and Peter met up with Andover Grammar School boy Chris Britton, who had been born not in Andover but in Watford on 21 January 1945, and a group was born. Reginald Maurice decided that Presley was obviously a commercial name, so he became Reg Presley, and handled the vocals. Ronnie Bultis was a Sean Connery fan and became Ronnie Bond, the drummer. He had a ready-made fan club already, his seven brothers and sisters Bill, Ted, Dennis, Vera, Iris, Kathy and Flo. Britton and Staples were happy with their surnames, and anyway Chris Britton had used his real name at his first public appearance at Wallop Village Hall, so he couldn't change it after a gig like that.

Then they met Larry Page and the 'Andover Sound' was born. The Troggs created two classic singles, **Wild Thing**, which reached number two and **I Can't Control Myself**, which did likewise. **With A Girl Like You** was the less interesting single issued between those two great tracks, and needless to say it went one better than the others. For a while in 1966, Larry Page and the Troggs were making money Andover fist.

222

YELLOW SUBMARINE/ELEANOR RIGBY

18 August 1966, for four weeks

The Beatles *Parlophone R 5493*

Writers (both sides): John Lennon and Paul McCartney
Producer: George Martin

The first single that the Beatles released to coincide with the release of the LP from which the tracks came was **Eleanor Rigby** and **Yellow Submarine**. The LP was 'Revolver'. It was said at the time that the Beatles issued the single to prevent others from covering songs from their LPs, as had happened, for example, with **Michelle** (see no. 209) and **Girl** from 'Rubber Soul', and was later to happen with **Ob-La-Di Ob-La-Da** (see no. 263) from the white album.

Yellow Submarine was the first Beatles single on which Ringo sang lead, and it was a simple children's tune, obviously mainly written by Paul McCartney. Despite issuing it as a single, the Beatles soon found that **Eleanor Rigby** was one of their most covered songs, and one of the most successful lyrically. The idea of loneliness regularly crops up in later Beatle songs, songs like **She's Leaving Home, Eleanor Rigby** and **Get Back**. Even in Beatle solo efforts, like Paul McCartney's first single **Another Day** or John Lennon's **Whatever Gets You Through The Night**, loneliness is the main theme.

While this single was at number one, the Beatles played their last live date, on 29 August 1966 at Candlestick Park in San Francisco.

223

ALL OR NOTHING

15 September 1966, for one week

The Small Faces *Decca F 12470*

Writers: Steve Marriott and Ronnie Lane
Producers: Steve Marriott and Ronnie Lane

The Small Faces had many hits in their career which are well remembered as typical sounds of the late sixties. Singles

Above **224 Jim Reeves**

226 Beachboys

221 Troggs

225 Four Tops

220 Chris Farlowe

Below **223 The Small Faces**

like **Whatcha Gonna Do About It?, Itchycoo Park, Sha La La La Lee** and **The Universal** were all hits, but the only time they topped the chart was with the less well-remembered **All Or Nothing**.

The Small Faces were small, and they were Steve Marriott, born 30 January 1947, Ronnie 'Plonk' Lane, born 1 April 1946, Kenny Jones, born 16 September 1948 and Ian McLagan, born 12 May 1946, who had replaced Jimmy Winston on organ after the release of their second single **I've Got Mine**, which missed the chart altogether. At their best they were highly original and able to produce a mod-rock sound that only the Who could equal. They based their sound on Steve Marriott's scratchy but versatile vocal chords, and the beautiful bass of Ronnie Lane. They broke up in 1968 almost as suddenly as they had formed in 1965. Marriott formed Humble Pie with Peter Frampton of the Herd, but that failed to match their high expectations. The others formed the Faces with Rod Stewart and Ron Wood, and went on to greater things. Ron Wood is now with the Rolling Stones, and Ronnie Lane picked up a couple of hits with his band Slim Chance.

224

DISTANT DRUMS

22 September 1966, for five weeks

Jim Reeves *RCA 1537*

Writer: Cindy Walker
Producer: Chet Atkins

Jim Reeves was born on 20 August 1924 in Texas. He had originally hoped to make his career as a professional baseball player and signed as a pitcher for the Houston Buffaloes, but a leg injury forced his retirement. He turned to broadcasting and became a successful disc jockey before his first big hit, a country song called **Mexican Joe** caused him to concentrate on a singing career. He soon became one of the most successful of all country stars, his deep and gentle voice producing hits like **He'll Have To Go, Four Walls, I Love You Because** and **I Won't Forget You**. At the height of his career, on 31 July 1964, Jim Reeves was killed when his private aeroplane crashed, but the sales of his records have not noticeably flagged in the years since. When **Distant Drums** became the third record to reach the top posthumously, it was the first time that a star had had a number one hit so long after his death, which proved the selling power of Jim Reeves. Buddy Holly, Eddie Cochran, Jimi Hendrix, Elvis Presley and John Lennon have all had number one hits after their death but always within a few weeks of the death. Jim Reeves' chart-topper came over two years later, and certainly did not rely on 'sympathy sales'. It was simply a very well made country ballad.

225

REACH OUT I'LL BE THERE

27 October 1966, for three weeks

The Four Tops *Tamla Motown TMG 579*

Writers: Brian Holland, Lamont Dozier and Eddie Holland
Producers: Brian Holland and Lamont Dozier

The day after the Beatles collected their MBE's from Buckingham Palace saw the Four Tops take over the top position, to give Tamla Motown their first number one in Britain. The Four Tops had first charted in Britain in 1965 with their American number one, **I Can't Help Myself**, but it took **Reach Out I'll Be There** to give them their first Top 20 hit in Britain, and Motown's largest selling single worldwide at the time.

Levi Stubbs, Renaldo Benson, Lawrence Payton and Abdul Fakir were the Four Tops. They formed in 1953 and in 1982 were still hitting the charts. Their first American hit was with a song covered by the Fourmost in Britain, called **Baby I Need Your Loving. Reach Out I'll Be There** was their ninth American hit, and their second US number one. It was their fourth British hit but curiously, despite their comparative lack of success in Britain up to then, their previous single **Loving You Is Sweeter Than Ever** was a bigger hit in Britain (no. 21) than in America (no. 45).

In 1972, they moved from Motown to Probe, a move that did them little chart good, but when in 1981 they issued the single **When She Was My Girl** on Casablanca they found themselves back in the Top 10 exactly 15 years after their greatest success, and 10 years after their preceding Top 10 hit.

226

GOOD VIBRATIONS

17 November 1966, for two weeks

The Beach Boys *Capitol CL 15475*

Writers: Brian Wilson and Mike Love
Producer: Brian Wilson

Perseverance paid off in the case of this classic. Originally planned by Brian Wilson in April of 1966, it took 6 months of work in four different studios to perfect. Layer upon layer of harmony was added before brother Carl recorded his lead vocal. Brian had been upset by the relative failure in the United States of 'Pet Sounds', the Beach Boys' album masterpiece that enjoyed greater chart success in Britain. He wanted to make sure that **Good Vibrations** was flawless, a sure-fire smash, before he released it. During the course of his ordeal he lost the complete comprehension of the group themselves, who on the one hand revered him and on the other couldn't understand some of his *avant garde* moves, such as using a Moog-theremin, which made eerie noises ordinarily associated with science-fiction films.

The final product was released in October 1966 and enjoyed instant success. **Good Vibrations** was a new peak for the Beach Boys, but it was also the beginning of their downfall as a recording act. As a consequence of drug use and personal problems Brian Wilson was unable or unwilling to make more material of this high standard. The Beach Boys would have more success, but none this glorious.

The original single release credited only Brian as the writer, but subsequent appearances of the song have also listed Love.

227

GREEN GREEN GRASS OF HOME

1 December 1966, for seven weeks

Tom Jones *Decca F 22511*

Writer: Claude Putman Jr.
Producer: Peter Sullivan

Tom Jones' second and final number one was the old country song of the condemned prisoner – **Green Green Grass of Home**. For Tom Jones, the grass in America had long seemed greener than at home, but as his chart career faltered slightly in 1967 and 1968 in America, everything started going right for him in UK. **Green Green Grass of Home** was only Tom Jones' second Top 10 hit in Britain, but over the next 3½ years the lad from Treforest chalked up nine more Top 10 hits, including three consecutive number two hits in 1967 and 1968. Not only that, he signed with ATV a contract to do 17 one-man shows a year for 5 years for a total of £9 million, which remains the largest TV contract ever signed in Britain.

In 1971 and 1972, Tom Jones had two more Top 10 hits, one of which was his fourth number two hit. Despite lack of significant chart success since then, Jones has become a show business institution and performs to packed houses of blue-rinsed matrons wherever he goes.

228

I'M A BELIEVER

19 January 1967, for four weeks

The Monkees *RCA 1560*

Writer: Neil Diamond
Producer: Jeff Barry

The Monkees were the American entertainment industry's deliberately manufactured 'answer' to the Beatles. After vast auditions at which Stephen Stills, among many others, was unsuccessful, four actors were brought together to make a TV series about a zany pop group – basically a rip-off of the Beatles 'Hard Day's Night' image – but their astonishing success was only partly a tribute to the system that created them. More credit must go to the Monkees themselves, Peter Tork (born Peter Thorkelson on 13 February 1942), Michael Nesmith (born 30 December 1942), Mickey Dolenz (born 8 March 1945) and the token Englishman Davy Jones (born 30 December 1946 in Manchester). **I'm A Believer** was their first English hit and their only number one. **Last Train To Clarksville**, their first American hit and their first release in England, finally made the British charts the week after **I'm A Believer** made number one.

Neil Diamond, the writer, never wrote another number one, although he wrote Top 10 hits for himself both solo and in duet with Barbra Streisand, and for Lulu among others. Jeff Barry, who wrote **Tell Laura I Love Her**, was as a producer musically more recognisable than the artists he produced. He was the supreme teenybop producer of the late 1960's, his work culminating in **Sugar Sugar** by the Archies (see no. 279)

229

THIS IS MY SONG

16 February 1967, for two weeks

Petula Clark *Pye 7N 17258*

Writer: Charles Chaplin
Producer: Ernie Freeman

Petula Clark, whose only other British number one had been **Sailor** (see no. 113) in 1961, returned to the top almost 6

Below **227 Tom Jones** *Right* **230 Engelbert Humperdinck**

232 Sandie Shaw

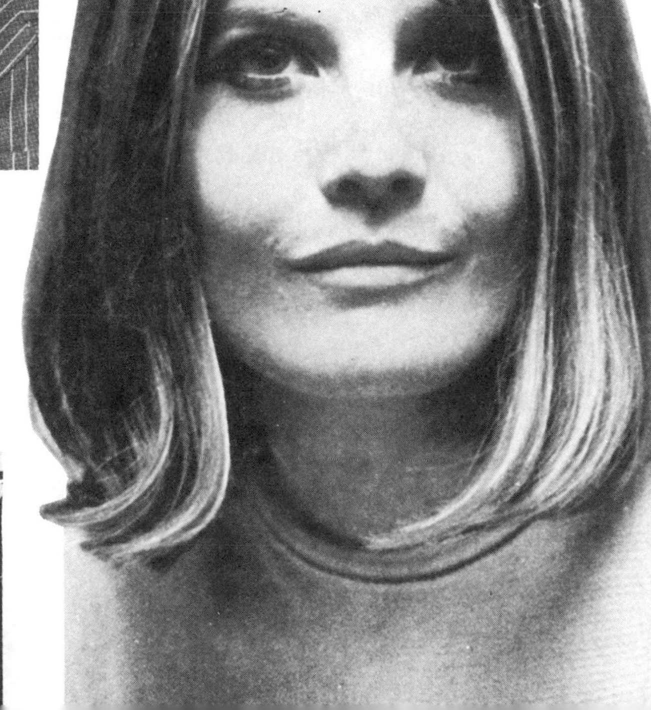

233 Tremeloes

234 Procul Harum

years later with the theme tune of the film, *A Countess From Hong Kong*, starring Marlon Brando and Sophia Loren and directed by the man who played a cameo role as a sea-sick waiter, Charlie Chaplin. Chaplin also wrote the theme song, which has sold more copies world-wide than even his famous 'Limelight' theme, and being well into his seventies when he wrote the tune, is probably the oldest person ever to write a number one hit.

Petula Clark first recorded **This Is My Song** in French, Italian and German for the European market. Then she made an English version, and thus managed to top the charts virtually all the way across Europe in four different languages. Her British success was despite strong competition from Harry Secombe, whose version climbed to number two to give him his biggest pop hit ever.

Petula Clark's last British hit was her version of **I Don't Know How To Love Him**, but her career continues in full swing. She celebrated her forty-eighth birthday by starring as Maria in the London revival of *The Sound Of Music*, and seems likely to extend indefinitely her showbusiness successes which began with her first film at the age of eleven, made before the end of World War II.

230

RELEASE ME

2 March 1967, for six weeks

Engelbert Humperdinck *Decca F 12541*

Writers: Eddie Miller and Dub Williams
Producer: Charles Blackwell

The transformation of Gerry Dorsey into Engelbert Humperdinck is the most famous 'if at first you don't succeed' story in show business. Alvin Stardust and Gary Glitter emerged triumphant in the 1970's from past failures, but Engelbert is the ultimate example of 'try, try again'. Arnold George Dorsey was born in Madras, India (venue of a Boomtown Rats concert in February 1982) on 2 May 1936, and moved with his family to England shortly after the end of the war. After completing his National Service in 1956, he began a show business career as Gerry Dorsey, which lasted for 9 years and covered occasional recording contracts, sporadic TV and radio spots and endless shows in provincial theatres on pop package tours. There was also a lot of resting between engagements.

In 1965, he met one of his former room-mates Gordon Mills who was by then managing Tom Jones. Mills took Gerry Dorsey on to his management roster and changed his name to Engelbert Humperdinck, which was the name of a German composer (1854-1921) who wrote the opera *Hansel and Gretel*. He recorded a couple of almost successful singles, one of which **Dommage Dommage**, was a big hit in Europe. Then he stood in for Dickie Valentine, who was ill, on 'Sunday Night At The London Palladium' and sang his latest single, **Release Me**. Over a year later, it finally dropped off the chart after the longest single stay in the top 50 ever by any record in Britain.

231

SOMETHING STUPID

13 April 1967, for two weeks

Nancy Sinatra and Frank Sinatra *Reprise RS 23166*

Writer: C. Carson Parks
Producers: Jimmy Bowen and Lee Hazelwood

For the first time ever, two acts who have already achieved a number one hit in their own right combined to produce yet another number one. The act was a father and daughter combination which had never been so successful before, and they became the first act to be one hit wonders on both sides of the Atlantic. Not that anyone in their senses would call either Frank or Nancy one hit wonders, but their only single together did reach the top both in Britain and America.

Like Elton John and Kiki Dee in later years, the duet was not really a duet, as the listing of two producers implies. Frank Sinatra cut the song with Billy Strange's orchestra, but Jimmy Bowen felt there was something missing. Nancy Sinatra was just off to entertain the troops in Vietnam, but she was asked to add a background vocal to her father's new record, which she did in 35 minutes work with the master tape. Nancy's producer Lee Hazelwood thought the result so good that it was agreed to issue the single as being sung by Nancy Sinatra and Frank Sinatra (somehow Nancy's background vocals got her top billing), produced by Jimmy Bowen and Lee Hazelwood. The unlikely but money-making formula was never repeated.

232

PUPPET ON A STRING

27 April 1967, for three weeks

Sandie Shaw *Pye 7N 17272*

Writers: Bill Martin and Phil Coulter
Producer: Ken Woodman

Sandie Shaw's third number one hit was the song with which she won the Eurovision Song Contest in 1967. It made her the only girl solo singer to top the British charts three times. The two girls from Abba have been on top much more often than Sandie Shaw, the girls from Brotherhood Of Man have been involved in three number ones. Olivia Newton-John has also had three number ones, two with John Travolta and one with ELO. But no solo female artiste has had three number ones. Winifred Atwell, Shirley Bassey, Cilla Black and Doris Day are among those who have had two, Dusty Springfield and Diana Ross among many others have had one, while Lulu, Toyah and Carole King have never had a chart topper.

Puppet On A String was in itself an excellent and immediately memorable song. Unfortunately it inspired so many inferior imitations from so many nations in subsequent Eurovision Song Contests (including the horrendous **Boom Bang A Bang** from Lulu in 1969) that the contest plumbed artistic depths in the late sixties and early seventies until revived temporarily by Abba's **Waterloo** (see no. 348) in 1974. By then Sandie Shaw was spending less time in a recording scene that she admitted no longer interested her.

233

SILENCE IS GOLDEN

18 May 1967, for three weeks

The Tremeloes *CBS 2723*

Writers: Bob Crewe and Bob Gaudio
Producer: Mike Smith

When Brian Poole and the Tremeloes (see no. 158) split up in 1966 there was no reason to suppose that the Tremeloes on their own would be any more successful than the Mindbenders without Wayne Fontana or the Hermits without Herman. But with a clever change of image and an astute choice of material, the Tremeloes launched themselves on a chart career which outdid anything they achieved backing Brian Poole.

The first move was to replace bass guitarist Alan Howard with Chip Hawkes, who was born in London on 11 November 1946 and was therefore 3 years younger than anybody else in the group. The hair grew longer and the clothes became more London and less Liverpool. Then they found a Cat Stevens song **Here Comes My Baby**, which producer Mike Smith turned into a very commercial pop record, and the Tremeloes had a Top 10 hit to start in 1967. Then they found a number which had originally been the B-side of the Four Season 1964 Top 10 hit **Rag Doll**, and they gave it a perfect Four Seasons treatment. **Silence Is Golden** gave the Tremeloes their only taste of a number one without Brian Poole, and more surprisingly a big American hit into the bargain. Another Top 10 hit followed before the summer was out, **Even The Bad Times Are Good**. No bad times for the Tremeloes in 1967.

234

A WHITER SHADE OF PALE

8 June 1967, for six weeks

Procol Harum *Deram DM 126*

Writers: Keith Reid and Gary Brooker
Producer: Denny Cordell

Procol Harum began life as the Paramounts, a Southend-based group who suffered immensely from having the reputation that their only hit, a revamping of **Poison Ivy** which reached number 35 in 1964, was hyped into the chart. The group split up, but Gary Brooker (born 29 May 1945) met Keith Reid who had written some lyrics which needed music. Brooker set **A Whiter Shade Of Pale** to music and then created a band to record it. The Procol Harum that actually performed on **Whiter Shade Of Pale** was Brooker on vocals, Matthew Fisher (born 7 March 1946), Ray Royer (born 8 October 1945), Bobby Harrison (born 28 June 1943) and Dave Knights (born 28 June 1945). When it came to recording the follow-up and an album, Royer and Harrison were considered unsuitable and were replaced by two ex-Paramounts, and Procol Harum never quite achieved the success that **Whiter Shade Of Pale** had promised. In March 1969, Dave Knights left the group, to be replaced by the final Paramount, Chris Copping, who had collected a University degree in the meantime. From then until 1971 when Robin Trower left, Procol Harum were the Paramounts plus Matthew Fisher.

235

ALL YOU NEED IS LOVE

19 July 1967, for three weeks

The Beatles *Parlophone R 5620*

Writers: John Lennon and Paul McCartney
Producer: George Martin

1 June 1967 was the day of the release in Britain of the 'Sergeant Pepper's Lonely Hearts Club Band' LP, the album that completed the process of transformation of the Beatles from the world's most exciting beat group to the makers of the world's most exciting records. The transformation was from a group who prided themselves in the early days on their ability to reproduce on stage any sound they put down on record into a group who had given up live performances in favour of the sophistication of recording techniques to produce brilliant popular music. 'Sergeant Pepper' not only led the way for groups to spend more time in the studios exploring new ideas in sound, it also was one of the very first 'concept' albums, and thus the album above all others to promote the 'concept' concept, which has been used by virtually everybody in pop and rock in the 15 years since its release.

24 days after the release of 'Sgt Pepper', the Beatles appeared on a BBC-TV show *Our World* that was beamed live by Satellite to all five continents. They sang **All You Need Is Love** in the Abbey Road studio, and within 2 weeks it became their next single and their twelfth number one.

236

SAN FRANCISCO (BE SURE TO WEAR SOME FLOWERS IN YOUR HAIR)

9 August 1967, for four weeks

Scott McKenzie *CBS 2816*

Writer: John Phillips
Producers: Lou Adler and John Phillips

The longest title of any song to reach number one was written by John Phillips, and was sung by the almost-one-hit-wonder Scott McKenzie. Scott McKenzie (born 1 October 1944) had been in an early sixties folk group called The Journeymen with John Phillips, who subsequently married the leggy Michelle Gilliam and with her, Cass Elliott and Denny Doherty created the Mamas and Papas, high priests of the California flower power phase of 1967.

The lyrics were trite and naive, but Scott McKenzie was quoted as saying that they were the basis of his lifestyle, which is probably how he managed to turn such a comparatively ordinary song into a superb single. It also explains why Scott McKenzie sank into the pit of oblivion at the end of 1967 despite 1 week at number 50 with the follow-up, **Like An Old Time Movie**. Flower power was a lovely idea, but as the most popular flower in San Francisco that summer was grass, it is not suprising that the movement never had any direction or unity. Bob Dylan's **Rainy Day Women Nos. 12 & 35** was nearer the true spirit of flower power, even though it was recorded a year earlier, in 1966.

237

THE LAST WALTZ

6 September 1967, for five weeks

Engelbert Humperdinck *Decca F 12655*

Writers: Les Reed and Barry Mason
Producer: Peter Sullivan

After **Release Me**, Engelbert Humperdinck found another country standard called **There Goes My Everything**, which had been a country smash for Jack Greene in 1966. That climbed to number three. For the next single, Engelbert chose a new song by the very successful British songwriters Les Reed and Barry Mason, called **The Last Waltz**. Within weeks it became the standard closing tune for every dance up and down the nation, and Engelbert had a hit that eventually sold even more copies worldwide than **Release Me**. It was a monster hit in Europe, too, where Mireille Mathieu recorded a French version, **La Dernière Valse** which even reached the British Top 50. Of all the late sixties ballads which seemed to dominate world markets as the Liverpool tide subsided, **The Last Waltz** is probably the best known, probably the biggest seller and certainly the biggest hit ever written by the prolific Les Reed and Barry Mason.

It was the last waltz for a revolutionary too. Che Guevara was killed by anti-guerilla forces in Bolivia on 9 October 1967. On the other hand, it was the first waltz for the Cunard liner, the *Queen Elizabeth II*, which was launched at the Clydebank shipyard on 20 September. And all the time Engelbert sang on.

Above **235 The Beatles,** *left* **236 Scott McKenzie,** *bottom left* **239 Foundations,** *below* **238 Bee Gees**

238

MASSACHUSETTS

11 October 1967, for four weeks

The Bee Gees *Polydor 56 192*

Writers: Barry, Robin and Maurice Gibb
Producers: Robert Stigwood and the Bee Gees

The first number one for the Bee Gees was co-written by Barry Gibb and his younger twin brothers, Maurice and Robin. Born in Douglas, Isle of Man, they had been raised in Manchester and later Australia. Returning to Britain in 1967, the protégés of entrepreneur Robert Stigwood achieved an international million-seller with **New York Mining Disaster 1941**.

They dwarfed that fine performance in less than half a year. **Massachusetts** reached number one in three of the four leading record markets, Britain, Germany and Japan, peaking at eleven in the United States. They learned of their first UK number one while setting up on a revolving stage just before a performance. They wondered whether they would regain their composure in time for the show. They did.

The song includes the lines 'I'm going back to Massachusetts' and 'Massachusetts is one place I have seen.' In fact, none of the brothers had ever been there. They wrote about the American state because they liked the sound of its name.

At the time of recording, the Bee Gees also included guitarist Vince Melouney and drummer Colin Petersen.

239

BABY NOW THAT I'VE FOUND YOU

8 November 1967, for two weeks

The Foundations *Pye 7N 17366*

Writers: Tony Macaulay and John McLeod
Producer: Tony Macaulav

The Foundations produced six chart hits in 2 years from September 1967 to September 1969, but none was as big as the first of all, **Baby Now That I've Found You**, which also gave Tony Macaulay the first of four number one hit productions. The Foundations were Clem Curtis (born 28 November 1940) on vocals, Eric Allandale (born 4 March 1936), Pat Burke (born 9 October 1937), Mike Elliott (born 6 August 1929), Tony Gomez (born 13 December 1948), Tim Harris (born 14 January 1948), Peter Macbeth (born 2 February 1943) and Alan Warner (born 21 April 1941).

Their second biggest hit was a year later, with a song by Tony Macaulay and Mike D'Abo, the lead singer of Manfred Mann, called **Build Me Up Buttercup** which reached number two but became one of those highly successful songs (like **My Sweet Lord, Fire** and **Hello Dolly**) which have become the victims of successful plagiarism suits by disgruntled writers of earlier, less successful but very similar songs.

240

LET THE HEARTACHES BEGIN

22 November 1967, for two weeks

Long John Baldry *Pye 7N 17385*

Writers: Tony Macaulay and John McLeod
Producer: John McLeod

It was perhaps apt that this song was at number one when the first heart transplant was performed, by Dr Christian Barnard at the Groote Schuur Hospital on 3 December 1967. However, this record has more claims to fame than just that. To begin with, it was one of the few occasions when writers have ousted another of their songs at the top. Macaulay and McLeod joined Bacharach and David, Lennon and McCartney and Bruce Welch (**Foot Tapper/Summer Holiday**) as writers who replaced themselves at number one, and even in 1981, when John Lennon wrote four number ones out of six, he still managed no more than two in a row. Macaulay and McLeod set an unequalled record, however, by taking over from each other as writer/producers at number one. The same producer has often produced consecutive top hits, but this is the only occasion when one half of a writing team has written and produced a song that took over from his partner's production.

Long John Baldry himself, born on 12 January 1941, is certainly the tallest act ever to make number one. His height is variously reported as between 6′6″ and 6′9″, but even the lower height is about double Little Jimmy Osmond. His singing career blossomed in the nineteen-sixties with his backing group, The Hoochie Coochie Men and then with Steampacket, a group that at various times contained Rod Stewart, Elkie Brooks and Elton John, who took his stage surname from Long John Baldry. Nevertheless, none of his white blues records ever made the charts. **Let The Heartaches Begin** was a big ballad totally unlike his previous music, and it was perhaps not surprising that he failed to consolidate his chart position. Three minor hits over the following year and a bit, were all that Long John could manage before he became Long Gone.

241

HELLO GOODBYE

6 December 1967, for seven weeks

The Beatles *Parlophone R 5655*

Writers: John Lennon and Paul McCartney
Producer: George Martin

Between **All You Need Is Love** and **Hello Goodbye** the Beatles' world changed. The man who they had sung about on the flip side of **All You Need Is Love** had died. Brian Epstein, the rich man of **Baby, You're A Rich Man** died in August 1967, and complete domination of the world's record shops achieved by 'Sgt. Pepper' meant that the world was looking forward to the Beatles' next record with all the anticipation that was there in 1963 and 1964. But with Epstein dead, the Beatles had nobody to tell them what to do, and therein lay the seeds of their disintegration.

Hello Goodbye was probably their most straightforward single since **Help!** (see no. 200) and its straightforwardness translated into commerciality. It was nowhere near as inventive as **Strawberry Fields Forever** or **Eleanor Rigby** but it stayed at number one for 7 weeks, the longest run by any Beatles single since **From Me To You**. Originality was expressed on the other side, **I Am The Walrus**, a track from their TV film *Magical Mystery Tour*, which hit the screens on Boxing Day 1967. *Magical Mystery Tour* was panned by the critics and the leadership that Paul McCartney had assumed after the death of Brian Epstein took its first knock.

242

THE BALLAD OF BONNIE AND CLYDE

24 January 1968, for one week

Georgie Fame *CBS 3124*

Writers: Mitch Murray and Peter Callander
Producer: Mike Smith

One of those film songs that was never in the film, like **Alfie**, **The Ballad of Bonnie and Clyde** gave Georgie Fame his third number one, Mitch Murray his third number one, and the performers of the actual theme music from *Bonnie and Clyde*, Lester Flatt and Earl Scruggs, a longer chart run than they might otherwise have had. We wonder how many fans went into a record shop to ask for 'The song from Bonnie and Clyde, please', and came out with **Foggy Mountain Breakdown** instead of the Georgie Fame single.

Georgie Fame disbanded the Blue Flames a few months after the success of **Get Away** (see no. 219) and early in 1967 switched labels from Columbia to CBS. His first few singles on his new label were unsuccessful, but then Georgie Fame lived up to his reputation of never getting into the Top 10 without going all the way to number one. His third Top 10 hit, **The Ballad of Bonnie and Clyde**, became his third number one.

His style had moved a long way from rhythm and blues at the Flamingo, and when later he teamed up briefly with another sophisticated ex-bluesman, Alan Price, their styles seemed entirely compatible for the production of frankly middle of the road material. The Animals and the Blue Flames were long forgotten.

243

EVERLASTING LOVE

31 January 1968, for two weeks

The Love Affair *CBS 3125*

Writers: Buzz Cason and Mac Gayden
Producer: Mike Smith

To cover the Robert Knight American hit, producer Mike Smith saw no reason actually to use the members of the teeny-bopper group Love Affair on the record. So apart from lead singer Steve Ellis, Mike Smith used session musicians rather than the members of the group whose instrumental talents at the time were charitably described as limited. The fact that session men were used was not unusual – at least one instrumental number one hit featured session musicians rather than the named artiste – but to admit it was then highly daring. It made no difference, however, as the record made it all the way to the top. What was more amazing was that Love Affair – by now using a higher percentage of their membership on record – managed four more Top 20 hits before breaking up and fading into the further recesses of the pop memory.

Not that **Everlasting Love** was a bad record: far from it. Producer Mike Smith was enjoying his second consecutive number one, while CBS joined Philips, RCA and MGM in having consecutive catalogue numbers (CBS 3124 and 3125) at number one. CBS obviously like the song. They reissued the Robert Knight original on their Monument label in 1974, and made the Top 20 with it. In 1981 a third CBS version of the song, this time by Rex Smith and Rachel Sweet, also hit the charts. This is the only time that there have been as many as three chart versions of a song, all from the same record company.

244

MIGHTY QUINN

14 February 1968, for two weeks

Manfred Mann *Fontana TF 897*

Writer: Bob Dylan
Producer: Mike Hurst

Manfred Mann liked Bob Dylan's songs, and Dylan is on record as saying he liked Manfred Mann's treatment of his songs. **If You Gotta Go, Go Now, With God On Our Side** and **Just Like A Woman** were three Dylan tunes that gave Manfred Mann big hits, but **Mighty Quinn** lay half-completed on tape for some months before Manfred himself could convince the rest of the band that it was a hit single.

But it was a massive hit, Manfred's third number one and the fourth of his seven Top 10 discs featuring the lead vocals of Old Harrovian and ex-Band Of Angels singer Mike d'Abo. Jack Bruce had by this time left Manfred, while the brief experiment with sax player Lyn Dobson and trumpeter Henry Lowther was also over. In Jack Bruce's place on bass was another wandering star, Klaus Voorman, who designed the 'Revolver' LP cover and who had been playing with the Hollies on a very temporary basis before joining Manfred Mann.

The Manfred Mann of the 1960's stayed together for three more Top 10 hits after **Mighty Quinn**, but they then split up. Mann and Hugg stayed together, forming firstly Manfred Mann Chapter III and then Manfred Mann's Earth Band. In the mid 1970's the hits started happening again, with three more Top 10 hits featuring Chris Thompson as lead vocalist. Manfred Mann remains the only number one hit group to have replaced their lead singer and had another number one.

245

CINDERELLA ROCKEFELLA

28 February 1968, for three weeks

Esther and Abi Ofarim *Philips BF 1640*

Writer: Mason Williams
Producers: Abi Ofarim and Chaim Semel

Only two husband and wife teams have ever topped the charts, and such is the transitoriness of life that both couples are now divorced. Sonny and Cher split up amidst vast publicity, but Esther and Abi Ofarim managed to go their own ways comparatively quietly, some years after their big success.

Esther Ofarim was born Esther Zaled in Safed, Israel on 13 June 1943, and her husband Abraham Reichstadt was born in Tel Aviv on 5 October 1939. Their marriage entitled Esther to leave the Israeli Army after serving only four months of her National Service, and enabled the pair to concentrate on a musical career. By 1963 they were a top attraction in Israel and rather confusingly that year, Esther Ofarim represented Switzerland in the Eurovision Song Contest. Their reputation throughout Europe grew as they recorded in French, German and English as well as Hebrew, and by mid-1967 they were appearing frequently on television programmes throughout Europe. It was one such appearance, on the Eamonn Andrews Show, that brought **Cinderella Rockefella** to the notice of the British public. The song had been written by Mason Williams, American composer and guitarist who hit in Britain with his **Classical Gas** later in 1968, and had been recorded by Esther and Abi in 1967. It was not issued as a single until early 1968, when public demand created the hit.

246

THE LEGEND OF XANADU

20 March 1968, for one week

Dave Dee, Dozy, Beaky, Mick and Tich *Fontana TF 903*

Writers: Ken Howard and Alan Blaikley
Producer: Steve Rowland

The band that set a trend that was followed by 70's bands like Sweet, Mud and Gary Glitter was the second group to be moulded for success by Ken Howard and Alan Blaikley.

Below **243 Love Affair**

251 Rolling Stones

246 Dave Dee, Dozy, Beaky, Mick and Tich

244 Manfred Mann

250 Union Gap featuring Gary Puckett

252 Equals

After their success with the Honeycombs (see no. 176) had faded, Howard and Blaikley looked for another vehicle for their commercial tunes and found a Wiltshire-based group, Dave Dee and the Bostons. The name was changed and the hits began for Dave Dee (born Dave Harman on 17 December 1943), Dozy (born Trevor Davies on 27 November 1944), Beaky (born John Dymond on 10 July 1944), Mick (Mick Wilson, born 4 March 1944) and Tich (born Ian Amey on 15 May 1944). Dave Dee was an ex-policeman which caused endless jokes about 'beat'. Their act was most unpolicemanlike, with whips and leather and double-meaning song titles like **You Make It Move** and **Bend It**.

There was talk in the musical press about a film based on the song **The Legend Of Xanadu** starring DD, D, B, M and T and the couple they deposed from the top spot, Esther and Abi Ofarim. It came to nothing and when asked about it years later, Dave Dee (now a successful record producer with Magnet Records) couldn't even recall the proposal. Another film called *Xanadu* a decade later provided another number one hit (see no. 461). Chart songs with 'Xanadu' in the title have never missed the number one spot.

247

LADY MADONNA

27 March 1968, for two weeks

The Beatles *Parlophone R 5675*

Writers: John Lennon and Paul McCartney
Producer: George Martin

The Beatles' last number one on the Parlophone label, their fourteenth number one in all, was by no means their most successful single. Certainly it reached the top, one place higher than Beatles' classics like **Strawberry Fields Forever** and **Let It Be** but **Lady Madonna** only stayed on the chart for a total of 8 weeks, the shortest-lived Beatles single ever. Furthermore, the similarities between **Lady Madonna** and Humphrey Lyttelton's 1956 Top 20 hit **Bad Penny Blues** (also on Parlophone) were such that a High Court judge agreed with Lyttelton's view that his copyright had been infringed, so a chunk of the royalties went to the Old Etonian trumpeter.

Lady Madonna did at least give the Beatles yet another hat-trick of number ones, and three more number ones were to follow on the Apple label. Between **Hello Goodbye** and **Lady Madonna**, the double EP 'Magical Mystery Tour' had been released. It reached number two and featured two of the Beatles' most successful songs, McCartney's **Fool On The Hill** and John Lennon's **I Am The Walrus**. It also included the only instrumental ever released by the Beatles, **Flying**. The critical reception of the Magical Mystery Tour film (which was panned) followed by the mediocre **Lady Madonna** made late in 1967 and early 1968 the low point in the Beatles' amazing career. But for the Beatles, even a low point is a number one hit.

248

CONGRATULATIONS

10 April 1968, for two weeks

Cliff Richard *Columbia DB 8376*

Writers: Bill Martin and Phil Coulter
Producer: Norrie Paramor

Cliff Richard's first attempt to win the Eurovision Song Contest resulted in his first number one hit for 3 years, but not in a second consecutive Eurovision victory for Britain. The winner of the Contest, held in London's Albert Hall on 6 April, was the Spanish singer Massiel, whose **La La La** pipped Cliff at the post amidst cries of foul from the British press about the voting of some of the foreign delegations.

Not that it really mattered. **Congratulations** was easily the biggest hit in Europe of all the Eurovision songs of 1968, and it has become a standard almost on the level of **Happy Birthday To You**. Cliff eventually recorded thirty different versions of the song for release in different countries around the world. Eurovision beamed the contest to seventeen countries in 1968, so despite this apparent overkill of languages, **Congratulations** rolled very quickly to its first million sales. It was Cliff's forty-first British single, and it proved to be his biggest worldwide seller, even reaching number 99 in the American Hot Hundred. In later years, both **Devil Woman** and **We Don't Talk Anymore** (see no. 441) have overhauled the sales figures of **Congratulations,** which is all the same one of the biggest hits in the history of the Eurovision Song Contest.

Despite this, Cliff's next four singles all missed the Top 10, giving Cliff his worst period of chart inaction since his career began 10 years earlier. It was to be another 10 years before he hit the top of the charts again.

249

WHAT A WONDERFUL WORLD/CABARET

24 April 1968, for four weeks

Louis Armstrong *HMV POP 1615*

Writers: What a Wonderful World – George David Weiss and George Douglas; Cabaret – John Kander and Fred Ebb
Producer: Bob Thiele

Born on 4 July 1900, Louis Armstrong was 67 years and 295 days old when his double-sided hit reached the top, making him the oldest artiste ever to have a number one hit. The most played side, **What A Wonderful World** was written by George Weiss, composer of **Can't Help Falling In Love** for Elvis, and George Douglas, whose real name was Bob Thiele. Douglas/Thiele produced the record. The flip-side of this double-sided hit was the theme tune of the hit musical *Cabaret*, which picked up a fistful of Oscars when translated into a film starring Liza Minelli, Michael York and Joel Gray. It followed Louis Armstrong's earlier hit with the theme of the musical *Hello Dolly* which reached number four in Britain in 1964, having earlier given him a number one hit in America.

What A Wonderful World reached number one 15 years and 127 days after Louis Armstrong's first hit **Takes Two To Tango**, entered the charts. At the time, this was the longest time that any chart artist had taken to hit the top. When Louis Armstrong died, 2 days after his 71st birthday, he still held that record, which was not beaten until Chuck Berry's **My Ding-A-Ling** (see no. 323) took over the number one spot on 25 November 1972.

250

YOUNG GIRL

22 May 1968, for four weeks

Union Gap featuring Gary Puckett *CBS 3365*

Writer: Jerry Fuller
Producer: Jerry Fuller, with arrangement by Al Capps

The Union Gap, like the Supremes and the First Edition, changed their billing to feature the lead singer more prominently as their success grew. On their first American hit, **Woman, Woman** they were simply Union Gap. They all wore American Civil War uniforms to remind their more erudite fans that they had taken their name from the site of a famous Civil War battle. For their second hit single, they became 'Union Gap featuring Gary Puckett' but by the time of their third smash they were 'Gary Puckett and the Union Gap'. Whatever the names, the line-up was the same for all the singles. Minnesota-born Gary Puckett was the vocalist, Dwight Bement played saxophone, Canadian Kerry Chater played bass, Paul Whitbread handled the drums and Gary Withem played keyboards. They had got together in San Diego, California in 1967, and through producer Jerry Fuller landed a recording contract almost immediately. Within a few months of their formation they had received their first Gold Discs for **Woman, Woman** and throughout 1968 their bandwagon rolled unstoppably along. Until it all stopped in 1969.

251

JUMPING JACK FLASH

19 June 1968, for two weeks

The Rolling Stones *Decca F 12782*

Writers: Mick Jagger and Keith Richard
Producer: Jimmy Miller

The Stones' first number one for 2 years, but what a record! To get the summer parties of 1968 going (in those pre-disco days), all you needed were copies of **Simon Says** by the 1910 Fruitgum Co., **Son Of Hickory Holler's Tramp** by O C Smith, and this one. Thirteen years later, **Jumping Jack Flash** was still the number used by the Stones to close the show on their American tour, still the number the fans were waiting for.

The first batch of the Rolling Stones drug problems were over by now, certainly for Mick Jagger and Keith Richard, whose jail sentences of 1 year and 3 months respectively imposed in June 1967 had been overturned on appeal. Brian Jones had also had a 9 month jail sentence reduced on appeal to merely a fine, but the strain of the court appearances told on him, an asthmatic, more than on the others. He spent much of the early part of 1968 in hospitals trying to recover his fitness, both mental and physical, but in May 1968, just a few days before the release of **Jumping Jack Flash**, he was arrested once again on drugs charges. **Jumping Jack Flash** is really Brian Jones' epitaph. Exactly a year after it dropped from the top, he drowned in his swimming pool. By that time he had already left the Stones but had shown few signs of sorting out his problems.

252

BABY COME BACK

3 July 1968, for three weeks

The Equals *President PT 135*

Writer: Eddie Grant
Producer: Ed Kassner

Less than a year after Robin and Maurice Gibb joined Herbie and Harold Kalin as the only twins at number one, a third pair added their names to the list. Lincoln and Derv Gordon (born 29 June 1948 in Jamaica) were 40 per cent of the Equals, the racially mixed London group who gave President Records their only number one hit. The other three members of the group were Eddie Grant (born 5 March 1948 in Guyana, then British Guiana) who wrote **Baby Come Back**, John Hall (born 25 October 1947 in Holloway, London) and Pat Lloyd (born 17 March 1948 also in Holloway).

The Equals were formed in 1965 in north-east London and by 1966 the Equals had a recording contract with President Records based on a demo tape of **Baby Come Back**. The song became a big hit in Europe, where the Equals performed very regularly, but was ignored by British fans until finally the song could be ignored no longer. It became one of the increasingly long list of songs which failed when originally released but hit the very top when re-activated, and provided the Equals with easily their biggest hit.

The group disbanded in the 1970's, but Eddie Grant is still very active as a composer and performer, hitting the British Top 20 even in the 1980's.

253

I PRETEND

24 July 1968, for one week

Des O'Connor *Columbia DB 8397*

Writers: Les Reed and Barry Mason
Producer: Norman Newell

Morecambe and Wise's favourite singer, Des O'Connor, reached number one for only 1 week, but the record enjoyed a total chart run of 36 weeks, longer than all but three of the 500 British Number One Hits. Born in January 1932, Des O'Connor is best known as a comedian of the Bob Monkhouse variety – the fixed smile and well-coiffed hair putting the finishing touches to the totally professional manner in which some of the world's worst jokes are delivered. But unlike Bob Monkhouse, Des O'Connor could sing, and in the late sixties followed Ken Dodd's lead up to the top of the charts. Like Ken Dodd, O'Connor never recorded humorous songs, but relied on his smooth voice and his smoothly produced material to infiltrate himself into the hearts and pockets of the record buyers.

I Pretend was written by the two Britons who most deserve the title of 'songsmiths', Les Reed and Barry Mason, whose other hits included **The Last Waltz** for Engelbert Humperdinck (see no. 237). For producer Norman Newell, whose only other recent number one had been Ken Dodd's **Tears** (see no. 204), **I Pretend** was the last number one production in a career that has included enough hit productions in the fifties to rank with Norrie Paramor.

254

MONY MONY

31 July 1968, for two weeks
and from 21 August 1968 for one week

Tommy James and The Shondells *Major Minor MM 567*

Writers: Bobby Bloom, Richie Cordell, Bo Gentry and Tommy James
Producers: Bo Gentry and Richie Cordell

The idea for the song is supposed to have come to Tommy James as he sat in a hotel in New York one night staring out of the window at a neon sign flashing on and off – MONY, MONY. The Mutual of New York Insurance Company not only looks after widows and orphans, it inspires pop writers.

Tommy James (born Tommy Jackson on 29 April 1946 in Dayton, Ohio) had his first hit in 1966 with **Hanky Panky** which reached number 38 in Britain and number one in America. Astonishingly, it was his only other chart hit in Britain, and Tommy James is one of the few people not to have followed up a number one in Britain. The Shondells were Ronnie Rossman (born 28 February 1945) on keyboards, Pete Lucia (born 6 February 1947) on drums, Eddie Gray (born 28 February 1948) on lead guitar, and Mike Vale (born 17 July 1943) on bass.

Mony Mony was the tenth American hit in a line which included two number ones and six other Top 10 hits between

1966 and 1969. When James left the Shondells and went solo, he came up with one superb single **Dragging The Line**, which also did nothing in Britain.

Mony Mony and **Hanky Panky** gave Tommy James a bubblegum image while classic tracks like **Crimson and Clover** and **Crystal Blue Persuasion** were ignored. A much underrated talent.

255

FIRE

14 August 1968, for one week

The Crazy World of Arthur Brown *Track 604022*

Writers: Vincent Crane, Arthur Brown, Peter Ker and Michael Finesilver
Producer: Kit Lambert

When Arthur Brown (born 24 June 1944) and his manager Vincent Crane wrote **Fire**, and built a stage act featuring facial make-up, a burning hat and many stage effects which later lived on through Alice Cooper and others, they hoped they were creating a hit, and launching Brown on a successful chart career. On both points they were wrong. Yes, the song was a hit, but two other writers, Peter Ker and Michael Finesilver, sued successfully to show that **Fire** was not an original creation but a variation of their song **Fire**. Furthermore, the song was Brown's only hit, and his popularity, unlike his hat, never really caught fire. The *New Statesman*, no less, thought that 'Arthur Brown could easily be the first genuine artist to come out of our local underground. He's disconcerting, even faintly perverse, but distinctly original and very very English'. But, as so often, the *New Statesman* showed that its finger was not really on the pulse of British popular music, not even at their local underground.

The record was produced by the late Kit Lambert, manager of the Who. On Arthur Brown's LP, associate producer credits went to Pete Townshend of the Who, but the official producer of the single was Kit Lambert, who owned the Track label.

256

DO IT AGAIN

28 August 1968, for one week

The Beach Boys *Capitol CL 15554*

Writers: Brian Wilson and Mike Love
Producer: Brian Wilson

The Beach Boys' career was already well in decline when **Do It Again**, a piece of nostalgia for the surfing summers of '64, '65 and '66, suddenly hit the top. Like all Beach Boys records, it was a masterly Brian Wilson production, but in retrospect there is no logical reason why it was their only Top 10 hit out of five singles issued between November 1967 and February 1969.

The Beach Boys had been swamped by the Beatles' 'Sergeant Pepper' album, which had topped their own brilliant 'Pet Sounds' album, issued a few months earlier. **Good Vibrations** (genuinely ahead of anything the Beatles had thus far done in production terms), was the last of thirteen Top 10 hits for the Beach Boys in America, while in Britain it was only the fifth of twelve. It has to be admitted that the Americans showed better taste in this, because they put classics like **Surfer Girl** and **Fun Fun Fun** into the Top 10 while in Britain they missed out altogether. In Britain, **Break Away**, an average single, reached number six, but in America it peaked at 63.

Perhaps that is why **Do It Again** hit number one. It was genuine good time surf music, the thing the Beach Boys knew best.

257

I'VE GOTTA GET A MESSAGE TO YOU

4 September 1968, for one week

The Bee Gees *Polydor 56 273*

Writers: Barry, Robin and Maurice Gibb
Producers: Robert Stigwood and the Bee Gees

A critic once observed that the Bee Gees of the late sixties were a gloomy bunch. When asked by Barry Gibb what songs could be cited to justify this remark, he replied '**New York Mining Disaster 1941 . . . I've Gotta Get a Message to You . . .**' 'And that's it!' Barry concluded.

The critic could be forgiven for having been overly affected by the two singles. They both concerned personal dilemmas of a desperate nature, the first that of a miner trapped below the surface and the second that of a killer who is about to be executed. At least the Gibbs were romantic to the end: both men facing death wanted to communicate with their women.

I've Gotta Get a Message to You came at a crucial moment for the Bee Gees. After hitting the American Top 20 with their first five singles there and the British equivalent with four out of the first five UK releases they had suffered their first international miss, **Jumbo**. **Message** proved them more than one-year wonders, marking their breakthrough to the US Top 10 and their return to the number one spot in Britain. There is no telling how many weeks this record may have spent at number one had the Beatles not launched their Apple label in the late summer of 1968.

258

HEY JUDE

11 September 1968, for two weeks

The Beatles *Apple R 5722*

Writers: John Lennon and Paul McCartney
Producer: George Martin

This song was inspired by Paul McCartney's fondness for Julian Lennon, son of John and Cynthia. While driving to Cynthia's house for a visit after she and John had broken up, he started singing 'Hey Jules.' He changed the title to **Hey Jude**, thinking Jude a name with more country and western flavour than Jules. Paul was uncertain about some of the lyric's obscure lines, such as 'the movement you need is on your shoulder,' but John and Yoko Ono considered them marvellously *avant-garde*. The Beatles' fifteenth number one, **Hey Jude** was the longest chart-topper ever, clocking in at approximately 7 minutes 10 seconds. It ruled the roost for 9 weeks in the United States, the Beatles' longest run at number one, but was held to 2 weeks in the UK by McCartney's own production, **Those Were the Days** by Mary Hopkin.

Hey Jude was made into a memorable promotional film, one of the very first widely seen, which debuted in Britain on the David Frost show and on the Smothers Brothers hour in the United States. It was the initial offering on the Beatles' Apple label, part of a debut issue of four. Despite being the first single for the company, it retained Parlophone's numbering system. Wilson Pickett scored a Top 20 hit with his soulful cover version mere months later. **Hey Jude** became the title track of an American anthology of Beatle singles.

259

THOSE WERE THE DAYS

25 September 1968, for six weeks

Mary Hopkin *Apple 2*

Writer: Gene Raskin
Producer: Paul McCartney

The story of Mary Hopkin is pure rags to riches schmaltz. Born in Pontardawe, South Wales, on 3 May 1950, she was noticed on Hughie Green's amateur talent TV show *Opportunity Knocks* by Twiggy, the model who did for London fashion what the Beatles did for British pop. Twiggy mentioned Mary Hopkin to Paul McCartney, who signed her to the infant Apple label. Her first single was a simple folk tune, sung in Hopkin's crystal clear voice and produced by Paul McCartney. It raced to the top of the charts and knocked her producer's **Hey Jude** out of the number one position.

Mary Hopkin never managed to match the vast success of her first single, but the hits continued for a few more years. She represented Britain in the Eurovision Song Contest in 1970 with a production line Eurovision number called **Knock Knock Who's There**. That song reached number two, but was kept off the top spot by the contest winner, **All Kinds of Everything** (see no. 284).

Subsequently Mary married producer Tony Visconti and has occasionally released singles, with scant success. Her recent involvement in the group Sundance, with Mike Hurst and Mike de Albuquerque has also proved unsuccessful. Her beautiful voice is no longer enough to carry a record into the charts of the 1980's.

260

WITH A LITTLE HELP FROM MY FRIENDS

6 November 1968, for one week

Joe Cocker *Regal-Zonophone RZ 3013*

Writers: John Lennon and Paul McCartney
Producer: Denny Cordell

The Ringo Starr track on the Sergeant Pepper album had been covered many times since the original version was released in mid 1967, and two versions, by Young Idea and Joe Brown, had been hits. Nevertheless Joe Cocker decided to follow up his inventive single **Marjorine** with this song, which became the title song of his LP. The title was apt – this track features among others, Jimmy Page on guitar, while other tracks on the LP featured the likes of Albert Lee, Stevie Winwood, Mathew Fisher and Henry McCullough. The backing vocals on **With A Little Help From My Friends** were by Madelene Bell, Rosetta Hightower and Sunny Wheetman, who in the late sixties were the queens of session vocals. The result was one of the few versions of Beatles' songs that can easily stand comparison with the original.

Joe Cocker never really won for himself the lasting success that his original and powerful singing style deserved. One of his problems was poor management. His performance at Woodstock was the high point of his career but his highly publicised, very popular and financially disastrous 'Mad Dogs and Englishmen' tour a year or so later, turned Leon Russell into a star but did little for Joe Cocker. His chart career finished in 1970 as far as the UK was concerned, although he enjoyed a fair amount of US Hot 100 success with records such as **You Are So Beautiful** (1975) in the seventies. His talent has survived even his exhausting lifestyle and it is to be hoped that the much-threatened Joe Cocker comeback will one day take place.

261

THE GOOD THE BAD AND THE UGLY

13 November 1968, for four weeks

Hugo Montenegro and his Orchestra and Chorus *RCA 1727*

Writer: Ennio Morricone
Producer: Hugo Montenegro

The Good The Bad and The Ugly was the first instrumental number one since 3 April 1963, when the Shadows' **Foot Tapper** gave way 4 weeks before the Beatles had their first chart topper. It had as its unlikely birthplace a spaghetti western starring Clint Eastwood. Montenegro himself was born in New York in 1925, but moved to California after serving in the US Navy and became known for the scores to films like *Hurry Sundown* and TV series like *The Man From U.N.C.L.E.* He also acted as arranger and conductor for label-mate Harry Belafonte.

The Good The Bad and The Ugly featured Elliott Fisher on electric violin, Manny Klein on piccolo trumpet, Tommy Morgan on electronic harmonica and Arthur Smith on ocarina, the instrument that produced the haunting introduction to the record. The grunting vocals were by Ron Hicklin, who led the chorus, and whistler Muzzy Marcellino also features on the record.

Hugo Montenegro managed to avoid the stigma of being a one hit wonder on 8 January 1969, when his theme to Clint Eastwood's next spaghetti western *Hang 'Em High* reached number 50, only to disappear from the charts the next week.

262

LILY THE PINK

11 December 1968, for three weeks
and from 8 January 1969 for one week

Scaffold *Parlophone R 5734*

Writers: John Gorman, Mike McGear and Roger McGough
Producer: Norrie Paramor

The Scaffold were John Gorman, poet Roger McGough and Paul McCartney's brother Mike McGear. They first hit the charts with **Thank U Very Much**, a top five hit at Christmas 1967 with the enigmatic first line, 'Thank U very much for the Aintree Iron'. Other equally unusual singles, like **Today's Monday**, failed completely, but at Christmas in 1968 they achieved their only number one, the saga of Lily The Pink and her Medicinal Compound.

It was Norrie Paramor's final number one production, his twenty-seventh, a total which remains unmatched today. At the time it meant that he had produced slightly more than one in ten number one hits, a phenomenal achievement. It was Paramor's only number one as an independent producer after years as staff producer for EMI. Uncredited vocals in the background on the verse about Jennifer Eccles and her terrible freckles were by Graham Nash of the Hollies, whose single **Jennifer Eccles** had been a Top 10 hit earlier that year. Also on background vocals was Norrie Paramor's assistant producer, Tim Rice. The production had been completed, ready to be pressed, when Mike McGear decided it needed a bass drum. The drum was added, the tape remixed and the single sold a million. Without that bass drum, would it have hit the charts quite as hard? No-one will ever know.

260 Joe Cocker

255 The Crazy World of Arthur Brown

262 Scaffold

263 Marmalade

263

OB-LA-DI OB-LA-DA

1 January 1969, for one week
and from 15 January 1969 for two weeks
Marmalade *CBS 3892*

Writers: John Lennon and Paul McCartney
Producer: Mike Smith

The third and final cover version of a Beatles song to reach number one was Marmalade's recording of the reggae track from the white album, 'Ob-La-Di, Ob-La-Da'. By composing and recording a tune with a reggae beat in 1968, the Beatles had as usual shown themselves to be one step ahead of the public taste, and Marmalade showed they were shrewd enough to spot a hit when they saw one.

Marmalade were originally called Dean Ford and the Gaylords and came from Scotland. Their first English single, **Loving Things** reached number six in the summer of 1968, to establish the group south of the border. **Ob-La-Di, Ob-La-Da** was their third chart single, and the personnel featured were vocalist Dean Ford (born Thomas McAleese on 5 September 1946), Junior Campbell (born 31 May 1947), Pat Fairley (born 14 April 1946), Graham Knight (born 8 December 1946) and Alan Whitehead (born 24 July 1946).

The group followed **Ob-La-Di** with another seven hits in a run that finished in 1972 with **Radancer**. The inevitable line-up changes were hitting the act by this time and one of those who left, Junior Campbell, scored a couple of chart successes by himself in 1972 and 1973. A version of Marmalade that bore little relation to the **Ob-La-Di** combination surprisingly brought the name back from the dead in 1976 with a Tony Macaulay/Roger Greenaway song and production that made no. 9 – **Falling Apart At The Seams** but since then success has been thinly spread upon Marmalade's slices.

264

ALBATROSS

29 January 1969, for one week
Fleetwood Mac *Blue Horizon 57 3145*

Writer: Peter Green
Producer: Mike Vernon

Fleetwood Mac's biggest British hit was the beautiful guitar instrumental **Albatross**. Like another blues performer, Long John Baldry, the biggest chart success was totally unlike their usual material, but unlike Long John Baldry, Fleetwood Mac had plenty of other chart success with their blues numbers.

At the time **Albatross** was recorded, Fleetwood Mac were Peter Green (born 29 October 1946) on guitar, Mick Fleetwood (born 24 June 1947) on drums, John McVie (born 26 November 1945) on bass, Jeremy Spencer (born 4 July 1948) on guitar and keyboards, and Danny Kirwan (born 13 May 1950) on guitar. After **Albatross**, two number two hits (both vocal) followed, giving Fleetwood Mac, like T Rex and Lulu, three consecutive hits on three different labels (Blue Horizon, Immediate and Reprise). **Albatross** itself nearly made number one for the second time when re-released in 1973.

Peter Green left the group he founded in May 1970. To replace him, John McVie's wife Christine Perfect joined from Chicken Shack. In February 1971, Jeremy Spencer joined the Children Of God cult in California, at which stage Bob Welch, an American, joined the band. By this time, Fleetwood Mac were based in the States, and when Danny Kirwan left, two more Americans, Lindsay Buckingham and Stevie Nicks joined. The massive hit album 'Rumours' in the late seventies established them as one of the largest selling groups in the world, and despite the departure of Bob Welch and recent solo efforts by Nicks, Lindsay and Fleetwood, they remain one of the biggest names on record in the world today.

265

BLACKBERRY WAY

5 February 1969, for one week
The Move *Regal Zonophone RZ 3015*

Writer: Roy Wood
Producer: Jimmy Miller

The Move claim a central position in the development of post-Beatles pop music. Formed in Birmingham in 1965, they were Roy Wood, Bev Bevan, Ace Kefford, Trevor Burton and vocalist Carl Wayne. Not only was a record of theirs **Flowers In The Rain** the first record played on the first Radio One programme, but also through Roy Wood especially, and Bev Bevan, they begat Wizzard and Electric Light Orchestra who have both reached number one in the 1970's. The Move also managed not only to be threatened with a libel suit over a caricature of then Prime Minister

Harold Wilson in the publicity material for **Flowers In The Rain**, they also lost the suit when it came to court.

Still, all publicity is good publicity, and by the time **Blackberry Way** became their third top five hit with a botanical title, and the only Move single ever to reach number one, they were one of the most innovative as well as one of the most popular groups in Britain. But internal dissension was already numbering their days. Little more than 3 years later, ELO's first single entered the chart even before Move's last one had disappeared. But Move were great while they lasted.

266

(IF PARADISE IS) HALF AS NICE

12 February 1969, for two weeks

Amen Corner *Immediate IM 073*

Writers: Lucio Battisti, English lyrics by Jack Fishman
Producer: Shel Talmy

Amen Corner came from Wales and were controlled by Andy Fairweather-Low, lead vocalist and majority shareholder. The others, Neil Jones, Blue Weaver, Clive Taylor, Mike Smith, Dennis Bryn and Allen Jones laid down a commercial backing at their leader's feet. They began life heavy on the blues, with singles like **Gin House Blues** which reached number 12. Andy Fairweather-Low discovered, however, that the fans liked bubblegum better than the blues, and established Amen Corner as a leading weenybop outfit with singles like **Bend Me Shape Me** and **High In The Sky**. At this point a change in labels, from Decca's progressive subsidiary Deram, to Immediate proved to be the final touch required for a number one hit. **(If Paradise Is) Half As Nice** was pure bubblegum, made interesting by Andy Fairweather-Low's voice, which sounded like Rod Stewart in tighter trousers than usual. When Immediate experienced financial difficulties Amen Corner more or less went down with them although Andy himself, operating next under the group name Fair Weather, soon came up with a Top Ten hit on RCA, **Natural Sinner**. Later still, in the mid-seventies, he had a further two hits as a solo act on A & M, including the memorable 1975 Christmastime biggie **Wide Eyed And Legless**.

267

WHERE DO YOU GO TO, MY LOVELY?

26 February 1969, for four weeks

Peter Sarstedt *United Artists UP2262*

Writer: Peter Sarstedt
Producer: Ray Singer

Peter Sarstedt's elder brother Richard had already had a number one hit, **Well I Ask You** (see no. 122) in 1961, when he sang under the name Eden Kane. Seven and half years later, Sarstedt was perfectly acceptable as a rock star's surname, especially one who sang so wistfully of the jet set and the meaning of life, so Peter resisted the temptation to become Peter Kane. All the same, he and Richard established a record that has only once been equalled. They were the first brothers to have separate solo number ones in Britain, a record that was equalled by Donny and Little Jimmy Osmond at the end of 1972. Paul McCartney and his brother Mike McGear have also had separate number one hits, but only as members of their groups. In 1976, the third Sarstedt brother, Robin, reached number three with his version of **My Resistance Is Low**, enabling the Sarstedt clan to become the only three brothers in British chart history with separate solo hits. Marie Osmond has of course had solo hits, making her the third solo hitmaking Osmond, but she most certainly is not a brother. Andy and Robin Gibb have had solo hits, and Barry Gibb has managed one with Barbra Streisand, but nobody yet has quite matched the Sarstedt achievement.

268

I HEARD IT THROUGH THE GRAPEVINE

26 March 1969, for three weeks

Marvin Gaye *Tamla Motown TMG 686*

Writers: Norman Whitfield and Barrett Strong
Producer: Norman Whitfield

Marvin Gaye was an undercharted artist and **I Heard It Through the Grapevine** an undercharted song in the United Kingdom until this single righted both wrongs. Gaye was the outstanding Motown male vocalist of the sixties, enjoying such success in America that in 1978 American chartologist Joel Whitburn computed that, according to his points

Above top to bottom **264 Fleetwood Mac, 265 Move, 266 Amen Corner,** *Right* **268 Marvin Gaye**

system, Gaye was the fifth most successful Hot 100 artist of the rock era.

In Britain, however, he had failed to penetrate the Top 40, and had only made it as far as the Top 20 with the assistance of occasional female partners. His style was too soulful for the mass British audience of the sixties.

So had been Gladys Knight and the Pips' gospel-tinged version of **I Heard It Through the Grapevine**. Jimmy Ruffin claimed that co-writer Barrett Strong had originally intended the song for him, and other artists had certainly recorded it before Gladys, but the family group's reading was the first to be issued. It topped the US soul chart for 6 weeks beginning in December, 1967, and was Motown's biggest domestic seller to date. Whitfield cut Gaye on the same tune, using a backing track first meant for another Pips performance. It appeared unheralded on a 1968 album, but when finally released topped the Hot 100 for 7 weeks and became in turn Motown's all-time US number one. It topped the UK list for 3 weeks and began Marvin's solo chart career in earnest.

269

THE ISRAELITES

16 April 1969, for one week

Desmond Dekker and the Aces *Pyramid PYR 6058*

Writers: Desmond Dekker and Leslie Kong
Producer: Leslie Kong

The first reggae number one was also probably the best. Written by Desmond Dekker and his Chinese-Jamaican producer, the late Leslie Kong, it was Dekker's second British hit, coming almost two years after his Top 20 record **007**. Dekker's diction was all that came to be expected of the reggae stars, largely unintelligible, but it made little difference. The disc came from nowhere to the top of the charts, bringing the reggae beat to British pop fans for the first time since Millie's 1964 number two hit, **My Boy Lollipop**. The time was right for reggae. The Beatles, as always the trendsetters, had recorded their own reggae-influenced song **Ob-La-Di**, which Marmalade took to number one, while other future stars like Rod Stewart and Eric Clapton were already aware of what was happening in Jamaica at Leslie Kong's studio.

Dekker had two more Top 10 hits over the next year, **It Miek** (not only unintelligible when sung but also when written down), and **You Can Get It If You Really Want**. When the Pyramid catalogue was acquired by Cactus in 1975, it was inevitable that **Israelites** would be re-issued, and not surprising that it hit the Top 10 once again in June of that year.

270

GET BACK

23 April 1969, for six weeks

The Beatles with Billy Preston *Apple R 5777*

Writers: John Lennon and Paul McCartney
Producer: George Martin

After thirteen consecutive number ones that reached the top in their second week on the charts, the Beatles finally came straight into the chart at number one with a song performed live on the roof of the Apple offices in London in February 1969. The version which was released was not recorded on the roof: that was produced as usual by George Martin at Abbey Road.

Billy Preston, who joined Tony Sheridan as the only individuals to have a performing credit on a Beatles' single, was born in Houston, Texas on 9 September 1946. He had by 1969 established a reputation as a brilliant session keyboards man, and it was George Harrison who brought him into the Beatle empire. John Lennon said of Billy Preston, 'we might have had him in the group', but the group was already breaking up. Preston put out a brilliant single on Apple in mid-1969, **That's The Way God Planned It**, which made number 11. Despite vocal and instrumental number ones in America in the early seventies, he faded chartwise in Britain until at the beginning of 1980 he reached number two in duet with Stevie Wonder's ex-wife Syreeta with the aptly titled **With You I'm Born Again**.

271

DIZZY

4 June 1969, for one week

Tommy Roe *Stateside SS 2143*

Writers: Tommy Roe and Freddy Weller
Producer: Steve Barri

Thomas David Roe, born in Atlanta Georgia on 9 May 1942, was one of the ranks of pop stars who admit that their biggest influence was Buddy. Holly. **Dizzy** was a brilliant piece of pure bubblegum, but early Tommy Roe hits, especially his first **Sheila**, were virtual duplications of Buddy Holly's phrasing, arrangements and sound. His first break came when, like Bobby Vee, he was asked to stand in on a date which Buddy Holly had been booked for, and a year later Roe had recorded and released **Sheila** on the tiny Judd label in Georgia. The record failed to attract any interest, but within two years Roe had signed with ABC-Paramount who re-recorded and re-released **Sheila**. This time it was a hit, and Roe was on his way.

His career was not very consistent after that. Some big hits, like **The Folk Singer**, in 1963, but a lot of failures, until Roe and Freddie Weller wrote one of the very best of the bubblegum songs of the late 1960's **Dizzy**. Roe had his first number one 7 years after his first hit. Co-writer Freddy Weller is now a highly successful country singer after a spell as one of Paul Revere's Raiders.

272

THE BALLAD OF JOHN AND YOKO

11 June 1969, for three weeks

The Beatles *Apple R 5786*

Writers: John Lennon and Paul McCartney
Producers: George Martin and the Beatles

The last number one hit by the Fab Four in fact only featured a Fab Two as only John and Paul actually played on **The Ballad Of John and Yoko** a hastily concocted but irresistibly catchy paean to some of the then recent events of John Lennon's life, the principal one being his marriage to the avant-garde Japanese artist, Yoko Ono.

The chorus had lines like 'Christ, you know it ain't easy' and 'The way things are going/They're going to crucify me', which immediately caused the media to criticize the increasingly erratic John Lennon, and to raise again the furore caused by his 'We're bigger than Jesus' remark in America a few years earlier. Not that this bothered the Beatles. By the time this record was released, they had all but split up. The later singles, **Something** and **Let It Be**, were both recorded before **The Ballad of John and Yoko**, which incidentally was the fourteenth of the Beatles' 17 number ones to reach the top in its second week on the chart.

And so the Beatles' reign of unprecedented success was over. John and Yoko climbed into their bag, Paul married Linda, George dug deeper into Indian music and Ringo went into films. Despite the brilliance and phenomenal success of many of their individual records since 1969, nothing has created the magic that 'the new Beatles single' always did.

273

SOMETHING IN THE AIR

2 July 1969, for three weeks

Thunderclap Newman *Track 604-031*

Writer: Speedy Keen
Producer: Pete Townshend

Described once as 'the song that bridges the gap between Woodstock and Kent State', whatever that may mean, **Something in The Air** was the only significant hit for Thunderclap Newman, a three piece band fronted by Speedy Keen (born 29 March 1945). One of Keen's songs, **Armenia, City In The Sky**, had been recorded by the Who on their album, 'The Who Sell Out', and it was Pete Townshend of the Who who produced the first single by Keen's group. The other members of the group were Andy 'Thunderclap' Newman on keyboards and Jimmy McCulloch on guitar, who later played in Wings for a while before his death. Speedy Keen was the drummer and vocalist.

The follow-up single, **Accidents**, scraped into the bottom of the charts, preventing anybody from describing Thunderclap Newman as one hit wonders, but they broke up soon afterwards. Speedy Keen put out an interesting first solo album called 'Previous Convictions', but has never lived up to the promise of his number one hit. The Who have never had a chart topper in Britain, so this Pete Townshend production is the only number one to have any direct connection with any member of the mod superstars. The song was a Top 40 hit in America as well, where it was featured prominently in a campus unrest semi-documentary film, *The Strawberry Statement*.

274

HONKY TONK WOMEN

23 July 1969, for five weeks

The Rolling Stones *Decca F 12952*

Writers: Mick Jagger and Keith Richard
Producer: Jimmy Miller

Just 3 weeks after the last Beatles chart-topper slid from the number one position, the last Rolling Stones number one (so far) took over. They went out with a bang, at least, as 5 weeks was their longest ever run at number one. The Stones' chart career is amazing in its consistency. Eight number ones puts them fifth on the all time list, but their unbeaten record is that over a period of 14 years and 8 months, every single official release by the Rolling Stones made the Top 10. When **Respectable** peaked at number 23 in late 1978, it marked the first time that the Stones had missed the Top 10 since **I Wanna Be Your Man** got no higher than number 12 at the end of 1963. It was also the lowest chart placing they had ever had – apart from a Decca cash-in single of **Out of Time** – in a 15 year career. But they are still making Top 10 hits, even in the 1980's.

Honky Tonk Women was the only Stones number one after Brian Jones left the group, and his subsequent death 20 days before this single reached the top. The replacement Stone on this record is Mick Taylor (born 17 January 1941), who came from John Mayall's Bluesbreakers. Taylor left the Stones at the end of 1974, and his replacement was, and still is, Ronnie Wood from the Small Faces.

275

IN THE YEAR 2525 (EXORDIUM AND TERMINUS)

30 August 1969, for three weeks

Zager and Evans *RCA 1860*

Writer: Rick Evans
Producers: Denny Zager and Rick Evans

The record that gave way to the Rolling Stones at the top of the American charts took over from them in Britain. One of the wierdest and therefore best known one-hit-wonder records in British pop history, **In the Year 2525** was a bleak vision of man's future written by Evans in half an hour one day in Lincoln, Nebraska. Denny Zager (born 1944) and Rick Evans (born 1943) had originally been part of a group called the Eccentrics, a country outfit from Nebraska, but had been performing as a duo for some years before the success of **In The Year 2525**. In November 1968, they borrowed $500 to record the song in Texas. They formed their own company, and hawked the initial pressing of 1000 copies around record shops and local radio stations. They sent copies of the record to all the major record companies as well, but it was RCA in New York that took the bait,and signed Zager and Evans to a national deal.

The result was a national release in June 1969 and a number one hit in America by July. In U.K., it also hit the top very quickly, but they disappeared just as fast, to join the growing list of one hit wonders. Exordium and Terminus.

276

BAD MOON RISING

20 September 1969, for three weeks

Creedence Clearwater Revival *Liberty LBF 15230*

Writer: John Fogerty
Producer: John Fogerty

The second of three consecutive number two hits in the United States gave Creedence Clearwater Revival their only number one hit in Britain. The band was led in all but name by John Fogerty (born 28 May 1945), their main writer and singer. His brother Tom (born 9 November 1941), Doug Clifford (born 24 April 1945) and Stu Cook (born 25 April 1945), made up the band, which for a couple of years was the tightest and most exciting rock band in the world. Their first hit in the UK, and their most successful song worldwide was the saga of the Mississippi paddlesteamer *Proud Mary*. That made number eight in England in the summer of 1969, and a version by Checkmates Ltd (no relation to Emile Ford's Checkmates) also hit our Top 30 six months later. By that time **Bad Moon Rising** had reached number one, helped considerably by the superb B-side **Lodi** which was never listed on the chart but which all the same gained a lot of airplay and generated significant sales.

Eight more chart hits by mid-1971 completed Creedence's singles successes in Britain, by which time the band had split up rather acrimoniously. By then they also created one of the best rock albums of all time 'Cosmo's Factory', which included a compelling 11-minute version of **I Heard It Through The Grapevine**. John Fogerty went on to have a few country flavoured hits in America under the name Blue Ridge Rangers, but Creedence Clearwater Revival was his masterpiece.

277

JE T'AIME . . . MOI NON PLUS

11 October 1969, for one week

Jane Birkin and Serge Gainsbourg *Major Minor MM 645*

Writer: Serge Gainsbourg
Producer: Jack Baverstock

In the week ending Saturday 11 October 1969, two events occurred that persuaded the older generation in Britain that

278 Bobbie Gentry

283 Simon and Garfunkel

272 Beatles/John and Yoko

275 Zager and Evans

life was sinking irretrievably into the bottomless pit. Firstly, the 50p piece was introduced, to highlight the inflation that decimilisation of the coinage would cause, and secondly this obscene record reached the very top of the charts.

Mind you, it had everything going for it. A very strong tune (which charted under the name **Love At First Sight** by a group called Sounds Nice when the BBC banned the original), a beautiful English girl, last seen romping naked with David Hemmings in a photographic studio in the film *Blow Up*, and for the first but not the last time on record, grunts and groans sounding remarkably like a gentleman and a lady entwined in mutual passion. Of course, it sold like hot cakes, and the only astonishing thing was that Fontana, who originally issued the record, were overcome with a burst of morality and deleted it when it was at number two in the charts. Major Minor, who had no such scruples, took over the master and were rewarded by a number one hit in the record's second week on their label.

Birkin and Gainsbourg never repeated their chart success and go down in the books as one hit wonders. The record was however re-issued in 1974 on the Antic label and enjoyed a further 9 weeks on the chart. This makes the record the only number one hit to chart on three different labels, and in racking up a total of 34 weeks on the chart, Birkin and Gainsbourg achieved the longest total chart run of any one hit wonder. Add the weeks achieved by Sounds Nice and Judge Dread, who subtly revived the song in 1975, and only 9 songs in chart history have been on the chart longer than **Je T'Aime**, the *Emmanuelle* of the British charts.

278

I'LL NEVER FALL IN LOVE AGAIN

18 October 1969, for one week

Bobby Gentry *Capitol CL 15606*

Writers: Burt Bacharach and Hal David
Producer: Kelso Herston

From the musical *Promises Promises* came yet another number one by Bacharach and David. There have been three different songs with this title in the charts, one of which was written by Lonnie Donegan and was the first of three consecutive number twos for Tom Jones in 1967. The third was Johnny Ray's last hit, which reached number 26 in 1959.

Bobbie Gentry first came to prominence in the summer of 1967 when her enigmatic saga of a deep South deep six **Ode To Billy Joe** took over the US airways and was top of the American charts. Surprisingly, it only reached number 13 in UK, and it was almost exactly 2 years later when this, her second hit, restored her to the charts. For a brief period Bobbie Gentry was very hot, as a duet with Glen Campbell of the Everly Brothers' number one **All I Have To Do Is Dream** reached number three at the turn of the year. Her solo follow-up was another Bacharach-David song, **Raindrops Keep Falling On My Head** but she was drowned by the bigger selling efforts of Sacha Distel and B J Thomas. On 6 March 1970, her duet single enjoyed its final week on the charts and the next week, her version of **Raindrops** finished its chart run. And that was the last the British charts have seen of Bobbie Gentry.

She has not been on the breadline, however, having married Las Vegas millionaire Bill Hurrah.

279

SUGAR SUGAR

25 October 1969, for eight weeks

The Archies *RCA 1872*

Writers: Jeff Barry and Andy Kim
Producer: Jeff Barry

Only two weeks after Jane Birkin and Serge Gainsbourg reached the top, in due course to become the most successful one-hit-wonder act ever, the Archies took over the number one position for 8 weeks, never to follow it up and thus earned for themselves the record of being the one-hit-wonder act that stayed longest at number one.

The Archies were not a real group. They were session musicians used on a children's TV cartoon series, *The Archies*, so they were never seen by the fans. Lead singer was a man called Ron Dante, who like England's Tony Burrows (see no. 281), was a session vocalist much in demand and who simultaneously was featured as lead singer on a hit by The Cuff-Links called **Tracy** which reached number four. Producer Jeff Barry wrote the song with Andy Kim, whose own hit single **Rock Me Gently** reached number two in 1974. Kim thus became one of more than 150 acts who have reached number two without ever having a number one hit, but for him at least immortality is assured by his writing efforts on **Sugar Sugar**.

280

TWO LITTLE BOYS

20 December 1969, for six weeks

Rolf Harris *Columbia DB 8630*

Writers: Theodore F Morse and Edward Madden
Producer: Martin Clarke

Anita, Emmylou, Jet, Major, Max, Rahni, Richard, Rolf and Ronnie are the acts that have helped make Harris one of the most widely used surnames in British chart history. Jet and Rolf are the only two Harrises to reach number one, and a more diverse pair of acts in British chart history would be hard to find. Sam The Sham and The Singing Nun perhaps.

Rolf Harris' recording of the 1903 song of the two boys, Joe and Jack, who share horses at all possible moments in their lives, from nursery to battlefield, was a perfect Christmas number one. The bearded Australian has always been considered something of a joke by pop fans, which is really a little unfair. Not even Rolf himself would say that he has a magnificent voice or a brilliant stage act, but he is very good at putting a song across. His first hit, **Tie Me Kangaroo Down Sport** in 1960, was pure Aussie hokum, but **Sun Arise** in 1962 was a fine pop record. His flop of 1963, **Fijian Girl**, sounds so like Adam and the Ants' **Prince Charming** (see no. 486) that you might suspect Rolf of being 18 years ahead of his time.

After **Two Little Boys**, Rolf Harris seems to have forsaken the charts, making him one of only ten acts (apart from the one-hit-wonders) who have failed to follow up a number one.

281

LOVE GROWS (WHERE MY ROSMARY GOES)

31 January 1970, for five weeks

Edison Lighthouse *Bell 1091*

Writers: Barry Mason and Tony Macaulay
Producer: Tony Macaulay

In 1970 if you wanted a hit record, you got Tony Burrows to sing lead. The king of the session singers, Burrows sang lead with the hastily assembled group, Edison Lighthouse, as well as on the Pipkins' Top 10 hit of the spring **Gimme Dat Ding**, and various other singles. **Love Grows** raced to the number one position in its second week on the chart, which was at the time the quickest rise by an act new to the charts. Seeing that Edison Lighthouse only existed in the studio, it was a tribute to the song itself, and to the usual faultless Tony Macaulay production, that it climbed so quickly. It was in brief, a perfect light pop song, and it sold accordingly.

A group of four anonymous-looking people, none of them Tony Burrows, was put together and given the name Edison Lighthouse to cash in on the success of **Love Grows**. It didn't work, because the voice was wrong. One brief week at number 49 with a song called **It's Up To You Petula** at the beginning of 1971 is all that stands between Edison Lighthouse and the stigma of being a one-hit wonder.

282

WAND'RIN' STAR

7 March 1970, for three weeks

Lee Marvin *Paramount PARA 3004*

Writers: Alan Jay Lerner and Frederick Loewe
Producer: Tom Mack

From the film version of *Paint Your Wagon* came Lee Marvin's only hit single, and among the three hundred and more number one hitmakers, he can readily claim with Telly Savalas to have the worst singing voice of them all. The movie also starred Clint Eastwood (arguably an even worse singer than Lee Marvin) and for a couple of weeks, Clint's version of **I Talk To The Trees**, which was the B-side of the single, was listed on the chart. By the time the song reached number one, however, the Eastwood side was no longer listed, and he missed the chance of adding yet another achievement to his long list of Hollywood successes, from *Rawhide* on TV to movies like *Every Which Way But Loose* and *Where Eagles Dare*.

Paint Your Wagon (the second Lerner-Loewe musical to provide a British number one) also starred Ray Walston, who like Eastwood and Marvin (Frank Ballinger in the cop series 'M Squad') had a long running TV success in the title role of *My Favourite Martian*. Walston also appeared in the film *South Pacific* in which his rendition of **Bloody Mary** helped to keep the soundtrack album at number one in Britain's LP charts for over a year.

283

BRIDGE OVER TROUBLED WATER

28 March 1970, for three weeks

Simon and Garfunkel *CBS 4790*

Writer: Paul Simon

Producers: Paul Simon, Arthur Garfunkel and Roy Halee

The song consistently voted Favourite Record Of All Time by readers of magazines and listeners to radio stations is Paul Simon's superlative **Bridge Over Troubled Water**. Paul Simon (born 13 October 1942) and Arthur Garfunkel (born 5 November 1942) worked together since they were kids together in New York, and had a fifties pop hit in America **Hey Schoolgirl** under the name Tom and Jerry.

Their first hit as Simon and Garfunkel in America was **Sounds Of Silence** which reached number one there, but was covered in Britain by the Bachelors and failed to make the charts. The follow-up **Homeward Bound** gave them their first British hit, and it was followed by influential LPs and singles which oddly failed to achieve high chart placings. Their soundtrack for the film *The Graduate* was a landmark in the use of rock in the movies, and their final album, 'Bridge Over Troubled Water' is probably the only LP consistently mentioned in the same breath as 'Sgt. Pepper's Lonely Hearts Club Band' as one of the great albums of rock.

The title track, featuring Art Garfunkel's singing at its very best, was the biggest hit, but **The Boxer** was another hit from the album. **El Condor Pasa** was also covered by Julie Felix, giving her her biggest hit. After the LP, the pair broke up. Art Garfunkel went into films (*Catch 22, Carnal Knowledge*) and solo recording success (see nos 379 and 436). Paul Simon recorded high quality albums, occasionally coming up with a brilliant song worthy of his heyday. In 1981 they reunited for a brilliantly successful concert in New York's Central Park in front of 500,000 people, and subsequently announced the permanent re-formation of Simon and Garfunkel.

284

ALL KINDS OF EVERYTHING

18 April 1970, for two weeks

Dana *Rex R 11054*

Writers: Denny Lindsay and Jackie Smith

Producer: Ray Horricks

The 1970 Eurovision Song Contest was won by Ireland, and the diminutive Dana became the first person to take a foreign entry in the Eurovision Song Contest to number one in Britain. The trick has subsequently been repeated by Abba (1974), Johnny Logan (1980) and by Nicole (1982), but before 1970, the highest a foreign Eurovision Song had climbed in the British charts was 17, by Italy's Gigliola Cinquetti in 1964 with her **Non Ho L'eta Per Amarti**.

After the success of **All Kinds Of Everything** a song very much along the lines of **My Favourite Things** from *The Sound Of Music* – her follow-up, called **Who Put The Lights Out** climbed to number 14. She obviously took her time finding the answer to the question because it was 4 more years before she hit the charts again, this time with a new label (Dick Leahy's GTO) and a new tougher image. Two Top 10 hits followed including a Christmas hit that climbed to number four in 1975, but further chart success has been elusive, despite a 1982 recording of Bobby Darin's **Dream Lover** (see no. 87) which nearly made it. She is still a regular face on television and has carved out a profitable career with her smiling, innocent face and crystal-clear voice. Not ingredients for chart action perhaps, but an excellent recipe for the BBC Saturday night audience.

285

SPIRIT IN THE SKY

2 May 1970, for two weeks

Norman Greenbaum *Reprise RS 20885*

Writer: Norman Greenbaum

Producer: Eric Jacobson

A song by an unknown New England Jew, with arguably the least commercial name among all the number one hitmakers (possibly excepting the St Winifred's Girls School Choir), praising Jesus and telling the world he was 'gonna recommend you to the spirit in the sky' was one of the most unlikely number ones in the history of the British charts. The only unsurprising thing was that Greenbaum proved to be a one hit wonder.

Born in Massachusetts in November 1952, Norman Greenbaum (it is, of course, his real name) put together a good time jug band, one step beyond Lovin' Spoonful, called Dr West's Medicine Show and Junk Band, which astonished America with the most unlikely Top 50 hit of 1966, **The Eggplant That Ate Chicago**. The group split up in 1967, but Greenbaum came up with **Spirit In The Sky** with its hypnotic reverberating guitar effect riff and became a one hit wonder all over again. The record was, accidentally, the start of the

'God Rock' boom, which included *Godspell* and *Jesus Christ Superstar* as well as singles like **Put Your Hand In The Hand** and **Amazing Grace**. *Jesus Christ Superstar* even featured the guitar effect on some tracks, consciously borrowed from **Spirit In The Sky**. Norman Greenbaum himself was last heard of goat-breeding in Petaluma.

286

BACK HOME

16 May 1970, for three weeks

The England World Cup Squad *Pye 7N 17920*

Writers: Bill Martin and Phil Coulter
Producers: Bill Martin and Phil Coulter

Probably because the England team song was written and produced by two Scots, Bill Martin and Phil Coulter, England failed to bring the World Cup **Back Home**. They almost failed to bring captain Bobby Moore back home, when a misunderstanding arose as to the whereabouts of a bracelet in a Colombian hotel. However, all was eventually well until they started kicking a football.

The England World Cup Squad members who sang on **Back Home** were, of course, the unsuccessful 1970 squad rather than the successful 1966 squad. Those people in both squads, like Bobby Moore, Geoff Hurst, Martin Peters, Nobby Stiles and the Charlton brothers, share the ludicrous record of having a World Cup Winner's medal and a number one hit. Not even Rod Stewart (Brentford FC) or Julio Iglesias (Real Madrid) can equal that.

When the 1982 squad took their single **This Time (We'll Get It Right)** to number two, the England World Cup Squad removed themselves from the one hit wonder list after 12 years of stigma.

287

YELLOW RIVER

6 June 1970, for one week

Christie *CBS 4911*

Writer: Jeff Christie
Producer: Mike Smith

Yellow River was written for the Tremeloes but they turned it down, so Jeff Christie decided that the only way he could get the song recorded, was to do it himself. He put together a three-piece group consisting of himself, a brother of a Trem, Mike Blakely, and Chris Elms and managed to persuade Mike Smith, the Tremeloes' producer (see no. 233) to record them. This was a good move, as Smith had already produced five number ones, including the only four UK-produced CBS number ones to date (nos. 233, 242, 243 and 263). The success of **Yellow River** meant that from the middle of 1967 until the beginning of 1972, almost 5 years, Mike Smith was the only British producer to come up with a number one for CBS, and he did it five times.

Perhaps it is not surprising that a group put together so hurriedly to record rather than to perform, did not last long. The follow-up to **Yellow River** was **San Bernadino**, a song very similar to its chart-topping predecessor. It reached number seven. But that was the end of the story, apart from one week at number 47 over a year later with a song called **Iron Horse**. All the same, it might have given Christie some satisfaction that this last week on the charts was some eight months after the last Tremeloes hit had dropped off the chart. They should never have turned down **Yellow River**.

288

IN THE SUMMERTIME

13 June 1970, for seven weeks

Mungo Jerry *Dawn DNX 2502*

Writer: Ray Dorset
Producer: Barry Murray

1970 was a year in which three songs stayed at number one for 6 weeks (something that did not happen at all in 1980 or 1981), but the longest stay at number one was by a group who were completely unknown until they stole the show at the Hollywood Festival (Newcastle, not Los Angeles) in the early summer of 1970 and found themselves with a million seller on their hands.

Mungo Jerry were named after one of the Cats in T S Eliot's verses, later popularised by Andrew Lloyd Webber's musical. Their leader and only permanent fixture during their years of chart success in the early seventies was a gap-toothed singer with a bush of curly hair and a permanent smile, called Ray Dorset. He wrote Mungo Jerry's material and controlled the destiny of the group, which for a year or two at least was a very profitable destiny. **In The Summertime** was the anthem of the youth of Britain in what was admittedly not a very summery summer, weatherwise. There

Above **286 The England World Cup Squad**

293 Jimi Hendrix

Above left to right **308 New Seekers, 298 T Rex, 290 Smokey Robinson and the Miracles**

Left **305 Rod Stewart,** *Above* **303 Diana Ross**

have been four number one hits with the word 'summer' in the title, but the others hit the top in the spring or the autumn (see nos. 90, 148 and 427). There were other number ones about summer (excluding **Just Walkin' In The Rain** and **The Day The Rains Came**) which managed to hit in the right season, songs like **Sunny Afternoon, San Francisco** and **Barbados**, but **In The Summertime** remains the most successful and most instantly recognisable summer song.

289

THE WONDER OF YOU

1 August 1970, for six weeks

Elvis Presley *RCA 1974*

Writer: Baker Knight
Producers: Elvis Presley and Felton Jarvis, arranged by Glen D Hardin

Elvis' penultimate UK number one (his 16th) took place 5 years after his previous chart-topper, **Crying In The Chapel** (see no. 197). A lot had happened in those 5 years. Elvis' career had slipped to its lowest point (1967) with the quality of his output on both wax and celluloid below mediocre at best. Then in 1968 he began a major comeback that was to continue until his death in 1977. He recorded songs that were not featured in abysmal films, and more important, gave up making the abysmal films. He starred in his own excellent TV spectacular and returned to live concerts in Las Vegas in 1969. His records began to sell again, on merit. In June 1969 **In The Ghetto** made number two in Britain – his first to get higher than number 13 for 3 years. In November he was very unlucky to miss number one with **Suspicious Minds**, one of the best singles of his entire career, although this track did bring him back to the US top spot for the first time since **Good Luck Charm** in 1962. **The Wonder Of You** was the single that did the trick for him in Britain and it did so in style, staying at the top for no less than 6 weeks. It was recorded live at the International Hotel, Las Vegas as part of 4 days of recording of Presley concerts there from 16-19 February 1970. The Joe Guercio Orchestra, the Sweet Inspirations (a black girl vocal group), The Imperials Quartet (a white vocal group) and Millie Kirkham (vocals) were all with Elvis during these shows and key rhythm section players were James Burton (guitar), Glen D Hardin (piano), Jerry Scheff (bass) and Ronnie Tutt (drums). **The Wonder Of You** was written by Baker Knight and was originally a hit in 1959 and again in 1964 for Ray Peterson in the US, and for Ronnie Hilton and Peterson in the UK in 1959. On Elvis' version Glen D Hardin (a former Cricket) is credited with the arrangement of the track.

290

TEARS OF A CLOWN

12 September 1970, for one week

Smokey Robinson and the Miracles *Tamla Motown TMG 745*

Writers: Henry Cosby, William Robinson and Stevie Wonder
Producers: Henry Cosby and Smokey Robinson

During the sixties William 'Smokey' Robinson had written several songs that had become pop standards, including the miraculous double **My Guy** and **My Girl**, but he had never enjoyed a number one. His only UK Top 10 hit, the 1969 winner **Tracks Of My Tears**, was in fact a re-release of a 1965 American smash. Tamla Motown executive John Marshall, noticing that the group's career needed a stimulus, decided to follow up on the 'Tears' motif. He issued **Tears of a Clown**, a track from the 1967 album 'Make It Happen'. Not only had this clearly commercial cut been lost on an LP, it had been buried at the end of side two. Marshall's choice was a stroke of genius. It went to number one in Britain and as a consequence was put out in America, where it duplicated the feat, becoming the group's first number one there as well. Ironically, this peak came near the end of the act's life, as Smokey and the Miracles parted in 1972.

Tears of a Clown was re-issued and enjoyed a second Top 40 run in 1976. The Beat took their version to the Top 10 in early 1980.

Stevie Wonder, Motown's most successful male vocalist, did not have any of the first 500 number ones as a solo artist. His four number twos were more than any other frustrated act had logged. However, he did get there as co-writer of **Tears of a Clown**, and in duet with Paul McCartney, another person who failed to achieve a solo number one.

291

BAND OF GOLD

19 September 1970, for six weeks

Freda Payne *Invictus INV 502*

Writers: Ron Dunbar and Edith Wayne
Producers: Brian Holland, Lamont Dozier, and Eddie Holland

If all the people who bought this single did so because they related to the personal difficulties expressed in the lyric, Britain would have experienced a severe drop in population during the seventies. Quite simply put, the Freda Payne character and her husband couldn't consummate their marriage, and no matter how hard the man tried, he could never perform properly. 'I wait in the darkness of my lonely room', Payne pined. Indeed.

Invictus was formed by ex-Motown songwriter-producers Brian Holland, Lamont Dozier and Eddie Holland. It got off to a roaring start with **Give Me Just a Little More Time** by the Chairmen of the Board, a top three hit in both Britain and America, and **Band of Gold**, which spent six weeks at the top of the charts. (A previous American release of Freda's, **The Unhooked Generation**, had gone unnoticed in the UK). This great pop success caused Payne to concentrate on singles for two more years, during which time she released the top ten US anti-war hit **Bring the Boys Home** and the UK charters **Deeper and Deeper** and **Cherish What Is Dear to You**. She had previously worked in both jazz and theatre, and the late seventies again found her on the stage in America. The Invictus label itself could not maintain its momentum and folded.

Band Of Gold holds a special place in the heart of one of this book's authors. It was the first single he reviewed for Rolling Stone and, coincidentally, number one when he first arrived in Great Britain.

292

WOODSTOCK

31 October 1970, for three weeks

Matthews' Southern Comfort *Uni UNS 526*

Writer: Joni Mitchell
Producer: Ian Matthews

It was in a hotel bar in Manila that one of the co-authors of this tome heard the most exquisite version of Joni Mitchell's **Woodstock** by a tiny Filipino singer with nothing but a large guitar for accompaniment. Sad to say, she seems to have been a no-hit wonder (in the UK anyway) which is just one degree worse than the band put together by Ian Matthews when he left the folk-rock band Fairport Convention.

Woodstock is the story in song of the Woodstock music festival, the most successful, most populated and most widely publicised rock festival in history. The performers included Jimi Hendrix, Who, Joe Cocker, Jefferson Airplane, John Sebastian just free of Lovin' Spoonful, and the newly-formed Crosby, Stills and Nash. At the time, Joni Mitchell was close to the 'supergroup' trio, and was at Woodstock with them. From the lyrics of her song, you would hardly know it.

Matthews' Southern Comfort, originally the title of Ian Matthews' first solo album after leaving Fairport Convention, comprised at this time Ian Matthews, Gordon Huntley, Ramon Duffy, Andy Leigh, Carl Barnwell and Mark Griffiths. By 1971, Matthews had left the band to go solo and without setting the world alight he has remained a respected performer on both sides of the Atlantic. Few people will remember that **Woodstock** was number one when Charles de Gaulle died, on 9 November, 1970 at the less often celebrated in song venue of Colombey-les-deux-Eglises.

293

VOODOO CHILE

21 November 1970, for one week

Jimi Hendrix Experience *Track 2095 001*

Writer: Jimi Hendrix
Producer: Jimi Hendrix

A track from Jimi Hendrix's 'Electric Ladyland' gave him a number one hit 2 months after his death from suffocation. James Marshall Hendrix was born on 27 November 1942 in Seattle, Washington, and by the early 1960's was establishing himself as a brilliant if unpredictable guitarist.

In 1966, Chas Chandler, who had played bass with the Animals, became his manager and brought Hendrix to Britain. There he formed a three piece group, the Jimi Hendrix Experience, which featured Noel Redding on bass and Mitch Mitchell on drums. He was immediately recognised by his fellow-guitarists as a performer of genius, and his first single **Hey Joe** hit the charts in the first week of 1967.

His big singles year was 1967, when he had three Top 10

hits, but 1968 and 1969 put him in the superstar bracket as an album artist and for his live shows, which were erratic, vulgar and brilliant. The bond was crumbling by late 1969, but he came through with a masterful performance at Woodstock with his new band – The Band Of Gypsies. That broke up only a month or two later, and in the last year of his troubled life, personal, financial and musical disintegration set in. His last major live performance, at the Isle of Wight Festival in August 1970, was poorly received and when he died, choking on his own vomit, on 18 September 1970, the world lost a man who had already destroyed his own talent.

294

I HEAR YOU KNOCKIN'

28 November 1970, for six weeks

Dave Edmunds *MAM 1*

Writers: Dave Bartholomew and Pearl King
Producer: Dave Edmunds

Dave Edmunds has his own studio in South Wales, Rockfield, and one of the first productions at the studio was his own version of the Smiley Lewis 1955 soul hit **I Hear You Knockin'**, written by Fats Domino's co-writer Dave Bartholomew and Pearl King. John Lennon was asked about Bob Dylan's album 'New Morning' by Jann Wenner of Rolling Stone, and replied, 'It's alright, but I'd sooner have **I Hear You Knockin'** by Dave Edmunds. It's top in England now'.

Practically everybody agreed with John Lennon (as usual). Oddly though it was over two years before Edmunds followed up **I Hear You Knockin'** and now he had moved away from 50's rock to the Phil Spector sound. Two Ronettes-type productions put Edmunds back in the Top 10 in 1973, but his bursts of activity and his chart success remained very sporadic until 1979, when he teamed up with the Brinsley Schwartz bassist and Johnny Cash stepson-in-law, Nick Lowe, on a series of hits, beginning with the Elvis Costello song, **Girls Talk**, which reached number four in the summer of 1979. It is more than 13 years since Dave Edmunds was a member of the instrumental trio Love Sculpture, who made number five with **Sabre Dance**. But at last he has established himself.

295

GRANDAD

9 January 1971, for three weeks

Clive Dunn *Columbia DB 8726*

Writers: Herbie Flowers and Kenny Pickett
Producers: John Cameron and Clive Dunn.

10 January 1971 was the warmest day ever recorded in London in January, so nobody needed a number one hit you could dance frenetically to. Which was lucky, because Clive Dunn's **Grandad** was anything but a disco workout number.

Clive Dunn first collected his 'old man' image in the very popular and very funny TV series *Dad's Army* in which he played Jonesy, the local butcher and Africa wars veteran whose age in no way diminished his eagerness to get at the Huns. The song **Grandad** was written for him by Herbie Flowers, at that time a member of Blue Mink, and now a member of Sky, and Kenny Pickett. It moved into the charts on the day that **I Hear You Knocking** reached number one, but despite its perfect sentimentality for Christmas, failed to knock Dave Edmunds off his perch until the New Year. Clive Dunn then enjoyed 3 weeks of glory before disappearing forever, the fifth one-hit wonder of the 1970's.

296

MY SWEET LORD

30 January 1971, for five weeks

George Harrison *Apple R 5884*

Writer: George Harrison
Producers: George Harrison and Phil Spector

George Harrison's first solo effort after the break-up of the Beatles was a triple album, 'All Things Must Pass'. The first single from the album was **My Sweet Lord**, which took Harrison to number one in only his second week on the chart as a solo performer. The album was undoubtedly Harrison's masterpiece, although he was certainly helped by the musicians on the album who included Ringo Starr, Klaus Voorman (who also played on John Lennon's **Imagine** and Nilsson's **Without You**), Billy Preston, Eric Clapton, Dave Mason, Gary Brooker, Bobby Keyes and Carl Radle among others. The world seemed perfect for George Harrison.

However, the vast success of **My Sweet Lord** was soured by the fact that the writers of the Chiffons' hit **He's So Fine** successfully sued George Harrison for breach of copyright, and what is more, Bill Martin and Phil Coulter rightfully demanded and got royalties for the track **It's Johnny's Birthday** on the Apple Jam third LP of the three record set, which was to the tune of Cliff Richard's 1968 chart-topper **Congratulations**. A track on a later Harrison album **This Song**, wryly commented on the dangers of breach of another writer's copyright.

Weep not for George Harrison, however. You can't write **Something** and not have a regular and substantial royalty income. Furthermore, he has now become an extraordinarily successful film producer with Monty Python's *Life Of Brian* one of his most profitable movie ventures. And he remains a writer and performer of stature.

297

BABY JUMP

6 March 1971, for two weeks

Mungo Jerry *Dawn DNX 2505*

Writer: Ray Dorset
Producer: Barry Murray

Slowly but surely, Mungo Jerry's follow-up to **In The Summertime** climbed to number one, to put them on the very short list of acts whose first two hits both topped the charts. In fact, when **Baby Jump** reached number one, only Gerry and the Pacemakers had previously reached number one with their first two releases although now John Travolta and Olivia Newton-John have equalled this record.

Baby Jump was nowhere near as exciting as the brilliant **In The Summertime** and later Mungo Jerry records also failed to get close to the standard set by their first hit, the biggest British hit of 1970. They carried on having chart hits until 1974, including two more Top 10 hits and one more record with a 13 word title. No chart hit has had more than 13 words in the title, so **You Don't Have To Be In The Army To Fight In The War** gave Mungo Jerry one more little souvenir of their hit-making days.

Ray Dorset's hit-making days are not yet over. As writer of Kelly Marie's 1980 number one, **Feels Like I'm In Love** (see no. 466), Dorset is still very involved in the industry and has joined the select few who have written number one hits for themselves and for someone else – the mark of the truly successful singer-songwriter.

298

HOT LOVE

20 March 1971, for six weeks

T Rex *Fly BUG 6*

Writer: Marc Bolan
Producer: Tony Visconti

The transformation of Marc Bolan from the whimsical fairy-tale songweaver of Tyrannosaurus Rex into the hard-rocking electrified bopper of T Rex caused almost as many shouts of 'sell out' as the electrification of Bob Dylan had done a few years earlier. In fact, as with Bob Dylan, there was a logical progression from one to the other. Marc Bolan was born Mark Feld in London on 30 July 1947. In 1967, after working as an occasional male model and sometime member of John's Children, a marginally successful flower power group, he formed Tyrannosaurus Rex with Steve Took. Their first album 'My People Were Fair and had Sky In Their Hair', had liner notes by John Peel and contained acoustically rhythmical and lyrically banal songs. Two more similar albums appeared in 1968 and 1969, but in 1970 Steve Took left.

Marc Bolan brought in Micky Finn (born 3 June 1947) as a replacement, and went electric. The rhythms were the same as ever, but the lyrics became more basic – and much better – and the electricity flowed out to the fans. The first electric single **Ride A White Swan** reached number two, and the follow-up was **Hot Love**. The teeny-boppers, who had been looking for a successor to the recently split Beatles, turned T Rex into the hottest group of the early seventies.

299

DOUBLE BARREL

1 May 1971, for two weeks

Dave and Ansil Collins *Technique TE 901*

Writer: Winston Riley
Producer: Winston Riley

The Jamaican duo of Dave and Ansil Collins came from nowhere in the spring of 1971 to hit with only the second West Indian reggae record to top the British charts, 2 years after the first – Desmond Dekker's **Israelites** (see no. 269). There was considerable confusion about who they were and how to spell Ansil (Ansel? Ansell? Ansill?), but their anonymity made no difference to the record's success. Apart from its British sales, **Double Barrel** also climbed to number 22 in the American charts, to become one of the first reggae hits over there.

The early success of reggae in Britain in the first years of the 1970's was largely due to the popularity of the music among a growing section of white youth – the skinheads. The early basic sounds of reggae were too limited to appeal to the general record-buying public, but the enthusiasm of a comparatively small number of fans made sure that a few reggae records hit the charts. This in turn led to a greater interest in reggae among non-West Indian record producers and record company executives. Before long, the British music industry had created a smoother reggae sound that became the basis of hundreds of hits. By then, the skinheads had moved on to other things.

300

KNOCK THREE TIMES

15 May 1971, for five weeks

Dawn *Bell 1146*

Writers: Irwin Levine and L. Russell Brown
Producers: Dave Appell and the Tokens

Tony Orlando, born in New York City on 3 April 1944, was only 17 when his song **Bless You** made the Top 10 late in 1961. The song had been his second hit single in America, but the first, **Halfway To Paradise** was covered in Britain by Billy Fury, who took it to number three and left Orlando out in the cold. One more small American hit followed **Bless You** at the end of 1961, ironically titled, **Happy Times Are Here To Stay**, but by his eighteenth birthday, Tony Orlando was a has-been. By 1970, Orlando had switched to the business side of show business, and was working for a music publishing subsidiary of Columbia Records, April Blackwood.

Here, Hank Medress of the Tokens (**The Lion Sleeps Tonight** – number 11 at the beginning of 1962), now working as a record producer at Bell, asked Tony Orlando to do a vocal on a demo of a song Irwin Levine and Toni Wine had written, a song called **Candida**. Orlando did the demo, girls' voices were added and the demo was issued as a single by a group called Dawn. It was a huge hit, in America as well as in UK where it reached number nine, and Tony Orlando found himself to be an overnight sensation for the second time. The follow-up was called **Knock Three Times**, and it climbed eight places higher than **Candida**, probably because Orlando ironed all the soul out of his voice to produce a sound that became the prototype for Abba and all the other boy/girl vocal groups of the 1970's.

301

CHIRPY CHIRPY CHEEP CHEEP

19 June 1971, for five weeks

Middle of the Road *RCA 2047*

Writer: Lally Scott
Producers: Giacomo Tosti and Ignacio Greco

Middle of the Road were very unlikely hit makers. They were a group of four Scots, Ken Andrew, Eric and Ian Lewis and Sally Carr, who performed with reasonable success in Europe but who were completely unknown in Britain. They had originally concentrated on Latin-American music and were for a time known as Los Caracas, but it was as Middle of the Road that they recorded a song they had heard in Italy. The record was released in Europe, and became a big hit in Spain and Belgium, where the rougher-edged versions of the same song by composer Lally Scott and by Mac and Katie Kissoon failed to attract much attention.
attention.

It was released in UK at the end of May 1971, and within 3 weeks was at number one, where it stayed for 5 weeks. After that hit, Britain took them a little more seriously, and further hits followed. The follow-up **Tweedle Dee Tweedle Dum** reached number two. Had it made number one it would have joined **Chirpy Chirpy Cheep Cheep** as one of the very few songs with nonsense titles to reach number one. As it is, **Chirpy Chirpy Cheep Cheep** was the fourth and last nonsense title to get to the top, after **Do Wah Diddy Diddy, Mony Mony** and **Ob-la-di Ob-la-da**. Their third Top 10 hit had yet another nonsense title, **Soley Soley**, and it was not until their fourth chart hit **Sacramento** that they ventured into a recognised language. But by then the hits were coming to an end.

302

GET IT ON

24 July 1971, for four weeks

T Rex *Fly BUG 10*

Writer: Marc Bolan
Producer: Tony Visconti

T Rex's second number one was a track from their amazingly successful album 'Electric Warrior'. Marc Bolan and Micky

Finn, who was billed as providing 'vocal percussion', were joined by Steve Currie, Bill Legend and Burt Collins, with Howard Kaylan and Mark Volman on back-up vocals, to give a sound that was never bettered on subsequent albums. Howard Kaylan and Mark Volman were ex-members of the highly successful American group, the Turtles, whose two British Top 10 hits didn't match their success in their homeland. In America, they had eight Top 20 hits, including one number one, in a 4 year period from 1965 to 1969.

Get It On was T Rex's only major hit in the States. There it was titled **Bang A Gong**, and it made the Top 20. But like Slade, Sweet, Mud and even the Bay City Rollers, T Rex was essentially a British act, tailored to the British fans by whom Marc Bolan was adored for the first 3 years of the 1970's.

303

I'M STILL WAITING

21 August 1971, for four weeks

Diana Ross *Tamla Motown TMG 781*

Writer: Deke Richards
Producers: Deke Richards and Hal Davis

When Diana Ross and the Supremes parted company at the turn of the decade, Motown hoped it would have two star attractions instead of one, but faced the prospect both might fade. Ross' debut disc, **Reach Out and Touch** was not a good start. Intended to entreat parents of drug addicts to be understanding to their children, it was too vague to inspire the mass audience and was only a minor hit. Diana's extended reading of Marvin Gaye and Tammi Terrell's 1967 classic **Ain't No Mountain High Enough** provided her with the smash she needed. But after the next hit, **Remember Me**, there was no obvious follow-up and nothing new awaiting release.

BBC Radio 1 breakfast show DJ and self-confessed Diana Ross freak Tony Blackburn told Tamla Motown he would make the album track **I'm Still Waiting** his Record of the Week, playing it every morning for five days, if the company would release it as a single. The label did, Blackburn did, and the result was Tamla Motown's biggest UK seller to date.

The record was not a major hit in the United States, and when Ross performed it in her British act by request, she was baffled though pleased by the standing ovations greeting it. She had unknowingly found a personal anthem.

304

HEY GIRL DON'T BOTHER ME

18 September 1971, for three weeks

The Tams *Probe PRO 532*

Writer: Ray Whitley
Producer: Rick Hall

The Tams, five men from Atlanta Georgia, were already around 30 years old when they recorded **Hey Girl Don't Bother Me** in 1964. On the ABC label in America, it climbed to number 41 that year, to give them their fifth American hit, but in the UK it failed to make any impact. In 1968, the Tams' seventh American hit, **Be Young Be Foolish Be Happy** proved to be their last Stateside chart outing, but still nothing had hit the British charts. Then in 1970, Stateside re-issued **Be Young Be Foolish Be Happy** in UK, and for no obvious reason it reached number 32. Floyd Ashton (born 15 August 1933), Horace Key (born 13 April 1934), Charles Pope (born 7 August 1936) his brother Joseph Pope (born 6 November 1933) and Robert Smith (born 18 March 1936) were suddenly stars in Britain too.

In 1971, the newly independent Anchor Records acquired the rights to the American ABC catalogue, and re-issued **Hey Girl Don't Bother Me** on their Probe label. It soared to the very top, but proved to be the very last chart hit for the by now middle-aged Tams on either side of the Atlantic.

305

MAGGIE MAY

9 October 1971, for five weeks

Rod Stewart *Mercury 6052 097*

Writers: Rod Stewart and Martin Quittenton
Producer: Rod Stewart

The record that launched the solo career of the most successful British male vocalist of the 1970's was originally put out with the Tim Hardin song **Reason to Believe** as the A-side, and for two weeks that was the only side listed in the charts. On 18 September, airplay action and consumer reaction forced the BMRB chart compilers to flip the record, and 3 weeks later Rod Stewart had the first of his five number ones.

Rod Stewart was born in London of Scottish parents on 10 January 1945. In his teens Brentford FC offered him a place on their staff, but playing to 2000 people on Saturdays in West London had none of the lure of playing to tens of thousands of fans all over the world, so Stewart opted for a musical life. He joined Long John Baldry's Hoochie Coochie Men in 1964, which developed into Steampacket in 1965. At this time, Rod Stewart was also singing on countless budget price covers of hit singles, and occasionally issuing solo singles which sank without trace. He also reportedly played harmonica on Millie's 1964 hit **My Boy Lollipop**. From Steampacket he became a founder member of Shotgun Express in 1966, which included Peter Green, Mick Fleetwood and Beryl Marsden.

In 1967, he joined the Jeff Beck Group, and in 1969 moved with Ron Wood to the disintegrating Small Faces, who metamorphosed into the Faces. The album from which Rod's first solo hit came, 'Every Picture Tells a Story' did not feature the Faces, but only three months later his first hit with the Faces, **Cindy Incidentally** hit the charts.

306

COZ I LUV YOU

13 November 1971, for four weeks

Slade *Polydor 2058 155*

Writers: Noddy Holder and Jim Lea
Producer: Chas Chandler

Neville 'Noddy' Holder (born 15 June 1946), Jim Lea (born 14 June 1950), Dave Hill (born 4 April 1952) and Don Powell (born 10 September 1950) were four Wolverhampton lads who formed a group in the late sixties called the In-Betweens. They landed a recording contract with Columbia, and their first single, **You Better Run**, was produced by the man who was B Bumble and the Stingers, Kim Fowley. The great British public was unimpressed.

The group were called Ambrose Slade when Chas Chandler, looking for an act to follow Jimi Hendrix, found them. He dropped the Ambrose, gave them the full skinhead image, bovver boots and braces and all, and cut an LP with them. It was noticed, but the boys were not yet megastars. A single was issued, the only Slade single on Polydor that was not written by Noddy Holder and Jim Lea. It was called **Get Down And Get With It** (written by Bobby Marchan) and like the first chart single of many acts destined for greatness, it missed the Top 10 but stayed on the charts a long time, almost 4 months. By the time the follow-up was released, Slade were a hot property. The first of the misspelt hits, **Coz I Luv You**, banged and crashed its way to number one in its third week on the chart, and the most successful act of the early seventies was on its way.

307

ERNIE (THE FASTEST MILKMAN IN THE WEST)

11 December 1971, for four weeks

Benny Hill *Columbia DB 8833*

Writer: Benny Hill
Producer: Walter Ridley

Benny Hill is one of those rare comics who has had a hit with a comedy song. Ken Dodd and Des O'Connor, the two most successful comedians in chart terms, have never had a comedy hit record. Only Benny Hill and Billy Connolly (see no. 381) among funny men in the 1970's have had a number one hit.

Benny Hill, born on 21 January 1925, has had an erratic chart career. In 1961 he managed his first two chart hits, **Gather In The Mushrooms** and **Transistor Radio**. Neither reached the Top 10. Two years later the extremely weak **Harvest Of Love** touched the Top 20, but his best known comedy song of the 1960's **Pepys' Diary** never made the charts. After **Harvest Of Love**, Hill left the chart for 8 years. He still issued singles occasionally, and kept in the public eye with TV shows, films and so on, but the record buying fans moved on to the Beatles and their imitators.

At Christmas 1971, for no logical reason, his saga of a West Country milkman became the hit of the season and Benny Hill found himself at number one when sales are at their best. It was 10 years and 298 days since his chart debut, and at the time only Louis Armstrong (see no. 249) had taken longer to have a number one hit. Since then, Benny Hill has had continuing success as a comic, especially recently in America where he is something of a cult figure on the West Coast. But no more hits, which makes him one of ten acts (excluding the one-hit wonders) who failed to follow up a number one.

308

I'D LIKE TO TEACH THE WORLD TO SING

8 January 1972, for four weeks

The New Seekers *Polydor 2058 184*

Writers: Roger Cook, Roger Greenaway, William Backer, and Billy Davis

Producer: David Mackay for Leon Henry Productions

The most successful advertising jingle in history began as **I'd Like To Buy The World A Coke**, was transmogrified into **I'd Like To Teach The World To Sing** and gave the original jingle artists, the Hillside Singers, a big hit in America. It also gave the New Seekers their biggest hit on both sides of the Atlantic.

Advertising jingles had succeeded before. Georgie Fame's **Get Away** (see no. 219) was based on an advertisement for petrol. Cliff Adams' **Lonely Man Theme** in 1960 was probably the first chart hit advertising theme tune. It was the background music for the Strand cigarette advertisement whose punch line 'You're Never Alone With A Strand' became a national catchphrase, so much so that the advertisement featured in Cliff Richard's first starring movie *The Young Ones*. The advertisement also turned off the customers in such vast numbers that the Strand cigarette disappeared before cigarette advertising on TV went the same way.

The New Seekers were formed on the break-up of the Seekers (see nos. 188 and 206) by Seeker Keith Potger. They were Eve Graham (born 13 April 1943), Lyn Paul (born 16 February 1949), Peter Doyle (born 28 July 1949), Marty Kristian (born 27 May 1947) and Paul Layton (born 4 August 1947). The girls had been in an unsuccessful group called The Nocturnes before Potger created The New Seekers. The men, an Australian, a German and a Briton, took very much a back seat to the girls, on whose charms the group sold records by the bucketful. **I'd Like To Teach The World To Sing** was their third hit, and to follow up the corny commerciality of a Coke jingle, only one option was possible – they sang 1972's Song for Europe, **Beg, Steal Or Borrow**.

309

TELEGRAM SAM

5 February 1972, for two weeks

T Rex *T Rex 101*

Writer: Marc Bolan

Producer: Tony Visconti

T Rex's third consecutive number one came after a label change from Fly to EMI (where for this single only he was on the T Rex label). During the switchover period, Fly put out another track from the Electric Warrior album, **'Jeepster'** as an unauthorised single, and despite no promotion at all by T Rex, it went to number two.

The first EMI single was a track from the album 'The Slider', which had the same line-up as 'Electric Warrior' (see no. 302), but was not quite so successful either artistically or commercially. It had a better cover than the previous album, two grainy photographs of Marc Bolan taken by Ringo Starr. The songs themselves retained the same compulsive beat, a kind of pre-George McCrae disco beat, but the tunes were becoming boring and the lyrics were becoming less interesting the more that Marc Bolan was caught up in his own success.

310

SON OF MY FATHER

19 February 1972, for three weeks

Chicory Tip *CBS 7737*

Writers: Giorgio Moroder, Peter Bellotte and Michael Holm

Producers: Roger Easterby and Des Champ

The first UK produced CBS number one not to be produced by Mike Smith was a record co-written by a man destined to become one of the great producers of the disco sound, Giorgio Moroder (see nos 409 and 456). **Son Of My Father** was a song very much in the Europop idiom, and it was covered for the British market by a group as unknown then as they are again now, Chicory Tip.

The members of Chicory Tip were Peter Hewson on vocals, Rick Foster on guitar, Barry Mayger on bass and Brian Shearer on drums. They were playing in and around Maidstone in Kent when Roger Easterby discovered them and put them into the recording studio. The single is notable as the first chart-topper to feature a synthesizer, which was played on the session not by any members of Chicory Tip but by Chris Thomas, who engineered the session.

Son Of My Father sold a million but after two more Top 20 hits over the next 18 months, Chicory Tip disappeared from the charts. The group still plays together, no doubt hoping that Giorgio Moroder will write another hit for them.

311

WITHOUT YOU

11 March 1972, for five weeks

Nilsson *RCA 2165*

Writers: Pete Ham and Tom Evans

Producer: Richard Perry

Harry Nilsson, known officially merely as Nilsson, was born in Brooklyn, New York City, on 15 June 1941. He was in the late sixties and early seventies a respected and much covered singer-songwriter, but ironically the two songs for which he is best known were neither of them written by him.

His first hit, both in America and the UK, was the theme song of the Dustin Hoffman-Jon Voigt movie *Midnight Cowboy*. The song was called **Everybody's Talking**, written by Fred Neil, and it stayed 15 weeks on the British charts without ever climbing higher than number 23.

Without You is track one on side two of Nilsson's best album **Nilsson Schmilsson**, recorded in London in June 1971. It was written by two members of the Apple group Badfinger, who had played on George Harrison's 'All Things Must Pass' album and had scored the first of their three Top 10 hits with the theme tune from the Peter Sellers-Ringo Starr film, *The Magic Christian.* Also playing bass on **Without You** is Klaus Voorman, who designed the 'Revolver' album cover and was spoken of as a possible replacement for Paul McCartney when the Beatles split up late in 1969. It was not the Beatles connection that made the hit. Nilsson's **Without You** is quite simply one of the great pop records of the 1970's.

312

AMAZING GRACE

15 April 1972, for five weeks

The Pipes and Drums and Military Band of the Royal Scots Dragoon Guards *RCA 2191*

Writer: Traditional

Producer: Pete Kerr

The longest named act ever to reach number one (59 letters in their full title, 18 letters more than even Olivia Newton-John and Electric Light Orchestra) became the first military band to reach the very top, the first record featuring bagpipes, and the twenty-first instrumental, to make number one. Judy Collins' vocal version of the same song began its 67 weeks on the chart in December 1970, and the success of the instrumental version brought renewed interest in the Collins version, which after almost 4 months off the chart, returned for a further 19-week run on 22 April 72. The Royal Scots Dragoon Guards version totalled 27 weeks on the chart by the end of 1972, so the song in both versions has almost totalled 2 years on the chart.

Amazing Grace is one of the few songs to have reached the Top 10 in both vocal and instrumental versions. Other songs which have achieved this rare double are **Oh Mein Papa**, **Annie's Song**, and **Don't Cry For Me Argentina**.

313

METAL GURU

20 May 1972, for four weeks

T Rex *EMI MARC 1*

Writer: Marc Bolan

Producer: Tony Visconti

The fourth consecutive number one hit for T Rex was another track from 'The Slider' LP. It was on the EMI label, rather than the T Rex label on which EMI put out his previous single, so it gave T Rex the obscure record of having had three successive number ones on three different labels, and all within the space of 10 months. Rod Stewart equalled this unlikely record in 1977, but it took him almost 5 years and his hits were not with consecutive singles.

After **Metal Guru**, the chart career of Marc Bolan and T Rex was consistently downwards. His next two singles, EMI MARC 2 & 3, reached number two, and then every single up to EMI MARC 9 achieved a lower chart placing than the one before. EMI MARC 10, **New York City**, in 1975, restored him to the Top 20 for the first time for almost 18 months, but EMI MARC 12 failed to make the 50. The bubble had well and truly burst but Marc Bolan found it hard to accept. He died in a car crash in London in 1977, anticipating a comeback.

322 Gilbert O'Sullivan

317 Alice Cooper

324 Little Jimmy Osmond

326 Slade

Left 314 Don McLean
Right 323 Chuck Berry

314

VINCENT

17 June 1972, for two weeks

Don McLean *United Artists UP 35359*

Writer: Don McLean
Producer: Ed Freeman

It is one of the most commonly held wrong assumptions in chartdom that **American Pie** was Don McLean's number one from the LP 'American Pie'. In fact, that cryptic epic reached number two. The second single from the album, **Vincent**, took the extra step to the top. Considered one of the great achievements of the singer-songwriter era of the early seventies, **Vincent** was not one of the personal favourites of its writer. McLean thought his appreciation of the painter Vincent Van Gogh drew too detailed a picture, leaving little to the listener's imagination. **American Pie** had been a sensation partly because much of it was open to interpretation. Besides the devastating emotional effect McLean achieved, he also managed to work in references to particular Van Gogh works. This was acknowledged by the grateful Van Gogh museum in Amsterdam, which played the disc daily. A friend of McLean's made a film of the artist's paintings to illustrate the record.

After the runaway success of **American Pie** McLean retreated to make an album of songs about the effects of fame, an LP that was received with some hostility and cooled media interest in him for several years. He made an appearance at a broadcast concert in Hyde Park during this period before approximately seventy-five thousand fans.

315

TAKE ME BAK 'OME

1 July 1972, for one week

Slade *Polydor 2058 231*

Writers: Noddy Holder and Jim Lea
Producer: Chas Chandler

Slade never managed a hat-trick of number ones. Their six number ones were in the space of nine releases over a period of 2 years and 32 days. Furthermore, twelve consecutive Slade releases hit the Top 5. (This compares with the record 22 consecutive top five releases by the Beatles, 20 by Elvis, 19 by Cliff but only 10 by the Rolling Stones). But Slade, like Cliff, never had more than two number ones in a row. **Take Me Bak 'Ome**, their second number one, was the follow-up to what would become their biggest flop in 3 years, the misspelt *and* grammatically incorrect **Look Wot You Dun**, which only reached number four.

Take Me Bak 'Ome only managed one week at the top, sandwiched between the enigmatic and peaceful **Vincent** and the raw weenybop emotion of **Puppy Love**. All the same, it was Slade's style of music that won the day in the end. By 1973, with help from Gary Glitter, Sweet, Suzi Quatro and Wizzard, Slade made sure that gentle ballads were given as little room as possible at the top of the charts.

316

PUPPY LOVE

8 July 1972, for five weeks

Donny Osmond *MGM 2006 104*

Writer: Paul Anka
Producers: Mike Curb and Ray Ruff

Donny Osmond, fifth singing son of George and Olive Osmond, was born on 12 September 1957, when a record by an earlier teenaged heart-throb was at number one in Britain – **Diana** by Paul Anka (see no. 63). It was totally fitting, therefore, that Donny Osmond's first British hit and first British number one should have been written by Paul Anka, whose own version of the song had climbed only to number 33 in Britain, disappearing from the charts some 3 months before Donny Osmond's third birthday.

Puppy Love was the seventh in a list of 12 songs with animals in their titles to reach number one. Although a rat, a bear and a rooster among others have all reached number one, dogs are easily the chart freak's best friends, having scored four times, twice with very long titles and twice as puppies (see nos. 8, 316, 339 and 421). The cat family have three number ones (see nos 343, 421 and 496), as do birds (see nos. 182, 214 and 264), but no fish has yet made it to the number one slot.

317

SCHOOL'S OUT

12 August 1972, for three weeks

Alice Cooper *Warner Brothers K 16188*

Writers: Alice Cooper, Michael Bruce
Producer: Bob Ezrin

Vincent Furnier, the minister's son from Detroit, became Alice Cooper, the group took his name and the world was outraged. Members of Parliament teamed up with ordinary mothers to prevent Alice Cooper from touring Britain and the record shot to the top, the free publicity tailor-made for a number one hit.

Furnier, born on Christmas Day 1945, formed a group in 1965 called the Earwigs, who proved to be a rather less commercial bunch of insects than the Crickets or the Beatles. It is alleged that they became Alice Cooper after a session with a Ouija board when a spirit named Alice Cooper told them that she was Vincent Furnier. They were discovered by Frank Zappa in Los Angeles at a Lenny Bruce Memorial gig when the entire audience except Zappa and Shep Gordon, who became the group's manager, walked out. With a pedigree like that, how could they fail? By killing chickens on stage, they established a reputation that began to draw the crowds, and the quality of the music improved to a point where only a small percentage of the audience walked out. By this time they had a recording contract, and life began to look good for Alice Cooper – Vincent Furnier, Glen Buxton, Dennis Dunaway, Michael Bruce and Neal Smith. But it didn't last. The hype was too total and even Alice himself began to hate his image; he took up golf and made half-hearted attempts to become adorable. By 1982 he was back to touring in the old unpleasant style in pursuit of glories but he had been rumbled by then – he really is a nice guy who should leave animal destruction to Ozzy Osbourne.

318

YOU WEAR IT WELL

2 September 1972, for one week

Rod Stewart *Mercury 6052 171*

Writers: Rod Stewart and Martin Quittenton
Producer: Rod Stewart

Rod Stewart's second consecutive number one, almost a year after **Maggie May**, was the first single from his 'Never A Dull Moment' LP, which dominated the album charts at the end of 1972. Similar in style to **Maggie May**, it featured Ron Wood of the Faces on acoustic guitar and Mickey Waller, who had been with Rod Stewart in Steam Packet, on drums.

It was to be 3 years and 4 days until Rod Stewart's next number one hit, **Sailing** (see no. 377). In the meantime, he had three solo Top 10 hits but his biggest hits during the gap between chart toppers were as lead singer with Python Lee Jackson, whose **In A Broken Dream** reached number three as **You Wear It Well** dropped off the chart, and with the Faces, whose **Cindy Incidentally** climbed to number two in the spring of 1973. The Faces only ever had three Top 10 hits, all in a 2 year period from the beginning of 1972 to the beginning of 1974. During this time Rod Stewart also sang lead on four other Top 10 hits, of which just this one, **You Wear It Well** reached the very top.

319

MAMA WEER ALL CRAZEE NOW

9 September 1972, for three weeks

Slade *Polydor 2058 274*

Writers: Noddy Holder and Jim Lea
Producer: Chas Chandler

Slade's third number one failed to show any improvement in their spelling, but it did show an improvement in the selling power of the Wolverhampton lads. **Mama Weer All Crazee Now** hit the top in its second week on the chart, faster than either of their first two chart-toppers, and faster than any other act of 1972 except T Rex.

Mama Weer All Crazee Now was also, astonishingly, the first British chart topper with the word 'Mama' or 'Mother' or any variation of that word in the title. Dad has had three number ones, **Oh Mein Papa**, **My Old Man's A Dustman** and **Son Of My Father**. Vera Lynn's **My Son My Son** added to the family number one collection, which also includes **Little Sister**, **Grandad** and **There's No-One Quite Like Grandma**. Mum is still rather left out, as neither **Mama Weer All Crazee Now** nor Abba's **Mamma Mia** really refers to motherhood. The biggest genuine 'Mother' hit is Neil Reid's number two hit in 1972, **Mother Of Mine**. The Hollies took **He Ain't Heavy, He's My Brother** to number three and Tom Jones' **Daughter of Darkness** climbed to number five. Paul McCartney's US number one, **Admiral Halsey/Uncle Albert** was not issued as a single in England, but Hugo and Luigi's French aunt's pen reached number 29 in 1959, **La Plume De Ma Tante**. There's hits to be found by keeping it in the family.

320

HOW CAN I BE SURE

30 September 1972, for two weeks

David Cassidy *Bell 1258*

Writers: Felix Cavaliere and Eddie Brigati
Producer: Wes Farrell

How Can I Be Sure was an American Top 5 hit in the autumn of 1967 for the Young Rascals, but this group, who had three US number ones and ten other Top 40 entries, rarely registered in the UK. It was Dusty Springfield who introduced the composition to the British lists in 1970, but her version peaked at a mere 36.

David Cassidy finally took the tune to chart heights, but by the time he had done so his recording career had already peaked in America. He had scored five Top 20 hits with the Partridge Family and one on his own in the year and a half ending early 1972. However, barring 1 week in the British twenty with **I Think I Love You**, this was the beginning of his UK success. He proceeded to rack up eleven Top 20 solo or with the imaginary family group.

How Can I Be Sure was the first of two number ones for the actor/singer, though if one went purely by the teen hysteria that followed his every move in this country one would have thought he had scored as many of the number ones as Elvis. Cassidy's recording career was a spin-off of *The Partridge Family* television series. He himself preferred rock and blues and wanted to be taken seriously as a writer and musician but found that when he did betray his image his fans deserted him. He did have the distinction of scoring the first hit version of **I Write The Songs**, which Barry Manilow later took to number one in America.

321

MOULDY OLD DOUGH

14 October 1972, for four weeks

Lieutenant Pigeon *Decca F 13278*

Writers: Nigel Fletcher and Robert Woodward
Producer: Stavely Makepiece

Lieutenant Pigeon was born out of a group that used to be called Stavely Makepiece, the name they credited with production of their number one. Stavely Makepiece had not been successful on record, producing one single called **Edna** which did not change the course of popular music. The change of name to Lieutenant Pigeon, a memorable but scarcely more dynamic name than the sedate Stavely Makepiece, improved their luck and gave them a number one in their fifth week on the chart.

Mouldy Old Dough was the last but one instrumental to reach the top of the British charts, and its title summed up the song. **Mouldy Old Dough** is a corruption of 'vo-de-o-do', the phrase well loved by megaphone toting band vocalists of the twenties and thirties. The jangly piano played by Nigel Fletcher's mum was nostalgic pub singalong rather than mainstream pop. After **Mouldy Old Dough** (the first food, however unappetising, at number one since **Sugar Sugar**), the group went back to their childhood for their Top 20 follow-up, **Desperate Dan**. Thereafter, Lieutenant Pigeon homed in on the charts no more. Further singles like **Red River Rock**, an unusual version of the Johnny and The Hurricanes classic of 1959, fell on deaf ears.

Mouldy Old Dough attained some significance as Decca's 38th and final number one, and almost 10 years later, the label still holds second place among successful number one labels, behind EMI's now dormant Columbia label.

322

CLAIR

11 November1972, for two weeks

Gilbert O'Sullivan *MAM 84*

Writer: Gilbert O'Sullivan
Producer: Gordon Mills

Gilbert O'Sullivan was born in Ireland on 1 December 1946, and was enveloped by Gordon Mills' organisation, MAM, in 1970. Despite an image which involved short-trousers and a cloth cap covering a pudding-basin haircut, O'Sullivan produced two brilliant songs in his first 18 months in the recording studios. His first single, **Nothing Rhymed**, showed a remarkable deftness of lyrics which is by no means always a passport to record sales, but he did reach number eight over the New Year of 1971. His American number one, **Alone Again (Naturally)**, is generally considered his best song, but even that could not hit the top spot here. It peaked at number three, but two singles later Gilbert O'Sullivan's fifth Top 10 hit in seven releases became his first number one hit, **Clair**.

Clair was in the tradition of **The Naughty Lady of Shady Lane** and of the 1976 Eurovision winner, **Save Your Kisses For Me**. It was a coy, middle of the road tune about a young lady who turns out to be very young indeed. In fact, the Clair that inspired this song was the infant daughter of Gilbert's manager, Gordon Mills. Without the last verse, it was a pleasant boy-meets-girl love song. With the last verse, it was a Children's Favourite number one hit.

323

MY DING-A-LING

25 November 1972, for four weeks

Chuck Berry *Chess 6145 019*

Writer: Chuck Berry
Producer: Esmond Edwards

My Ding-a-Ling reached the Top 15½ years after Chuck Berry's chart début with **School Day**. The rock and roll pioneer's first important record, **Maybellene**, had started his American string of hits two years previously, in 1955.

My Ding-a-Ling was as inappropriate as it was late in coming. It was Berry's first live hit, having been recorded at the Lanchester Arts Festival; his classic singles had all been studio performances. The number one was also wildly different in being a rude novelty rather than a rock and roll story song. It was the musical equivalent of a ribald postcard from a seaside resort. Originally part of Berry's fifties concert set under the name **My Tambourine**, the song had once been rejected by the artist's record company. It should be noted, however, that in 1952 Dave Bartholomew recorded a remarkably similar song called **My Ding-a-Ling** for which he was listed as the author.

Despite the obvious reference to its being recorded in Britain ('That's future Parliament . . . '), **My Ding-a-Ling** was also a number one in the United States. There, too, it was Chuck Berry's first chart-topper. It is more reflective of his fifties success to say that it was his seventh million seller.

Only Johnny Mathis took more time after his chart début to achieve a number one single, but, unlike Berry, his greatest chart feats were in the US album tables.

324

LONG HAIRED LOVER FROM LIVERPOOL

23 December 1972, for five weeks

Little Jimmy Osmond *MGM 2006 109*

Writer: Christopher Dowden
Producers: Mike Curb and Perry Botkin

Little Jimmy Osmond, youngest son of the prolific George and Olive, was born on 16 April 1963, and was 9 years and 251 days old when his first British single release made it to the top of the charts. He thus became the youngest ever chart-topper, eclipsing by some 4 years the record held by Frankie Lymon since 20 July 1956 (see no. 48). Little Jimmy's song had been written at the peak of Beatlemania, and it was a reminder of how fast time disappears, even in the eternally young world of popular music, that Jimmy had been born 5 days after the first Liverpool number one hit, Gerry and the Pacemakers' **How Do You Do It?** (see no. 150) reached the top. Young Master Osmond, not so little any more, is still the youngest solo act ever to have a number one hit, although it is hard to be sure whether any of St Winifred's School Choir were younger than 9 years 251 days on 27 December 1980 when **There's No-one Quite Like Grandma** (see no. 472) became a British number one. If so, those girls would have been still in nappies when **Long Haired Lover** was at number one, and not even born when the Beatles broke up.

325

BLOCKBUSTER

27 January 1973, for 5 weeks

Sweet *RCA 2305*

Writers: Nicky Chinn and Mike Chapman
Producer: Phil Wainman

The only number one hit written by Nicky Chinn and Mike Chapman which was not also produced by them was Sweet's seventh hit, all of which had been Chapman/Chinn compositions. Sweet were formed in 1968, and in 1970 joined forces with Chinn and Chapman, who at that stage were unknown. Sweet were Brian Connolly, lead vocalist and guitarist, Steve Priest on bass, Andy Scott on guitar and Mick Tucker on drums. Their first hit, **Funny Funny** in March 1971 introduced Chapman and Chinn songs to the British charts, and within a year Sweet were established as a major chart act. By the time the hits finally ran out after their tenth Top 10 hit, **Love Is Like Oxygen** early in 1978, Sweet had racked up one number one and five number two hits, including three consecutive number two hits which followed up **Blockbuster**. This established a record for consecutive number two hits, which was equalled in 1978 by Darts. At least Sweet had the compensation of one chart-topper, which Darts never managed.

326

CUM ON FEEL THE NOIZE

3 March 1973, for four weeks

Slade *Polydor 2058 339*

Writers: Noddy Holder and Jim Lea
Producer: Chas Chandler

Number one when the last American soldier left Vietnam on 29 March 1973 was Slade's fourth chart-topper, **Cum On Feel The Noize**. By this time Slade were easily Britain's most successful chart act, having eclipsed the achievements of T Rex, and **Cum On Feel The Noize** became the first single to come in at number one for almost 4 years, since the Beatles **Get Back** (see no. 270) in April 1969. It followed **Gudbuy T'Jane**, which climbed to number two but was kept from the top by Chuck Berry and Little Jimmy Osmond. If **Gudbuy T'Jane** had reached number one, Slade would have achieved a hat trick of chart-toppers, which remained the only major chart achievement that Slade missed out on.

Noddy Holder and Jim Lea managed to hit on a style of songwriting which combined elements of teenybop, heavy metal and rebelliousness which the slick productions of Chas Chandler turned into brilliantly commercial singles. Slade's stage act was also a demonstration of carefully controlled excitement which made the four mild-mannered boys from Wolverhampton as popular on stage as on wax.

327

THE TWELFTH OF NEVER

31 March 1973, for one week

Donny Osmond *MGM 2006 199*

Writers: Jay Livingston and Paul Francis Webster
Producers: Mike Curb and Don Costa

The Twelfth of Never was part of Donny Osmond's spectacular string of successes in 1972-73. In an 18 month period he registered three number ones and three other Top 5 hits in six attempts, while in the same period he was scoring three top fivers out of three with his brothers The Osmonds.

As happened with Roy Orbison and Gene Pitney in the sixties, the consistent chart careers of Osmond and fellow weenybopper hero David Cassidy in each case began and ended a couple of years later than they did in the States. In Donny's case, he had already notched up two US Top 10 and a number one (**Go Away Little Girl**) before he even set tonsil in the British charts. He peaked earlier in America as well; hence **The Twelfth Of Never** only got to eight in the US.

Another reason for this disc's slightly less favourable placing in its country of origin was that the Johnny Mathis original was considered definitive. Although the Master of Make Out Music's 1957 version merely reached 51 in the *Billboard* Top 100, as it was then called, it was in the charts for 17 weeks and enjoyed heavy airplay. Cliff Richard's cover introduced the song to the UK, achieving a number eight placing in 1964.

328

GET DOWN

7 April 1973, for two weeks

Gilbert O'Sullivan *MAM 96*

Writer: Gilbert O'Sullivan
Producer: Gordon Mills

Gilbert O'Sullivan's second consecutive and final number one was **Get Down**. Unlike all the other songs, with **Get Down** in the title, like KC and the Sunshine Band's **Get Down Tonight** or Kool & The Gang's **Get Down On It**, O'Sullivan's song had nothing to do with dancing at the discotheque. It was a plea to his dog to get down off the furniture.

Get Down represented the peak of Gilbert O'Sullivan's popularity. Only one more Top 10 hit was to follow, and 2 years later the hits stopped. There then followed a bitter dispute with manager and producer Gordon Mills which resulted in a widely-reported court case early in 1982 with claims and counterclaims about how much money O'Sullivan had earned and how much of his earnings he had been able to get his hands on. In May 1982, the law found in favour of Gilbert (real name Ray O'Sullivan) describing him as 'a patently honest and sincere man' who had not received a just proportion of the vast income his songs had generated. Well before the case came to court, O'Sullivan had left MAM and even scored his fifteenth hit at the end of 1980, **What's In A Kiss** on CBS, his first hit for over 5 years.

329

TIE A YELLOW RIBBON ROUND THE OLD OAK TREE

21 April 1973, for four weeks

Dawn featuring Tony Orlando *Bell 1287*

Writers: Irwin Levine and L Russell Brown
Producers: The Tokens and Dave Appell

According to the *Guinness Book of Records*, the most recorded songs in history are the Lennon/McCartney song, **Yesterday** and **Tie A Yellow Ribbon Round The Old Oak Tree**, which gave Dawn their second number one hit and 40 weeks on the chart. In the original version, the song was the biggest selling single in the world in 1973, so if you add to that the sales of the one thousand and more other versions, we can assume that Irwin Levine and L Russell Brown are now wealthy men.

The two girls backing Tony Orlando were Detroit-born Joyce Vincent (born 14 December 1946) and Thelma Hopkins, born 28 October 1948 in Louisville, Kentucky, the home town of Muhammad Ali. Both girls had worked as session singers at Motown before the success of **Candida** changed their lives, but by the end of Dawn's run of success, they were back to being little more than session singers for by the time Dawn's chart career had finished after two songs with titles only one letter shorter than **Tie A Yellow Ribbon**, they were just background ooby dooby girls.

Both Dawn number ones were about unusual ways for a girl to get a message to her man. 'Knock three times on the ceiling if you want me' must be the most bizarre advice to any girl until she is told to 'tie a yellow ribbon round the old oak tree'. What's wrong with the telephone system in America?

330

SEE MY BABY JIVE

19 May 1973, for 4 weeks

Wizzard *Harvest HAR 5070*

Writer: Roy Wood
Producer: Roy Wood

Roy Wood, who claims his real name is Ulysses Adrian Wood, was the driving force behind three groups, Move, Electric Light Orchestra and Wizzard. In retrospect, for Roy Wood the most successful was probably Move, even though with the short-lived Wizzard he achieved two number ones.

Roy Wood left Electric Light Orchestra after two singles had been released, **10538 Overture** and **Roll Over Beethoven**. Both were Top 10 hits, but the conflict of style between Roy Wood and Jeff Lynne meant that something had to give. Between the spring of 1973 and early 1976, for almost 3 years after Wood left ELO, they had only two hits, neither of which reached the top 10. It took them a long while to get over the departure of the gentle bearded rocker with an ear for commercial productions. During those three years, Wizzard came and went, but they packed two number ones and four more top ten hits into almost exactly two years.

Wizzard was Roy Wood just as much as Wings were Paul McCartney, but Wood still needed to issue solo singles. In December 1973, he had two top ten hits at the same time, one by Wizzard and one under his own name. The Wizzard song was **I Wish It Could Be Christmas Every Day**, which was rereleased at Christmas 1981 to give Roy Wood another chance to appear on Top Of The Pops.

331

CAN THE CAN

16 June 1973, for one week

Suzi Quatro *RAK 150*

Writers: Nicky Chinn and Mike Chapman
Producers: Nicky Chinn and Mike Chapman

Suzi Quatro was born in Detroit on 3 June 1950, the daughter of Art Quatro whose jazz band attained a certain popularity in the American mid-West in the 1950's. In her early teens, Suzi became a go-go dancer on TV called Suzi Soul, and thereafter formed Suzi Soul and the Pleasure Seekers with her sisters Patti and Nancy. For 5 years they played all over the country and overseas (including for American troops in Vietnam), being appreciated as much for their looks as for their music. Nevertheless, Suzi Quatro was becoming a very competent rock guitarist and singer, and when Mickie Most happened to hear her in Detroit in 1970, he persuaded her to come to Britain. Her first releases were flops, and she appeared to be fated to a career touring Britain just as she had toured America for the previous 5 years. Then Mickie Most asked Nicky Chinn and Mike Chapman to produce her, and the immediate result was **Can The Can**. Suzi Quatro and her backing musicians, Alastair

Mackenzie, Dave Neal and Len Tuckey, her husband, had their first number one.

332

RUBBER BULLETS

23 June 1973, for one week

10 CC *UK 36*

Writers: Kevin Godley, Lol Creme and Graham Gouldman
Producers: 10 CC at Strawberry Studios

Rubber Bullets represented a first taste of number one hit-making for the four members of 10 CC, which must have been particularly gratifying for Eric Stewart, the only member of the group who does not have writing credit on this song. Stewart had been a member of Wayne Fontana and the Mindbenders, who reached number two with **The Game Of Love** in 1965. When the Mindbenders split from their leader their first solo hit, **A Groovy Kind Of Love**, reached number two in 1966. The Mindbenders later broke up, and Eric Stewart formed Hotlegs with Kevin Godley and Lol Creme. Their only hit, **Neanderthal Man**, in 1970, also got as high as number two. When 10 CC's first hit, **Donna**, also reached number two, Eric Stewart must have felt doomed never to reach the very top. 23 June 1973 not only gave him and 10 CC their first number one, but it also gave Jonathan King's label, UK, its only number one. None of Jonathan King's many efforts under many names and on many labels ever reached number one, and this record is his only claim to a number one hit.

333

SKWEEZE ME PLEEZE ME

30 June 1973, for three weeks

Slade *Polydor 2058 377*

Writers: Noddy Holder and Jim Lea
Producer: Chas Chandler

This record was Slade's fifth number one, and established a record which has yet to be equalled of being the group's second consecutive record to enter the chart at number one. Only Elvis Presley and Jam, apart from the Wolverhampton lads, have had more than one record that went straight into the charts at number one. Slade have had three of the 13 records which hit the chart at the top, all of them in 1973.

Between 1962 and 1973, only the Beatles in 1969 with **Get Back** managed to come straight in at number one, and after 1973 nobody managed the trick until Jam in 1980. In 1973, four records came in at number one; three by Slade and one by Gary Glitter, so Slade seem to have been very lucky to have been the teenyboppers' heroes at a time when the method of compilation of the chart made instant number ones slightly more possible to attain.

It is really surprising that more records have not gone straight in at number one. Many records by big name artists probably sell enough in the week following their release to justify a number one position, but the chart often fails to reflect massive sales very quickly.

334

WELCOME HOME

21 July 1973, for one week

Peters and Lee *Philips 6006 307*

Writers: Jean-Alphonse Dupre, Stanislas Beldone, English lyrics by Bryan Blackburn
Producer: Johnny Franz

The last number one produced by Philips' resident A & R man, the late Johnny Franz, was a sentimental ballad from Italy sung by the vocal duo of Lenny Peters and Di Lee. Lenny Peters is blind, an East Ender whose sudden success was very popular among the recording fraternity. It was a success that could not be maintained, however. The song and the treatment were very mid-sixties, in the style of Engelbert Humperdinck or Ken Dodd, while in the early seventies the competition in sentimental ballads was from Donny Osmond and David Cassidy. It was a remarkable achievement of Peters and Lee to manage even one week at the top, squeezed in between Slade and Gary Glitter, the ultimate purveyors of glam-rock who were then at the very peak of their popularity.

Over the next 3 years Peters and Lee scored four more hits, including one top tenner in 1974, **Don't Stay Away Too Long**. Not a very impressive record perhaps, but better than most of the other male/female vocal duos to hit the top. There have been seven in all, of whom three, Jane Birkin and Serge Gainsbourg, Frank and Nancy Sinatra and Elton John and Kiki Dee, were one-hit wonders.

335

I'M THE LEADER OF THE GANG (I AM)

28 July 1973, for four weeks

Gary Glitter *Bell 1321*

Writers: Gary Glitter and Mike Leander
Producer: Mike Leander

The emergence of Gary Glitter as a major pop act of the mid-seventies was one of the more pleasant surprises of that unpredictable and generally uninspired period. Born Paul Gadd on 8 May 1940, Glitter had failed for years to be successful under the name Paul Raven (see no. 130), although he kept in work and released a few unremarkable singles. He succeeded as Gary Glitter because he was a showman rather than a rocker, and he refused to take his image seriously. He took his music seriously, however, and worked and worked on getting his music and his image across. The slightly pudgy, outrageously hairy chest scarcely encased in a rhinestone and glitter jacket, the painfully tight silver trousers and the orthopaedically dangerous high heels made Glitter the most imitated act of the time, but nobody could get near enough to the tight and exciting productions of Mike Leander which showcased Glitter's talents as well as possible.

Glitter's first eleven singles all hit the Top 10 – a record – beginning with one of the real sleepers of the seventies **Rock and Roll (Part Two). I'm The Leader Of The Gang** was Glitter's fifth single and his first number one. It may not have been the best of all his records, but it is Glitter's personal favourite, 'because it was my first number one'.

336

YOUNG LOVE

25 August 1973, for four weeks

Donny Osmond *MGM 2006 300*

Writers: Carole Joyner and Ric Cartey
Producers: Mike Curb and Don Costa

The first song ever to be a number one hit twice on two completely separate occasions was the Tab Hunter smash of 1957, **Young Love** (see no. 56). Donny Osmond was the king of revivals of old songs, doing for the sentimental ballads of the fifties what, nearly a decade later, Shakin' Stevens would do for the squarer rock songs of the fifties. Donny Osmond revived three old number ones in his chart career (the others were **Why** and **Too Young**) but only **Young Love** made the top again. Donny Osmond's entire chart career, which consisted of seven hits over 2 years, consisted of old tunes revived. Three number ones, three top tenners and one at number 18 is quite a good return on a search through the back catalogues. Add to that the four oldies that Donny made hits with his sister Marie, Marie's only solo hit **Paper Roses** (number two at the end of 1973, number seven for the Kaye Sisters in 1960) and Little Jimmy Osmond's two oldies out of three hits, and you can see how Mike Curb and Don Costa operated. Strangely when the brothers sang as a group, they only sang new songs, which gave them ten hits in 4½ years.

Don Costa's production career peaked when he produced Paul Anka's multi-million selling hit **Diana** in 1957. By the time **Young Love** was a hit, it was easy to see how far he had eased off. Mike Curb's career probably peaked with **Young Love**. He is now Lieutenant-Governor of California.

337

ANGEL FINGERS

22 September 1973, for one week

Wizzard *Harvest HAR 5076*

Writer: Roy Wood
Producer: Roy Wood

Roy Wood is one of the very few people who have been members of two groups who have had number one hits. There is Paul McCartney (Beatles and Wings), Denny Laine (Moody Blues and Wings), Bev Bevan (Move and ELO) and Roy Wood (Move and Wizzard). After that, you have to look very hard indeed.

Angel Fingers was Wizzard's second consecutive number one hit, and it was the peak of Roy Wood's success. 1973 was dominated by the RAK/Bell/Donny Osmond school of Teenybop, but Roy Wood managed to introduce subtleties of production into his basically simple pop tunes that makes them stand up to the test of time. He also knew that he was not producing great art and was happy to joke about his music. **I Wish It Could Be Christmas Every Day** (number four at Christmas 1973) features Wizzard with 'vocal backing by the Suedettes plus the Stockland Green Bilateral School First Year Choir, with additional noises by Miss Snob and Class 3C'.

343 **Mud**

330 **Wizzard**

335 **Gary Glitter**

344 **Suzi Quatro**

332 **10 CC**

338

EYE LEVEL

29 September 1973, for four weeks

Simon Park Orchestra *Columbia DB 8946*

Writers: Simon Park and Jack Trombey
Producer: Simon Park

In the autumn of 1972, a new TV series went out on the ITV network, based on the detective thrillers of Nicholas Freeling. The series was called *Van Der Valk* and the theme music was written by Simon Park and Dutchman Jan Stoeckhart, writing under the name of Jack Trombey. The theme proved popular with viewers, and a single was issued, which reached number 41 in November 1972.

In the autumn of 1973, a second season of the *Van Der Valk* series was broadcast. Again viewer reaction to the theme was strong, so EMI re-activated the single. This time, it roared to the top in its third week of re-entry, which was nevertheless 307 days since it had first hit the chart. Only three records have taken longer to reach number one, **Rock Around The Clock, Space Oddity** and **Imagine**. Simon Park's only hit with his studio orchestra took so long to hit that in the meantime the label it was on had been virtually discontinued, so Columbia's 50th and final number one hit was by far the most surprising of all. **Eye Level** is the only TV theme tune to reach number one, by the only one hit wonder orchestra, which never really existed anyway. Astonishingly, it is also the 23rd and last instrumental to reach the top spot, unless you count **Guns of Navarone** on the Specials **Special AKA Live** EP (no. 450).

339

DAYDREAMER/THE PUPPY SONG

27 October 1973, for three weeks

David Cassidy *Bell 1334*

Writers: Daydreamer – Terry Dempsey/The Puppy Song – Harry Nilsson
Producer: Rick Jarrard

David Cassidy's second number one at least had the merit of giving Harry Nilsson a writing credit on a number one hit, to match his singing credit on **Without You** (no. 311).

Looking back on 1973, it is easy in hindsight to see it as a fallow period in British pop creativity. A succession of faces rather than voices recording sounds rather than songs soared to the top as the record companies began to use marketing techniques that other branches of the entertainment industry had been using for years. The British and American charts, which throughout most of the 1960's and early 1970's had been influencing each other strongly, began to drift apart as acts like Slade, T Rex and the Chinnichap artistes failed to hit in the States. American acts like Tommy James and Three Dog Night missed out almost entirely here, but the TV-backed weeny-bop heroes, David Cassidy and Donny Osmond, crossed the Atlantic in triumph. David Cassidy did so quite literally, flying in for one TV spot on *Top Of The Pops* to perform this record, which hit the top in 2 weeks as a result.

Shortly after this final number one, he tried to be taken more seriously as a singer. His 'I Write The Songs' LP (most of which he didn't) in 1975, slowed down his career to a virtual full stop, but at least his hits lasted a full year longer than Donny Osmond's.

340

I LOVE YOU LOVE ME LOVE

17 November 1973, for four weeks

Gary Glitter *Bell 1337*

Writers: Gary Glitter and Mike Leander
Producer: Mike Leander

One of the songs for which Gary Glitter is best remembered is **I Love You Love Me Love**. Blessed with a title as confusing as Lulu's **Love Loves to Love Love** and a beat as subtle as Hotleg's **Neanderthal Man**, it went to number one in its week of release, one of four singles to do so in 1973. Glitter was by this stage the most successful British male vocalist of all, and the days of Paul Raven were long gone. The days of the original Gary Glitter were fast disappearing too, as the act and the records became more outrageous, the chest became hairier, the trousers tighter and the heels higher. **I Love You Love Me Love** was the last of the great Glitter records, the only one to rank with **Rock & Roll (Parts 1 & 2)**.

By late 1973, Gary Glitter's backing group, the Glitter Band, were preparing their own recording career. For a variety of reasons, the Glitter Band were never credited on Gary Glitter's singles, even though they played on most of them, so it was a logical step to let them record their own singles. From 1974 to early 1976, almost 2 years, they produced solid pop singles which earned them six Top 10 hits. The last of them reached number five in March 1976, 8 months after Gary Glitter's last top tenner, **Doing Alright with the Boys**.

341

MERRY XMAS EVERYBODY

15 December 1973, for five weeks

Slade *Polydor 2058 422*

Writers: Noddy Holder and Jim Lea
Producer: Chas Chandler

Slade had earlier in 1973 succeeded in having consecutive singles enter the charts at number one, a unique achievement. A few months later, **Merry Xmas Everybody** followed Gary Glitter's **I Love You Love Me Love** in entering at number one, the only time consecutive number ones have done that. All it really proves is that in 1973, the charts were calculated in an unusual manner, although nobody would deny that Slade were the biggest selling act of that year.

Merry Xmas Everybody has proved to be one of the most successful of Christmas records. It sold a million at the end of 1973, and re-appeared at Christmas 1980, re-recorded by 'Slade and the Reading Choir'. In 1981, at the end of Slade's most successful chart year since 1975, the original version re-entered the charts and returned to the Top 40. In 1981, only three million-selling singles hit the chart of which two were re-issues, **Merry Xmas Everybody** and John Lennon's **Imagine**, showing how far singles sales have declined since the peak of the mid-seventies.

342

YOU WON'T FIND ANOTHER FOOL LIKE ME

19 January 1974, for one week

The New Seekers *Polydor 2058 421*

Writers: Tony Macaulay and Geoff Stephens
Producer: Tommy Oliver

The New Seekers matched the old Seekers by having two number ones when the Tony Macaulay/Geoff Stephens song **You Won't Find Another Fool Like Me** reached the top in its ninth week on the chart.

By this stage the break-up of the New Seekers was inevitable. At the end of 1972, their remake of the Fleetwoods/Frankie Vaughan and the Kaye Sisters hit of 1959 **Come Softly To Me**, which reached number 20, billed 'The New Seekers featuring Marty Kristian'. Two singles later, **Nevertheless** was officially by 'Eve Graham and the New Seekers'. Lyn Paul was also expressing a desire to do solo recording, so it was no surprise that the follow-up to **You Won't Find Another Fool Like Me** was their last New Seekers single before the split. It was called **I Get a Little Sentimental Over You** and reached number five. This gave the New Seekers 125 weeks on the chart in all, including two number one hits, and four more Top 10 hits. The old Seekers managed two number ones, four more Top 10 hits and 120 weeks on the chart.

Lyn Paul then went solo and her hit **It Oughta Sell A Million** didn't, but still reached number 37. At the end of 1976, the New Seekers re-formed (minus Lyn Paul) and had three more small hits before disappearing off the charts forever at the end of September 1978. We await the New New Seekers.

343

TIGER FEET

26 January 1974, for four weeks

Mud *RAK 166*

Writers: Nicky Chinn and Mike Chapman
Producers: Nicky Chinn and Mike Chapman

As Slade and Gary Glitter moved away from the position of total chart domination that they had enjoyed in 1973, a new phenomenon began a period of success that was even more total. The phenomenon was not a new group but a combination of writer/producers and a record label with the golden touch. The producers were 'Chinnichap' Mike Chapman and Nicky Chinn, and the label was Mickie Most's RAK. **Tiger Feet** was not the first Chapman and Chinn number one (Sweet and Suzi Quatro had already scored). **Tiger Feet** was not the first RAK number one, that was Suzi Quatro's **Can The Can** (see no. 331). But **Tiger Feet** was the first number one by Mud, the biggest of the Chinnichap/RAK acts, and was the first number one hit among ten Top 20 hits by the Mud/Chinnichap/RAK combination between March 1973 and July 1975.

Mud were Les Gray, the vocalist, Rob Davis on guitar,

Roy Stiles on bass and Dave Mount on drums. They were far more basic than Slade or Sweet on hits like **Tiger Feet**, but by the time they moved from RAK to Private Stock, they had developed a smoothness and subtlety that Slade and Sweet never had.

344

DEVIL GATE DRIVE

23 February 1974, for two weeks

Suzi Quatro *RAK 167*

Writers: Nicky Chinn and Mike Chapman
Producers: Nicky Chinn and Mike Chapman

RAK 167 followed RAK 166 at number one. This time it was Suzi Quatro's second number one, another Chapman/Chinn composition and production. It was probably their weakest number one hit, but in early 1974 every little thing they did was magic.

Devil Gate Drive was Suzi Quatro's fourth chart hit, and it proved to be her last number one. She joins the ranks of female soloists with two number ones – Doris Day, Kay Starr, Connie Francis, Helen Shapiro, Petula Clark, Cilla Black, Shirley Bassey, Rosemary Clooney and Winifred Atwell are the others – all of them one hit behind Sandie Shaw. Suzi Quatro has had ten more hits since **Devil Gate Drive**, including two more Top 10 hits. She also managed an American smash with Chris Norman, lead vocalist of Smokie, called **Stumblin' In**. For some reason it never rose higher than number 41 in Britain.

Suzi Quatro was the first act beginning with the letter Q to have a number one hit, but the day that **Devil Gate Drive** dropped from the top of the charts, another Q act made its first entry into the chart, an act which would be the only Q act more successful than the leather-clad Miss Quatro – Queen.

345

JEALOUS MIND

9 March 1974, for one week

Alvin Stardust *Magnet MAG 5*

Writer: Peter Shelley
Producer: Peter Shelley

Factory productions were not limited to RAK. Late in 1973, Peter Shelley had persuaded Michael Levy to start an independent record label called Magnet based on a demonstration tape of a song called **My Coo-Ca-Choo** which looked like a sure-fire hit. **My Coo-Ca-Choo** became Magnet MAG 1, and it climbed to number two. The singer was Alvin Stardust, né Bernard Jewry in 1942, a.k.a. Shane Fenton. The hair had changed from blonde to black in the years since Shane's **Cindy's Birthday** hit the Top 20 in the summer of 1962, but the face and the voice were the same.

My Coo-Ca-Choo was Alvin Stardust's best single, but as in so many cases (for example the Troggs and Billy J Kramer) it is not the best single that is always the biggest hit. The follow up was **Jealous Mind**, and it reached the number one spot. Thereafter, Magnet prospered as a record company, with hits for Guys and Dolls, Susan Cadogan and producer-turned-performer Peter Shelley, and more for Alvin Stardust. In 1981 he followed Shakin' Stevens' lead in reviving pop hits of the fifties, and came up with two more hits, a Top 10 version of Nat King Cole's **Pretend**, and a smaller hit with Pat Boone's **Wonderful Time Up There**. That song gave Alvin Stardust the greatest honour of his career: he sang it on Morecambe and Wise's Christmas Show.

346

BILLY DON'T BE A HERO

16 March 1974, for three weeks

Paper Lace *Bus Stop BUS 1014*

Writers: Mitch Murray and Peter Callander
Producers: Mitch Murray and Peter Callander

Nottingham-based group Paper Lace took an American Civil War saga to the very top of the charts to give the Bus Stop label its biggest ever hit. This emotional song, with the inevitable heroic ending, was written by two very successful but thoroughly British writers, and enjoyed the unusual distinction of being covered by an unknown American group, Bo Donaldson and the Heywoods, who took their version to number one in America. Paper Lace may have missed out with **Billy Don't Be A Hero** in America, but their follow-up, **The Night Chicago Died**, gave them their own US chart-topper. In Britain, **The Night Chicago Died** reached number three, but thereafter Paper Lace died. Their third single **The Black Eyed Boys** peaked at Number 11, and that was their lot. Or at least, it was the last the charts heard of them until they teamed up with their hometown's pride and joy, Nottingham Forest FC, to help the European Cup-winners put their version of **We've Got The Whole World In Our Hands** into the Top 30 in March 1978.

—347—

SEASONS IN THE SUN

6 April 1974, for four weeks

Terry Jacks *Bell 1344*

Writers: Jacques Brel, English lyrics by Rod McKuen
Producer: Terry Jacks

Terry Jacks is a Canadian, who was at one stage in his career married to a lady called Susan, née Pesklevits. In the late summer of 1970, a single featuring Susan Jacks as lead singer, and called **Which Way You Goin' Billy** by the Poppy Family, climbed to number seven in the charts. The Poppy Family then, like Billy, went, and so nothing more was heard from Terry Jacks until early in 1974.

He then came upon a Jacques Brel song which had been given English lyrics by the self-proclaimed most popular poet in the world, Rod McKuen. Terry Jacks' arrangement and production made **Seasons In The Sun** more than just a sentimental song in the tradition of **Green Green Grass of Home**, and it gave him a huge number one hit. He followed it up almost immediately with his version of that most melodramatic of torch songs, **If You Go Away** (another Jacques Brel song), which gave him another Top 10 hit. After that, he went away.

—348—

WATERLOO

4 May 1974, for two weeks

Abba *Epic EPC 2240*

Writers: Bjorn Ulvaeus, Benny Andersson, Stig Anderson
Producers: Bjorn Ulvaeus and Benny Andersson

Benny Andersson (born in Stockholm on 16 December 1946) began his musical career with a group called the Hep Stars, who were for some years very popular in Sweden. Bjorn Ulvaeus (born in Gothenberg on 25 April 1948) was with an outfit called the Hootenanny Singers, but in the late sixties the two combined to form the duo Bjorn and Benny. It was hardly the obvious foundation for the most popular group in the world since the break-up of the Beatles. By the early seventies, Bjorn and Benny had achieved considerable popularity in Scandinavia at which time they brought their girlfriends into the group. They were Agnetha Faltskog (born in Janskoping on 5 April 1950) and Annifrid Lyngstad (born in Norway on 15 November 1945) and by the original ploy of taking the initial letters of the quartet's first names, the name Abba was born. Up to this moment, the only thing that could be said about the new group was the startling lack of originality displayed by all concerned throughout their musical careers. The music that Abba actually produced was therefore all the more unexpected.

Waterloo was Sweden's Eurovision entry for 1974. It won easily, and became probably the biggest international hit in the history of the contest. It created a new stereotype of Eurovision song, which continued into 1981 with Buck's Fizz, another two men–two girls group. At least this stereotype was more listenable to than the **Boom-Bang-A-Bang** late sixties brand of Eurovisionism.

—349—

SUGAR BABY LOVE

18 May 1974, for four weeks

Rubettes *Polydor 2058 442*

Writers: Wayne Bickerton and Tony Waddington
Producer: Wayne Bickerton

The Rubettes were another studio group. Session singer Paul da Vinci sang lead on a number written by Polydor producer Wayne Bickerton and Tony Waddington (not the same Tony Waddington who used to manage Stoke City FC), and they put the single out under the group name Rubettes. It was a falsetto rock song modelled on the type of white fifties rock that groups like the Diamonds did so well. In fact, their imitation of the Diamonds was carried a stage further when the Rubettes' sixth hit even had the same title as the Diamonds biggest hit (in Britain their only hit), **Little Darling**. It was not the same song.

The Rubettes' success had two immediate effects. It encouraged Bickerton and Waddington to set up State Records, so that 10 months after the release of **Sugar Baby Love**, the fourth Rubettes single and third Top 10 hit was **I Can Do It** on State STAT 1. They managed seven hits on State in all, the last one being their fourth Top 10 hit, **Baby I Know**, which fell off the chart at the end of April 1977. The other effect of **Sugar Baby Love**'s success was to encourage Paul da Vinci to try a solo career. He did not

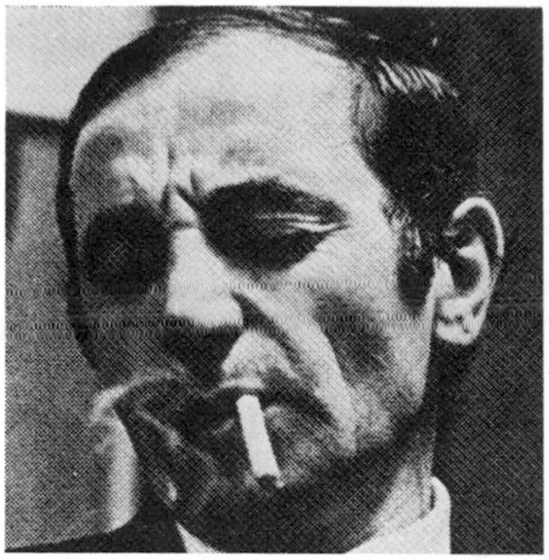

Left **352 Charles Aznavour**

Right **345 Alvin Stardust**

Above **346 Paper Lace**

Below **349 Rubettes**

become a Rubette when the group was created after the success of **Sugar Baby Love**, but his attempts at solo stardom began and ended with a single which hit the chart one week after the Rubettes' follow-up **Tonight**. It was called **Your Baby Ain't Your Baby Anymore**, and climbed to number 20.

350

THE STREAK

15 June 1974, for one week

Ray Stevens *Janus 6146 201*

Writer: Ray Stevens
Producer: Ray Stevens

Ray Stevens, born in Clarksdale, Georgia about the time that Hitler invaded Poland, has earned himself the title of the most successful comic in pop music, although his list of hits in Britain is not as long as you might expect, while a few of his hits have veered away from comedy and into country sentimentality. His American hits of the early sixties, like **Harry The Hairy Ape** and **Ahab The Arab** (covered by Jimmy Savile) all failed in Britain, and his first hit on this side of the Atlantic was the cloyingly sentimental **Everything Is Beautiful** in 1970. Other 'significant' songs like **Mr Businessman** mercifully failed to register here, and his first comedy hit was the Chipmunk-like **Bridget The Midget**, which climbed to number two in 1971. It was the switch to the Janus label that gave him his biggest hit, **The Streak**, involving the attempts of a young man wearing nothing but a smile to offend an elderly lady named Ethel.

Further hits by Ray Stevens have included an amusing country version of **Misty**. It was the Johnny Mathis version that the girl in the Clint Eastwood film wanted the DJ to play, but it was the Ray Stevens version that made the bigger chart impact in Britain. His final hit in Britain has been a tune put out under the name 'Henhouse Five Plus Two' in the States, but as Ray Stevens in Britain. It was **In The Mood** as performed by chickens, with the Mason Williams tune **Classical Cluck** on the B-side. It all but laid an egg.

351

ALWAYS YOURS

22 June 1974, for one week

Gary Glitter *Bell 1359*

Writers: Mike Leander and Gary Glitter
Producer: Mike Leander

Gary Glitter's final number one was not of the quality of **I Love You Love Me Love** (see no.340), and the message of his songs was becoming more and more straight which spelled the beginning of the end. The humour of titles like **Do You Wanna Touch Me (Oh Yeah)** and **I'm The Leader Of The Gang (I Am)** was being replaced by unexciting messages like **Always Yours** and **Love Like You And Me**. Anybody can sing that sort of stuff. What Gary Glitter always did best was to create a solidly self-mocking rock sound. **Always Yours** was a more sincere Gary Glitter that wasn't going to capture the fans' hearts for long.

The end came suddenly. After his first eleven singles hit the Top 10, the best start to a chart career in British pop history, his twelfth single **Papa Oom Mow Mow** was not included on the BBC Radio One playlist. It peaked at number 38. A small comeback was achieved in 1981, thanks to a medley single **All That Glitters** and the release of an old track as a single, **Then She Kissed Me**. But no new Glitter recording has hit the charts since 1977.

That's a pity, because he's one of the nice guys of pop and a highly original entertainer. As these words are written he is hosting Radio 4's chat programme 'Start The Week', a task that few other UK chart-toppers would tackle with equanimity.

352

SHE

29 June 1974, for four weeks

Charles Aznavour *Barclay BAR 26*

Writers: Charles Aznavour and Herbert Kretzmer
Producers: Eddie Barclay, arranged by Del Newman

The theme from the TV series *The Seven Faces Of Woman* gave French superstar Charles Aznavour his biggest international hit. In Britain, it was his only hit apart from **The Old Fashioned Way**, which despite climbing no higher than number 38 in the charts, gave Aznavour 15 weeks of chart glory, one week longer than **She**.

Charles Aznavour (born 22 May 1924) is the only French solo singer to top the British charts, although Serge Gainsbourg partnered his English friend, Jane Birkin, to number one in 1969. It gave Eddie Barclay and his Barclay Records, which had for years been hugely successful in France, his biggest international hit, and put the not obviously attractive Aznavour into the upper reaches of worldwide superstardom. Aznavour is now beyond needing chart success, like Sinatra, Tom Jones and a few others. This is lucky for him as he has had none since 1974.

She joined Anthony Newley's **Why** as the shortest title to reach number one, although less than 9 months later, a two letter title took over the honour of being the shortest at number one. British lyricist Herbert Kretzmer, in 1982 the Daily Mail TV critic, had come near to a number one in 1960 with his witty words for Peter Sellers and Sophia Loren's hit **Goodness Gracious Me**, but this time he reached the very top.

353

ROCK YOUR BABY

27 July 1974, for three weeks

George McCrae *Jayboy BOY 85*

Writers: Harry W Casey and Richard Finch
Producers: Harry W Casey and Richard Finch

Eras in popular music are quite often signalled by individual records. **Rock Your Baby** clearly began the disco craze of the seventies. The first number one by a black artist since **My Ding-a-Ling** in 1972, it was followed by five soul and reggae chart-toppers by the end of the year.

Rock Your Baby was originally intended for McCrae's wife Gwen, but when she couldn't make the session, engineer H W Casey cut the record with George, allegedly on scrap tape. The unusual production, distinguished by a lengthy introduction and the vocalist's falsetto delivery, found fast favour in Puerto Rican and gay clubs in New York. Purchases by their clientele forced the record onto WABC, then the nation's most important Top 40 outlet. Other radio stations had to follow suit, and **Rock Your Baby** became a worldwide smash with total sales estimated in excess of ten million.

McCrae had come a long way from his first group, The Fabulous Stepbrothers. Ironically, his producer and record company went on to more lasting success than he did. Casey won fame as KC of KC and the Sunshine Band while TK, an American label distributed in Britain by Jayboy, was a leading label of the mid-seventies.

354

WHEN WILL I SEE YOU AGAIN

17 August 1974, for two weeks

The Three Degrees *Philadelphia International PIR 2155*

Writers: Kenny Gamble and Leon Huff
Producers: Kenny Gamble and Leon Huff

The Three Degrees, in 1974 Fayette Pickney, Sheila Ferguson and Valerie Thompson, are Prince Charles' favourite group, if Mike Yarwood is to be believed. In 1972, after recording on a variety of American labels with little success, they moved to Philadelphia International, and success finally caught up with them. Their style was a slightly silkier version of Gladys Knight and the Pips, but definitely better looking.

When Will I See You Again was their second British hit, and it remains their only number one. By the end of 1975 the hits had stopped coming, so the group moved to Epic. That was even less successful, and by 1978 they were recording for Ariola, and concentrating on the European market where their popularity had always been greater than in their homeland. Suddenly, between October 1978 and February 1980, they had six hits, three of which made the Top 10. 1979 was their best chart year since 1974, but after **My Simple Heart** dropped off the charts in February 1980, it all stopped again as quickly as it had restarted. Even worse, Prince Charles got married.

355

LOVE ME FOR A REASON

31 August 1974, for three weeks

Osmonds *MGM 2006 458*

Writer: Johnny Bristol
Producer: Mike Curb

Five of the sons of George and Olive Osmond of Utah sang together at church functions from an early age. They are Alan, born 22 July 1949, Wayne, born 28 August 1951, Merrill, born 30 April 1953, Jay, born 12 September 1955 and Donny, born exactly two years later on 12 September 1957. Andy Williams' father heard them perform, and it was not long before the brothers became regulars on his TV show. They sang sweet harmony songs and recorded with success totally unrelated to the popular trends of the day.

In 1971 they signed with MGM and Mike Curb produced their first single on that label, **One Bad Apple**. It was a complete departure from their past (even more total than the Nolans' change of image a decade later) and they scored a number one hit in USA by sounding like a white Jackson Five. The disc flopped totally in Britain, but by the end of 1972 the Osmonds had turned disaster into triumph. That Christmas, Donny Osmond's version of the Anthony Newley/Frankie Avalon hit **Why** reached number three, The Osmonds **Crazy Horses** reached number two and Little Jimmy Osmond reached number one (see no. 324). 1973

Below left to right **356 Carl Douglas, 357 John Denver, 359 Ken Boothe, 355 Osmonds, 358 Sweet Sensation**

The Three Degrees

gave the Osmonds two more Top 10 hits, and in 1974 they reached number one with a song which entered the charts on the same day as writer Johnny Bristol's only solo hit as a performer, **Hang On In There Baby**.

—356—

KUNG FU FIGHTING

21 September 1974, for three weeks

Carl Douglas *Pye 7N 45377*

Writer: Carl Douglas
Producer: Biddu

One of the biggest hits world-wide of 1974 was the discotized tribute to the legacy of Bruce Lee by a black Londoner who came from nowhere with his self-penned song to take number one on both sides of the Atlantic. Indian producer Biddu who was later to get back to number one with his production of Tina Charles' hit **I Love To Love** (see no. 386), is the first Asian to have written, produced or performed a number one hit in Britain, unless you include Cliff Richard or Engelbert Humperdinck, for example, who were both born in India. Since Biddu's success, only Yoko Ono has brought further Asian inscrutability to the number one slot.

After the million-selling success of **Kung Fu Fighting**, Carl Douglas displayed no originality whatsoever in coming up next with **Dance The Kung Fu**. The same rhythm, virtually the same tune, practically the same words but in a different order, **Dance The Kung Fu** reached number 35 and then receded. So did Carl Douglas, who managed to run back to number 25 at Christmas 1977 with **Run Back** but who has since hidden his light under a bushel.

—357—

ANNIE'S SONG

12 October 1974, for one week

John Denver *RCA APBO 0295*

Writer: John Denver
Producer: Milt Okun

John Denver was born John Deutschendorf in New Mexico in 1933, but took his stage name from the biggest city in Colorado, the state whose natural beauty inspired many of his songs. It is an astonishing fact that this song of praise to his wife Ann is his only solo hit in Britain. Over 7 years later, a duet with Placido Domingo, **Perhaps Love**, brought him back into the charts, but his American hits like **Rocky Mountain High**, **Take Me Home Country Roads** (covered by Olivia Newton-John) and **Sunshine On My Shoulder** all failed in Britain.

Probably John Denver has reconciled himself to this failure. In the States his popularity in the early seventies was such that he eventually rated a cover of *Time* magazine. He wrote songs for other artistes, for example, **Leavin' On A Jet Plane** for Peter, Paul and Mary. He starred in the box-office smash movie *Oh God* with George Burns and continues to play sell-out concerts all over America and many other parts of the world. He can still afford to live in Aspers, Colorado, the town with the most expensive house prices in the world.

—358—

SAD SWEET DREAMER

19 October 1974, for one week

Sweet Sensation *Pye 7N 45385*

Writer: D E S Parton
Producers: D E S Parton and Tony Hatch

The Manchester-based soft soul band Sweet Sensation recorded a song which proved to be Tony Hatch's final number one production, and became one of the first of the highly choreographed British soul acts to hit the Top 10. They were the forerunners of many similar acts from the Real Thing (see no. 391) to Imagination.

At the time of their success, Sweet Sensation were an eight man outfit, like their successors at number one Showaddywaddy and Dexy's Midnight Runners. They featured four vocalists, Vincent James, Junior Daye, St Clair Palmer and Marcel King, who at 16 was the youngest member of the band. The music came from Barry Johnson on bass, Leroy Smith on piano, Roy Flowers on drums and Gary Shaughnessy, the only white man in the band, on lead guitar.

David Parton, who wrote and co-produced **Sad Sweet Dreamer** under the more formal name of D E S Parton, went on to hit the Top 10 as a vocalist in 1977 with his version of the Stevie Wonder song, **Isn't She Lovely**. Wonder had refused to allow this track, a tribute to his infant daughter, to be released as a single, and in consequence probably denied himself a number one hit. His style has over the years inspired many very successful acts, including Sweet Sensation, who climbed one step higher than Stevie Wonder has ever climbed on his own.

359

EVERYTHING I OWN

26 October 1974, for three weeks

Ken Boothe *Trojan TR 7920*

Writer: David Gates
Producer: Lloyd Chalmers

Ken Boothe was born in Jamaica in 1949, recorded a version of **Puppet On A String** in 1967 and finally climbed to the top with a song by David Gates, which Gates' group, Bread, had already taken to number 32 in Britain in the spring of 1972. Throughout the song, Ken Boothe sings **Anything I Own** rather than **Everything I Own**, thus making this record one of the few in which the title is never actually sung. There are other examples of this at number one, like **Annie's Song** and **Space Oddity**, but Ken Boothe's record is the only record on which the title should have been sung, but wasn't by mistake.

Ken Boothe seemed to have the makings of a longer lasting hitmaker than most of the reggae acts. His smoother style gave him wider appeal, and his choice of songs to record showed the breadth of his musical taste. But he only managed one more hit, **Crying Over You**, which reached number 11, and dropped off the chart at the end of February 1975.

Four days after Ken Boothe hit the top for the first time, Mohammad Ali did so for the second time, by knocking out George Foreman in Kinshasa, Zaire.

360

GONNA MAKE YOU A STAR

16 November 1974, for three weeks

David Essex *CBS 2492*

Writer: David Essex
Producer: Jeff Wayne

David Essex was born in London on 23 July 1947. He began his recording career in the mid-sixties with a series of singles that seemed destined to put him in the same bracket as David Ballantine or Wayne Gibson – almost but not quite a success. Then he landed the lead role in the musical *Godspell*, which made him a critical and popular hit, and the actor/singer David Essex became a star. After *Godspell* he made one of the best British pop films, *That'll Be The Day* in 1973, and then turned movie fiction into reality with a succession of hits. **Rock On** began the list, on which **Gonna Make You A Star** was the fourth. All his singles up to this time were self-penned and produced by Jeff Wayne. For over 2 years, the string of hits never flagged, and Essex temporarily abandoned acting to concentrate on being a pop star.

Five days after **Gonna Make You A Star** hit number one, John Stonehouse MP temporarily abandoned the world by leaving his clothes on Miami Beach and hoping the world would think he had drowned. It didn't. He was found in Australia 33 days later by somebody who thought he was Lord Lucan. Still, his disappearance made him a star.

361

YOU'RE THE FIRST THE LAST MY EVERYTHING

7 December 1974, for two weeks

Barry White *20th Century BTC 2133*

Writers: Barry White, Tony Sepe and Peter Radcliffe
Producer: Barry White

Barry White, the fat man with the deep sexy voice, was born in the Glen Campbell hit town of Galveston in 1944, and first found success as the producer of Felice Taylor, who reached number 11 with her only British hit **I Feel Love Comin' On** in 1967. Barry White mentioned on American radio, in an interview with rock DJ Jim Pewter, that Felice Taylor had had four number one hits in Britain with his productions. This is neither the first nor the last time people have claimed more chart-toppers than they have achieved.

Five years later Barry White reappeared in Britain as the voice on the telephone (and producer) on Love Unlimited's hit **Walkin' In The Rain With The One I Love**. Barry White's preference for long titles was confirmed in mid 1973 when his first solo hit **I'm Gonna Love You Just A Little Bit More, Baby**, hit the British charts. **You're The First The Last My Everything** was his fourth hit in Britain, and although it has been his only number one, his deep sexy growls with the lush string backing and the long titles produced fourteen hits in Britain between June 1973 and April 1979.

362

LONELY THIS CHRISTMAS

21 December 1974, for four weeks

Mud *RAK 187*

Writers: Nicky Chinn and Mike Chapman
Producers: Nicky Chinn and Mike Chapman

The second number one single for Mud capped a triumphant year for Les Gray and the lads, for Chinn and Chapman and for Mickie Most's RAK label. The four singles issued by Mud in 1974 gave them two number ones, a number two, (**The Cat Crept In**) and a weak single that nevertheless reached number six, **Rocket**. **Lonely This Christmas** kept Gary Glitter's **Oh Yes You're Beautiful** at number two and became the second consecutive Christmas number one with the word 'Christmas' in the title, the third and last in all. The other two are, of course, Dickie Valentine's **Christmas Alphabet** in 1955 (see no. 40) and Slade's **Merry Xmas Everybody** in 1973 (see no. 341).

RAK in 1974 had hits by Mud, Suzi Quatro, Hot Chocolate, Arrows and Kenny, all of whom managed at least one Top 10 hit. Virtually half of all RAK releases that year were hits, and this was before acts like Smokie, Racey or Kandidate had come on to the RAK roster of hitmakers. As the small labels proliferate, some very successfully like Magnet, Stiff and Ensign, and some less brilliantly, it should not be forgotten that RAK led the way towards making the independent labels respectable and respected in the music industry.

363

DOWN DOWN

18 January 1975, for one week

Status Quo *Vertigo 6059 114*

Writers: Francis Rossi and Robert Young
Producers: Status Quo

Status Quo have been making hit records for years. Francis Rossi (born 29 May 1949), Rick Parfitt (born 12 October 1948), Alan Lancaster (born 7 February 1949) and John Coghlan (born 19 September 1946) began life as the Spectres in the mid-sixties, became Traffic Jam and then finally Status Quo in 1967. They first hit the charts at the beginning of 1968 with a Francis Rossi composition **Pictures of Matchstick Men**. Four more hits came quickly, but then two hitless years followed. Status Quo seemed to be commercially dead as a group.

But, no. They developed from a post-flower power act into your actual basic rockers, the first of the heavy metal kids. Early in 1973, **Paper Plane** reached number eight, and since then the hits have just gone on and on. **Down Down** is still their only chart topper, but like the Hollies or Dave Dee, Dozy, Beaky, Mick and Tich, they have always achieved chart consistency rather than massive sellers. The style has developed slowly over the years, too. At the end of 1981, their umpteenth hit **Rock and Roll** was a very subtle tune, living up to its title, but peacefully.

364

MS. GRACE

25 January 1975, for one week

The Tymes *RCA 2493*

Writers: John and Johanna Hall
Producer: Billy Jackson

The Tymes share the perhaps useless distinction of being one of the few acts to have one and only one chart-topper in both the US and UK with different titles. Their American triumph came in 1963 with their very first single, **So Much In Love**, which only managed to reach 21 in Britain. It was on the Philadelphia-based Parkway label, part of Cameo-Parkway in the United Kingdom. The group had been spotted by a company representative at a talent show run by a rhythm and blues radio station.

After two more US Top 20 hits, a re-make of Johnny Mathis' **Wonderful! Wonderful!** and a version of **Somewhere** from *West Side Story*, the group went into obscurity, to resurface on CBS in 1968 (1969 in the UK) with an internationally popular version of Barbra Streisand's classic **People**. This time it was straight back to limbo, where they languished for 5 years before mounting a string of successes for RCA. Ironically, the one that gave them their British list leader, **Ms Grace**, was not a hit in their home country.

Perseverance pays. The Tymes' number one came 19 years after two members of the group met at a summer camp in 1956 and drafted the three others of the original quintet that autumn.

Above **365 Pilot,** *Below left to right* **361 Barry White, 367 Telly Savalas, 364 The Tymes,** *bottom* **366 Steve Harley and Cockney Rebel**

365

JANUARY

1 February 1975, for three weeks

Pilot *EMI 2255*

Writer: David Paton
Producer: Alan Parsons

With perfect timing **January** reached number one on 1 February, to give Alan Parsons his first number one production ever. His second followed immediately, but his third is yet to come. Pilot were David Paton, Ian Bairnson, Billy Lyle and Stuart Tosh. They first hit the charts with **Magic** at the end of 1974, which spent 11 weeks on the chart without reaching the Top 10, but promised great things for the future. The great things came at once, with **January** which hit number one in its third week on the charts. It was a major surprise when neither of the next two singles hit the Top 30, and the band died a natural death. The song's arranger Andrew Powell went on to record Kate Bush, and both David Paton and Ian Bairnson played on her first LP which included **Wuthering Heights** (see no. 420), but as a group Pilot was grounded.

January was the first month to appear in a number one title, apart from Rod Stewart's **Maggie May**. A year later, the Four Seasons took **December '63** (see no. 385) to number one, but otherwise months have been unsuccessful chart-toppers.

366

MAKE ME SMILE (COME UP AND SEE ME)

22 February 1975, for two weeks

Steve Harley and Cockney Rebel *EMI 2263*

Writer: Steve Harley
Producers: Steve Harley and Alan Parsons

Alan Parsons's second consecutive number one as a producer was the only chart-topper by a group who at one time looked set to be very big indeed. The line up for **Make Me Smile (Come Up And See Me)** was Steve Harley, Stuart Elliott on drums, Jim Cregan on guitar, Duncan Mackay on keyboards, and George Ford on bass. Tina Charles (see no. 386) sang back-up vocals. Jim Cregan later joined Rod Stewart and plays on **Da Ya Think I'm Sexy?** (no. 429) while Duncan Mackay moved up to Strawberry Studios when Kevin Godley and Lol Creme left 10 CC., and is to be heard on **Dreadlock Holiday** (no. 426). If this band had stayed together, they might have lived up to the promise of the first few hits. **Make Me Smile** was their third Top 10 hit, but already the group had reformed once, changing title from Cockney Rebel on **Judy Teen** and **Mr Soft** to Steve Harley and Cockney Rebel for the number one hit. Then the disintegration was rapid. One more single off the LP, **Mr. Raffles (Man It Was Mean)** made the Top 20 as the follow-up, but then Cockney Rebel disbanded. Harley had one more Top 10 hit on his own with the Lennon/McCartney tune **Here Comes The Sun**, but his career has not yet been a true reflection of a fine talent.

367

IF

8 March 1975, for two weeks

Telly Savalas *MCA 174*

Writer: David Gates
Producer: Snuff Garrett

If written by David Gates of Bread, produced by Snuff Garrett and performed by television's Kojak, Telly Savalas, created various firsts in British chart history. It was the shortest song title ever to reach number one; it was the only spoken record ever to reach number one and it was the first major hit to be broken by local radio, in this case Capital Radio in London. There are some cynics who regard this recording to be one of the less distinguished offerings to hit the top slot, but those who have heard Telly's album realise just how good **If** is.

Telly Savalas (born 2 January 1924) is one of quite a few TV cops to have hit the charts. David Soul, of *Starsky and Hutch*, is the most successful with two number ones to his name, but there is also Lee Marvin, once the hero of *The Streets Of San Francisco* and Dennis Waterman of *Sweeney* who hit number 3 at the end of 1980. Cops on TV today are a far cry from *Dixon Of Dock Green.*

Telly Savalas, who first shaved his head for a part in the Burt Lancaster film *Birdman Of Alcatraz* is not of course the only bald man to reach number one. Errol Brown of Hot Chocolate (see no. 408) is equally hairless.

368

BYE BYE BABY

22 March 1975, for six weeks

The Bay City Rollers *Bell 1409*

Writers: Bob Crewe and Bob Gaudio
Producer: Phil Wainman

The Bay City Rollers were for two years in 1974 and 1975 the teen sensation of Britain. Their talent was not limitless, but their looks and style were marketable, as Jonathan King had known when he gave them a one-off Top 10 hit in late 1971 with **Keep On Dancing**. It took two personnel changes and Bill Martin and Phil Coulter to give their records the consistent commerciality that took them to the top, and with a succession of plaintively bouncy tunes, the Bay City Rollers had four Top 10 singles in 1974. At the beginning of the new year, they switched producers again and recorded the old Four Seasons US hit **Bye Bye Baby**, a number 44 hit in Britain for the Symbols in 1967, with Phil Wainman. At last the Bay City Rollers had a number one hit.

Leslie McKeown (born 12 November 1955) was lead vocalist, with Eric Faulkner (born 21 October 1955) and Stuart 'Woody' Wood (born 25 February 1957) on guitars, Alan Longmuir (born 20 June 1953) on bass and his brother Derek (born 19 March 1955) on drums. These are the official dates of birth, but it should be noted that Derek Longmuir, for example, would have been only 16½ when **Keep On Dancing** was a hit, yet none of the group were then said to be very young. When the group was formed, in Edinburgh in 1969, most of them must have been too young to work professionally, full-time. Still, youth was one of the attractions of the Bay City Rollers, so they had to be young.

369

OH BOY

3 May 1975, for two weeks

Mud *RAK 201*

Writers: Sonny West, Norman Petty and Bill Tilghman
Producers: Nicky Chinn and Mike Chapman

Mud had already arranged their move away from the Chapman and Chinn hit production line when **Oh Boy** was released. Before they were able to record anything for their new label, Private Stock, RAK issued the track as a follow up to their St Valentine's Day single **The Secrets That You Keep**, which had been their sixth consecutive Top 10 hit. There were to be two further RAK singles after **Oh Boy** and before the first Private Stock single **L-L-Lucy** which gave Mud the ninth of their 11 Top 10 hits.

Oh Boy was the song that the Crickets had taken to number three early in 1958 as the follow-up to **That'll Be The Day** (see no. 64). Written by Sonny West and Bill Tilghman, it was one of those songs on which the writing credits became jumbled, and Norman Petty, the Crickets' producer, found his name in the brackets under the song title even though he did not write it. Nor did Chapman and Chinn, and the song became the first number one hit produced by the superproducers that they did not also write. It was also the last number one that Nicky Chinn produced, although Mike Chapman has gone on to produce four more for Blondie.

Mud and their producers had been brave to tackle such a well-known rock classic, originally sung by one of the music's greatest legends, but in doing so this sometimes underrated group came up with an inspired single, their striking multipart harmonies taking the song a long way from Holly in every aspect except that of commercial appeal. Mud's chart career ended at the beginning of 1977 when their last hit **Lean On Me** dropped off the chart after peaking at number seven. Lead-vocalist Les Gray had one more small solo hit a couple of months later, and from time to time still comes up with interesting but so far unsuccessful singles.

370

STAND BY YOUR MAN

17 May 1975, for three weeks

Tammy Wynette *Epic EPC 7137*

Writers: Billy Sherill and Tammy Wynette
Producer: Billy Sherrill

Tammy Wynette (born Wynette Pugh on 4 May 1942) of the cascading blond curls and worldy-wise country songs has been married often enough (including a tempestuous few years with country superstar George Jones) to prompt one cynical reviewer to ask "Stand By Which Man?" Her songs have always been middle-aged in outlook, dealing with the problems of marriage more often than any other theme and she was hammering away at this even when she was in her early twenties at the start of her staggeringly successful country career. For many years in the late sixties and early seventies her success in this market were unmatched by any other female. Not surprisingly in Britain, where country records usually spell commercial death, her hits have been few. The re-release of a 1968 American country number one early in 1975 turned out to be a brilliant move by Epic Records, a label with perhaps the biggest country catalogue of all. **Stand By Your Man** soared to the very top, and set up not only two more re-release hits for Miss Wynette (**D.I.V.O.R.C.E.** and **I Don't Wanna Play House**) but also number one hits for cover versions of her **No Charge** (see 389) and Billy Connolly's very funny **D.I.V.O.R.C.E.** (see no. 381). Other country hits for such people as Billie Jo Spears, Slim Whitman and Dolly Parton made the mid-seventies a boom time for country music in Britain.

371

WHISPERING GRASS

7 June 1975, for three weeks

Windsor Davies and Don Estelle *EMI 2290*

Writers: Fred and Doris Fisher
Producer: Walter Ridley

Two of the stars of one of the many successful BBC-TV comedy series by Jimmy Perry and David Croft, *It Ain't Half Hot, Mum* were Windsor Davies and Don Estelle. Welshman Windsor Davies played the Sergeant Major and tiny Don Estelle, needless to say, took the part of Lofty. Among the other stars of the show was father of five Melvyn Hayes, who had also had large roles in Cliff Richard's films, *The Young Ones*, *Summer Holiday* and *Wonderful Life*.

Don Estelle has a fine singing voice, and only his less than dominant physical presence prevented him from becoming a profesional singer. Instead he went into comedy acting, and it was an inspired move by veteran producer Walter Ridley to record Don Estelle singing **Whispering Grass** despite the background interruptions of Windsor Davies. The result was the second number one of the year by TV stars, and the first hit by actors playing comic soldiers since Michael Medwin, Bernard Bresslaw, Alfie Bass and Leslie Fyson took **The Signature Tune Of The Army Game** to number five in the summer of 1958. Davies and Estelle even had a follow-up hit, **Paper Doll**, which reached number 41 in the autumn of 1975.

372

I'M NOT IN LOVE

28 June 1975, for two weeks

10 CC *Mercury 6008 014*

Writers: Graham Gouldman and Eric Stewart
Producers: 10 CC

One of the great records of the 1970's, and certainly the best of 10 CC's many outstanding songs, was **I'm Not In Love**, the second single taken from their most adventurous album, 'Original Soundtrack'. The album was their first release on their new label, Mercury, who paid a lot to lure 10 CC away from Jonathan King's UK label, but who were rewarded by two number ones and five other Top 10 hits in the only seven singles released by 10 CC on Mercury.

Like many acts before and since, they failed to pick the best track as the first single from the album, and put out the excellent but less original **Life Is A Minestrone**, which reached number seven. The mistake was soon realised, and with a speed that would have made even Police proud, released **I'm Not In Love** as the second single only 7 weeks later. Four weeks after that it became 10 CC's second number one. After that, the gap between single releases grew longer, and only four singles by 10 CC were issued in the 3 years between **I'm Not In Love** and their last chart-topper **Dreadlock Holiday** (see no. 426). In that period Kevin Godley and Lol Creme left, leaving the writers of **I'm Not In Love** to carry on alone. They did not become 5 CC.

373

TEARS ON MY PILLOW

12 July 1975, for one week

Johnny Nash *CBS 3220*

Writer: Ernie Smith
Producer: Johnny Nash

John Lester Nash Jr, born in Houston Texas on 19 August 1940, first hit the British charts in 1968 when his reggae-flavoured **Hold Me Tight** reached number five in the autumn of that year. He had been a successful recording star in America since the end of 1957 when his first hit, **A Very Special Love**, reached number 46 in the Billboard charts. At the end of 1958, he released a single with ABC Paramount stable mates, Paul Anka and George Hamilton IV called

The Teen Commandments, which gave him his biggest hit until **Hold Me Tight** and which is now a collectors' item.

A succession of hits followed **Hold Me Tight**, oddly enough in batches of three every 3 years. After three hits in 1968/69, and three more in 1972 (including his US number one hit **I Can See Clearly Now**), **Tears On My Pillow** was the first of three hits in 1975-6. These proved to be the last he could manage. 1979 passed without Nash's distinctive voice returning to the charts, and the cycle was broken. He remains one of the most successful reggae acts in British chart history, and his early recordings of the late Bob Marley's songs certainly contributed to the subsequent success that came to Marley and the Wailers a little later.

374

GIVE A LITTLE LOVE

19 July 1975, for three weeks

The Bay City Rollers *Bell 1425*

Writers: Johnny Goodison and Phil Wainman
Producer: Phil Wainman

The second and last BCR number one was the follow up to **Bye Bye Baby** at the peak of the thankfully shortlived Rollermania. By the end of 1976, they had had their last of ten Top 10 hits, and 8 months later, they dropped off the British charts forever. Nevertheless, in two amazing years they had sold records by the truckload, and had even confounded the critics by having a number one American hit, **Saturday Night**, in 1976.

By 1980, when the authors of this book wished to invite the group to the party to celebrate the publication of the *Guinness Book Of Hits Of The 70's*, the only contact with the group was their lawyer, an Australian who refused to divulge contact numbers or addresses, no doubt for fear of writs. So the lads missed a good party. In 1981, lead singer Leslie McKeown was working steadily in Japan where his style continues to exert some appeal to the young ladies. But second billing to the Nolans is all he can command even there. How are the mighty fallen!

375

BARBADOS

9 August 1975, for one week

Typically Tropical *Gull GULS 14*

Writers: Jeffrey Calvert and Max West
Producers: Jeffrey Calvert and Max West

The saga of Coconut Airways Flight 372 to Barbados, captained by Tobias Willcock, gave two white Englishmen, Jeffrey Calvert and Max West the chance of going higher than 32 000 feet, all the way to number one.

It was a one-off reggae summer hit, but it proved what Rod Stewart had already suggested with his harmonica-playing on Millie's big hit **Lollipop**, and what Jonathan King and his very English Piglets had shown with their **Johnny Reggae**: reggae is a black music which whites can play excitingly. Perhaps there will never be a white Bob Marley, although Police have created very powerful songs in West Indian rhythms, but simple and lighthearted reggae is no worse performed by Typically Tropical than by Pluto Shervington, for instance.

Almost from the moment **Barbados** was released, it was obvious that Typically Tropical were one-hit wonders. Calvert and West continue to be active and successful in production, but as recording stars, they were never able to strike twice.

376

CAN'T GIVE YOU ANYTHING (BUT MY LOVE)

16 August 1975, for three weeks

The Stylistics *Avco 6105 039*

Writers: Hugo Peretti, Luigi Creatore and George David Weiss
Producers: Hugo Peretti and Luigi Creatore

The leftovers of two defunct Philadelphia groups, the Percussions and the Monarchs, combined at the beginning of the 1970's to create the Stylistics, a five man vocal group which built its hits around the falsetto singing of their lead vocalist, Russell Thompkins Jr. The other members of the group, James Dunn, Aaron Love, Herbie Murrell and James Smith, provided a slick backing but the only real distinction of the group sound was Thompkins' lead vocal.

When first they signed for Hugo and Luigi's Avco label, their singles were produced by Thom Bell, and in the main written by Bell and Linda Creed. Records like **I'm Stone In Love With You** and **You Make Me Feel Brand New** made the Stylistics one of the hottest groups in the world by the mid-seventies, and when Hugo and Luigi themselves (with more than a little help from the late Van McCoy) took over production of Stylistics singles, the hits carried on uninterrupted. **Can't Give You Anything (But My Love)** was the group's tenth chart single, and was co-written by George David Weiss, who had also co-written **Can't Help Falling In**

Love for Elvis Presley (see no. 133). It was no surprise, therefore, that the Stylistics recorded **Can't Help Falling In Love** in 1976 and made it one of those very rare songs to have been a Top 10 hit three times.

—377—

SAILING

6 September 1975, for four weeks

Rod Stewart *Warner Brothers K 16600*

Writer: Gavin Sutherland
Producer: Tom Dowd

Sailing had more weeks on the chart than any record from the second half of the seventies except Boney M's **Rivers of Babylon/Brown Girl in the Ring**. It had 11 weeks in its first go, which included 4 weeks at number one, and 20 weeks in the second run the following year when it crawled back to number three. The comeback was spurred by the use of the record as the theme for a BBC television series about HMS *Ark Royal*.

This song originally appeared on an album by the Sutherland Brothers. Gavin knew he had penned a catchy tune and used it with joke lyrics for a flimsy single distributed as a Christmas greeting, now a collectable for trivia buffs and Stewart aficionados.

Rod, who had realised his recording career needed a shot in the arm, went to record in the United States with legendary producer Tom Dowd. Arriving at the Muscle Shoals Studio, he inquired where the famous rhythm section was. Told they were present before him, he blurted out in surprise that they were white men. He had assumed such soulful players had to be black.

Stewart intended his version of **Sailing** to be "one for the terraces," one whose popularity would be enhanced by its use by football crowds. He was proved correct by supporters around the country.

—378—

HOLD ME CLOSE

4 October 1975, for three weeks

David Essex *CBS 3572*

Writer: David Essex
Producer: Jeff Wayne

Eleven months and three singles later, David Essex followed up his first chart-topper (see no. 360) with a second. By this time his style had developed from echoing bop-rock to Cockney-accented music reminiscent of other actor/singers like Tommy Steele and Anthony Newley. **Hold Me Close** held the top of the charts for three weeks, but proved to be the last David Essex number one. It did not prove to be the beginning of the end of his career, however. He returned to acting, and became Variety Club Personality Of The Year in 1978 thanks to his role as Che in *Evita*. His single of **Oh What A Circus** from that musical reached number three in the autumn of that year. In 1980, the theme from his motorcycling movie *Silver Dream Machine* gave him his eighth top ten hit. He continues to record regularly and tours the UK with unflagging enthusiasm and to great response, but music is only one of the strings to his bow; stage and screen are liable to see as much of Essex as the world of wax will during the next decade or so.

—379—

I ONLY HAVE EYES FOR YOU

25 October 1975, for two weeks

Art Garfunkel *CBS 3575*

Writers: Harry Warren and Al Dubin
Producer: Richard Perry

After splitting with Paul Simon, Art Garfunkel followed a film career, starring in such successes as *Catch 22* and the Jack Nicholson–Ann-Margret–Candice Bergen film *Carnal Knowledge*. He recorded only sporadically, and his first solo hit in Britain came after Paul Simon had already had four solo outings on our charts, including two Top 10 hits. Garfunkel did better than his former partner, however, by reaching the very top with a song from the 1930's which had been an American hit for the Flamingos in 1959.

The writers of this song, Harry Warren and Al Dubin, also wrote such standards as **September In The Rain** and **You're Getting To Be A Habit With Me**, but **I Only Have Eyes For You** was their only major success on the British charts. Art Garfunkel's chart career then went into total collapse until his next hit and his next number one in 1979 (see no. 436). Once again, Eyes were the secret of his success.

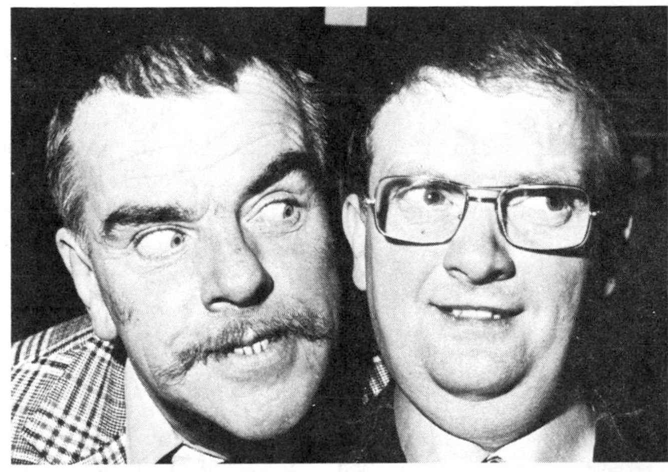

Clockwise from top left **371 Windsor Davies and Don Estelle, 374 Bay City Rollers, 381 Billy Connolly, 378 David Essex, 370 Tammy Wynette, 373 Johnny Nash, 380 David Bowie**

380

SPACE ODDITY

8 November 1975, for two weeks

David Bowie *RCA 2593*

Writer: David Bowie
Producer: Gus Dudgeon

Space Oddity was for years the only record to go to number one as a re-issue. Seeing that it first charted in 1969, it had the further distinction of being the only single to have taken more than 1 year to reach number one after its initial appearance in the best-sellers until equalled by John Lennon's **Imagine**. It was a slower moving hit than even these statistics suggest. Bowie wrote the number in 1968 for a proposed German television special, *Love You Till Tuesday*.

Space Oddity was eventually released to tie in with the 1969 Apollo moon landing, but Americans shied away from the terrible tale of Major Tom; they wished Neil Armstrong and company success, not doom. The single finally charted in Britain the first week of September, but then dropped out. It re-entered later in the month, eventually earning a placing of number five. The song finally made the American Top 10 in 1972. Upon re-issue as part of a series of RCA oldies it made its glorious British flight in 1976. Bowie re-recorded it in sparser style for a 1980 B-side. That year his **Ashes to Ashes**, which continued the story of Major Tom, became the only sequel to a number one hit to make number one itself.

Space Oddity was the only Bowie A-side produced by Gus Dudgeon, who later worked on Elton John's hits, including, ironically, **Rocket Man**. Rick Wakeman plays synthesizer on this disc.

381

D.I.V.O.R.C.E.

22 November 1975, for one week

Billy Connolly *Polydor 2058 652*

Writers: Billy Connolly, Claude Putman Jr and Bobby Braddock
Producer: Phil Coulter

Six months after Tammy Wynette hit the top of the charts with her classic moral clarion call (see no. 370), Billy Connolly adapted one of her biggest American hits to his own purposes and took it all the way to the top, bleeped language and all. The original song, which went to number 12 as the follow-up to **Stand By Your Man** in the summer of 1975, is one of the most sickly yet compulsive of all Tammy Wynette's recordings, but Billy Connolly transformed the song into the saga of a scruffy Scottish dog breaking up an otherwise happy and civilised Glasgow couple.

Billy Connolly has been so successful as a comedian that his record sales, though considerable, are merely a sideline. He has only had three chart singles, and his main success on record is on the album charts. After **D.I.V.O.R.C.E.**, he attacked another Tammy Wynette song which had in the meantime reached number one when covered by J J Barrie (see no.389). Billy Connolly's version was called **No Chance (No Charge)**. His final single hit was an abortive amalgam of the Village People's **Y.M.C.A** and **In The Navy**, called **In The Brownies**. It only reached number 38.

382

BOHEMIAN RHAPSODY

29 November 1975, for nine weeks

Queen *EMI 2375*

Writer: Freddie Mercury
Producers: Roy Thomas Baker and Queen

The success of **Bohemian Rhapsody** surprised Queen as much as anyone else. It was placed as the last track on side two of their album 'Night at the Opera' and was originally considered too long (6 minutes) and too *avant garde* for single release. But it was so well made, and the multi-tracked harmony section so intoxicating, that the decision was made to put it out as the first 45 from the set.

The results were staggering. **Bo Rhap**, as the group came to call it, spent 9 weeks at number one, including the 1975 Christmas period. Not since **Rose Marie** by Slim Whitman had ruled the roost for 11 weeks in 1955 had a single been number one for so long. The record was an international monster, selling over three million copies. 'Night at the Opera' was also propelled over the million mark.

Bohemian Rhapsody was the model for a subsequent single, **Somebody to Love**, which reached number two. Queen became associated with exquisite group harmonies and Brian May's raunchy guitar sound, both featured on this record. Ironically, the multi-tracked singing could not be duplicated on stage, so when the group came to that part of the song in live performance they would simply leave the stage while a tape played. They then returned to finish.

383

MAMMA MIA

31 January 1976, for two weeks

Abba *Epic EPC 3790*

Writers: Stig Anderson, Benny Andersson and Bjorn Ulvaeus
Producers: Benny Andersson and Bjorn Ulvaeus

The record that changed Abba from just another European group into the Superswedes whose sales exceeded those of Volvo was **Mamma Mia**. Not that **Mamma Mia** was itself a massive worldwide smash, but by giving Abba their second number one in Britain, almost 2 years after the first, it established a base of international popularity on which they built their incredible sales of the late seventies and early eighties.

Between **Waterloo** and **Mamma Mia** had been some flops and three hits. Two of those hits did not even make the Top 30, but **SOS**, the release before **Mamma Mia**, climbed to number six to return Abba to the Top 10 after 18 months absence. When **Mamma Mia** hit the top, Abba became the first act to have a number hit after their Eurovision number one, a feat that has since been equalled by Brotherhood Of Man, Cliff Richard and Buck's Fizz but never by a foreign act. Abba have changed the popular music of recent years by making record executives realise that European groups can sell, whether or not they are Abba imitators. Acts like Pussycat, Baccara and Kraftwerk owe a lot of their international success to the success of Abba, which really began with **Mamma Mia**, the 383rd record and 400th different song to reach number one.

384

FOREVER AND EVER

14 February 1976, for one week

Slik *Bell 1464*

Writers: Bill Martin and Phil Coulter
Producers: Bill Martin and Phil Coulter

Bill Martin and Phil Coulter, composers of **Puppet On A String** and **Congratulations** among countless other smaller hits moved into the early seventies looking for an outlet they could control for their writing and productions. They found the Jonathan King discards, the Bay City Rollers, and wrote and produced four Top 10 hits for them before the group moved on to Phil Wainman who gave them two number ones. Before their year with the Rollers, Martin and Coulter had been working with an Irish singer, Kenny, who had two smallish hits in 1973. When Kenny left Bill and Phil, they retained rights to the name, so when they found another group to replace the Rollers, they naturally enough called the group Kenny. That combination produced four hits in '74 and '75, three of which made the Top 10. Then Kenny and Martin and Coulter went their separate ways for the second time. Enter four more lads from Scotland, this time called Slik, and a Martin/Coulter song and production called **Forever and Ever**. At last, a number one! The song title seemed aptly named for the popularity of Slik.

But no. The follow-up single was even more aptly named **Requiem**. It reached number 24 and marked the end of Slik's career. One extremely talented lad however emerged from the ashes – the man behind both Ultravox and Visage – Midge Ure.

385

DECEMBER '63 (OH WHAT A NIGHT)

21 February 1976, for two weeks

Four Seasons *Warner Brothers K 16688*

Writers: Bob Gaudio and Judy Parker
Producer: Bob Gaudio

By December 1963, the Four Seasons had already scored four hits in Britain and many more in America. The famous line-up of Frankie Valli, Bob Gaudio, Nick Massi and Tommy de Vito which had been responsible for the sensational chart achievements of the Four Seasons in the sixties was not however the gang that brought the group's name to the top of the British charts for the first and only time. On **December '63** there were in fact five Seasons, including Messrs. Valli and Gaudio but also Don Ciccone, John Paiva and Gerry Polci, who sang lead vocal. The great Frankie Valli is only on this hit in a minor vocal role, and the truth is that by this time the Four Seasons had become little more than a studio group run by Bob Gaudio (but a very good one).

The Four (or Five) Seasons, then, finally reached number one with their thirteenth British hit, 13 years and 140 days after their first hit entered the chart, the week before the Beatles first hit. Only four acts have ever taken longer to reach the top, and even then the Four Seasons nearly didn't make it. The British Market Research Bureau computer went haywire on that week's computations, and the chart which Johnny Walker announced on Radio 1 at lunchtime on 17 February 1976 showed **Rodrigo's Guitar Concerto d'Aranjuez** by Manuel and his Music of the Mountains at number one, with the Four Seasons staying still at number three. Three hours later, a corrected chart was announced, and poor Manuel (Geoff Love) found himself at number four while Frankie Valli and company moved up to number one. The next week Manuel moved up to number three, but he never did get to the top.

386

I LOVE TO LOVE (BUT MY BABY LOVES TO DANCE)

6 March 1976, for three weeks

Tina Charles *CBS 3937*

Writers: Jack Robinson and James Bolden
Producer: Biddu

Tina Charles is perhaps the smallest adult to have reached the number one spot, although full statistics are not available on this point. Certainly she was taller than Little Jimmy Osmond (who would now tower over her) and many of the St Winifred's School Choir, but as Brenda Lee never had a number one hit, Tina Charles or Don Estelle must be considered the most petite of them all.

Her voice was far from small. She sang lead on **I'm On Fire**, as a session singer, which became a number 4 hit under the group name 5000 Volts in the autumn of 1975. 5000 Volts never performed their first hit live or on TV with the record's lead vocalist. Tina Charles then teamed up with producer Biddu, who had also had a hit late in 1975 with his orchestra and the theme from the film *Summer Of '42*. The result was Biddu's second chart-topping production (see also no. 356) and the first of seven hits for Miss Charles in the following 2 years. 5000 Volts' only other hit (without Tina) was a song called **Dr Kiss Kiss** which reached number eight in summer '76. Tina topped this 5 months later as far as medical tunes were concerned by hitting number 4 with **Dr Love**.

387

SAVE YOUR KISSES FOR ME

27 March 1976, for six weeks

Brotherhood of Man *Pye 7N 45569*

Writers: Tony Hiller, Martin Lee and Lee Sheriden
Producer: Tony Hiller

More than **Waterloo**, more than **Puppet On A String**, more than **Non Ho L'Eta Per Amarti**, **Save Your Kisses For Me** was a runaway Eurovision Song Contest winner even before the voting had started. The coy little song of Daddy going to work and leaving his 3-year-old daughter at home for the day not only smashed through the charts and into the hearts of Europe, but marked an astonishing and surprisingly long-lived comeback for Brotherhood of Man.

In 1970, Brotherhood of Man were a two men, two girl vocal group rather hurriedly put together around a session hit, **United We Stand**. That reached number 10 in Britain, but gained notoriety in America as an anthem of homosexuality in the early seventies. There is nothing in the lyrics to assume that the subject might be homosexuality, but it's an easy song to sing along with and the group's name could be made to fit the cause. Anyhow, that was to all intents and purposes the beginning and the end of Brotherhood of Man Mark One.

Then in 1976 Mark Two won Eurovision.

388

FERNANDO

8 May 1976, for four weeks

Abba *Epic EPC 4036*

Writers: Stig Anderson, Benny Andersson and Bjorn Ulvaeus
Producers: Benny Andersson and Bjorn Ulvaeus

Abba's third number one, their second in succession, was **Fernando**. It knocked Brotherhood of Man off the top, but they retaliated by modelling their style ever closer on Abba, and even coming up with two more chart-toppers, **Angelo** and **Figaro** (see nos. 410 and 418) whose titles bore a more than coincidental similarity to **Fernando**.

Fernando was a gentle anti-war song, featuring the only mistake in English in Bjorn Ulvaeus' lyrics, when he wrote 'Since many years I haven't seen a rifle in your hand'. It

Right **382 Queen**

390 The Wurzels

391 Real Thing

may seem churlish to point out the mistakes in English, but it is worth mentioning only because it is unique. How many English writers could write nine number one hits in a foreign language virtually without error? Albert Hammond (writer of **When I Need You** – no. 401) speaks fluent Spanish, but even he prefers to write about the rain in Southern California rather than the rain in Spain. Abba have also had hits with song titles in Italian, **Mamma Mia**, and French, **Voulez-vous**, but the nearest they have got to their native Swedish was their ode to Stockholm, **Summer Night City**.

389

NO CHARGE

5 June 1976, for one week

J J Barrie *Power Exchange PX 209*

Writer: Harlan Howard
Producer: Bill Amesbury

Canadian J J Barrie, an executive at the small Power Exchange label, decided to make a version of the Tammy Wynette and Tina classic, **No Charge**. There is no simple explanation why his husky version should have shot to the top of the charts, but it did. The sickly sentimentality of the song, which is as hard to take as **Deck of Cards** or Red Sovine's **Teddy Bear**, is saved only in Tammy Wynette's version by the voice of her daughter Tina and by the way Miss Wynette obviously thinks the sentiments are second only to those of the Lord's Prayer as a guide to a moral life. Mr Barrie misses all this in his version, which sounds like a DJ reading the traffic news on the air, all sincerity and smiles into the microphone, with no thought about what he is actually saying.

Fortunately for Western civilisation, Mr Barrie's attempts at a follow-up in a similar vein failed to attract the cash from the pockets of the public. Mr Barrie is thus a one-hit wonder, the twenty-first on the list at that time.

390

COMBINE HARVESTER (BRAND NEW KEY)

12 June 1976, for two weeks

Wurzels *EMI 2450*

Writer: Melanie Safka
Producer: Bob Barratt

Melanie Safka has been greatly underrated by the British record-buying public, possibly because she recorded for Buddah, the American teenybop label. Her versions of oldies like **Ruby Tuesday** or **Will You Love Me Tomorrow** show a vocal style not unlike Toyah Willcox and the punk ladies of the 1980's, while her compositions, like **Brand New Key** and **What Have They Done To My Song, Ma** convey a sense of bewilderment about this modern world that matches Pete Townshend's **I Can't Explain** or **Substitute**.

The Wurzels, who had been Adge Culter's backing group until his death in a car crash, were Tommy Banner, Tony Baylis and Pete Budd. Although they gave themselves no writing credit on the label, they transformed Melanie's **Brand New Key** into a saga of a West Country farmer courting his ladylove. It took over the top spot for two weeks during the scorching summer of 1976 which was bad news for most farmers, with or without combine harvesters. A follow-up, **I Am A Cider Drinker**, based on the George Baker song, **Paloma Blanca**, hit number three, but **I Was Farmer Bill's Cowman** was the last straw between the Wurzel's teeth.

391

YOU TO ME ARE EVERYTHING

26 June 1976, for three weeks

Real Thing *Pye International 7N 25709*

Writers: Ken Gold and Micky Denne
Producer: Ken Gold

The Real Thing, four Liverpool lads, were first noticed on *Opportunity Knocks*, the Hughie Green TV talent show, by Tony Hall, the ex-Radio Luxenbourg DJ who also played a significant part in the early career development of budding songwriter Tim Rice.

Success was not immediate for the Real Thing, lead singer Chris Amoo, his brother Eddie, Dave Smith and Ray Lake. Contracts with a couple of major record labels led to nothing, and it was not until Pye signed the foursome and Ken Gold produced **You To Me Are Everything** that they first tasted success. It climbed quickly to number one and led off a list of nine hits on Pye over a 3 year period, including **Can't Get By Without You**, which reached number two, and over 2 years later, **Can You Feel The Force** which climbed to number five.

A label change to Calibre in 1980 produced the small hit **She's A Groovy Freak**. The Real Thing also tour with David Essex as his vocal backing group.

—392—

THE ROUSSOS PHENOMENON (EP)

17 July 1976, for one week

Demis Roussos *Philips DEMIS 001*

Writers: Forever and Ever – Stylianos Vlavianos, Robert Constandinos, Sing An Ode To Love – Stylianos Vlavianos, Robert Constandinos and Charalampe Chalkitis, So Dreamy – Stylianos Vlavianos and Robert Constandinos, My Friend The Wind – Stylianos Vlavianos and Robert Constandinos
Producer: Demis Roussos

Demis Roussos, like Vangelis a former member of the group Aphrodite's Child whose million-selling **Rain and Tears** hit the British Top 30 late in 1968, is possibly the largest performer ever to reach number one. He is certainly the first Greek performer to reach number one, the first performer to reach number one with an EP and the first person to reach number one with a song title that has been used before to take a different song to number one. He remains the only Greek among the chart-toppers, but the Specials have equalled his achievement in taking an EP to the top (see no. 450) and **Forever and Ever** is no longer the only title to have been used for two different chart-toppers. Frankie Laine and Barbra Streisand have both scored with a different **Woman In Love**.

The vast Mr Roussos, clad only in kaftan and much hair, is an unlikely sex object for the female of the species, but like the almost equally enormous Barry White, for a while he was the breaker of a million hearts with every song he sang. Born on 15 June 1947, he began his chart career with **Happy To Be On An Island In The Sun**, a Top 10 hit at the end of 1975, and in 1976, scored with **Can't Say How Much I Love You**, his number one EP and **When Forever Has Gone** which reached number two. In 1977, his magic touch deserted him, and despite a popularity which remains, he has been hitless for 5 years.

—393—

DON'T GO BREAKING MY HEART

24 July 1976, for six weeks

Elton John and Kiki Dee *Rocket ROKN 512*

Writers: Elton John and Bernie Taupin
Producer: Gus Dudgeon

Elton John was the world's most prominent and best-selling recording artist in the early and mid-1970's. But for all his global success he had never reached number one in his home country, coming closest with the 1972 number two **Rocket Man**. In March of 1976 he recorded his part of the duet at Eastern Sound in Toronto, Canada. The tape was then brought to London where Kiki Dee added her vocal. As usual, Gus Dudgeon produced and Bernie Taupin supplied the lyric. The difference was the use of the songwriting pseudonyms Anne Orson and Carte Blanche, which Elton and Bernie sometimes used when penning material for Kiki.

Elton's first release on his Rocket label, the record exploded in the summer, going to number one in Britain for 6 weeks and America for 4. It penetrated international markets previously closed to Elton as a soloist. **Don't Go Breaking My Heart** was the world number one for 1976.

Bizarrely, there was never a proper follow-up. The pair considered recording the Four Tops' **Loving You Is Sweeter Than Ever** but didn't get around to it until 1981, and even then only as an album track. The release of **Don't Go Breaking My Heart** came as Elton entered a period of voluntary retirement, with no original studio material emerging for 2 years. The team of Elton John and Kiki Dee joined Frank and Nancy Sinatra and Paul McCartney with Stevie Wonder as the one-hit wonders who had a number one with their only release.

—394—

DANCING QUEEN

4 September 1976, for six weeks

Abba *Epic EPC 4499*

Writers: Stig Anderson, Benny Andersson and Bjorn Ulvaeus
Producers: Benny Andersson and Bjorn Ulvaeus

Abba completed their first hat-trick of number ones in Britain with **Dancing Queen**, which also became their only American number one. Abba had been quoted as saying that they would never tour America until they had had a number one hit there, so the success of **Dancing Queen** gave them the excuse to sample the delights of motels and fast food in the United States. We can only assume that the failure of Abba to manage a second number one in America is directly due to the fact that they don't like Big Macs or Holiday Inns, and thus have never spent long enough in the States to make the big breakthrough.

The follow-up to **Dancing Queen** was their only single in 3 years not to make the top. It was called **Money Money**

Money and reached number three. It confirmed the jinx on 'money' records. The Bay City Rollers followed up two number ones with **Money Honey** which also reached number three. Elvis Presley's first flop after five consecutive number ones in 1961 and 1962 was **One Broken Heart For Sale**, and only the Beatles with **Can't Buy Me Love** have managed to sing about money without a drop in popularity.

395

MISSISSIPPI

4 September 1976, for four weeks

Pussycat *Sonet SON 2077*

Writer: Werner Theunissen

Producer: Eddy Hilberts

Pussycat became the third European act to hit number one in Britain in 1976, the only year until 1982 in which so many of our chart-toppers came from the continent. Pussycat, who began life in Limburg in South Holland, became the first Dutch act to top the UK charts with the third number one song about an American state, after **Carolina Moon** (see no. 75) and **Massachusetts** (see no. 238).

The line up on **Mississippi** was Lou Willé, his wife Tony who sang lead, her two sisters Marianne Hensen and Betty Dragstra, Theo Wetzels, Theo Coumans and John Theunissen. The three girls had been telephone operators in Limburg, while John and the two Theos had begun as a three-piece outfit called Scum. Lou Willé played with his brothers in a group called Ricky Rendell and his Centurions until he married Tony and helped create a band called Sweet Reaction.

When this band signed to EMI-Bovema in Holland and producer Eddy Hilberts took them into the studio, he changed their name to Pussycat and gave them a song written 6 years earlier by Werner Theunissen, who was guitar tutor to the three girls in Pussycat. The song, **Mississippi** was their first single and sold a reputed 4½ million copies worldwide, making Pussycat the biggest thing to come out of Limburg since the cheese.

396

IF YOU LEAVE ME NOW

16 October 1976, for three weeks

Chicago *CBS 4603*

Writer: Pete Cetera

Producer: James Guercio

Chicago began life in the late sixties as Chicago Transit Authority, which persuaded one co-author to release a couple of singles under the name Huddersfield Transit Authority. For a while it looked as though the two organisations would enjoy equal success in UK, but then CTA became just plain Chicago and hit with the Spencer Davis hit, **I'm A Man**. The follow-up was another Top 10 hit, **25 or 6 to 4** which was either the odds on the winner in the 1927 Derby or else the time of the last train to San Fernando. Six hitless years followed (for both Huddersfield and Chicago; Huddersfield were also during this period relegated to Division Four), and then at the end of 1976, **If You Leave Me Now** climbed to the very top.

The prime movers of Chicago were Pete Cetera, the vocalist, born on 13 September 1944, Robert Lamm on keyboards (born 13 October 1944) and Terry Kath on guitar (born 31 January 1946) who was killed in a shooting accident. The rest of the line-up was Lee Loughnane, Jim Pankow, Walter Parazaider, Dan Seraphine and Laudir Oliviera, a Brazilian who joined in 1974. They made a string of original albums, Chicago I, Chicago II, Chicago III and so on until by 1982 they had reached Chicago 16, by which time they had abandoned Roman numerals. **If You Leave Me Now** was a lovely song from Chicago X.

397

UNDER THE MOON OF LOVE

4 December 1976, for three weeks

Showaddywaddy *Bell 1495*

Writers: Tommy Boyce and Curtis Lee

Producer: Mike Hurst

Showaddywaddy are eight lads from Leicester who first appeared on ITV's *New Faces* television show and from there brought rock and roll back into the charts. Since the success of Showaddywaddy, masterminded by ex-Springfield Mike Hurst, old rock songs, Teddy Boy DA's, velvet collars and creepers, have become regular chart entrants. Acts like Darts, who revived black rock songs of the fifties and sixties, Shakin' Stevens, who revives pre-rock songs in rock style, Alvin Stardust and Jets all owe some of their commercial success to the pioneering oldies revamp work done by Showaddywaddy.

Under The Moon Of Love had been co-writer Curtis Lee's follow-up to his Top 10 American smash, **Pretty Little Angel Eyes** in 1961. Lee's version of that song reached number 47 in Britain, but the follow-up failed. **Pretty Little Angel Eyes** was revived in 1978 by Showaddywaddy to give them their

Above **398 Johnny Mathis**

Right **397 Showaddy-waddy**

Above **393 Elton John and Kiki Dee**

Below **395 Pussycat**

seventh consecutive Top 10 hit, but since then there have been no more top tenners for Malcolm Allured, Dave Bartram, Romeo Challenger, Rod Deas, Russ Fields, Billy Gask, Al James and Trevor Oakes, who together make Showaddywaddy.

398

WHEN A CHILD IS BORN (SOLEADO)

25 December 1976, for three weeks

Johnny Mathis *CBS 4599*

Writers: Fred Jay and Di Damicco Ciro
Producer: Jack Gold

Eighteen years and 216 days after the first chart appearance of Johnny Mathis (born in San Francisco on 30 September 1935) he finally hit the number one spot with a million-selling Christmas hit. Eighteen years earlier he had recorded another Christmas song, which only took him to number 17 in the British charts but which has sold probably more records in all versions than any Christmas song except **White Christmas**. That song was **Winter Wonderland**.

Mathis racked up nine hits between May 1958 and the end of 1960, including three Top 10 hits and possibly his best known hit of all **Misty**, which only reached number 12. Then the bottom fell out of the Mathis market, and apart from one week at number 49 on 4 April 1963, he was hitless until early 1975 when his remake of the Stylistics 1972 hit **I'm Stone In Love With You** climbed to number 10. All the time, Johnny Mathis had not been starving, however. His albums never stopped selling, including his 'Johnny's Greatest Hits' album which stayed on the American charts for 490 weeks from April 1958. Now his career is steaming along on all fronts, with two hit singles in duet with Deniece Williams and another solo Top 20 hit in 1979 to make him one of the select few artists whose British chart career spans over 20 years.

399

DON'T GIVE UP ON US

15 January 1977, for four weeks

David Soul *Private Stock PVT 84*

Writer: Tony Macaulay
Producer: Tony Macaulay

The record which topped the charts on 6 February 1977, the actual date of the Queen's Silver Jubilee which dominated the year in Britain, was by David Soul, Hutch of the very popular television detective series, *Starsky and Hutch*. Tony Macaulay, one of the most successful writers and producers in British chart history, noticed the potential of David Soul and came up with a very strong song for the blond actor to record. Soul has by far the best voice of any chart-topping actor-turned-singer, with the possible exception of Anthony Newley, and given such outstanding material to match his voice and looks, it was no surprise to see his debut single at number one.

Don't Give Up On Us was also a monster hit in Soul's homeland, making him the second Soul brother to hit high up the American charts. In 1963, Jimmy Soul's song in praise of fat and ugly women, **If You Wanna Be Happy** had taken the Soul name into the American top ten for the first time. Surprisingly, the surnames, Reggae and Country have never been used by chart acts, although there have been two Blues, and Sir Monti Rock III who contributed to the success of Disco Tex and the Sex-O-Lettes.

400

DON'T CRY FOR ME ARGENTINA

12 February 1977, for one week

Julie Covington *MCA 260*

Writers: Tim Rice and Andrew Lloyd Webber
Producers: Tim Rice and Andrew Lloyd Webber

The hit tune from the staggeringly successful musical *Evita* was not given its title, which has now passed into the realms of popular cliché, until almost the final take of the final recording session of the original 'Evita' album.

An extensive search for a girl to take the title role on the record ended when the performance of Julie Covington in the TV series *Rock Follies* persuaded Rice and Lloyd Webber that this was the girl they wanted for the role. The recording went very well, but for the strongest tune Rice wanted a title that would make the song a hit out of the context of *Evita*. Covington even recorded the title line as 'It's Only Your Lover Returning'. This just didn't sound right so, with the deadline for completion of the album approaching, it was decided that **Don't Cry For Me Argentina** would have to do; a good title for the story line but a rotten one (so everybody thought) for a single release from the album.

Nobody need have worried. The single sold 980 000 copies in UK alone and made Covington an even bigger star than her fellow members of Cambridge University's Footlights Club of the mid-sixties, people like Clive James, Germaine Greer, Rob Buckman and Jo Rice.

401

WHEN I NEED YOU

19 February 1977, for three weeks

Leo Sayer *Chrysalis CHS 2127*

Writers: Albert Hammond and Carole Bayer Sager
Producer: Richard Perry

Leo Sayer, born in Shoreham in Sussex on 24 May 1948, first came to the notice of the record-buying public early in 1973. That was when the début solo LP by Roger Daltrey of the Who was released featuring songs by Leo Sayer and Dave Courtney. A single culled from the LP, **Giving It All Away**, took Roger Daltrey to number five in the late spring of that year. Leo Sayer, like Sandie Shaw, had been discovered by Adam Faith, but unlike Sandie Shaw, Sayer was also managed by Adam Faith, who by the early seventies had given up singing.

At the end of 1973, Leo Sayer's first single **The Show Must Go On** was released. He performed the song with whitened face and a clown's outfit and the song shot up to number two. In America it was covered by Three Dog Night who also enjoyed a Top 10 smash with the song. It might have been difficult to throw off the clown image, which like Gilbert O'Sullivan's short trousers and pudding basin haircut was fine for attracting public attention but not much good for sustaining a musical career. However, Sayer followed up with hit after hit – **One Man Band** (another song originally recorded by Roger Daltrey), **Long Tall Glasses, Moonlighting** and his first American chart-topper **You Make Me Feel Like Dancing**. After three number two hits in his first five singles, Sayer must have despaired of ever topping the charts. But on 19 February 1977, his sixth hit (and the first not co-written by Leo Sayer) gave the Chrysalis label their first ever number one hit.

402

CHANSON D'AMOUR

12 March 1977, for three weeks

Manhattan Transfer *Atlantic K 10886*

Writer: Wayne Shanklin
Producer: Richard Perry

Richard Perry's second consecutive number one as a producer was track three on side one of Manhattan Transfer's second LP, 'Coming Out'. Manhattan Transfer are a two men, two girls vocal group (then Alan Paul, Tim Hauser, Laurel Massé and Janis Siegel), but there the similarity with Abba ends. Except that Tim Hauser has a beard like Bjorn and Benny.

Chanson d'Amour is an American song, dating from 1958, and not a French song translated. It is unlikely that correct French pronunciation would stand for the rhyme of 'amour' with 'je t'adore', which is the basis of this song. The tenor sax solo by Jay Migliori adds to the French flavour of the record, but it is actually as American as **Que Sera Sera**. Manhattan Transfer can sing in a wide variety of styles, but in terms of popularity this has probably been of as little help as it was to Bobby Darin. Bobby Darin lost one lot of fans and found another as he moved from **Dream Lover** to **Mack The Knife** to **Things** and Manhattan Transfer have not found an audience which can accept not only **Chanson d'Amour** but also **Don't Let Go, Operator, Tuxedo Junction** or **Who What When Where Why**, all brilliantly performed but all quite different.

403

KNOWING ME KNOWING YOU

2nd April 1977, for five weeks

Abba *Epic EPC 4955*

Writers: Benny Andersson, Stig Anderson and Bjorn Ulvaeus
Producers: Benny Andersson and Bjorn Ulvaeus

Despite the small hiccup in Abba's stream of chart successes when **Money Money Money** reached only number three, the boys and girls from snowy Sweden showed their ability to bounce back when their next single, **Knowing Me Knowing You**, hit the top on 2 April 1977, in its sixth week on the chart. It then stayed there for 5 weeks, and became the first number one in Abba's second hat-trick of chart-toppers. That second hat-trick took 46 weeks to complete, the third slowest hat-trick after the Beatles' **Lady Madonna/Hey Jude/Get Back** hat-trick which covered 56 weeks, and Police, who took 52 weeks in 1979 and 1980 over the hat-trick. The Beatles took 46 weeks over their **Help/Day Tripper/Paperback Writer** hat-trick as well. John Lennon completed his posthumous hat-trick in 7 weeks.

404

FREE

7 May 1977, for two weeks

Deniece Williams *CBS 4978*

Writers: Deniece Williams, Hank Redd, Nathan Watts and Susaye Green
Producers: Maurice White and Charles Stepney

Deniece Williams, no relation of Andy, David, Billy, Danny, Don, Iris, John, Kenny, Larry, Lenny, Mason, Maurice or even Kenneth, was discovered by Maurice White of Earth, Wind and Fire and joined CBS on his recommendation. Although Earth, Wind and Fire have become one of the most successful chart acts in Britain since 1978, by the time Deniece Williams hit number one with **Free**, EWF had managed only one small chart hit on this side of the Atlantic, **Saturday Nite**, which reached number 17 about the time **Free** was released. Their reputation was more Windy than Earthy or Fiery, and it took the classic single **September** at the very end of 1978 to establish them in Britain.

Deniece Williams had three hits in 1977, but since then her solo career has collapsed. In 1978, she and the rejuvenated Johnny Mathis took the nonsensically titled **Too Much Too Little Too Late** to number three but apart from a smaller follow-up hit, the duo have not been seen in the charts again. Miss Williams remains active however, and may well return to her old chart-busting ways in the future.

405

I DON'T WANT TO TALK ABOUT IT/FIRST CUT IS THE DEEPEST

21 May 1977, for four weeks

Rod Stewart *RIVA 7*

Writers: I Don't Want To Talk About It – Danny Whitten. First Cut Is The Deepest – Cat Stevens
Producer: Tom Dowd

Here was a case where the artist really had to thank his fans for his number one. Without their participation, **I Don't Want To Talk About It** would never even have been released. It originally appeared on the album 'Atlantic Crossing' leading off the slow side of the set that included **This Old Heart Of Mine** and concluded with **Sailing**. The massive success of the latter track tended to obscure the remaining material, and Stewart's new label Riva began issuing singles from the following album, 'Night On The Town' in the summer of 1976.

But at the Christmas concerts Rod gave in London that year he and his associates were startled when fans sang along with the chorus of **I Don't Want To Talk About It**, even continuing when Rod dropped out to watch them. Clearly the artist had a potential hit of which he had been unawares. The track was made his next single, and it went to number one for 4 weeks. Since so many fans already had 'Atlantic Crossing', a track from 'Night On The Town', **First Cut Is The Deepest**, was made part of a double-A disc, but **Talk** was far and away the lead side.

Sadly, Danny Whitten, a member of Neil Young's Crazy Horse and author of the song, did not live to see it become a hit. He was dead of a drug overdose.

406

LUCILLE

18 June 1977, for one week

Kenny Rogers *United Artists UP 36242*

Writers: Roger Bowling and Hal Bynum
Producer: Larry Butler

Kenny Rogers, like Barry McGuire a graduate of the New Christy Minstrels, first hit the recording big-time in the States with a single called **Just Dropped In (To See What Condition My Condition Was In)** which was by a group in which Rogers sang lead, First Edition. It failed in Britain, but a follow-up (much more country than the psychedelic **Just Dropped In**) reached number two in Britain in 1969. This was the epic saga of the wounded Vietnam war veteran no longer capable of satisfying his wife, **Ruby Don't Take Your Love To Town**. The aching Kenny Rogers voice was perfect for the maudlin, some would say tasteless, sentiments of the song. The follow-up single was **Something's Burning** (written by Mac Davis), and that too reached our Top 10. Then First Edition disbanded and no more was heard of Kenny Rogers in Britain until **Lucille** in 1977.

By then, Kenny Rogers had become America's leading country male vocalist, and under the expert guidance of Larry Butler, was creating a string of mammoth country and pop hits that turned the bearded and burly Mr Rogers into the biggest selling pop act in America in the late seventies and early eighties. The sad story of the girl he met in a bar in Toledo was but one of those mammoth hits.

400 Julie Covington

Left **401 Leo Sayer**

Below **404 Deniece Williams**

406 Kenny Rogers

Below **408 Hot Chocolate**

407

SHOW YOU THE WAY TO GO

25 June 1977, for one week

Jacksons *Epic EPC 5266*

Writers: Kenny Gamble and Leon Huff
Producers: Kenny Gamble and Leon Huff

At the end of 1976, the Jackson 5 left Tamla-Motown, where they had been taken by their discoverer Diana Ross. Their recording career was in a slump. Jermaine Jackson, who had married Berry Gordy's daughter, stayed in Detroit, but the Jackson Four plus Randy Jackson, the youngest of them all, completed the move to Epic and became the Jacksons. Almost immediately, under the guidance of Kenny Gamble and Leon Huff (see no. 354 **When Will I See You Again**), they hit form again and achieved their only British chart-topper.

Show You The Way To Go was not their greatest single, but it had an energy that had been lacking from their later Motown efforts, and in a year of often uninspiring number ones, it managed to grab the top for one short week at the end of June.

Regular hits have followed for the Jacksons and for lead singer Michael Jackson on his own, but only two of these hits have reached the Top 10. At the end of 1980 they came up with possibly the most stupid choice of title ever for a new song – the same as that of the immortal Elvis number – **Heartbreak Hotel**.

408

SO YOU WIN AGAIN

2 July 1977, for three weeks

Hot Chocolate *RAK 259*

Writer: Russ Ballard
Producer: Mickie Most

Only three acts had hits on the British charts in every year of the seventies. They were Elvis Presley, Diana Ross and the very under-rated but consistently successful Hot Chocolate. Beginning in 1970 with **Love Is Life**, which climbed to number six, Hot Chocolate produced a string of fourteen hits, six of which hit the Top 10, before **So You Win Again** finally put them at number one.

Only thirteen of the 319 acts to have hit the top have taken ten or more hits to achieve their first number one. Top of the list of slow starters is the late Jim Reeves, whose **Distant Drums** (see no. 224) was his sixteenth chart single. Second equal, the acts who took 15 hits each to come up with a chart-topper, are Wings and Hot Chocolate. For Mickie Most, 2 July 1977 must have been a very satisfying day, as it was for Hot Chocolate and their lead singer Errol Brown, whose distinctive voice has done as much as Mickie Most's productions to keep them on top. Since **So You Win Again**, the hits have carried on almost as consistently, including their biggest American hit, **Every 1's A Winner**. But perhaps Hot Chocolate had their greatest moment with their classic 1974 offering **Emma** which peaked at number three.

409

I FEEL LOVE

23 July 1977, for four weeks

Donna Summer *GTO GT 100*

Writers: Giorgio Moroder, Pete Bellotte and Donna Summer
Producers: Giorgio Moroder and Pete Bellotte

Giorgio Moroder was first heard of as the composer and original performer in Italy of the Chicory Tip number one **Son Of My Father** (see no. 310). Five and a half years later he turns up in California as the composer and producer of disco goddess Donna Summer, whose **I Feel Love** was only marginally more subtle than her semi-pornographic **Love To Love You Baby** which gave her her first British hit at the beginning of 1976.

The disco craze was perhaps started by George McCrae but the most successful of all the disco performers has been Donna Summer. Disco music gave female performers back the popularity that had been largely wiped out by the Beatles and their followers throughout the sixties and early seventies. Since **I Feel Love**, over 25 records featuring female lead singers have hit number one, mainly disco sounds from people like Anita Ward and Fern Kinney, Blondic and Gloria Gaynor, Aneka and Barbra Streisand. All of them owe a debt to Donna Summer, whose 20 hits in a 5 year period between January 1976 and November 1980 made disco music the most popular music in the world.

410

ANGELO

20 August 1977, for one week

Brotherhood of Man *Pye 7N 45699*

Writers: Tony Hiller, Martin Lee and Lee Sheriden
Producer: Tony Hiller

The sad story of the Mexican shepherd boy Angelo gave Brotherhood of Man their second number one and confirmed their style of music as Abba-inspired. Their Eurovision chart-topper of 1976, **Save Your Kisses For Me** (see no. 387) was obviously in the style of Abba, but then so were practically all the successful Europop songs of the mid-seventies. Brotherhood Of Man's third post-Eurovision single had been an imaginative cover of Diana Trask's big US country hit, **Oh Boy (The Mood I'm In)**, which led fans to assume that the Abba influence had waned as far as the Brotherhood were concerned. This proved not to be the case when their next single, **Angelo**, came out. But they answered their critics in the best possible way – the record shot to number one.

Angelo lived high on a mountain in Mexico, and when he and his rich girlfriend ran away together, they ran and ran until they reached the coast where they chose to die in the sand. The cause of death is not stated, but one must suspect exhaustion.

411

FLOAT ON

27 August 1977, for one week

Floaters *ABC 4187*

Writers: Arnold Ingram, James Mitchell Jr and Marvin Willis
Producer: Woody Wilson

The Floaters were four starstruck men with unusual tastes in women. Ronnie Floater was an Aquarius who liked 'a woman who can hold her own'. Many Aquarians also like women who buy their own. Charles Floater was a Libra (and everybody knows that Aquarians and Librans are incompatible) and he liked 'a woman who carries herself like Miss Universe'. Don't we all. Paul Floater was a Leo, and much less fussy. He liked 'All women of the world'. The fourth Floater was Larry, a Cancer who was rather optimistically looking for 'a woman that loves everything and everybody'. It was a pity that he had stipulated that the object of his desires had to be a woman. Otherwise Paul Floater would have fitted his bill. As nobody loved the Floaters' follow-up single, one can assume that Larry Floater has failed to find his ideal woman. Perhaps he has been able to make do with one of Paul Floater's flotilla.

412

WAY DOWN

3 September 1977, for five weeks

Elvis Presley *RCA PB 0998*

Writer: Layng Martine, Jr
Producers: Elvis Presley and Felton Jarvis

Elvis 17th and final UK number one was the single that had been issued shortly before his tragic death on 16 August 1977. It had not shown signs of being more than a minor chart entry when the King died and immediately it shot to number one. It was ironic that his death should have resulted in his equalling the Beatles' all-time record of 17 number one records. The song was written by Layng Martine, Jr and is the only Elvis number one to carry a production credit, as follows: 'Executive producer: Elvis Presley; Associate Producer: Felton Jarvis.' Vocal accompaniment is by J D Sumner and the Stamps quartet, Kathy Westmoreland, Sherrill Neilson and Myrna Smith. The track was recorded at Elvis' home, Graceland, in Memphis during sessions at the end of October 1976. James Burton is one of the guitarists on the sessions. These were the last studio recordings of Presley's life – all that was to come in 1977 were some indifferent concert tapings of previously recorded material. Since his death Elvis has had several more hits, two of which made the Top 10. An 18th number one is obviously not impossible but as the years go by, becomes less and less likely. It is probably right that Elvis and the Beatles should remain the all-time joint UK number one champions.

413

SILVER LADY

8 October 1977, for three weeks

David Soul *Private Stock PVT 115*

Writers: Tony Macaulay and Geoff Stephens
Producer: Tony Macaulay

David Soul's face is his fortune, but his first big career break came in 1966 on the American TV talk show, *The Merv*

Griffin Show, when he sang with a hood over his head. After thirty or so appearances on the Merv Griffin Show, singing as the 'Covered Man', David Soul uncovered himself and quickly signed a TV contract for a series called *Here Come The Brides*.

This led to appearances on *The Streets of San Francisco* and *Encyclopaedia Britannica Presents* before he landed the starring role in *Starsky and Hutch*.

Silver Lady was his third single release in UK. The second, **Going In With My Eyes Open**, peaked at number two, and although nobody realised it at the time, David Soul thus missed by a whisker the equalling of Gerry and the Pacemakers' record of three number ones with their first three singles.

414

YES SIR I CAN BOOGIE

29th October 1977, for one week

Baccara *RCA PB 5526*

Writers: Frank Dostal and Rolf Soja
Producer: Rolf Soja

Astonishingly, it took 414 number ones over all but 25 years for the first female vocal duo to hit the very top. There have been plenty of male vocal duos at the top, from the Everly Brothers to Typically Tropical, plenty of male/female vocal duos at the top, beginning with Sonny and Cher, and even female vocal trios such as the Supremes and the Three Degrees. But it took two leggy Spanish girls singing a Dutch production in English to make the breakthrough in the British charts, and by an extraordinary coincidence one record that their success kept out of the top spot was **Black Is Black**, a song originally recorded by a German/Spanish vocal group in English but this time revived by La Belle Epoque, a French female vocal duo.

Baccara were also the first Spanish act to hit the top in Britain, and they remained the only Spanish people to have a number one until Julio Iglesias actually sang in his native tongue all the way up to number one 4 years later (see no. 490).

415

NAME OF THE GAME

5 November 1977, for four weeks

Abba *Epic EPC 5750*

Writers: Stig Anderson, Benny Andersson and Bjorn Ulvaeus
Producers: Benny Andersson and Bjorn Ulvaeus

It was perhaps fitting that one of the biggest chart names of all time should be at number one on 14 November 1977, on the twenty-fifth birthday of the singles charts in Britain. Abba's sixth number one hit brought them level with Slade in the all-time rankings, behind only Elvis and the Beatles (seventeen each), Cliff Richard (then nine number ones) and the Rolling Stones (eight). Abba have subsequently overtaken the Stones, and the race with Cliff Richard for third place is hotting up. At Christmas 1981, Cliff Richard's **Daddy's Home** peaked at number two, his ninth number two hit to go with his ten number ones. At the same time, Abba's **One Of Us** stopped at number three, both records being kept off the top by the first number one by Human League, **Don't You Want Me** (see no. 491). So Abba still have nine number ones and two number two hits.

By the beginning of 1982, Abba had produced eighteen consecutive Top 10 hits, which puts them fifth behind Cliff (26), Elvis (25) and the Beatles (23) and the Rolling Stones (19). But the nineteenth potential Top Tenner, **Head Over Heels**, missed even the Top 20. Like the Stones, no record by Abba has ever re-entered the chart after once dropping out. The champions of this negative achievement are, however, the Hollies. All 29 of their hit records have enjoyed only one spell on the charts.

416

MULL OF KINTYRE/GIRLS' SCHOOL

3 December 1977, for nine weeks

Wings *Capitol R 6018*

Writers: Paul McCartney and Denny Laine
Producer: Paul McCartney

Paul McCartney had registered ten post-Beatle Top 10 singles by the end of 1976, but none had gone all the way. Three, **Another Day, Silly Love Songs** and **Let 'Em In**, had peaked at number two. To add to this frustration, he had

420 **Kate Bush**

412 **Elvis Presley**

Above **419 Abba**

Below **416 Wings**

scored five US chart toppers in the same period, **Silly Love Songs** being the American number one of the year 1976, without crossing over to the head of the UK list. The pattern changed drastically with **Mull of Kintyre**. McCartney wrote the song because he felt Scotland needed a contemporary anthem and, quite simply, because he loved his home there. Denny Laine helped complete the composition. At the time of recording Wings were between membership changes. The trio of Paul and Linda McCartney and Laine was as small as the group ever got.

Paul was not certain **Mull of Kintyre** would be a hit, so he made it part of a double A-side with the up-tempo **Girls' School**. Though this title was also credited in the printed charts, it was patently obvious that **Mull of Kintyre** was the popular side. It was the first single to sell more than two million copies in the United Kingdom, surpassing the Beatles' **She Loves You** to become the nation's all-time number one.

417

UP TOWN TOP RANKING

4 February 1978, for one week

Althia and Donna *Lightning LIG 506*

Writers: Althia Forest, Donna Reid and Errol Thompson
Producer: Joe Gibson

Only three hits after the first female vocal duo to hit number one, a second pair hit the top. This time it was two Jamaican girls, Althia Forest and Donna Reid, with their own composition, **Up Town Top Ranking**. Baccara, the first female vocal duo to hit the top, at least managed one follow-up hit, **Sorry, I'm A Lady**, which was climbing into the Top 10 while Althia and Donna were at number one. But the Jamaican girls joined the growing list of one hit wonders.

At the time, Althia and Donna were the twenty-fifth act on the one-hit wonder list, of whom seven were vocal duos. Nine weeks later an eighth vocal duo, Brian and Michael, joined the list which also at the time included half a vocal duo, Art Garfunkel. Since then, Paul McCartney and Stevie Wonder have joined the list, and after 500 number ones, almost a quarter of all the one hit wonders have been vocal duos, even though far less than a quarter of the number ones have been by duos. There must be a moral there somewhere, although being a duo certainly didn't upset the career of the Everly Brothers, who remain the only duo in British chart history to have clocked up more than 100 weeks on the chart.

418

FIGARO

11 February 1978, for one week

Brotherhood of Man *Pye 7N 46037*

Writers: Tony Hiller, Lee Sheriden and Martin Lee
Producer: Tony Hiller

The third number one for Brotherhood Of Man was the third written by Messrs Hiller, Sheriden and Lee, and the third produced by Tony Hiller. It was their second consecutive number one about a foreign man with a six-letter name ending in O. It must be admitted that Figaro was not as strong a song as Angelo and despite being a happy, uncontroversial record for the discos, immaculately performed and produced, it only stayed at the top for one week before being pushed out by the group the Brotherhood so successfully sounded like, Abba, whose **Take A Chance on Me** was also to prove their final number one for a while.

The follow-up to **Figaro**, **Beautiful Lover** was still singing the praises of foreign men (is this what the British public wants to hear?) but only just made the Top 20. The next single was their last hit to date, climbing to number 41 and ending a second chart career for the group which had lasted 2½ years. Nevertheless they still tour Britain and the world with great gusto, having carved for themselves a secure place in the almost recession-proof MOR appearance stakes.

419

TAKE A CHANCE ON ME

18 February 1978, for three weeks

Abba *Epic EPC 5950*

Writers: Benny Andersson and Bjorn Ulvaeus
Producers: Benny Andersson and Bjorn Ulvaeus

Abba completed a hat-trick of increasing uncertainty on 18 February 1978. The first record of the hat-trick had the positive title **Knowing Me Knowing You** and stayed at the top for 5 weeks. The second record had the less certain, but still unworried title **The Name Of The Game**, and stayed on top for 4 weeks. The third record was much less optimistic, pleading **Take A Chance On Me**, which the British public did for 3 weeks. Logically, Abba should have recorded **Maybe Baby** and **God Only Knows** as their next two singles, which would have held the top spot for 2 weeks and 1 week respectively, but they didn't. They recorded **Summer Night City** which became the first of six consecutive Abba singles to hit the Top 5 without any reaching the very top. It was therefore quite a surprise to chartwatchers if not to Epic Records executives when at the end of 1980 two singles from the 'Super Trouper' album hit number one, to put Abba back on top after 2½ years.

420

WUTHERING HEIGHTS

11 March 1978, for four weeks

Kate Bush *EMI 2719*

Writer: Kate Bush
Producer: Andrew Powell

Wuthering Heights, a musical version of the Brontë classic story, launched the career of one of the few original talents to hit popular music in the nineteen-seventies. With its weird but haunting chorus of 'Heathcliff, it's me, I'm Cathy come home again', sung almost unintelligibly by the diminutive Miss Bush, it became an airplay favourite almost at once and a number one hit in its fifth week on the charts. It became the final track on the first side of Kate Bush's first LP 'The Kick Inside', which also included her second single and second Top 10 hit, **Man With The Child In His Eyes**. Among the musicians on the album were guitarists David Paton and Ian Bairnson, both from Pilot, number one hitmakers with **January** (see no. 365) three years earlier.

Kate Bush has consolidated her position as one of Britain's most successful female vocalists in chart terms with hits like **Wow, Babooshka** and **December Will Be Magic Again**, but she is really best known for her stage performances which combine song, dance and theatre in a production which leaves audiences not quite sure what they've seen, but screaming for more.

421

MATCHSTALK MEN AND MATCHSTALK CATS AND DOGS

8 April 1978, for three weeks

Brian and Michael *Pye 7N 46035*

Writer: Michael Coleman
Producer: Kevin Parrott

The song with the second longest title to reach number one was the saga of the Ancoats painter L S Lowry, whose death on 23 February 1976 had inspired Mick Coleman to write the song. He took it to producer Kevin Parrott, and the pair recorded the song. Kevin Parrott decided that Brian and Michael sounded more commercial than Kevin and Michael, so the chance of a Kevin reaching number one was lost. A year later, England soccer captain Kevin Keegan climbed to number 31 with **Head Over Heels In Love** and Australian Kevin Johnson had a number 23 hit in 1975, but otherwise Mr Parrott seems to have been proved correct in his opinion of the lack of commerciality of the name Kevin.

Matchstalk Men (not to be confused with Status Quo's first hit in 1968 **Pictures Of Matchstick Men**) features the St Winifred's School Choir (see no. 472) singing with Brian and Michael, and the subsequent careers of both Kevin Parrott and Mick Coleman have continued to involve children. All follow-ups to their number one hit were failures, but Kevin produced the hit by the Ramblers, from the Abbey Hey Junior School, called **The Sparrow** which reached number 11 at the end of 1979. Mick Coleman also wrote the song recorded at Christmas 1981 by both Ken Dodd (who made it a hit) and the St Winifred's School Choir (who flopped) called **Hold My Hand**.

422

NIGHT FEVER

29 April 1978, for two weeks

The Bee Gees *RSO 002*

Writers: Barry, Robin and Maurice Gibb
Producers: Barry, Robin and Maurice Gibb, Karl Richardson and Albhy Galuten

The Bee Gees were at the Chateau d'Herouville in France working on the follow-up to their 'Children of the Universe' album when they received a phone call from manager Robert Stigwood. He was making a film of a Nik Cohn article in *New York* magazine and needed a few songs. He couldn't send them a script but needed the numbers within a fortnight.

The Gibbs worked in the black music based groove that had recently brought them great success with **Jive Talkin'** and **You Should Be Dancing**. Without really knowing how the songs would be used, they presented Stigwood with **How Deep Is Your Love, Staying Alive, Night Fever, More Than a Woman**, and **If I Can't Have You**, the last of which was ultimately given to Yvonne Elliman. Stigwood was unhappy he did not have a title track for the film, which he thought he would call *Saturday Night*. The Bee Gees noted they did have a song called **Night Fever**, so the movie became *Saturday Night Fever*.

The double album soundtrack went on to become the world's biggest-ever seller, passing the thirty million mark. The Gibbs became so associated with the film many people assumed they had appeared in it, but this was not the case. The Bee Gees music got more straight-laced middle aged people dancing in popular styles than any phenomenon since the Twist.

423

RIVERS OF BABYLON

13 May 1978, for five weeks

Boney M *Atlantic/Hansa K 11120*

Writers: Traditional, arranged by Frank Farian and Hans-Georg Mayer
Producer: Frank Farian

The second biggest-selling single in British history, and the only other record after **Mull Of Kintyre** to sell over two million in Britain, is the single culled from Boney M's 'Night Flight To Venus' LP, **Rivers Of Babylon**. The song is an age-old lament, and has been used by pop artists before. Don McLean included a version on his 'American Pie' LP, but as it has never been copyrighted, producer Frank Farian was able to create his own version and put his name down as one of the authors.

The single was released with **Rivers Of Babylon** as the A-side, and it reached the top of the charts purely on sales of that track. After it had begun to fall, however, the other side, **Brown Girl In The Ring**, began picking up airplay and the record climbed up the chart again; it lasted in all 40 weeks on the chart, the second longest consecutive run by any number one hit in history (Engelbert Humperdinck's **Release Me** (see no. 230) lasted 56 weeks), and together with the success of **Rasputin** and **Mary's Boy Child – Oh My Lord** (see no. 430) made Boney M the chart champions of 1978.

424

YOU'RE THE ONE THAT I WANT

17 June 1978, for nine weeks

John Travolta and Olivia Newton-John *RSO 006*

Writer: John Farrar
Producer: John Farrar

John Travolta (born 18 February 1954) and Olivia Newton-John (born in Cambridge on 26 September 1948) lay claim to being the most successful chart act in recording history, if statistics are cunningly manipulated. Together they released only two singles, both of which topped the charts, for a combined total of 16 weeks. No other act has done so well with 100% of their singles releases. Individually, John Travolta starred in two of the biggest box office successes of all time, *Saturday Night Fever* and *Grease*, as well as the film which did for country music what his earlier two had done for disco and fifties rock n'roll, *Urban Cowboy*. Miss Newton-John's acting career has been less spectacular, but this has been more than compensated for by her singing career. She has had hits with Cliff Richard and with ELO (see no. 461) but on her own has become the most successful female singer the US record charts have ever seen, winning three Grammies in 1974 and topping the charts with monotonous regularity. As the eighties got into their stride Olivia's hits got even bigger. At the end of 1981 **Physical** stayed at number one in America for no less than ten straight weeks. In the UK her solo offerings have never done quite as well but in the country of her origin (she is technically British, having emigrated with her family from the UK to the land of Foster's and boomerangs when she was four) her (extremely attractive) face and voice could hardly be better known. She has the OBE too.

425

THREE TIMES A LADY

19 August 1978, for five weeks

Commodores *Motown TMG 1113*

Writer: Lionel Richie, Jr.
Producers: James Carmichael and the Commodores

The world owes this classic love song to Leo Sayer, who had nothing to do with the writing or making of it. In 1977 the

Grammy Award for Best Rhythm and Blues Song went to Sayer and Vini Poncia for Leo's worldwide hit **You Make Me Feel Like Dancing**. Among the defeated writers were the Commodores. Shaken that white men could defeat him in this category, Commodore Lionel Richie vowed to write pop. It had always been the intention of the Commodores to earn as much as the top rock bands. Now Richie set out to develop his craft as a songwriter for all formats.

Three Times a Lady followed **Sweet Love** and **Just to Be Close to You**, all hit Commodore ballads that originally appeared as the last track on side one of an album. The group figured that after a few up-tempo dance numbers, this was wise placement. The tracks were always far too long for single release, and it was left to co-producer James Carmichael to edit them. Richie was only too willing to let him handle the chore, but with the passage of time and the development of his reputation and skills he finally began to write ballads with the proper length in mind.

Three Times a Lady replaced **I'm Still Waiting** as Motown's best UK seller. It was also number one in America.

426

DREADLOCK HOLIDAY

23 September 1978, for one week

10 CC *Mercury 6008 035*

Writers: Eric Stewart and Graham Gouldman
Producers: Eric Stewart and Graham Gouldman

Kevin Godley and Lol Creme left 10 CC in 1977, and so 10 CC became a duo, just Eric Stewart and Graham Gouldman. In August 1978, they put out an LP Bloody Tourists, which featured as performers and co-writers Rick Fenn, Stuart Tosh and Duncan Mackay, but the writers and producers of the only hit single from the album were Stewart and Gouldman. It was their last hit.

Since **Dreadlock Holiday**, Graham Gouldman has scored one minor hit **Sunburn,** but 10 CC, although officially still in existence, have done nothing. Kevin Godley and Lol Creme came back strongly after a couple of flops with two songs from their Ismism album which both made the top ten at the end of 1981. By this time, they were more involved with video work (including the production of the much-talked about video for Duran Duran's **Girls On Film** single), and the success of the two singles was a distraction.

The disappearance of 10 CC from the charts was very sudden, but the influence of records like **Rubber Bullets, I'm Not In Love** and **Art For Art's Sake** carries on.

427

SUMMER NIGHTS

30 September 1978, for seven weeks

John Travolta and Olivia Newton-John *RSO 18*

Writers: Warren Casey and Jim Jacobs
Producer: Louis St. Louis

The only male/female vocal duo to have two number one hits is John Travolta and Olivia Newton-John. In achieving their second number one, they broke all sorts of chart records. They hit number one with all the records they ever released, which has never been achieved by any act that has released more than one single. They reached number one with their first and last chart hits, equalling the record set by Kay Starr in the fifties, and they find themselves on the short list of artists who hit number one with their first two releases (3 acts), artists who failed to follow up a number one (10 acts) and artists with 15 or more weeks on top in one year (4 acts). Olivia Newton-John, who has never climbed higher than number two as a solo singer, has also achieved one-hit wonder status in combination with Electric Light Orchestra (see no.461). John Travolta, a singing movie star in the tradition of Tab Hunter and Lee Marvin, also achieved a number two hit on his own. The film *Grease*, from which both the duo's chart-toppers came, has also proved to be the most successful film in terms of original hits in British chart history. Two number ones, two number twos (**Hopelessly Devoted To You** and **Sandy**), a number three (Frankie Valli's **Grease**) and a number eleven (**Greased Lightnin'**) give it a list of hits that far outstrips its nearest rivals, **Summer Holiday** and **The Young Ones.**

428

RAT TRAP

18 November 1978, for two weeks

Boomtown Rats *Ensign ENY 16*

Writer: Bob Geldof
Producer: Mutt Lange

The Boomtown Rats had Top 20 hits with their first four releases, but even this streak did not prepare them for the

427 John Travolta and Olivia Newton-John

Left 433 Blondie

425 Commodores

432 Ian Dury

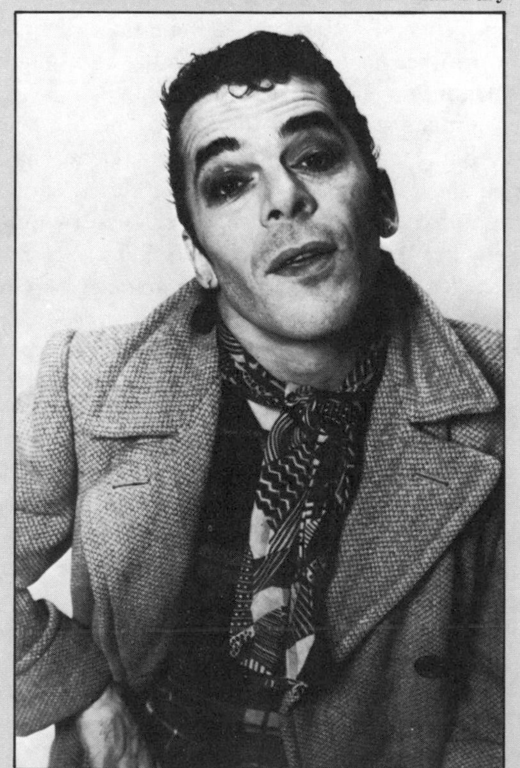

428 Boomtown Rats

success of **Rat Trap**. The third A-side from the top ten album 'Tonic For the Troops', it was put out to show that the Irish sextet wasn't just a pop band. Its nearly 4 minute length and complex structure were considered natural impediments to significant sales.

Viewing a videotaped Rats performance at the Hammersmith Odeon months later, lead singer and writer Bob Geldof noticed that even shortly after the release of 'Tonic' concert-goers were calling for **Rat Trap**. At the time, this indication of a possible hit was missed.

When **Rat Trap** replaced **Summer Nights** at the top it was hailed as the triumph of local talent over a highly hyped Hollywood hit. Conveniently overlooked was the fact that the Boomtown Rats were, in fact, Irish, though they had come to London specifically for the purpose of making it in the international capital of rock music. **Rat Trap** was the first New Wave number one.

With the success of **Rat Trap** Geldof, already a proven charismatic figure on *Top of the Pops,* found himself in heavy demand from television chat hosts who were relieved to find an articulate representative of, if not spokesman for, New Wave.

429

DA YA THINK I'M SEXY

2 December 1978, for one week

Rod Stewart *Riva 17*

Writers: Rod Stewart and Carmen Appice
Producer: Tom Dowd

The question of unintentional plagiarism raised in the **My Sweet Lord** case surfaced again with Rod Stewart's 1978 disco hit. The artist originally claimed full credit for himself and band member Appice until a complaint was made that the music clearly borrowed from Jorge Ben's **Taj Mahal**, a tribute to the American blues singer who himself used the name of the Indian monument. The issue never blew up in the media because Stewart donated the song to UNICEF in the historic January, 1979 United Nations concert. There was, however, a temporary wrangle over how much of the song's rights he had actually assigned to the children's charity.

Da Ya Think I'm Sexy was a startling departure for Stewart, placing him directly in the mainstream of the 1978 disco boom. He enjoyed soul and disco chart success with this multi-million seller. Ironically, it temporarily took his career off the rails, as he became broadly typed as a leering stud, rather like a Benny Hill of rock. In 7 years he had only missed the Top 10 once, and that only by one place. For the following 3 years he fell short, often well short, every time. **Da Ya Think I'm Sexy** was a rare example of a number one that might not have been worth the price.

430

MARY'S BOY CHILD – OH MY LORD (medley)

9 December 1978, for four weeks

Boney M *Atlantic/Hansa K 11221*

Writers: Jester Hairston, Fred Jay, Frank Farian and Lorin
Producer: Frank Farian

Boney M's second number one was a massive Christmas seller combining one former number one song with a negro spiritual which was updated, just like **Rivers Of Babylon** had been, by Boney M's producer Frank Farian. **Mary's Boy Child** (see also no.65) became the fifth song to top the charts twice, and the gap of just over 21 years between the two chart topping versions was a record, beaten in 1981 by the Rosemary Clooney and Shakin' Stevens versions of **This Ole House** (see nos. 25 and 411).

After **Mary's Boy Child – Oh My Lord**, Boney M seemed to lose some of the magic that had made them chart champions of 1978. Liz Mitchell, Marcia Barrett, Maizie Williams and Bobby Farrell have continued to make technically faultless Euro-disco singles under the guidance of Frank Farian (né Franz Reuther), but apart from **We Kill The World**, which just broke into the Top 40 in 1981, their British hit singles seem to be a thing of the past.

431

YMCA

6 January 1979, for three weeks

Village People *Mercury 6007 192*

Writers: Jacques Morali, Henri Belolo and Victor Willis
Producer: Jacques Morali

When Frenchman Jacques Morali saw Felipe Rose wearing Indian dress in a New York gay discotheque, then saw him in a second club a week later with other costumed characters, he got an idea. He told *Rolling Stone*, 'I say to myself, "You know, this is fantastic—to see the cowboy, the Indian, the construction worker with other men around." And also, I think to myself that the gay people have no group, nobody to personalise the gay people, you know?'

What a New Yorker might take for granted the foreigner saw as an exciting fantasy: a group of young men dressed as stereotypical American males. He recruited an ensemble, mostly models, to front songs about US gay capitals. The name Village People represented the men of Greenwich Village in New York City. When the first album sold 100 000 copies and a single, **San Francisco (You've Got Me)** made the British charts, Morali quickly found himself Village persons who could sing as well as pose, retaining Felipe Rose and lead vocalist Victor Willis. The unpredictable happened. **Macho Man** became a pop hit in America and **YMCA** an international smash, selling several million copies, including approximately 150 000 in one day in Britain alone over the 1978 Christmas period. All types of audiences could relate to this ode to the Mecca of Manhood, and the group quickly became a mass appeal fad. In so doing they lost touch with their original supporters and went the way of all fads, falling out of fashion and, even worse, the charts.

432

HIT ME WITH YOUR RHYTHM STICK

27 January 1979, for one week

Ian and the Blockheads *Stiff BUY 38*

Writers: Ian Dury and Chas Jankel
Producer: Chas Jankel

Ian Dury first came to public attention with an outrageous LP, 'New Boots and Panties,' containing songs like **Billericay Dickie** and other sagas of the unemployed and unconsidered East Enders which had never previously been subjects for pop LPs. But then Ian Dury was no average pop star. Partly paralysed from childhood, this diminutive college lecturer stumbles onto the stage, uses the microphone as a crutch and then sings his own brand of disco. The musical inspiration is Chas Jankel, whose song **Ai no Corrida** provided Quincy Jones with a 1981 hit and whose rhythms are those of the discotheque. The lyrical content is supplied by Ian Dury. **Hit Me With Your Rhythm Stick** is funny, obscene or incomprehensible as you choose, but consistently original. Dury is the only person who could have rhymed 'Ich Liebe dich' with 'rhythm stick', and in doing so became the first person since Elvis Presley to sing in German on a number one hit.

Perhaps the best Ian Dury song of all, combining lyrical originality, musical sophistication and belligerent working classness is **Common As Muck**, the B-side of **Reasons To Be Cheerful Part 3**, which was the follow-up to **Rhythm Stick** and his last Top 10 hit so far.

433

HEART OF GLASS

3 February 1979, for four weeks

Blondie *Chrysalis CHE 2275*

Writers: Chris Stein and Debbie Harry
Producer: Mike Chapman

Track 4 on side 2 of the highly successful album 'Parallel Lines' was the third single taken from the album, following **Picture This**, which reached number 12, and **Hanging On The Telephone**, which climbed as high as number five, giving Blondie their second Top 10 hit. It is hard to understand why **Heart Of Glass** reached number one, when so many people had already bought the album, but it was certainly a stronger single release than either of the earlier cuts.

Blondie were then fronted by the artificially blonde Debbie Harry, whose instantly recognisable vocals were the key to the band's success. Playing behind her were co-writer Chris Stein, on 'guitar, 12-string and E-bow' (according to the liner notes), Jimmy Destri on keyboards, Frank Infante on guitar, Nigel Harrison on bass and Clem Burke on drums. **Heart Of Glass** was produced by Mike Chapman, who was now embarking on a run of success in the States to compare with the golden touch he and his partner Nicky Chinn had displayed in the early seventies with Mud, Suzi Quatro, Smokie and the rest. Apart from Blondie, Chapman produced American number ones for Exile, called **Kiss You All Over** (number six in UK) for Nick Gilder (**Hot Child In The City** – a flop in UK) and **My Sharona** for the Knack (number six in UK). Blondie too were hot. **Heart Of Glass** was the first of five number ones within 21 months.

434

TRAGEDY

3 March 1979, for two weeks

Bee Gees *RSO 27*

Writers: Barry, Robin and Maurice Gibb
Producers: The Bee Gees, Karl Richardson and Albhy Galuten

The Bee Gees dominated the international record business in 1978 as no act had done since the heyday of the Beatles. Not only was 'Saturday Night Fever' the best-selling album of all-time, several records the brothers wrote and produced in varying combinations with different artists were worldwide hits and the title song of the film *Grease* allegedly earned writer and co-producer Barry Gibb more money than anyone had ever received from a single song.

The age-old show business question asking what one does for an encore was never more apt. The Bee Gees replied with 'Spirits Having Flown', an album recorded in Florida with Galuten and Richardson. They chose to change pace with the first single from the set, preceding the LP's release with **Too Much Heaven**. This ballad, its publishing rights donated to UNICEF, reached number three in Britain and one in America.

The second 45 from the package, **Tragedy**, scaled the summit in both countries. At the time, the group was concerned that every single they released be a potential US number one. In this case they got the top spot at home, too. **Tragedy** was the last UK smash in the late seventies string of Bee Gees hits. Their first number one of the eighties would come, not with their own voices, but with that of Barbra Streisand.

435

I WILL SURVIVE

17 March 1979, for four weeks

Gloria Gaynor *Polydor 2095 017*

Writers: Dino Fekaris and Freddie Perren
Producers: Dino Fekaris in association with Freddie Perren

Because of the subsequent rise to superstardom by Donna Summer many fans forget that Gloria Gaynor was the original Disco Queen of the seventies. The entire first side of her late 1974 album début became popular programming in the western world's leading discotheques. There were only three extended numbers on this LP face, leading directly to the lengthy mixes and 12-inch singles that became the characteristic forms of disco music. One of the tracks, **Never Can Say Goodbye**, became an international hit single in edited form, reaching number two in Britain in early 1975. **Reach Out I'll Be There**, another Motown standard from the same sequence, followed it into the Top 20.

Gaynor's shooting star seemed to burn out when Donna Summer moaned her way to the top in 1976. Just when it seemed she had become a past tense figure Gloria recorded **I Will Survive**, a personal testament to self-sufficiency. This was a perfect record for The Me Decade, known for its short-term affairs and love of therapy. The Gaynor character, having resisted a nervous breakdown, shuns the man who once deserted her and now wants her back. The sentiments seemed so universal the record was a global success, reaching number one in both the US and UK. It was the favourite disc of nightclub mogul Regine, who recorded her own version. Gaynor headlined at the London Palladium; Regine did not.

436

BRIGHT EYES

14 April 1979, for six weeks

Art Garfunkel *CBS 6947*

Writer: Mike Batt
Producer: Mike Batt

This number one represented great personal triumphs for both Garfunkel and Batt, yet it was almost never released as a single. The vocalist, always intensely concerned with his image and craft, did not feel the theme from the film *Watership Down* would make a worthy single. He also had no intention of putting it on his new album, 'Fate For Breakfast'. It was only when CBS executives in the UK showed him photographs of fans queuing to see the film that he relented.

Bright Eyes became the best selling single of 1979 in Great Britain. It was the last of the five hundred number ones in this book to achieve a 6 week run. It also went to number one in several other European countries, though it never made the American Hot 100.

This second solo UK number one gave Garfunkel a 2-0 edge over ex-partner Paul Simon. Even during their glorious partnership their only British number one was a solo vocal by Art, making the tally 3-0, most odd in view of Simon's esteemed reputation as a writer and great success as an album artist.

For Mike Batt it was an even sweeter triumph. His eight hits as the Wombles had typed him as a talented lightweight, despite a few other successes. **Bright Eyes** established him as a serious talent.

437

SUNDAY GIRL

26 May 1979, for three weeks

Blondie *Chrysalis CHS 2320*

Writer: Chris Stein
Producer: Mike Chapman

Ex-Bunny Girl Debbie Harry and her band continued their phenomenal run of success with tracks from the 'Parallel Lines' album by culling track 3 on side 2 as the fourth single from the album. It quickly became their second chart-topper. Only Michael Jackson, with his 'Off The Wall' platinum album, and Human League, with 'Dare' (see no. 491) have in recent years had four major hit singles from one album, besides Blondie, and only Blondie have scored two number ones, and three top tenners out of the four. Fleetwood Mac had four minor hits from 'Rumours'.

Sunday Girl was the first number one to include a day of the week in the title, and was almost immediately followed by **I Don't Like Mondays** (see no. 440). No other days of the week have reached number one, although they have featured in hit record titles. For example, **Ruby Tuesday** reached number three by the Rolling Stones in 1967 and number nine by Melanie in 1970. There was **Wednesday Week**, a number 11 hit from the Undertones in 1980, and **Friday On My Mind** which the Easybeats took to number six in 1966. **Saturday Night At the Movies**, number three for the Drifters in 1972 is one of many hit Saturdays, but no song with the word Thursday in the title has ever been a hit, although the B-side of a flop single by the Evening Standard Girl Of The Year of 1967, Ross Hannaman, was called **Probably On Thursday**.

438

RING MY BELL

16 June 1979, for two weeks

Anita Ward *TK TKR 7543*

Writer: Frederick Knight
Producer: Frederick Knight

Anita Ward was a young teenager singing a capella gospel in a Memphis Tennessee church choir when Chuck Holmes discovered her and got her a recording contract. Very little happened for a long time, as acknowledged by Miss Ward on the liner notes to her 'Songs Of Love' album which included **Ring My Bell**. 'Special thanks to my manager Chuck Holmes', she wrote, 'for his persistent determination' which eventually led to producer Frederick Knight and recording sessions in Jackson, Mississippi.

The result of those sessions was a mediocre collection of songs, written for the most part by Frederick Knight, Chuck Holmes and Anita herself, with one outstanding track, **Ring My Bell**. It was perfect midsummer disco music and it raced to the top of the charts. The hook was the synthesiser of Carl Marsh which produced a sound – impossible to translate into words but instantly recognisable to the ear – which became almost as copied as Donna Summer's referee's whistle. After the success of **Ring My Bell**, absolutely nothing. Anita Ward is now a member of the one-hit wonder club, with little prospect of releasing herself from it. A sad fate for a girl who used three studios, four engineers, two remixers and a 'midnight mix by Richie Rivera' as well as a producer to come up with a number one.

439

ARE 'FRIENDS' ELECTRIC?

30 June 1979, for four weeks

Tubeway Army *Beggars Banquet BEG 18*

Writer: Gary Numan
Producer: Gary Numan

Gary Numan was largely responsible for one of 1979's oddest chart statistics: three out of four consecutive number ones were by men whose name at birth was Webb but who used a different name on record. Gary Webb and Harry Webb (Cliff Richard) were protagonists in this web of suspense; the Boomtown Rats were the intruders.

Above left **435 Gloria Gaynor,** *right* **434 Bee Gees,** *below right* **444 Buggles**

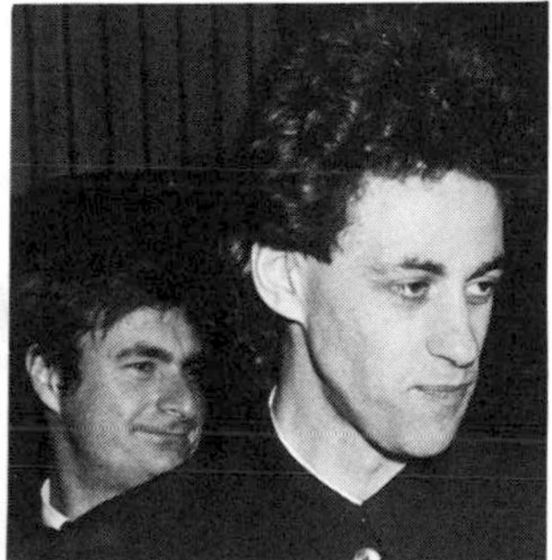

Above left **436 Art Garfunkel,** *right* **440 Boomtown Rats**

Left **441 Cliff Richard**

Tubeway Army, Numan's group, had recorded without chart success. A fan following developed without support from the music press. For the band's second LP there were only Numan, his uncle and another musician on board, so there was little subsequent need to retain a group name. **Are 'Friends' Electric?** was Numan's song, produced by Numan, and it was his charismatic performance that sold the song on *Top of the Pops*. Sandwiched between Roxy Music and David Bowie, he more than held his own. Many commentators found the new star overly derivative of Bowie, but Numan himself claimed his main influence had been John Foxx. Numan temporarily ceased being a bleached blonde after the release of **Are 'Friends' Electric?** Beginning with the follow-up single, **Cars**, he issued his discs under his own name. His twin number ones were separated by only two other 45s. This seems at first like a speed record for returning to the top, but in fact John Travolta and Olivia Newton-John had achieved the same feat the previous year. Several artists had done the same or even better in the early sixties and, amongst other stars, Jimmy Young had managed it in the fifties.

440

I DON'T LIKE MONDAYS

28 July 1979, for four weeks

Boomtown Rats *Ensign ENY 30*

Writer: Bob Geldof
Producer: Phil Wainman

The Boomtown Rats had been spoiled when their very first recording, **Looking After Number One**, received airplay from a New Wave sampler and became a Top 20 single. They were even more fortunate with **I Don't Like Mondays**. Entering the chart at number 15, it spent the next 4 weeks at number one and was chosen the Best Single of 1979 in the British Rock and Pop Awards sponsored by Radio One, *Nationwide* and the *Daily Mirror*. Bob Geldof had been in the United States on a promotional visit when he noticed a bizarre story coming over the wire services. A teenage Californian had sniped at her school playground, causing death and injury. When asked why she had gone on her homicidal rampage, she replied 'I don't like Mondays.' Shaken by her reply as much as her crime, Geldof penned his highly dramatic million seller.

Mondays was a worldwide hit, with the glaring exception being the United States. Fear of lawsuits and charges of bad taste kept radio stations from playing the record as much as any aversion to New Wave. The unofficial boycott was front page news in *Variety*, the only time the Rats earned such prominent coverage in the show business Bible.

This song was given its pre-release live premiere at the 1979 Loch Lomond festival.

441

WE DON'T TALK ANYMORE

25 August 1979, for four weeks

Cliff Richard *EMI 2975*

Writer: Alan Tarney
Producer: Bruce Welch

Twenty years and 25 days after his first number one hit (see no. 88), Cliff Richard reached the top for the tenth time with the record that has turned out to be his biggest-selling worldwide hit. It marked a second period of strong resurgence for the ageless Cliff, who has come up with four more Top 10 hits in the next 2 years. Among those hits was his ninth number two hit, his version of his own favourite song of all time, **Daddy's Home**, which just failed to push Human League off the top at Christmas 1981.

The song was written by Alan T[illegible], who had already written successfully for Leo Sayer, and who was to write and produce Cliff's next few singles. **We Don't Talk Anymore** was produced by Shadow Bruce Welch, who thus joined Paul McCartney as the only people to have written and produced number one hits for others, and to have written and performed number one hits themselves. McCartney has also produced his own number ones, which Bruce Welch has not achieved.

Sadly, during the weeks that **We Don't Talk Anymore** was at number one, Norrie Paramor, the man who was most responsible for the recording success of Cliff Richard and the Shadows, died. He was then, and remains now, the man who has produced more British number ones than any other person.

442

CARS

22 September 1979, for one week

Gary Numan *Beggars Banquet BEG 23*

Writer: Gary Numan
Producer: Gary Numan

Gary Numan changed his performing title from Tubeway Army, but the result was the same, another number one. He thus became the tenth, and so far the last, act to reach number one with his first two chart hits, joining a select band that began with the Stargazers on 12 March 1954 (see no. 17). **Cars** proved to be Numan's biggest American hit and his final British number one. The hits continued, with computerised precision and enigmatic titles like **We Are Glass** and **I Die: You Die**, but they tended to reach their highest chart placing in the week of issue and to tumble downwards and out within 7 weeks or so. The high standards he set himself with **Are 'Friends' Electric?** and **Cars** could not be maintained.

Late in 1981, Gary Numan switched his attention from cars to aeroplanes. He attempted to fly around the world solo in his Cessna, but was forced to land on the East coast of India in what turned out to be a restricted military zone. The Indian authorities impounded the aircraft and detained Gary for a few days in a hotel in Visakhapatnam, until he persuaded them that he was not a spy. He then flew back to UK on a scheduled flight, leaving **This Wreckage** in India.

443

MESSAGE IN A BOTTLE

29 September 1979, for three weeks

Police *A & M AMS 7474*

Writer: Sting
Producers: Police and Nigel Gray

The Police are Andy Summers, Stewart Copeland and Sting, and their first of four number one hits in the first 500 number ones was also the first UK number one for the A&M label.

Andy Summers obviously buys elixir of youth from Cliff Richard's chemist, because despite his youthful appearance, he was playing (as Andy Somers) in Zoot Money's Big Roll Band as long ago as 1964. He was also briefly with Eric Burdon's New Animals. Stewart Copeland, the drummer, is American and the brother of the group's manager, Miles Copeland. Their father ran the CIA in Beirut for many years, a fact which gave them the idea of the name Police. Sting, real name Gordon Sumner, is the star, the only personality in British pop to match Adam Ant in 1981. Sumner was a schoolteacher in Newcastle-upon-Tyne, playing part time with a jazz fusion band which Stewart Copeland happened to see one night. The two got together, formed Police with guitarist Henry Padovani and released a single, **Fall Out/Nothing Achieving**, one of the most accurately titled records of all time. Padovani left, Andy Summers took his place, and the next single was the amazing **Roxanne**. The Police were a force to be reckoned with.

444

VIDEO KILLED THE RADIO STAR

20 October 1979, for one week

Buggles *Island WIP 6524*

Writers: Bruce Woolley, Trevor Horn and Geoff Downes
Producers: Trevor Horn and Geoff Downes

Trevor Horn and Geoff Downes joined the ranks of producers-turned hitmakers, called themselves Buggles and took their very danceable first single, **Video Killed The Radio Star**, to the very top. Unlike other producers-turned-hitmakers, for example Typically Tropical (see no. 375), Hugo & Luigi or Pete Wingfield, Buggles then had more hits and even for a while joined Yes in one of the more surprising rock personnel shifts. That experiment was not entirely successful, probably because the Buggles style is too pop for Yes, but Horn and Downes continue both as performers and producers to contribute to the 1980's charts.

Trevor Horn has produced many Top 10 hits for Dollar, the duo that emerged from the seventies group Guys and Dolls to become the most popular duo of the early eighties in Britain. In 1982 he was also producing Spandau Ballet and ABC's Top 10 hits **Poison Arrow** and **Look of Love**, proving once again as he did with Buggles that Pop and New Wave can live together on the same piece of wax.

445

ONE DAY AT A TIME

27 October 1979, for three weeks

Lena Martell *Pye 7N 46021*

Writer: Kris Kristofferson
Producer: George Elrick

One track from Lena Martell's thirteenth LP for Pye was the Kris Kristofferson gospel song, **One Day At A Time**. Miss Martell had been for some years (as 13 LPs would indicate) a consistent seller in the easy listening category. Her LPs contain her versions of the popular middle-of-the-road hits of the day, all exquisitely performed and painstakingly produced, but never expected to contain a track which could have given Miss Martell a hit in the singles charts. **One Day At A Time** changed all that. Considerable TV and radio exposure for her version of the song, which had never been a British hit before, created a public demand which suddenly gave Lena Martell her one and only British hit single.

The Andrew Lloyd Webber–Tim Rice combination has launched the careers of many a female vocalist – Yvonne Elliman, Helen Reddy and Julie Covington to name but three. But for Lena Martell they were not so lucky. Her version of **Don't Cry For Me Argentina** was the on–off follow-up to **One Day At A Time** and it missed completely. But her albums still sell as well as ever.

446

WHEN YOU'RE IN LOVE WITH A BEAUTIFUL WOMAN

17 November 1979, for three weeks

Dr Hook *Capital CL 16039*

Writer: Even Stevens
Producer: Ron Haffkine

Dr Hook began life as Dr Hook and the Medicine Show, and are one of the few groups (the Beatles and Three Dog Night are others) which have more than one lead singer. Ray Sawyer (born 1 Feb 1937) and Dennis Locorriere (born 13 June 1949) are the two regularly featured lead vocalists, the rest of the band being Rik Elswit on guitar, John Wolters on drums, Billy Francis on keyboards and Jance Garfat on bass. Their first hit in Britain was that piece of telephonic agony in conversation with the long-distance operator and Mrs Avery, **Sylvia's Mother**, written by Playboy cartoonist Shel Silverstein, which reached number two in 1972. Silverstein wrote many more songs for Dr Hook, including the very funny **Cover Of Rolling Stone**, which was banned from broadcast in Britain because it was classed as advertising, and thus flopped totally.

By 1975, the band had gone bankrupt, but they stuck together (apart from the original drummer, John David, who bailed out) and the hits began to start again. Their version of **Only Sixteen** (see no. 89) was a massive hit in America in 1975, but in Britain their comeback hit was **A Little Bit More** which entered the charts 4 years and 2 days after **Sylvia's Mother** and again peaked at number two. **When You're In Love With A Beautiful Woman** (one of the longest titles in number one history) reached number one for an hour or two on 10 November 1979, until a computer error was revealed, and it fell back to number two. A week later, the computer worked properly and gave Dr Hook their only number one to date.

447

WALKING ON THE MOON

8 December 1979, for one week

Police *A & M AMS 7494*

Writer: Sting
Producers: Police and Nigel Gray

The second chart-topper for Police was the second single from their second LP 'Regatta de Blanc'. By this time Police were big, and people were beginning to realise that they weren't just popular, they were good. Their first album, 'Outlandos d'Amour' contained **Can't Stand Losing You** which had eventually climbed to number two in August 1979, 10 months after it originally hit the chart. There was also **Roxanne**, a brilliant single that was the only single to miss the Top 10 (it reached number 12) until **Spirits In The Material World** peaked at number 13 early in 1982. They have yet to issue a single with their present line-up which has missed the Top 20.

After **Walking On The Moon**, Police went back into the studios to work on what became their third LP, 'Zenyatta Mondatta'. This gave A & M the chance to re-activate the single **So Lonely** which had for some reason originally failed as the follow-up to **Can't Stand Losing You**. **So Lonely** reached number six and a 'six-pack' of six separate singles (their first five singles plus **The Bed's Too Big Without You**) even reached number 17. It was weird marketing but it worked. It kept the fans happy until **Don't Stand So Close To Me** (see no. 467).

448

ANOTHER BRICK IN THE WALL (PART II)

15 December 1979, for five weeks

Pink Floyd *Harvest HAR 5194*

Writers: Roger Waters and Bob Ezrin
Producers: Roger Waters, Bob Ezrin and Dave Gilmour

Pink Floyd are the creators of the biggest-selling British album of all time, 'Dark Side Of The Moon', which has sold an estimated thirteen million copies. But **Another Brick In The Wall (Part II)** was their first single hit for 12½ years, since **See Emily Play** reached number six in the flower-power summer of 1967. In those far-off days, Pink Floyd were led by the erratic Syd Barrett, and the other members were Roger Waters (born 6 September 1944) on bass, Richard Wright (born 28 July 1945) on keyboards and Nick Mason (born 27 January 1945) on drums. Shortly after **See Emily Play** was released, Barrett was replaced by Dave Gilmour (born 6 March 1944), and Pink Floyd began recording the succession of hit albums that has made them one of the supergroups of the 1970's.

Originally there was no plan to release a single from their late 1979 album, 'The Wall', but eventually the first Pink Floyd single in years was issued, the anti-education anthem, **Another Brick In The Wall (Part II)**. It took barely 3 weeks to become the first '(Part II)' single ever to top the British charts. Bob Ezrin, co-writer and co-producer, also produced Alice Cooper's smash **School's Out** (see no. 317). Obviously school themes work for Mr Ezrin.

449

BRASS IN POCKET

19 January 1980, for two weeks

Pretenders *Real ARE 11*

Writers: Chrissie Hynde and James Honeyman-Scott
Producer: Chris Thomas

The Pretenders were ex-journalist Chrissie Hynde from Akron, Ohio on guitar and vocals, and three Englishmen, James Honeyman-Scott (guitar and keyboards), Pete Farndon on bass and Martin Chambers on drums. Miss Hynde's distinctive vocal style quickly attracted attention in the clubs where they performed, and chart success came early in 1979 with their brilliant version of the Ray Davies' song, **Stop Your Sobbing**. It only reached number 34 in the charts, but attracted a lot of airplay and increased the popularity of the Pretenders as a live act. That was followed by the self-penned **Kid** which sounded very like lots of other tunes but it was hard to pin down which. The third single from the 'Pretenders' album (which was not released until late in 1979) was **Brass In Pocket**, the hymn of the late seventies modern girl. It started very slowly, climbing the charts at the same consistent but unexciting rate as the two earlier singles, and then over Christmas and the New Year it raced upwards. It was not until its tenth week on the chart that it hit the top, making it one of the slowest-climbing chart-toppers of all. Hits continued after **Brass In Pocket**, including two more Top 10 hits, **Talk Of The Town** in 1980 and **I Go To Sleep** at the end of 1981. **I Go To Sleep** was another Ray Davies song (Chrissie Hynde and Ray Davies being emotionally involved with one another). It had been recorded in the mid-sixties by the Applejacks, who missed out completely with it.

In June 1982, James Honeyman Scott died suddenly, casting doubts over the future of the Pretenders.

450

THE SPECIAL A.K.A. LIVE (EP)

2 February 1980, for two weeks

Specials *2 Tone CHS TT 7*

Writers: Too Much Too Young – Jerry Dammers and Lloyd Chalmers, Guns Of Navarone – Dmitri Tiompkin and Paul Francis Webster, Long Shot Kick De Bucket – Sydney Roy Crooks and Jackie Robinson, Liquidator – Harry Johnson, Skinhead Moonstomp – Monty Naismith and Roy Ellis
Producers: Jerry Dammers and Dave Jordan

The Coventry-based Specials reached number one with their third hit, and joined Demis Roussos (see no. 392) in taking an EP to number one. The EP was officially called 'The Special A.K.A. Live!' but track 1 on side 1, **Too Much Too Young** was given top billing on the EP cover. The first side, featuring **Too Much Too Young** and the last instrumental to reach the top, **Guns Of Navarone**, was recorded at the Lyceum in London. The B-side, the **Skinhead Symphony** was recorded at Tiffany's in Coventry, late in 1979.

The Specials were, at this time, Terry Hall, Neville Staples, Roddy Radiation, Lynval Golding, John Bradbury, Jerry Dammers and Sir Horace Gentleman. Rico Rodriguez, who had been featured on the previous Specials release, **A Message To You Rudy**, played trombone on **Guns Of Navarone** and **Long Shot Kick De Bucket**, and Dick Cuthell played flugelhorn on **Guns Of Navarone**.

451

COWARD OF THE COUNTY

16 February 1980, for two weeks

Kenny Rogers *United Artists UP 614*

Writers: Roger Bowling and B E Wheeler
Producer: Larry Butler

Almost three years after **Lucille** (see no. 406) Kenny Rogers returned to the top of the charts with the inspiring tale of the convict's son Tommy who was known as the **Coward Of The County**, but still whipped the Gatlin boys because they had performed unspeakable acts upon his wife. It was another great performance by Kenny Rogers, who tells these little homespun sagas so well, and the only surprise about the success in Britain of this particular record was that other Rogers singles, for example the best of them all **The Gambler**, had failed to register in Britain.

After **Coward Of The County**, Kenny Rogers has moved on to hits produced by Lionel Richie of the Commodores, and also a huge hit in America in duet with that female Rod Stewart, Kim Carnes, which unaccountably did nothing in Britain. By the early nineteen-eighties, Kenny Rogers had become the first country superstar to move firmly across the dividing line into pop. Other country acts, notably that fine duo Dolly Parton, have had major pop successes but remain basically country stars. Kenny Rogers, who had psychedelic hits in the sixties before moving to country, is now an Easy Listening superstar, although his records are still country hits as well.

———*452*———

ATOMIC

1 March 1980, for two weeks

Blondie *Chrysalis CHS 2410*

Writers: Chris Stein and Debbie Harry
Producer: Mike Chapman

Blondie's third number one **Atomic** was, like their first, **Heart Of Glass** (see no. 433) written by Debby Harry and Blondie guitarist Chris Stein, and produced by Mike Chapman. It was Blondie's ninth hit single, all of which had reached the Top 20, with all but two reaching the Top 10. It was the follow-up to one of those two comparative failures, **Union City Blue**, and it must have been reassuring for the band to see **Atomic** leap to number one in its second week on the chart. It proved also to be the first of a hat-trick of number ones.

In 1979, despite missing number one with two of the four singles they issued that year, Blondie tied with Abba and Chic to be the acts on the chart for most weeks of the year. In 1980, all three Blondie singles hit number one, but the band did not even feature in the Top 10 of 'Most Weeks On Chart: 1980'. The reason was that the heavy and rapid sales of each Blondie single gave them high chart placings, but a short chart life. **Atomic** and **Call Me** each spent only 9 weeks on the chart, while **The Tide Is High** lasted only a little longer, 12 weeks.

———*453*———

TOGETHER WE ARE BEAUTIFUL

15 March 1980, for one week

Fern Kinney *WEA K 79111*

Writer: Ken Leray
Producers: Carson Whitsett, Wolf Stephenson and Tommy Couch

Together We Are Beautiful had been recorded by British vocalist Steve Allan 18 months before Fern Kinney hit the charts, and at the beginning of 1979 he enjoyed 2 weeks of chart action with his version. Some 364 days after Mr Allan dropped out of the charts for ever, Fern Kinney's rendition came on to the charts via the discos, and within a month was number one. Six weeks later, she became the twenty-eighth current member of the one-hit wonder club, the third consecutive female vocalist to join this exclusive band, and the first of five one-hit wonders of 1980.

In her native land, Miss Kinney is not quite as obscure as she has been for all but 11 weeks of her life in Britain. She was first noticed when she had a big disco hit with her version of King Floyd's 1970 American R & B number one, **Groove Me**. But it must be admitted that the decline in the careers of disco megastars like Donna Summer and the Bee Gees has been paralleled by a decline in the career of smaller but equally heavenly bodies like Fern Kinney.

———*454*———

GOING UNDERGROUND/DREAMS OF CHILDREN

22 March 1980, for three weeks

Jam *Polydor POSP 113*

Writer: Paul Weller (both sides)
Producer: Vic Coppersmith-Heaven

Three lads from Sheerwater in Surrey, Bruce Foxton, Rick Buckler and Paul Weller, startled the music world by entering the chart with their first number one at number one. It was their tenth hit single since **In The City** climbed to number 40 in May 1977. Their first eight hits had missed the Top 10, but the popularity of their concerts had eventually to be translated into record sales. **The Eton Rifles** climbed to number three, and **Going Underground/Dreams Of Children** completed the success story by hitting the very top.

Jam's early success was based on three songs with similar titles, **All Around The World, The Modern World** and **News Of The World**, all of which were reissued in early April 1980 and all re-entered the charts. Ronnie Hilton is another number one hit maker who hit with 'World' songs, in his case **Two Different Worlds**, **Around The World** and **The World Outside**. Ronnie Hilton did not also have a succession of London songs as Jam did – their hits like **'A' Bomb in Wardour Street**, **Strange Town**, **In The City** and **Down In The Tube Station At Midnight** showed that these articulate punks based their music firmly on the experiences of city life. The word 'Love' doesn't appear anywhere in the themes of Paul Weller.

455

WORKING MY WAY BACK TO YOU

12 April 1980, for two weeks

Detroit Spinners *Atlantic K 11432*

Writers: Sandy Linzer and Denny Randell
Producer: Michael Zager

The Spinners were called the Motown Spinners and then the Detroit Spinners in Britain to avoid confusion with the folk singers of the same name. They survived several personnel changes and finally achieved their British number one 25 years after the original group began singing together in high school in Ferndale, Michigan. At that point they went by yet another name, the Dominicos.

Initially protégés of Harvey Fuqua, they scored their first American Top 40 hit in 1961 on his Tri-Phi label with **That's What Girls Are Made For**. When Fuqua went to Motown so did the Spinners, who hit the forty again in 1965 with **I'll Always Love You** and then in 1970 with the Stevie Wonder-produced **It's a Shame**. This disc, also co-written by Wonder, gave the group their first British entry. In 1972, now on Atlantic Records, they began a memorable string of hits with producer Thom Bell, including **Could It Be I'm Falling In Love, Ghetto Child**, and their US number one with Dionne Warwicke, **Then Came You**.

Great glory in Britain was reserved for their work with yet another mentor, Michael Zager. He coupled the old Four Seasons hit **Working My Way Back to You** with his own **Forgive Me Girl** to reach the top spot, though oddly his own composition was not credited on the original label. A medley of old and new was not only appealing to listeners, it gave Zager a share of the composer's royalties, and he repeated the trick later in 1980 by joining **Cupid** with **I've Loved You For a Long Time**.

456

CALL ME

26 April 1980, for one week

Blondie *Chrysalis CHS 2414*

Writer: Giorgio Moroder and Debbie Harry
Producer: Giorgio Moroder

Call Me is the only one of Blondie's five number one hits not produced by Mike Chapman. It was produced by the mastermind of Donna Summer's disco hits, Giorgio Moroder. The reason for the temporary switch of producers was that this was a song from a film, the film being *American Gigolo*. It was Blondie's second single of a film tune, the first being the theme from the under-rated film *Union City*, starring Deborah Harry. The single, **Union City Blue** was not underrated, and rose only to number 13 in Britain.

Call Me was to prove to be the second number one in Blondie's hat-trick of number ones, all in 1980. It was a hat-trick completed with only a total of 5 weeks at number one for the three singles together, which is the fewest weeks ever spent at number one in completing a hat-trick by any of the ten acts who have so far managed it. **Call Me** had one more distinction. It was the third number one written or co-written by Debbie Harry, who thus became the only woman in British chart history to write three number ones.

457

GENO

3 May 1980, for two weeks

Dexy's Midnight Runners *R 6033*

Writers: Kevin Rowlands and Al Archer
Producer: Pete Wingfield

In the mid-sixties, Geno Washington and his Ram Jam Band had a club reputation that was second to none, but their inability to capture on vinyl 3 minutes of the excitement of their live performances meant that their singles chart career never reflected their popularity or their influence on later bands. In fact, the only chart record that Washington held when his final single, **Michael**, fell off the listings in March 1967 was that of most weeks on the chart (20) without ever hitting the Top 30. His band's highest singles chart placing ever was number 39 although his albums were Top 10 items.

Suddenly, 13 years later, a band of politically aware young men, too young to have seen Geno in his prime, produced a single as a tribute to the sixties soul man, which raced to number one. The secret was probably the production of Pete Wingfield, solo hitmaker with **Eighteen With A Bullet** and member of the Olympic Runners (no relation), who was old enough and interested enough in rock history to know all about Geno Washington. So with their second chart single, Kevin Rowlands, Big Jimmy Patterson, Seb Shelton, Micky Billingham, Steve Wynne, Paul Speare, Brian Morris and Billy Adams, a.k.a. Dexy's Midnight Runners achieved their only number one.

458

WHAT'S ANOTHER YEAR

17 May 1980, for two weeks

Johnny Logan *Epic EPC 8572*

Writer: Shay Healy
Producers: Bill Whelan and Dave Pennefather

The Irish entry in the 1980 Eurovision Song Contest was sung by an Australian, Johnny Logan. There had been many precedents for a country to be represented by an artist of different national origin, though the notion seemed strange in Britain, which traditionally gave the nod to a native.

The photogenic and personable Logan real name Sean Sherrard, proved an overnight sensation with his well-made recording of the tune. The single shot in and out so quickly it only registered 8 weeks on the chart. Johnny consequently earned the dubious distinction of having had the shortest chart career of any artist who had a number one hit.

He might have shed that onus were it not for legal complications. He had previously contracted to another record company, and with two different labels throwing out material to capitalise on the Eurovision victory, radio programmers, rarely enthusiastic about the follow-ups to Eurovision winners anyway, threw up their hands and ignored them all. Only subsequent years would determine if the likeable Logan could relaunch his career.

Although Eurovision Song winners have a reputation for going to number one, **What's Another Year** was in fact only the fifth victor to do so.

459

THEME FROM M*A*S*H* (SUICIDE IS PAINLESS)

31 May 1980, for three weeks

Mash *CBS 8536*

Writers: Mike Altman and Johnny Mandel
Producer: Thomas Z. Shepherd

The film *M*A*S*H** (which stands for Mobile Army Surgical Hospital) starred Donald Sutherland. Sutherland also starred in *The Eagle Has Landed* with Michael Caine, the star of *Alfie*, which inspired Burt Bacharach and Hal David to write the song which proved to be a hit for Cilla Black. Another co-star of *The Eagle Has Landed* was Jenny Agutter, who also starred in *The Railway Children*, directed by Lionel Jeffries who starred in *Chitty Chitty Bang Bang* written by Ian Fleming whose James Bond books have, in their film versions, provided theme song hits for Nancy Sinatra, Shirley Bassey, John Barry, Sheena Easton, Carly Simon, Wings, Matt Monro and others. Elliott Gould, another star of *M*A*S*H**, was married to Barbra Streisand who starred in *Hello Dolly* which provided a hit for Louis Armstrong who starred in *High Society*, a film which contained the hit song **Samantha**, a hit for Bing Crosby and Grace Kelly, and for Kenny Ball who also had a hit with **March Of The Siamese Children** from *The King And I* which originally starred in the Broadway production Gertrude Lawrence, who was portrayed in the biopic *Star* by Julie Andrews, who has never had a hit single.

The M*A*S*H* theme single came from nowhere, via Noel Edmonds' persistent plugging, to reach number one a decade after it was recorded. It was co-written by the son of the film's director, Robert Altman, but all it proves is that films feature a lot of music, some good, some bad.

460

CRYING

21 June 1980, for three weeks

Don McLean *EMI 5051*

Writers: Roy Orbison and Joe Melson
Producer: Larry Butler

The odyssey of this track to number one rivals that of Kraftwerk's **The Model** (see no. 494) as one of the strangest ever. Originally recorded in 1978 as part of the 'Chain Lightning' album, it was rejected by McLean's American record company, whose chief executive suggested it be sped up to make it more commercial. McLean resisted, having intentionally dropped the Latin beat of Roy Orbison's 1961 original to create a reflective ballad. He was further resistant to change because he thought **Crying** was one of his best performances as a singer.

Over a year later, McLean made a personal trip to Israel, stopping over in Northern Europe for a television appearance that would pay for the journey. One of the numbers he performed was **Crying**, which received such viewer reaction the cut was released as a single. When it went Top 5 in a couple of countries, EMI put it out in Britain, where it went to number one. With this success McLean made a deal with a new US record company and enjoyed an American Top 5 hit in 1981. American buyers were unaware it had taken three years and an international trek to get there. Always a top concert attraction around the world, McLean was now restored as a media favourite.

The 7 years and 357 days that had elapsed between McLean's number one hits was the fourth longest in chart history. He had gone to number one in Ireland during the interim with **Mountains O'Mourne**.

461

XANADU

12 July 1980, for two weeks

Olivia Newton-John and Electric Light Orchestra *Jet 185*

Writer: Jeff Lynne
Producer: Jeff Lynne

'The most dreadful, tasteless movie of the decade. Indeed, probably of all time,' Felix Barker wrote in the London *Evening News*, dismissing the Olivia Newton-John film *Xanadu*. Barker's criticism was only slightly more severe than the typical reaction to the musical extravaganza, in which Olivia, a daughter of Zeus, inspired Gene Kelly to open a roller disco in California.

The film may have been a folly, but the music from it was spectacularly successful. Four tracks became hits in both Britain and the United States, with **Xanadu** a UK number one and **Magic** an American chart-topper. But whereas **Magic** was Olivia's solo, **Xanadu** was a duet with the Electric Light Orchestra. Indeed, the record was written and produced by ELO leader Jeff Lynne. It was Newton-John's third UK number one, all in tandem with somebody else. For the ELO, who had two hits from the film on their own, it was their first appearance in the number one position in any form. They had previously scored thirteen top tenners without ever going all the way.

462

USE IT UP AND WEAR IT OUT

26 July 1980, for two weeks

Odyssey *RCA PB 1962*

Writers: Sandy Linzer and L Russell Brown
Producer: Sandy Linzer

Though it had occasionally happened through the years, in the post-punk era it became commonplace: an American record could get to number one in Britain without even penetrating the Top 100 at home. It was so with three 1980 number ones, **Together We Are Beautiful** by Fern Kinney, **Theme From M*A*S*H*** by Mash and **Use It Up And Wear It Out** by Odyssey.

In the last case the clear reason was that the British chart reflected sales with no airplay factor. If a disco record caught on and sold, it made the chart. In the States, the radio spin element was also important. **Use It Up And Wear It Out** had in fact done fairly well in the US disco chart but was blocked from spreading to pop because the other side, **Don't Tell Me, Tell Her**, was the stronger deck on black radio. There was no such divided chart action in Britain. **Use It Up And Wear It Out** which had received heavy disco attention on import, won quick radio acceptance from programmers fond of the group's 1975 Top 5 hit **Native New Yorker**. Odyssey were happy to have a number one but slightly dismayed that the side of their work they preferred, the ballad, was not recognised. They need not have worried:

Left **463 Abba,** *Above* **457 Dexys Midnight Runners**

462 Odyssey

Below left **464 David Bowie,** *right* **458 Johnny Logan**

the follow-up, the down tempo **If You're Looking For a Way Out**, was also one of the year's Top 40 sellers.

This triumph was also sweet for co-writer Sandy Linzer. The veteran author had helped pen the Detroit Spinners' number one only 3 months earlier. His patience had paid off.

463

THE WINNER TAKES IT ALL

9 August 1980, for two weeks

Abba *Epic EPC 8835*

Writers: Benny Andersson and Bjorn Ulvaeus
Producers: Benny Andersson and Bjorn Ulvaeus

Abba's return to the top after a 2½ year absence was a surprise to chart form-watchers who felt that Abba would fade slowly into the sunset after a long, hugely successful but no longer chart-topping career. The first of two singles taken from Abba's 'Super Trouper' album changed all that by leapfrogging to the top in only its second week on the chart. The group had come a long way since those far off days of Hep Stars, Hootenanny Singers and the Anni-Frid Four.

By the time the group recorded 'Super Trouper' both romantic partnerships within Abba had come to an end; Benny and Frida, Bjorn and Agnetha were no longer lovers and/or husband and wife. Yet the quartet seemed to be able to handle the complications of such breakdowns with the skill with which they made records – families had broken up but the hits kept coming. **The Winner Take It All** was Abba's eighth number one.

464

ASHES TO ASHES

23 August 1980, for two weeks

David Bowie *RCA BOW 6*

Writer: David Bowie
Producers: David Bowie and Tony Visconti

Eleven years after he left Major Tom stranded in **Space Oddity**, David Bowie continued his saga on an even more pessimistic note. Left 'floating in my tin can' in 1969, out of radio contact with Ground Control, Major Tom now stood revealed as 'a junkie . . . hitting an all-time low'.

The hapless astronaut moaned 'I've never done good things/I've never done bad things/I've never done anything out of the blue.' Bowie told the *New Musical Express* the words could be applied to himself, representing a 'continuing, returning feeling of inadequacy over what I've done.' Reflecting the discontent many thoughtful artists feel, he added 'I'm not awfully happy with what I've done in the past.' At least he gave himself credit for 'the idea that one doesn't have to exist purely on one defined set of ethics and values, that you can investigate other areas and other avenues of perception and try and apply them to everyday life.'

The New Romantic movement, which owed its existence to Bowie's past, was just beginning to exert its influence, and Bowie turned to it for his **Ashes to Ashes** video. He wore a Pierrot costume and featured the mentor of the movement, Steve Strange. Unlike **Space Oddity, Ashes to Ashes** was not a great success in the United States, but there Bowie scored an even more important triumph when he successfully took over the title role in the Broadway production of *The Elephant Man.*

465

START

6 September 1980, for one week

Jam *Polydor 2059 266*

Writer: Paul Weller
Producer: Vic Coppersmith-Heaven

Born on 23 May 1958, Paul Weller's main influence in music has, he says, been Ray Davies of the Kinks, and his favourite record of all time is the Kinks' **Waterloo Sunset**, a song about London, the city that has been the subject of many of Jam's biggest hits. Ray Davies and the Kinks emerged from a bleak period in the early seventies to become a very popular live act in America, and also a big influence on eighties rock. The influence of Ray Davies is sometimes direct, as for example with the Pretenders and their versions of his compositions **Stop Your Sobbing** and **I Go To Sleep**, and sometimes indirect, as for example through the songs of Paul Weller.

Jam have a remarkable chart pedigree. It took them nine singles to reach the Top 10, but since the success of **The Eton Rifles** at the end of 1979, they hit the Top 10 with every single, usually in the first week on the chart, and they have hit the very top three times. Like Gary Numan, Jam have tended to sell in vast quantities in the week the new single is released, and then sales tail off. This means they regularly enter the chart at their highest position, and just go down from there. Both **Start** (which took 2 weeks to reach number one) and their third number one, **A Town Called Malice/Precious** (see no. 495) lasted only 8 weeks on the chart, the fewest number of weeks of chart action for any number one since the introduction of the Top 75, and second only to **Christmas Alphabet** (see no. 40) since the chart began.

466

FEELS LIKE I'M IN LOVE

13 September 1980, for two weeks

Kelly Marie *Calibre PLUS 1*

Writer: Ray Dorset
Producer: Pete Yellowstone

Ray Dorset, former lead singer of Mungo Jerry and composer of their two number one hits (see nos. 288 and 297), wrote **Feels Like I'm In Love** and when Kelly Marie took it to number one, Dorset not only gave the Calibre label a number one with its first single (not as rare a feat as you might think. Warner Brothers started the trend with **Cathy's Clown**), but he also joined the ranks of singer/songwriters whose compositions have been number one for themselves and for other performers.

Kelly Marie began life on 23 October 1957 in Paisley, Scotland as Jacqueline McKinnon. **Feels Like I'm In Love** was her first British hit, but she had already earned herself a French Gold Disc for her hit, **Who's That Lady With My Man** and had hit the charts across much of Europe before Ray Dorset's disco offering established her in Britain. More surprisingly, she has become a disco favourite in America too, where she has toured extensively since the success of **Feels Like I'm In Love**. She has been out of Britain almost as much as she has been at home since her number one, which is perhaps why her follow-up singles have been not so successful.

467

DON'T STAND SO CLOSE TO ME

27 September 1980, for four weeks

Police *A&M AMS 7564*

Writer: Sting
Producers: Nigel Gray and Police

The first track from Police's third album, 'Zenyatta Mondatta' gave Police their third consecutive number one single and won them a Grammy. They thus became the eighth act to complete the hat-trick, and were joined 2 months later by the ninth, Blondie (see no. 469). This was Police's first single release for 10 months, but the lay-off seemed to have done them no harm. The second single from the album, however, missed the top spot. That was **De Do Do Do, De Da Da Da**, which as titles go is no dafter than **Chirpy Chirpy Cheep Cheep** or **Do Wah Diddy Diddy**. Unfortunately, it failed to climb as high as those other titles.

The titles of the first two Police albums stretched the average record-buyer's knowledge of inaccurate French to the limit, but the third title proved to be something of a debating point among linguists. First of all, what language was it meant to be? A majority opinion favoured Swahili or some other African tongue, but a few distinguished scholars argued that it might be bad mediaeval Japanese, meaning something like, 'It was a matter of money'. The reply from the Police was obscure. 'De Do Do Do, De Da Da Da, is all I want to say to you.'

468

WOMAN IN LOVE

25 October 1980, for three weeks

Barbra Streisand *CBS 8966*

Writers: Barry and Robin Gibb
Producers: Barry Gibb, Karl Richardson and Albhy Galuten

At the peak of their success in 1978 the Bee Gees were approached to produce Bob Dylan and Barbra Streisand. Shortly thereafter Dylan began his series of religious albums, but Streisand remained interested. She was in the duet phase of her career, having recently scored with team-ups co-starring Neil Diamond and Donna Summer. Though two tracks from the 'Guilty' album featured Barry Gibb and became American hits, the international number one was **Woman in Love**. Streisand, born 24 April 1942, who had enjoyed a US Top 5 smash in 1964 with **People**, had made her British chart debut in 1966 with **Second Hand Rose**. The 14 year 279 day interval between her first chart appearance and her first number one was the fourth longest wait in UK history.

Considered by many to have the finest female voice of her time, Streisand co-operated with other artists so often because she preferred filming to making records, and sometimes had to be lured into the studio. She has also recently avoided the Broadway stage, where she first won acclaim in 1962 for a supporting role in the musical *I Can Get It For You Wholesale.*

The success of the Streisand-Gibb collaboration was such that the 'Guilty' album remained in the British album chart well into 1982.

469

THE TIDE IS HIGH

15 November 1980, for two weeks

Blondie *Chrysalis CHS 2465*

Writer: John Holt
Producer: Mike Chapman

The record that many would pick out as the best of Blondie's five number ones completed their hat-trick and has proved to be their last single to top the charts. It was written by Jamaican John Holt, ex-lead singer with the Paragons and solo hitmaker with his version of Kris Kristofferson's **Help Me Make It Through The Night** early in 1975. It gave Mike Chapman his ninth British number one as a producer, putting him behind only Norrie Paramor, George Martin and Johnny Franz on the list of British producers of number one hits.

The Tide Is High joined songs like **Sailing**, **Message In A Bottle**, **Albatross** and **Yellow Submarine** on the rather absurd list of number one hits with a nautical flavour. Clearly, songs like **Sailor** and **Kon-Tiki** are also on that list, but what about **Dreamboat** and **Float On**?

Shortly after the success of this single, Debbie Harry began work on her solo album **Koo Koo** produced by Chic masterminds Edwards and Rodgers. Had this album done as well as the Chic-produced Diana Ross LP, or as most of Blondie's albums, it is possible that Blondie the group might have been no more. But it didn't and by 1982 they were back together again with another new album **The Hunter**.

470

SUPER TROUPER

29 November 1980, for three weeks

Abba *Epic EPC 9089*

Writers: Benny Andersson and Bjorn Ulvaeus
Producers: Benny Andersson and Bjorn Ulvaeus

The second single from the 'Super Trouper' album was the title track, which gave Abba their ninth and to date final number one. It took a week longer than **The Winner Takes It All** to climb to the top, but was only knocked off the top by the tragedy of John Lennon's death, which put his otherwise unremarkable single to number one. It was perhaps a fitting reminder to the biggest group in the world since the break-up of the Beatles that the Beatles always were, and always will be, bigger than any other group in popular music history.

At the time of writing, Abba have definitely slipped into a phase of less than mega-sales (their 1981 album **The Visitors** failed to yield a number one single) but it would be unwise to write off the genius of the writing talents of Benny and Bjorn. Some of their songs have been so expertly crafted that they would have been hits in almost any era sung by almost anybody.

As the lights dim after the concert and the musicians make their way backstage, the echoes of the latest Abba hit ring clear across the emptying auditorium. 'Tonight the super trouper lights are gonna find me/ shining like the sun/ smiling have fun/ feeling like a number one.' The signs are there that Abba believe in their own myth, but then it's quite a myth to believe in.

471

(JUST LIKE) STARTING OVER

20 December 1980, for one week

John Lennon *WEA/Geffen K 79186*

Writer: John Lennon
Producers: John Lennon, Yoko Ono and Jack Douglas

(Just Like) Starting Over had reached number eight in the British charts, and had fallen back to number 21 when the tragic news of Lennon's senseless murder broke. The next week the song was at number one, to give John Lennon his first British chart-topper since the Beatles split, one week too late.

The long-awaited 'Double Fantasy' album had many good tracks, and all in all proved that John Lennon was in pretty good musical form after his long lay-off. But **(Just Like) Starting Over** was by no means the best track on the album, and its original peak position of number eight was a truer reflection of its real merit as a hit single. Both **Woman** (see no. 474) and **Watching The Wheels**, the second and third singles from the album would have been most people's choices for release before **(Just Like) Starting Over**.

But what does that matter? The death of John Lennon deprived the world of a man who had made a matchless contribution to twentieth-century music and who clearly still had a great deal more to give.

472

THERE'S NO-ONE QUITE LIKE GRANDMA

27 December 1980, for two weeks

St Winifred's School Choir *Music For Pleasure FP 900*

Writer: Gordon Lorenz
Producer: Peter Tattersall

One hit wonders come in all shapes and sizes, but probably the smallest in individual shape but the largest in total size was a girls' school choir whose first single was at the time the only single ever released, or ever planned for release by the budget LP label, Music For Pleasure. MFP's 100 per cent success with single releases was not unique, however. The T Rex label only ever issued one single, **Telegram Sam** (see no. 309) and that was a number one hit too.

At Christmas 1981, the girls issued an LP which sold well and another single, also on MFP, featuring the song that Ken Dodd turned into a minor hit, **Hold My Hand**, but it flopped completely. MFP's reign as the joint most successful singles label of all time was over. The St Winifred's girls are only just one-hit wonders, though. The children singing on the Brian and Michael hit, **Matchstalk Men and Matchstalk Cats and Dogs** (see no. 421) are the St Winifred's School Choir, who thus become the only act whose only chart appearances have been on two one-hit wonder singles.

There's No-One Quite Like Grandma was, incidentally, the 500th track to to be listed at number one, thanks to double-sided hits and two EPs which swelled the total above 472.

473

IMAGINE

10 January 1981, for four weeks

John Lennon *Parlophone R 6009*

Writer: John Lennon
Producers: John Lennon, Yoko Ono and Phil Spector

The death of John Lennon created a demand for his records that compares only with the sales of Elvis records in 1977, and one result was that Lennon's masterpiece, **Imagine**, reached number one in Britain.

It was originally recorded in 1971 for the album of which it was the title track, but it was not released as a single in Britain until 1975, when it reached number six. It was released then only because Lennon had gone into retirement which was to last until 1980, so **Imagine** was actually his final single release for 5 years. Produced by Phil Spector, who had also worked on the Beatles' 'Let It Be' album and George Harrison's 'All Things Must Pass', the 'Imagine' album featured many of the musicians who were on George's album, including Klaus Voorman and Alan White on the title track.

Imagine was the second of three consecutive number ones for John Lennon, and on 7 February 1981 he equalled a record set by the Beatles at the end of 1963 when he took over from himself at the top of the charts.

474

WOMAN

7 February 1981, for two weeks

John Lennon *Geffen K 79195*

Writer: John Lennon
Producers: John Lennon, Yoko Ono and Jack Douglas

By far the strongest song on the 'Double Fantasy' LP, it is hard to understand why **Woman** was not released as the first single off the album. When it was released, it quickly completed a hat-trick of number ones for John Lennon within a period of 7 weeks, which is of course by far the quickest hat-trick of number ones ever completed.

The sales of John Lennon records in the weeks after his death were staggering. On 10 January, in the chart which first reflected immediate post-Christmas sales, three of the Top 5 singles were by Lennon (**Imagine, Happy Christmas**

Top
467 Police,
centre
472 St Winifred's School Choir,
left
468 Barbra Streisand,
right
484 Aneka

(**War Is Over**) and (**Just Like**) **Starting Over**). That same week, the 'Double Fantasy' album was at number two in the LP charts, behind Abba. 'Imagine' was at number 39 and 'The Beatles 1962-1966' was at number 58. By the beginning of February, there were five Lennon singles in the Top 40, the extra two being **Woman** and **Give Peace A Chance**. There were also three Lennon albums on the Top 15, as well as two Beatles albums in the Top 75. A little later came the Roxy Music single (see no. 476) and even the John Lennon/Elton John live duet single of **I Saw Her Standing There**. In chart terms it was the most spectacular monopoly of the charts since the Beatles in their heyday. Small compensation for the loss of such a musical giant.

475

SHADDUP YOU FACE

21 February 1981, for three weeks

Joe Dolce *Epic EPC 9518*

Writer: Joe Dolce

Producers: Joe Dolce and Ian McKenzie

The unlikely one-hit wonder who kept John Lennon songs off the top for 3 weeks early in 1981 was an Italian-American born in Painesville, Ohio in 1947. From 1966 he was in a group called Sugarcreek, who recorded an unsuccessful album on the Metromedia label in America in 1969. By 1974, Joe Dolce had formed a 'poetry-music fusion group' and was touring the East Coast of America, 'creating popular songs out of poetry classics' by Dylan Thomas, Yeats and Sylvia Plath. No gold discs were earned.

1978 found Joe Dolce in Australia, where he formed the Joe Dolce Music Theatre Show, and created the character Giuseppi. As Giuseppi he recorded **Shaddup You Face**, which became a big hit in Australia and was picked up by Epic for the UK market. It became the first comedy record to hit the top since **D.I.V.O.R.C.E.** (see no. 381) and Joe Dolce became the first one-hit wonder of 1981 when all his follow-up singles, including the weird **Reggae Matilda**, missed and the face of Joe Dolce was shut up.

476

JEALOUS GUY

14 March 1981, for two weeks

Roxy Music *Polydor ROXY 2*

Writer: John Lennon

Producers: Bryan Ferry and Rhett Davies

The only words printed on the sleeve of this single were the title, the artist, and the phrase 'a tribute'. That is precisely what this record was. When John Lennon was murdered Roxy Music were in Germany rehearsing for a television show. Their natural instinct, as was the reaction of many top artists performing that week, was to include a Lennon number in their set. Bryan Ferry suggested one of his great favourites, **Jealous Guy** from the 'Imagine' album.

The song went well on the show, and one of the German executives enthused that it must be made a single. At first Roxy declined, having only intended to pay homage to the slain hero. But upon returning to Britain they realised it might not be a bad idea and, at Ferry's further suggestion, they cut the tune at a studio near guitarist Phil Manzanera's home in Chertsey. Saxophonist Andy Mackay was the other group member heavily involved in the arrangement and recording.

Roxy Music had accumulated eight Top 10 hits before this chart-topper, all of them of their own authorship. The explanation of this record's success could not be simply that it was a Lennon composition released shortly after his death, since **Jealous Guy** was the only single written by Lennon alone but not performed by him alone to ever go to the top.

This 45 was the last appearance with Roxy Music by bassist Gary Tibbs, who went on to take part in two very different number ones with Adam and the Ants later in the year.

477

THIS OLE HOUSE

28 March 1981, for three weeks

Shakin' Stevens *Epic EPC 9555*

Writer: Stuart Hamblen

Producer: Stuart Colman

Shakin' Stevens was born Michael Barrett in Cardiff on 4 March 1951, so he was not yet 4 years old when Rosemary Clooney took the song **This Ole House** to number one (see no. 25). He apparently never heard the song until the end of 1980, by which time he had had two small hits, **Hot Dog** and **Marie Marie**. He took the song to his producer Stuart Colman and the rest is history.

Stevens' first break in the business came in 1969 when he appeared on the same bill (rather lower down) as the Rolling Stones at the Saville Theatre. But he failed to capitalise on that opportunity and found himself trailing up and down the country, playing in thousands of half-empty halls for almost 8 years. The second big break came in 1977, when he was

Above **474 John Lennon**
Below **478 Buck's Fizz**

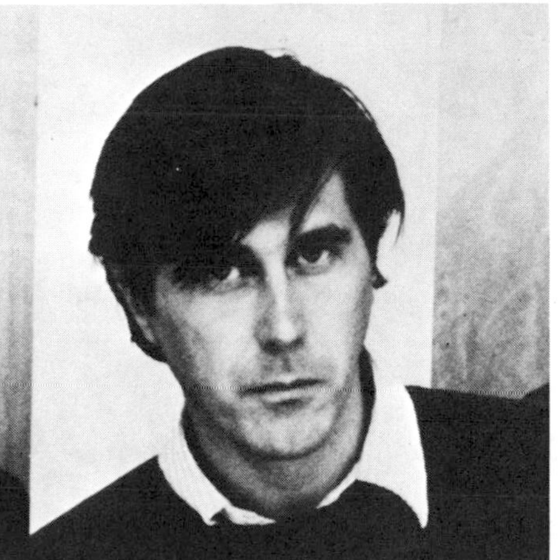

476 Roxy Music

Above **475 Joe Dolce,**
Below **477 Shakin' Stevens**

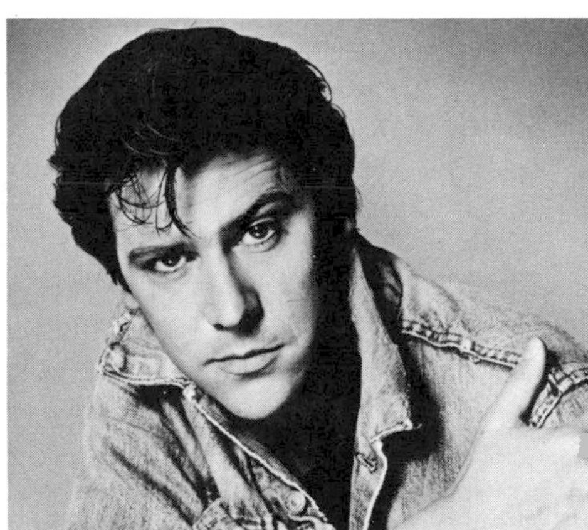

480 Smokey Robinson

one of three artists asked to play the title role in the West End musical *Elvis*. He was very successful and it led to a residency on Jack Good's revamped *Oh Boy* TV show and another series called *Let's Rock*. That led to the Epic recording contract and a lot of hard work by Stevens, his manager Freya Miller and his record company to turn Shaky into a recording star. It finally paid off with **This Ole House** which thus became the sixth song in British chart history to hit number one in two different versions.

478

MAKING YOUR MIND UP

18 April 1981, for three weeks

Buck's Fizz *RCA 56*

Writers: Andy Hill and John Danter
Producer: Andy Hill

Buck's Fizz – Bobby Gee, Mike Nolan, Cheryl Baker and Jay Aston – won the Eurovision Song Contest in 1981 with **Making Your Mind Up**. They became the fourth British winners, after Sandie Shaw, Lulu and Brotherhood of Man, and the fourth British act to take their Eurovision song to number one. **Making Your Mind Up** was in fact the first UK entry to reach the British Top 10 since 1976 and **Save Your Kisses For Me** (see no. 387). For the first time since 1968, Eurovision provided a number one hit in consecutive years, but unlike 1980's Johnny Logan, who proved to be the shortest lived one-hit-wonder of them all, Buck's Fizz were conspicuously successful with their follow-up singles. Perhaps it was the song, far stronger than most Eurovision entries and a runaway winner in Dublin, or perhaps it was the way Cheryl and Jay discard their skirts as they perform the song, but the most likely reason for their success was that they filled a gap in the young teen market which was widening as Abba became more sophisticated and Adam and the Ants more aggressive. By the end of 1981, only Shakin' Stevens and Dollar could begin to match Buck's Fizz in the pre-pubescent popularity stakes.

479

STAND AND DELIVER

9 May 1981, for five weeks

Adam and The Ants *CBS CBSA 1065*

Writers: Adam Ant, Marco Pirroni
Producer: Chris Hughes

The event that Adam Ant says made him want to become a rock star was a Roxy Music concert at the Rainbow in 1972. It took a while for 27-year-old Stuart Goddard to become Adam and to form his Ants, but by the start of 1981, 'Marco, Merrick, Terry Lee, Gary Tibbs and yours truly' had become Britain's biggest act, following in the tradition of Herman's Hermits, T Rex and the Bay City Rollers as teeny bop heroes.

Adam Ant is a star. Only time will tell whether he can continue to create original sounds or whether he will find that like Marc Bolan, one sound can be strung out to create a lot of hits. A lot of 'Antmusic' is clever media hype and determined CBS marketing, which ensured an entry at number one for **Stand And Deliver**. And yet a lot of it is exciting too. It was the addition of Marco Pirroni to the group, as guitarist and writer, that changed them from giving live shows 'with a very clandestine atmosphere, where "Antpeople" gather to be entertained' into chart-topping stars. Nobody has accused Adam and The Ants of selling out, even though the difference between **Young Parisians** (recorded in 1978) written by Adam Ant, and **Stand And Deliver** (by Ant and Pirroni) is even greater than the difference between **Debora** and **Hot Love**. Besides their videos are wonderful.

480

BEING WITH YOU

13 June 1981, for two weeks

Smokey Robinson *Motown TMG 1223*

Writer: William "Smokey" Robinson
Producers: George Tobin in association with Mike Piccirillo

Smokey Robinson's first number one solo single came about as a consequence of a song he had written over a dozen years before. **More Love** had been a US Top 40 hit for Robinson and the Miracles in 1967. Kim Carnes took it to the Top 10 in 1980 in a version produced by George Tobin, who had overseen Robert John's US number one **Sad Eyes**. Robinson always made a point of sending additional songs to artists who had hits with his material. In this case he sent a batch to Tobin, who was well-known for the firm control he asserted over his charges. The embarrassed producer had to reply that he was no longer working with Carnes, but that he would love to cut the number **Being With You** with Smokey himself. Robinson, who had liked the Carnes version of **More Love**, consented, and enjoyed his biggest success since the 1970 winner **Tears of a Clown**.

Bizarrely, **Being With You** was held at number two in

America by the number one hit of 1981, **Bette Davis Eyes** by . . . Kim Carnes. The success of **Being With You** prompted Motown to celebrate Smokey's twenty-fifth anniversary in show business, though literally speaking they were jumping the gun by nearly a year.

481

ONE DAY IN YOUR LIFE

27 June 1981, for two weeks

Michael Jackson *Motown TMG 976*

Writers: Sam Brown III and Renée Armand
Producer: Sam Brown III

Michael Jackson was born on 29 August 1958, 2 weeks before Cliff Richard first hit the charts in Britain. At the age of 11, he sang lead on the first hit (and first American number one) for the Jackson Five, **I Want You Back**. For several years, even after Michael's voice broke, Motown had the hottest black act in the world with the Jackson family, who hit the charts both as a group and with Michael's solo hits, none of which ever reached number one in Britain, however.

Michael and his brothers, excluding Jermaine, had moved to Epic in 1976, but Motown still had a lot of old material on file. For no apparent reason, an old single was reactivated from 5 years before, and this time hit the very top. For the only time in the label's history, Tamla Motown achieved consecutive number ones in Britain. Both were solo records by lead singers of successful Motown groups, but the Michael Jackson track was so old that one fifth of all Motown singles were released between the day **One Day In Your Life** hit the British market and the day it became a hit.

482

GHOST TOWN

11 July 1981, for three weeks

The Specials *2 Tone CHS TT 17*

Writer: Jerry Dammers
Producer: John Collins

The second and, as it turned out, final number one for the Specials represented a considerable change from the previous chart-topper, the EP of reggae favourites (see no. 450). It was still imbued with the basic Jamaican beat, but far from being a rude boy bash, it was an original, subtle and very clever comment on inner city problems, which hit number one at a time when Brixton, Bristol and Toxteth brought the realities of Britain's ghost towns into every household in Britain.

Then the Specials broke up. They got their names on the fairly short list of acts whose last hit was a number one, and then they went their several ways. Terry Hall, Neville Staples and Lynval Golding became the Funboy Three, and quickly launched their chart career with an unusual single, **The Lunatics Have Taken Over The Asylum**. The next single, recorded with the female vocal trio Bananarama, was a revival of the old tune **It Ain't What You Do It's The Way That You Do It** and it hit the Top 3. Every Specials single hit the Top 10, and it only took the Funboy Three two singles to get back into the habit.

483

GREEN DOOR

1 August 1981, for four weeks

Shakin' Stevens *Epic EPCA 1354*

Writers: Bob Davie and Marvin Moore
Producer: Stuart Colman

Shakin' Stevens' architecture fixation continued with **Green Door**, the second old song that the Welsh rocker had resurrected and taken to the top. **Green Door** had not been a number one the first time round in 1956. Three versions had made the chart, the most successful being Frankie Vaughan's, which gave the high-kicking Liverpudlian his first Top 10 hit and finally climbed to number two. The original, by Jim Lowe, made number eight, and another cover by Glen Mason, hit number 24.

Green Door was the follow-up to **You Drive Me Crazy** which Shaky took to number two but couldn't quite push up that final notch. It came on to the chart at number 22, and then made the second biggest leap to number one of all the first 500 number ones. John Lennon's **Starting Over** jumped from 21 to the top in the week following his death, but apart from the records that have come straight in to number one, only Elvis Presley's **Surrender** (see 119), which jumped from 27 to 1, beats Shaky's leap to the top.

All this happened a couple of days after one of the authors of this book had told Mr Stevens that **Green Door** was a great sound but would not make number one. But another had already predicted on the radio that it would go all the way, thus salvaging some of the GRRR Books reputation.

—484—

JAPANESE BOY

29 August 1981, for one week

Aneka *Hansa HANSA 5*

Writer: Bobby Heatlie
Producer: Neil Ross

There was no sense writing to *Jim'll Fix It* asking for a number one record, so Scottish folk singer Mary Sandeman went out and got it herself. A respected traditional vocalist who sang with the Scottish Fiddle Orchestra, Sandeman felt she'd like the thrill of having a pop hit record but didn't want to do so under her own name. Mary had taught herself to sing in Gaelic; pretending she was Japanese for a few minutes was by comparison easy.

Having recorded **Japanese Boy** she needed an oriental-sounding name to use as a pseudonym. She looked through the Edinburgh phone book and found Anika. Rather than risk upsetting the real Anika, she changed the middle vowel and became Aneka. She wore a kimono and Japanese wig on *Top of the Pops* to further the illusion. Ironically, the Japanese music business wasn't too impressed, thinking the record sounded more like a Chinese effort. But the single was a hit on the European continent as well as in the UK. It was the first number one in Britain by a British artist for Hansa, a large German-based company.

When her game was over Sandeman remarked she found singing to Edinburgh Festival Fringe audiences more frightening than *Top of the Pops*. She returned to performing her Gaelic music.

—485—

TAINTED LOVE

5 September 1981, for two weeks

Soft Cell *Bizarre BZS 2*

Writer: Ed Cobb
Producer: Mike Thorne

Soft Cell, a duo consisting of Marc Almond and David Ball, came to attention in Britain via their contribution to a futurist compilation album on the Some Bizarre label. In America **Memorabilia**, the B-side of their first single, proved a surprise top thirty disco hit.

The next effort, **Tainted Love**, was a worldwide dance smash that topped the best sellers as well. The twosome had been introduced to the song through the version by Gloria Jones. Perhaps because Marc Bolan's last girl friend was known as a Motown songwriter, some fans assumed she had penned **Tainted Love**. It had in fact been written years before by Ed Cobb, previously best known for **Dirty Water**, a Stateside smash by the Standells in 1966. All this mattered not. Soft Cell spent 2 weeks at number one with the tune, aided by Marc's histrionic *Top of the Pops* performance. Though ousted by Adam and the Ants' **Prince Charming**, Almond and Ball had the last laugh as **Tainted Love** ended up at number one for the year 1981. A lasting dance floor favourite, it returned at Christmastime for a further run of 10 weeks after its initial stay of 16 weeks. **Tainted Love** also became number one in, among other countries, Germany, Australia and Canada.

—486—

PRINCE CHARMING

19 September 1981, for four weeks

Adam and the Ants *CBS CBSA 1408*

Writers: Marco Pirroni and the Ants
Producers: Chris Hughes, Marco Pirroni and the Ants

By the time the 486th chart-topper eased into a month at number one, video was beginning to be a major feature of singles promotion, and Adam and the Ants were the trendsetters in video. As far back as **I Don't Like Mondays** (see no. 440) in the summer of 1979, videos were selling records by the bucket-load, but in 1981 video promotional films were often costing much more to make than the records they were promoting. The video of **Prince Charming** revolved around the Cinderella story, with Adam Ant as an androgynous Cinderella/Prince Charming swinging from chandeliers in slow motion after Fairy Godmother Diana Dors had waved her magic wand. All this to point out the moral that 'ridicule is nothing to be scared of'.

The next question on everybody's lips was, 'Will Adam and the Ants complete a hat-trick of number ones?' The answer was not long in coming. Another track from the third Ants LP, 'Prince Charming', was put out as a single to catch the Christmas market. It was called **Antrap**. Despite an

Top left **482 Specials,** *top right* **486 Adam and the Ants,** *bottom left* **485 Soft Cell,** *bottom right* **487 Dave Stewart and Barbara Gaskin**

astonishing video featuring Lulu and knights in armour, **Antrap** stopped at number three.

487

IT'S MY PARTY

17 October 1981, for four weeks

Dave Stewart with Barbara Gaskin *Stiff BROKEN 2*

Writers: Herb Wiener, Wally Gold and John Gluck Jnr.
Producer: Dave Stewart

The town of Hatfield is famous for Hatfield House, seat of the Marquess of Salisbury, and for the British Aerospace factory by the A1 where the first flights of such famous aircraft as the Vampire and the Comet took place. In British chart history, it is known as the home town of the Zombies and Scots-born Donovan. It is also featured heavily on the motorway signs known to millions of drivers coming out of London – 'Hatfield and the North'.

The motorway sign became the name of a travelling band in the early 1970's. Hatfield and The North were Richard Sinclair, Phil Miller, Pip Pyle and Dave Stewart, who played piano, organ and tone generator. A female vocal backing group, The Northettes, worked with the band. They were Amanda Parsons, Ann Rosenthal and Barbara Gaskin.

The band broke up, hitless but with a cult following, in the mid-seventies. In 1981 Dave Stewart emerged on a new chart version of Jimmy Ruffin's top ten hit of 1966 and 1974, **What Becomes Of The Broken Hearted?**, which featured Hatfield-born Colin Blunstone, an ex-Zombie, on vocals. A few months later, an extraordinary version of Lesley Gore's 1963 smash, **It's My Party** climbed right to the top, with vocals by Northette Barbara Gaskin.

488

EVERY LITTLE THING SHE DOES IS MAGIC

14 November 1981, for one week

Police *A&M AMS 8174*

Writer: Sting
Producers: Hugh Padgham and Police

The fourth Police LP produced three hit singles in an astonishingly short space of time. No matter that they had waited 10 months between **Walking On The Moon** and **Don't Stand So Close To Me**, or another 10 months between **De Do Do Do De Da Da Da** and **Invisible Sun** – once the LP 'Ghosts In The Machine' was completed the singles were peeled off like fivers at the Ritz. **Invisible Sun** was released, climbed to number two, and immediately the follow-up, **Every Little Thing She Does Is Magic** was in the shops. **Invisible Sun** became rapidly invisible, but **Every Little Thing She Does** was magic and Police climbed to the top for the fourth time. Not content with that, a few weeks later a third single, **Spirits In The Material World** was taken from the album, but this was too much even for the most devout Police fans to take. Most of them had bought the LP anyway. The single peaked at number 13, and Police's run of consecutive Top 10 singles stopped at eight.

In the process, however, Police had become the most successful trio in British chart history. The Bee Gees are now a trio, but for their number ones in the sixties, they were a five piece outfit. The only other trio to have scored even three number ones in Britain are Jam. Police now have four.

489

UNDER PRESSURE

21 November 1981, for two weeks

Queen and David Bowie *EMI 5250*

Writers: Queen and David Bowie
Producers: Queen and David Bowie

Under Pressure marked only the second occasion in which two makers of number one hits came together for the first time to record another number one. The previous case was when Frank Sinatra and daughter Nancy teamed up on **Something Stupid** (see. no. 231). Bowie, like Frank, had scored two prior number ones; Queen, like Nancy, had achieved one.

Under Pressure was written and recorded when Bowie and Queen met in a German studio. Since it was an act of on-the-spot inspiration, no album was ever recorded. Indeed, no B-side was made. Since it was Queen's session, one of their tracks went on the flip and they got lead billing on the disc.

Because **Another One Bites The Dust** had been a long-lived hit in the United States in late 1980, selling over three million copies in that country alone, the 'Queen's Greatest Hits' album planned for Christmas had to be postponed until 1981, even in Britain; imports would otherwise have flooded

America. EMI had a long time to plan their UK marketing strategy and pressed hundreds of thousands of 'Hits' in anticipation of a television campaign. This meant they could not put **Under Pressure** on the album: the LP was already sitting in the warehouse. In the States, where no such problem existed, the cut did appear on the set.

490

BEGIN THE BEGUINE (VOLVER A EMPEZAR)

5 December 1981, for one week

Julio Iglesias *CBS CBSA 1612*

Writers: Cole Porter, Spanish lyrics by Julio Iglesias
Producer: Ramon Arousa

On 12 October 1935, the new musical, *Jubilee*, with music and lyrics by Cole Porter and book by Moss Hart, opened at the Imperial Theater, New York. The show was a comparative failure, but it has two claims to theatrical immortality. Firstly, it featured Montgomery Clift, one of Adam Ant's heroes, in his first professional role as Prince Peter, and secondly the hit song of the show was **Begin The Beguine**.

Despite countless versions of the song recorded since 1935, no version appeared on the British charts until a man who had been Real Madrid's reserve team goalkeeper translated the words rather loosely into Spanish and romped up to number one. Julio Iglesias, born on 23 September 1943, had been the idol of Spanish middle-of-the-road fans for some time, filling the niche in Spanish hearts that Charles Aznavour (see no. 352) has cornered in France. Iglesias is, however, taller than Aznavour, as it is hard to be a goalie, even a reserve one, when of similar stature to Aznavour. CBS also claim that by 1980 Iglesias was the top selling male singer in the world and 'the top-selling artist in the history of CBS records – ever'. Names on CBS include Barbra Streisand, Simon and Garfunkel, Frankie Laine, Guy Mitchell and Adam and the Ants, so the sales of Julio Iglesias records must indeed have been quite sensational.

491

DON'T YOU WANT ME?

12 December 1981, for five weeks

Human League *Virgin VS 466*

Writers: Jo Callis, Phil Oakey and Philip Adrian Wright
Producers: Martin Rushent and Human League

The only single issued in 1981 that sold a million copies in Britain was the Human League's **Don't You Want Me?** It was the fourth single taken from their massive selling LP 'Dare', and it marked the translation of Human League from another New Wave band into rivals to Police and Adam and the Ants as the most popular British group of the 1980's.

Human League are Phil Oakey, Ian Burden, Jo Callis, Joanne Catherall, Susanne Sulley and Philip Adrian Wright. Sheffield-born Phil Oakey's vocals offset the synthesisers which provide all the backing and tend to hide the fact that Human League's appeal is much more to the fans of Abba and Adam Ant than to the fans of the Stranglers or even Toyah. Phil Oakey's admitted influences are Abba, Chic and Donna Summer, and the success of the 'Dare' album was the synthesis of modern musicmaking with straightforward good songwriting and almost traditional rock vocals. 'Dare' was a brilliant album and **Don't You Want Me?** became the only single in the final year of the 500 number ones to stay on top for as long as five weeks.

492

LAND OF MAKE BELIEVE

16 January 1982, for two weeks

Buck's Fizz *RCA 163*

Writers: Andy Hill and Peter Sinfield
Producer: Andy Hill

The group responsible for bringing the 1982 Eurovision Song Contest to Harrogate managed a second number one early in 1982 with a song which rapidly became a favourite on children's television and radio shows. It was a children's song along the lines of the Seekers' **Morningtown Ride** (a number 2 hit 15 years earlier) and even ended with a poem read by 11-year-old Abby Kimber, a member of the Mini-Pops children's group who had some success with their album over Christmas 1981. To complete the child connections, the wife of Bobby Gee of Buck's Fizz had her first baby a few days before the record hit the top.

The Eurovision Song Contest has proved a mixed blessing for the British contestants. The established acts, like Sandie Shaw, Lulu, Cliff Richard, Olivia Newton-John and the Shadows all found that Eurovision gave them one hit single but little more. The unknowns, like Co-Co, the Allisons or Prima Donna, have mostly disappeared back into obscurity once the last television set had been switched off. Only Brotherhood of Man and Buck's Fizz have successfully used Eurovision to launch a career. Dana from Ireland also

Far left **491 Human League, 490 Julio Iglesias,** *above* **494 Kraftwerk** and *below* **488 Police**

turned one Eurovision success into the basis of a good career, as did that quartet from Sweden who won in 1974, Abba.

493

OH JULIE

30 January 1982, for one week

Shakin' Stevens *Epic EPCA 1742*

Writer: Shakin' Stevens
Producer: Stuart Colman

Elvis Presley's seventeenth number one, **Way Down** (see no. 412) was on top when Sir Freddie Laker inaugurated his London to New York Skytrain on 25 September 1977. Shakin' Stevens' third number one, **Oh Julie** was on top when Laker Airways went bankrupt 4 years later. Airlines may come and airlines may go, but rock and roll goes on forever.

After the comparative failure of Shaky's follow-up to **Green Door** (see no. 483), a revival of **It's Raining** that only just made the Top 10, Epic decided to put out a self-penned song to revive the Shaky fortunes, and it did just that. It was very much in the rock idiom that Shaky had so completely appropriated from the fading Showaddywaddy, and it sneaked a week at the top at a time when outstanding singles were in very short supply.

One unlikely fact about Shakin' Stevens is that his real name at the time **Oh Julie** reached the top was Clark Kent, a name he adopted by deed poll a few years ago. Superman is alive and well at the top of the charts.

494

THE MODEL/COMPUTER LOVE

6 February 1982, for one week

Kraftwerk *EMI 5207*

Writers: Ralf Hutter, Karl Bartos and Emil Schultz
Producers: Ralf Hutter and Florian Schneider

The Model is one of the strangest success stories of recent years. A 1978 track that had received considerable club play, it was placed on the B-side of the new number **Computer Love** when that title was issued in 1981. Buyers are more likely to purchase a single if they are partial to the B-side as well as the top deck.

The tactic was only partially successful, as **Computer Love** was only a minor hit. But it refused to die and featured in sales reports for several months. Clubs still preferred **The Model**. Finally the picture sleeve was altered with the colours changed, the title **Computer Love** taken off the front and the words **The Model** put in the computer screen. Sufficient sales pushed the record into the Top 75 and subsequent radio plays exploded the disc. Though a double-sided hit, this was never a double-A: **The Model** was always the official B-side. The group's time had simply come; the synthesiser music long triumphed by the German ensemble had come to dominate the UK market.

During the first 2 months of 1982 the BMRB altered its method of chart computation. The traditional Monday-Saturday tally was dropped in favour of Friday-Thursday on the grounds that the sales diary collectors charged too much for Saturday working. With the impact of weekend sales and *Top of the Pops* appearances now delayed until a fortnight after they occurred, bizarre yo-yo performances were observed. **The Model** went 10-2-3-1, the first single to drop on the chart and then go to number one since the 1981 re-appearance of **Imagine**.

495

A TOWN CALLED MALICE/PRECIOUS

13 February 1982, for three weeks

Jam *Polydor POSP 400*

Writer: (both sides) Paul Weller
Producers: Pete Wilson and the Jam

The thirteenth single ever to come straight in at number one was the second Jam single to achieve this feat. Only Slade, with three direct hits, and Elvis with two, can match Jam's achievement of bringing two singles in at the very top. They achieved a further weird record of quickest rise and fall when the record slipped out of the Top 10 two weeks after being at number one, so it spent only 4 weeks in the Top 10, of which three were at number one. It lasted in total only 8 weeks on the chart, joining the short list, which already included **Start** (see no. 465) of number ones which spent only one week more in the chart than the record-holder at 7 weeks, Dickie Valentine's **Christmas Alphabet** (see no. 40). Just to add to the chart significance of the single, for the first time ever, consecutive number one hits (numbers 494 and 495) were double-sided hits.

The success of this single also caused EMI to ask for

'clarification' of the method of calculation of sales of 7-inch and 12-inch singles for chart purposes. The Jam single was issued in a studio-recorded 7-inch version, which received the airplay, and a 12-inch live version. EMI felt that Jam fans were buying both versions of the song, thereby greatly increasing sales of **A Town Called Malice/Precious**, and keeping EMI's big hit, **Golden Brown** by the Stranglers, from number one. Whatever the merits of the argument, Jam had the number one and the Stranglers had to make do with a number two.

496

THE LION SLEEPS TONIGHT

6 March 1982, for three weeks

Tight Fit *Jive 9*

Writers: Hugo Peretti, Luigi Creatore, George David Weiss, Solomon Linda, Paul Campbell and Albert Stanton
Producer: Tim Friese-Greene

There has been a Top 3 version of **The Lion Sleeps Tonight** every 10 years. The Tokens went to number one in America with it in 1962, Robert John got to three in the States in 1972, and Tight Fit went to the top in Britain in 1982. Though the latter version was the first UK Top 10 rendering, the Tokens having stopped just short of the charmed circle, Karl Denver had reached number five in '62 with a wild reading of **Wimoweh**, a Zulu folk song on which **The Lion Sleeps Tonight** was based. Denver's performance of this at private parties was said to be unforgettable. Most rock scribes are unaware that the Weavers popularised **Wimoweh** in the pre-rock era.

The Tight Fit smash was notable for three odd reasons. First, it was the first number one of the eighties not recorded by the people who publicly promoted it. Studio singers and musicians frequently toiled without credit in the sixties and early seventies, but in the late seventies and early eighties it had become common practice for everyone, even St. Winifred's School Choir, to make their own records. The medley mania of 1981, begun by Jaap Eggermont's Star Sound, changed that. Roy Ward, formerly of City Boy, sang lead on **The Lion Sleeps Tonight**, and here is where the second distinction of this disc emerged. The studio group who made Tight Fit's medley success **Back To The Sixties** were a different lot from those who made the number one. Tight Fit had scored two Top 5 hits with studio groups made of different singers and musicians. Thirdly, the song is the only number one to have as many as six names on the writing credits. One of those six was Paul Campbell, which in turn is a collective pseudonym for the Weavers – Pete Seeger, Fred Hellerman, Lee Hayes, and Ronnie Gilbert. Thus nine writers participate in the royalties. It is just as well that the song is a hit as often as it is.

497

SEVEN TEARS

27 March 1982, for three weeks

The Goombay Dance Band *Epic EPCA 1242*

Writers: Wolff-Ekkehardt Stein and Wolfgang Jass
Producer: Jochen Petersen

The Goombay Dance Band, a German-based outfit fronted by its fire-eating leader 35-year-old Oliver Bendt, took up the mantle of Boney M to top the British charts with a piece of Caribbean Europop. Only a few weeks after Kraftwerk had become the first German act to hit number one in UK, the Goombay Dance Band became the second. They proved to be another group like Tight Fit, who had a different line-up in the studios from the one on TV and live dates.

The Goombay Dance Band officially comprises Bendt, his wife Alicia, Dorothy Hellings, Wendy Doorsen and Mario Slijngaard. The Bendt's two children, Danny and Yasmin, often appear on stage as background vocalists. Bendt learned his fire-eating and his calypso rhythms on St Lucia in the West Indies, and by 1980 had established his band as one of the most successful acts in Germany. **Seven Tears** was originally recorded in Germany in mid-1980, and its success soon after its release in January 1982 was the culmination of a long and determined effort by their management and their record company to move into the slot that Boney M had begun to vacate. After many flops in Britain, their patience was rewarded.

498

MY CAMERA NEVER LIES

17 April 1982, for one week

Buck's Fizz *RCA 202*

Writers: Andy Hill and Nicola Martin
Producer: Andy Hill

My Camera Never Lies was the third number one in a 12-month period for Buck's Fizz. They became the first act to

Left
497 Goombay Dance Band,
right
495 Jam,
below
498 Buck's Fizz

achieve three number ones within a year since Shakin' Stevens. Of all Eurovision winners, only Abba have scored more number ones; the Brotherhood of Man also managed three, but over a 2-year period.

The melody of **My Camera Never Lies** was written by Andy Hill and the lyric by Nicola Martin. Hill took Buck's Fizz into the studio and recorded the boys' lines first, since they were the most straightforward. He then cut the girls' part. Finally came the complicated middle sections where the members are chanting 'my cam-er-a' at each other. Hill gave the quartet full credit for mastering this complex sequence without prior rehearsal.

Both authors felt the attention-getting hooks in the song were the repeated phrases rather than the lyric as a whole. The title, a reference to a frustrated lover who was going to follow his lady and find out the meaning of her movements, also won audience interest.

With the success of this single Buck's Fizz suddenly found themselves critical as well as commercial favourites, favourably reviewed in music papers usually damning of middle-of-the-road pop. Along with Dollar they were the centre of a new school of hip mass appeal groups.

499

EBONY AND IVORY

24 April 1982, for three weeks

Paul McCartney with Stevie Wonder *Parlophone R 6054*

Writer: Paul McCartney
Producer: George Martin

The final track on the second side of 'Tug Of War', the album that reunited George Martin and Paul McCartney in the recording studio featured Stevie Wonder (born Saginaw, Michigan on 13 May 1950). When it was released as a single, Motown refused to allow Stevie Wonder full billing on the single, so Paul McCartney with, rather than and, Stevie Wonder was the name of the act that shot to the top and gave McCarney his 24th songwriting credit at number one. He is the only performer to be featured in three different chart-topping combinations (see also Beatles and Wings), but still McCartney has not managed a solo number one in UK. **Ebony and Ivory** gave George Martin his 26th number one production, to bring him one behind Norrie Paramor on the all-time list. It was all but 21 years since his very first number one production (see no. 118), which was by far the longest spell of number one success for any producer. It gave Stevie Wonder his first taste of the top of the British charts as a performer, but he, like Paul McCartney, Elton John and Olivia Newton-John, has still to enjoy his first solo number one. He co-wrote **Tears Of A Clown** (see no. 290), but over 16 years after his first solo hit in Great Britain, he has only this duet to claim as a number one hit.

Despite the fact that Paul McCartney did not appear on the singles charts in any guise in 1981 (he released no singles), and thus was absent from the charts for a whole year for the first time since 1961, McCartney and Stevie Wonder between them have racked up about 900 weeks on the charts – rather more than any other one-hit wonders!

500

A LITTLE PEACE

15 May 1982, for two weeks

Nicole *CBS A 2365*

Writers: Ralph Siegel and Bernd Meinunger, English lyrics by Paul Greedus
Producer: Robert Jung

For the third year in a row, the Eurovision Song Contest winner topped the British charts. This time it was 17-year-old Nicole Hohloch from Saarbrücken who was a runaway winner for Germany in the contest held in Harrogate on 24 April 1982. She became the seventh winner to top the British charts in the 27 years of the contest, but the first of those seven winners who did not sing in English to win. Chance awarded Nicole the extra prize of having the 500th British Number One.

For co-writer Ralph Siegel, it was a triumph of persistence. He had composed Germany's Eurovision entry for 4 years in a row, and came second in 1980 and 1981 before finally providing his country with their first ever winning song in 1982. Nicole proved to be such a linguist that she was able to reprise her winning song in German, English, French and Dutch at the close of the contest: it meant a massive seller all across Europe with only her second record. Her first, **Flieg Nicht So Hoch Mein Freund**, was a hit in Germany and led her to the Eurovision opportunity. Only time will tell whether Nicole, the sixth solo female singer known only by her first name to win Eurovision, will fare better than Massiel, Salome, Severine, Dana, or even Lulu.

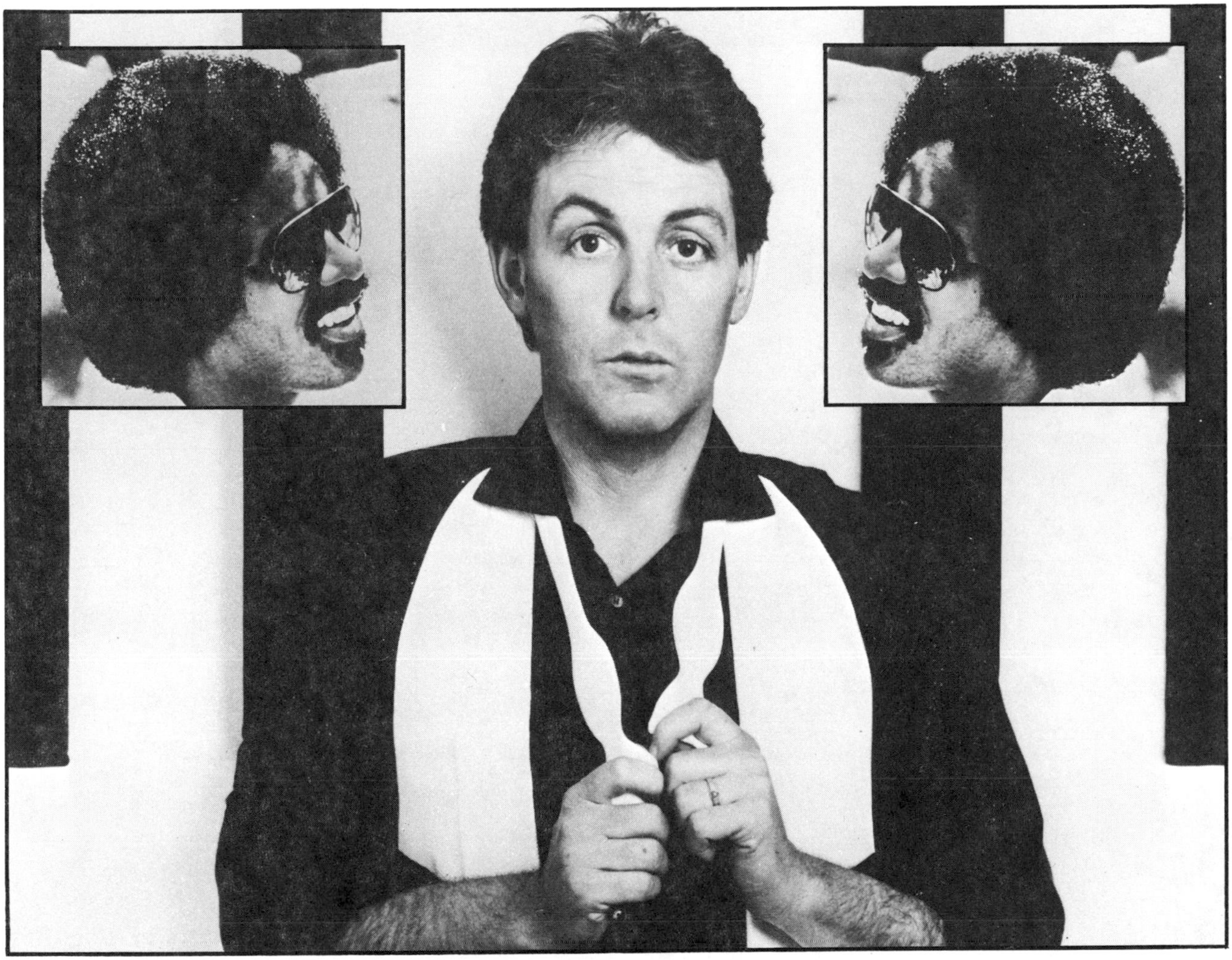

499 Stevie Wonder and Paul McCartney,
500 Nicole

PART 2

The Five Hundred Number Ones: Listed Alphabetically by Artist

The information given in this part of the book is as follows: the date that the record first reached number one, the title, label, catalogue number and the number of weeks at number one. We do not, in this book, record the entire chart career of the number ones, only their time at the top.

Describing a recording act in one sentence is often fraught with danger, but we have attempted to do so above each act's list of hits. Although we are aware that many of the vocalists thus described also play an instrument, we have only mentioned this fact where the artist's instrumental skills were an important factor in the record's success.

We have also listed acts under the name they used for their number one hits, which is not necessarily their usual styling. Thus for example Ian Dury is listed under 'Ian And The Blockheads', which is how he was billed for **Hit Me With Your Rhythm Stick**. Cross-references will also be found under 'Blockheads' and 'Ian Dury'.

ABBA Sweden, male/female vocal/instrumental group

4 May 74	WATERLOO	Epic EPC 2240	2 wks
31 Jan 76	MAMMA MIA	Epic EPC 3790	2 wks
8 May 76	FERNANDO	Epic EPC 4036	4 wks
4 Sep 76	DANCING QUEEN	Epic EPC 4499	6 wks
2 Apr 77	KNOWING ME KNOWING YOU	Epic EPC 4955	5 wks
5 Nov 77	NAME OF THE GAME	Epic EPC 5750	4 wks
18 Feb 78	TAKE A CHANCE ON ME	Epic EPC 5950	3 wks
9 Aug 80	THE WINNER TAKES IT ALL	Epic EPC 8835	2 wks
29 Nov 80	SUPER TROUPER	Epic EPC 9089	3 wks

ACES – *See* Desmond DEKKER and the ACES

ADAM and THE ANTS U.K., male vocal/instrumental group

9 May 81	STAND AND DELIVER	CBS A 1065	5 wks
19 Sep 81	PRINCE CHARMING	CBS A 1408	4 wks

ALICE COOPER U.S., male vocal/instrumental group

12 Aug 72	SCHOOL'S OUT	Warner Brothers K 16188	3 wks

ALTHIA and DONNA Jamaica, female vocal duo

4 Feb 78	UP TOWN TOP RANKING	Lightning LIG 506	1 wk

AMEN CORNER U.K., male vocal/instrumental group

12 Feb 69	(IF PARADISE IS) HALF AS NICE	Immediate IM 073	2 wks

ANEKA U.K., female vocalist

29 Aug 81	JAPANESE BOY	Hansa HANSA 5	1 wk

ANIMALS U.K., male vocal/instrumental group

9 Jul 64	THE HOUSE OF THE RISING SUN	Columbia DB 7301	1 wk

Paul ANKA Canada, male vocalist

30 Aug 57	DIANA	Columbia DB 3980	9 wks

ANTS – *See* ADAM and the ANTS

ARCHIES U.S., male/female vocal/instrumental group

25 Oct 69	SUGAR SUGAR	RCA 1872	8 wks

Louis ARMSTRONG U.S., male vocalist

24 Apr 68	WHAT A WONDERFUL WORLD/CABARET	HMV POP 1615	4 wks

Winifred ATWELL U.K., female instrumentalist – piano

3 Dec 54	LET'S HAVE ANOTHER PARTY	Philips PB 268	5 wks
13 Apr 56	POOR PEOPLE OF PARIS	Decca F 10681	3 wks

Charles AZNAVOUR France, male vocalist

29 Jun 74	SHE	Barclay BAR 26	4 wks

BACCARA Spain, female vocal duo

29th Oct 77	YES SIR I CAN BOOGIE	RCA PB 5526	1 wk

BACHELORS Ireland, male vocal group

20 Feb 64	DIANE	Decca F 11799	1 wk

Long John BALDRY U.K., male vocalist

22 Nov 67	LET THE HEARTACHES BEGIN	Pye 7N 17385	2 wks

J J BARRIE Canada, male vocalist

5 Jun 76	NO CHARGE	Power Exchange PX 209	1 wk

Shirley BASSEY U.K., female vocalist

20 Feb 59	AS I LOVE YOU	Philips PB 845	4 wks
21 Sep 61	REACH FOR THE STARS/CLIMB EV'RY MOUNTAIN	Columbia DB 4685	1 wk

BAY CITY ROLLERS U.K., male vocal/instrumental group

22 Mar 75	BYE BYE BABY	Bell 1409	6 wks
19 Jul 75	GIVE A LITTLE LOVE	Bell 1425	3 wks

BEACH BOYS U.S., male vocal/instrumental group

17 Nov 66	GOOD VIBRATIONS	Capitol CL 15475	2 wks
28 Aug 68	DO IT AGAIN	Capitol CL 15554	1 wk

BEAKY – *See* Dave DEE, DOZY, BEAKY, MICK and TICH

BEATLES U.K., male vocal/instrumental group

2 May 63	FROM ME TO YOU	Parlophone R 5015	7 wks
12 Sep 63	SHE LOVES YOU	Parlophone R 5055	4 wks
28 Nov 63	SHE LOVES YOU	Parlophone R 5055	2 wks
12 Dec 63	I WANT TO HOLD YOUR HAND	Parlophone R 5084	5 wks
2 Apr 64	CAN'T BUY ME LOVE	Parlophone R 5114	3 wks
23 Jul 64	A HARD DAY'S NIGHT	Parlophone R 5160	3 wks
10 Dec 64	I FEEL FINE	Parlophone R 5200	5 wks
5 Aug 65	HELP!	Parlophone R 5305	3 wks
22 Apr 65	TICKET TO RIDE	Parlophone R 5265	3 wks
16 Dec 65	DAY TRIPPER/WE CAN WORK IT OUT	Parlophone R 5389	5 wks
23 Jun 66	PAPERBACK WRITER	Parlophone R 5452	2 wks
18 Aug 66	YELLOW SUBMARINE/ ELEANOR RIGBY	Parlophone R 5493	4 wks
19 Jul 67	ALL YOU NEED IS LOVE	Parlophone R 5620	3 wks
6 Dec 67	HELLO GOODBYE	Parlophone R 5655	7 wks
27 Mar 68	LADY MADONNA	Parlophone R 5675	2 wks
11 Sep 68	HEY JUDE	Apple R 5722	2 wks
23 Apr 69	GET BACK	Apple R 5777	6 wks
11 Jun 69	THE BALLAD OF JOHN AND YOKO	Apple R 5786	3 wks

"Get Back" is 'with Billy Preston'. See also George HARRISON, John LENNON, WINGS, Paul McCARTNEY with Stevie WONDER

BEE GEES U.K., male vocal/instrumental group

11 Oct 67	MASSACHUSETTS	Polydor 56 192	4 wks
4 Sep 68	I'VE GOTTA GET A MESSAGE TO YOU	Polydor 56 273	1 wk
29 Apr 78	NIGHT FEVER	RSO 002	2 wks
3 Mar 79	TRAGEDY	RSO 27	2 wks

Harry BELAFONTE U.S., male vocalist

22 Nov 57	MARY'S BOY CHILD	RCA 1022	7 wks

Tony BENNETT U.S., male vocalist

13 May 55	STRANGER IN PARADISE	Philips PB 420	2 wks

Chuck BERRY U.S., male vocalist/instrumentalist – guitar

25 Nov 72	MY DING-A-LING	Chess 6145 019	4 wks

Jane BIRKIN and Serge GAINSBOURG U.K./France female/male vocal instrumental group

11 Oct 69	JE T'AIME...MOI NON PLUS	Major Minor MM 645	1 wk

Cilla BLACK U.K., female vocalist

27 Feb 64	ANYONE WHO HAD A HEART	Parlophone R 5101	3 wks
28 May 64	YOU'RE MY WORLD	Parlophone R 5133	4 wks

BLOCKHEADS – *See* IAN and the BLOCKHEADS

BLONDIE U.S./U.K., female/male vocal/instrumental group

3 Feb 79	HEART OF GLASS	Chrysalis CHE 2275	4 wks
26 May 79	SUNDAY GIRL	Chrysalis CHS 2320	3 wks
1 Mar 80	ATOMIC	Chrysalis CHS 2410	2 wks
26 Apr 80	CALL ME	Chrysalis CHS 2414	1 wk
15 Nov 80	THE TIDE IS HIGH	Chrysalis CHS 2465	2 wks

BLUE FLAMES – *See* Georgie FAME

BONEY M Various West Indian Islands, male/female vocal group

13 May 78	RIVERS OF BABYLON	Atlantic/Hansa K 11120	5 wks
9 Dec 78	MARY'S BOY CHILD – OH MY LORD (medley)	Atlantic/Hansa K 11221	4 wks

BOOMTOWN RATS Ireland, male vocal/instrumental group

18 Nov 78	RAT TRAP	Ensign ENY 16	2 wks
28 Jul 79	I DON'T LIKE MONDAYS	Ensign ENY 30	4 wks

Pat BOONE U.S., male vocalist

15 Jun 56	I'LL BE HOME	London HLD 8253	5 wks

Ken BOOTHE Jamaica, male vocalist

26 Oct 74	EVERYTHING I OWN	Trojan TR 7920	3 wks

David BOWIE U.K., male vocalist

8 Nov 75	SPACE ODDITY	RCA 2593	2 wks
23 Aug 80	ASHES TO ASHES	RCA BOW 6	2 wks

BRIAN and MICHAEL U.K., male vocal duo

8 Apr 78	MATCHSTALK MEN AND MATCHSTALK CATS AND DOGS	Pye 7N 46035	3 wks

BROTHERHOOD OF MAN U.K., male/female vocal group

27 Mar 76	SAVE YOUR KISSES FOR ME	Pye 7N 45569	6 wks
20 Aug 77	ANGELO	Pye 7N 45699	1 wk
11 Feb 78	FIGARO	Pye 7N 46037	1 wk

Crazy World of Arthur BROWN U.K., male vocal/instrumental group

14 Aug 68	FIRE	Track 604022	1 wk

BUCK'S FIZZ U.K., male/female vocal group

18 Apr 81	MAKING YOUR MIND UP	RCA 56	3 wks
16 Jan 82	LAND OF MAKE BELIEVE	RCA 163	2 wks
17 Apr 82	MY CAMERA NEVER LIES	RCA 202	1 wk

BUGGLES U.K., male vocal/instrumental duo

20 Oct 79	VIDEO KILLED THE RADIO STAR	Island WIP 6524	1 wk

B BUMBLE and the STINGERS U.S., male instrumental group

17 May 62	NUT ROCKER	Top Rank JAR 611	1 wk

Kate BUSH U.K., female vocalist

11 Mar 78	WUTHERING HEIGHTS	EMI 2719	4 wks

BYRDS U.S., male vocal/instrumental group

22 Jul 65	MR TAMBOURINE MAN	CBS 201765	2 wks

Eddie CALVERT U.K., male instrumentalist – trumpet

8 Jan 54	OH MEIN PAPA	Columbia DB 3337	9 wks
27 May 55	CHERRY PINK AND APPLE BLOSSOM WHITE	Columbia DB 3581	4 wks

David CASSIDY U.S., male vocalist

30 Sep 72	HOW CAN I BE SURE	Bell 1258	2 wks
27 Oct 73	DAYDREAMER/THE PUPPY SONG	Bell 1334	3 wks

Ray CHARLES U.S., male vocalist/instrumentalist – piano

12 Jul 62	I CAN'T STOP LOVING YOU	HMV POP 1034	2 wks

Tina CHARLES U.K., female vocalist

6 Mar 76	I LOVE TO LOVE (BUT MY BABY LOVES TO DANCE)	CBS 3937	3 wks

CHECKMATES – *See* Emile FORD and the CHECKMATES

CHER – *See* SONNY and CHER

CHICAGO U.S., male vocal/instrumental group

16 Oct 76	IF YOU LEAVE ME NOW	CBS 4603	3 wks

CHICORY TIP U.K., male vocal/instrumental group

19 Feb 72	SON OF MY FATHER	CBS 7737	3 wks

CHRISTIE U.K., male vocal/instrumental group

6 Jun 70	YELLOW RIVER	CBS 4911	1 wk

Dave CLARK FIVE U.K., male vocal/instrumental group

16 Jan 64	GLAD ALL OVER	Columbia DB 7154	2 wks

Petula CLARK U.K., female vocalist

23 Feb 61	SAILOR	Pye 7N 15324	1 wk
16 Feb 67	THIS IS MY SONG	Pye 7N 17258	2 wks

Rosemary CLOONEY U.S., female vocalist

26 Nov 54	THIS OLE HOUSE	Philips PB 336	1 wk
14 Jan 55	MAMBO ITALIANO	Philips PB 382	1 wk
4 Feb 55	MAMBO ITALIANO	Philips PB 382	2 wks

Eddie COCHRAN U.S., male vocalist

23 Jun 60	THREE STEPS TO HEAVEN	London HLG 9115	2 wks

Joe COCKER U.K., male vocalist

6 Nov 68	WITH A LITTLE HELP FROM MY FRIENDS	Regal-Zonophone RZ 3013	1 wk

COCKNEY REBEL – *See* Steve HARLEY and COCKNEY REBEL

Alma COGAN U.K., female vocalist

15 Jul 55	DREAMBOAT	HMV B 10872	2 wks

Dave and Ansil COLLINS Jamaica, male vocal duo

1 May 71	DOUBLE BARREL	Technique TE 901	2 wks

COMETS – *See* Bill HALEY and his COMETS

COMMODORES U.S., male vocal/instrumental group

19 Aug 78	THREE TIMES A LADY	Motown TMG 1113	5 wks

Perry COMO U.S., male vocalist

6 Feb 53	DON'T LET THE STARS GET IN YOUR EYES	HMV B 10400	5 wks
28 Feb 58	MAGIC MOMENTS	RCA 1036	8 wks

Billy CONNOLLY U.K., male vocalist

22 Nov 75	D.I.V.O.R.C.E.	Polydor 2058 652	1 wk

Russ CONWAY U.K., male instrumentalist – piano

27 Mar 59	SIDE SADDLE	Columbia DB 4256	4 wks
19 Jun 59	ROULETTE	Columbia DB 4298	2 wks

Don CORNELL U.S., male vocalist

8 Oct 54	HOLD MY HAND	Vogue Q 2013	4 wks
19 Nov 54	HOLD MY HAND	Vogue Q 2013	1 wk

Julie COVINGTON U.K., female vocalist

12 Feb 77	DON'T CRY FOR ME ARGENTINA	MCA 260	1 wk

Floyd CRAMER U.S., male instrumentalist – piano

18 May 61	ON THE REBOUND	RCA 1231	1 wk

CREEDENCE CLEARWATER REVIVAL U.S., male vocal/instrumental group

20 Sep 69	BAD MOON RISING	Liberty LBF 15230	3 wks

CRICKETS U.S., male vocal/instrumental group

1 Nov 57	THAT'LL BE THE DAY	Vogue Coral Q 72279	3 wks

Although not credited on the record, Buddy Holly was the vocalist. See also Buddy Holly.

DAKOTAS – *See* Billy J. KRAMER and the DAKOTAS

Vic DAMONE U.S., male vocalist

27 Jun 58	ON THE STREET WHERE YOU LIVE	Philips PB 819	2 wks

DANA Ireland, female vocalist

18 Apr 70	ALL KINDS OF EVERYTHING	Rex R 11054	2 wks

Bobby DARIN U.S., male vocalist

3 Jul 59	DREAM LOVER	London HLE 8867	4 wks
16 Oct 59	MACK THE KNIFE	London HLE 8939	2 wks

Windsor DAVIES and DON ESTELLE U.K., male vocal duo

7 Jun 75	WHISPERING GRASS	EMI 2290	3 wks

Spencer DAVIS GROUP U.K., male vocal/instrumental group

20 Jan 66	KEEP ON RUNNING	Fontana TF 632	1 wk
14 Apr 66	SOMEBODY HELP ME	Fontana TF 679	2 wks

DAWN U.S., male/female vocal group

15 May 71	KNOCK THREE TIMES	Bell 1146	5 wks
21 Apr 73	TIE A YELLOW RIBBON ROUND THE OLD OAK TREE	Bell 1287	4 wks

'Tie A Yellow Ribbon Round The Old Oak Tree' credits Dawn featuring Tony Orlando.

Doris DAY U.S., female vocalist

16 Apr 54	SECRET LOVE	Philips PB 230	1 wk
7 May 54	SECRET LOVE	Philips PB 230	8 wks
10 Aug 56	WHATEVER WILL BE WILL BE	Philips PB 586	6 wks

Dave DEE, DOZY, BEAKY, MICK and TICH U.K. male vocal/instrumental group

20 Mar 68	THE LEGEND OF XANADU	Fontana TF 903	1 wk

Kiki DEE – *See* Elton JOHN and Kiki DEE

Desmond DEKKER and the ACES Jamaica, Male vocal/instrumental group

16 Apr 69	ISRAELITES	Pyramid PYR 6058	1 wk

John DENVER U.S., male vocalist

12 Oct 74	ANNIE'S SONG	RCA APBO 0295	1 wk

DETROIT SPINNERS U.S., male vocal group

12 Apr 80	WORKING MY WAY BACK TO YOU	Atlantic K 11432	2 wks

DEXY'S MIDNIGHT RUNNERS U.K., male vocal/instrumental group

3 May 80	GENO	R 6033	2 wks

Dr HOOK U.S., male vocal/instrumental group

17 Nov 79	WHEN YOU'RE IN LOVE WITH A BEAUTIFUL WOMAN	Capital CL 16039	3 wks

Ken DODD U.K., male vocalist

30 Sep 65	TEARS	Columbia DB 7659	5 wks

Joe DOLCE U.S., male vocalist

21 Feb 81	SHADDUP YOU FACE	Epic EPC 9518	3 wks

Lonnie DONEGAN U.K., male vocalist

12 Apr 57	CUMBERLAND GAP	Pye Nixa B 15087	5 wks
28 Jun 57	GAMBLIN' MAN/PUTTING ON THE STYLE	Pye Nixa N 15093	2 wks
31 Mar 60	MY OLD MAN'S A DUSTMAN	Pye 7N 15256	4 wks

DONNA – *See* ALTHIA and DONNA

Carl DOUGLAS U.K., male vocalist

21 Sep 74	KUNG FU FIGHTING	Pye 7N 45377	3 wks

Craig DOUGLAS U.K., male vocalist

11 Sep 59	ONLY SIXTEEN	Top Rank JAR 159	4 wks

DOZY – *See* Dave DEE, DOZY, BEAKY, MICK and TICH

DREAMWEAVERS U.S., male/female vocal group

16 Mar 56	IT'S ALMOST TOMORROW	Brunswick 05515	2 wks
6 Apr 56	IT'S ALMOST TOMORROW	Brunswick 05515	1 wk

Clive DUNN U.K., male vocalist

9 Jan 71	GRANDAD	Columbia DB 8726	3 wks

Ian Dury – *See* IAN and the BLOCKHEADS

EDISON LIGHTHOUSE U.K., male vocal/instrumental group

31 Jan 70	LOVE GROWS (WHERE MY ROSEMARY GOES)	Bell 1091	5 wks

Dave EDMUNDS U.K., male vocalist/multi-instrumentalist

28 Nov 70	I HEAR YOU KNOCKIN'	MAM 1	6 wks

Tommy EDWARDS U.S., male vocalist

7 Nov 58	IT'S ALL IN THE GAME	MGM 989	3 wks

ELECTRIC LIGHT ORCHESTRA – *See* Olivia NEWTON-JOHN and ELECTRIC LIGHT ORCHESTRA

ENGLAND WORLD CUP SQUAD U.K., male vocal group

16 May 70	BACK HOME	Pye 7N 17920	3 wks

EQUALS U.K. male vocal/instrumental group

3 Jul 68	BABY COME BACK	President PT 135	3 wks

David ESSEX U.K., male vocalist

16 Nov 74	GONNA MAKE YOU A STAR	CBS 2492	3 wks
4 Oct 75	HOLD ME CLOSE	CBS 3572	3 wks

Don ESTELLE – *See* Windsor DAVIES and Don ESTELLE

EVANS – *See* ZAGER and EVANS

EVERLY BROTHERS U.S., male vocal duo

4 Jul 58	ALL I HAVE TO DO IS DREAM/CLAUDETTE	London HLA 8618	7 wks
5 May 60	CATHY'S CLOWN	Warner Brothers WB 1	7 wks
2 Mar 61	WALK RIGHT BACK	Warner Brothers WB 33	3 wks
20 Jul 61	TEMPTATION	Warner Brothers WB 42	2 wks

Adam FAITH U.K., male vocalist

4 Dec 59	WHAT DO YOU WANT	Parlophone R 4591	3 wks
10 Mar 60	POOR ME	Parlophone R 4623	1 wk

Georgie FAME U.K., male vocal/instrumentalist, keyboards

14 Jan 65	YEH YEH	Columbia DB 7428	2 wks
21 Jul 66	GET AWAY	Columbia DB 7946	1 wk
24 Jan 68	THE BALLAD OF BONNIE AND CLYDE	CBS 3124	1 wk

'Yeh Yeh' and 'Get Away' credit the Blue Flames backing Georgie Fame.

Chris FARLOWE and the THUNDERBIRDS U.K., male vocal/instrumental group

28 Jul 66	OUT OF TIME	Immediate IM 035	1 wk

Eddie FISHER U.S., male vocalist

30 Jan 53	OUTSIDE OF HEAVEN	HMV B 10362	1 wk
26 Jun 53	I'M WALKING BEHIND YOU	HMV B 10489	1 wk

FLEETWOOD MAC U.K., male instrumental group

29 Jan 69	ALBATROSS	Blue Horizon 57 3145	1 wk

FLOATERS U.S., male vocal/instrumental group

27 Aug 77	FLOAT ON	ABC 4187	1 wk

Emile FORD and the CHECKMATES U.K., male vocal/instrumental group

18 Dec 59	WHAT DO YOU WANT TO MAKE THOSE EYES AT ME FOR?	Pye 7N 15225	6 wks

Tennessee Ernie FORD U.S., male vocalist

11 Mar 55	GIVE ME YOUR WORD	Capitol CL 14005	7 wks
20 Jan 56	SIXTEEN TONS	Capitol CL 14500	4 wks

FOUNDATIONS U.K., male vocal/instrumental group

8 Nov 67	BABY NOW THAT I'VE FOUND YOU	Pye 7N 17366	2 wks

FOUR PENNIES U.K., male vocal/instrumental group

21 May 64	JULIET	Philips BF 1322	1 wk

FOUR SEASONS U.S., male vocal/instrumental group

21 Feb 76	DECEMBER '63 (OH WHAT A NIGHT)	Warner Brothers K 16688	2 wks

FOUR TOPS U.S., male vocal group

27 Oct 66	REACH OUT I'LL BE THERE	Tamla Motown TMG 579	3 wks

Connie FRANCIS U.S., female vocalist

16 May 58	WHO'S SORRY NOW	MGM 975	6 wks
26 Sep 58	CAROLINA MOON/STUPID CUPID	MGM 985	6 wks

Serge GAINSBOURG – *See* Jane BIRKIN and Serge GAINSBOURG

Art GARFUNKEL U.S., male vocalist

25 Oct 75	I ONLY HAVE EYES FOR YOU	CBS 3575	2 wks
14 Apr 79	BRIGHT EYES	CBS 6947	6 wks

See also SIMON and GARFUNKEL

Barbara GASKIN – *See* Dave STEWART with Barbara GASKIN

Marvin GAYE U.S., male vocalist

26 Mar 69	I HEARD IT THROUGH THE GRAPEVINE	Tamla Motown TMG 686	3 wks

Gloria GAYNOR U.S., female vocalist

17 Mar 79	I WILL SURVIVE	Polydor 2095 017	4 wks

Bobbie GENTRY U.S., female vocalist

18 Oct 69	I'LL NEVER FALL IN LOVE AGAIN	Capitol CL 15606	1 wk

GERRY and the PACEMAKERS U.K., male vocal/instrumental group

11 Apr 63	HOW DO YOU DO IT?	Columbia DB 4987	3 wks
20 Jun 63	I LIKE IT	Columbia DB 7041	4 wks
31 Oct 63	YOU'LL NEVER WALK ALONE	Columbia DB 7126	4 wks

Gary GLITTER U.K., male vocalist

28 Jul 73	I'M THE LEADER OF THE GANG (I AM)	Bell 1321	4 wks
17 Nov 73	I LOVE YOU LOVE ME LOVE	Bell 1337	4 wks
22 Jun 74	ALWAYS YOURS	Bell 1359	1 wk

The GOOMBAY DANCE BAND

27 Mar 82	SEVEN TEARS	Epic EPCA 1242	3 wks

GORDON – *See* PETER and GORDON

Norman GREENBAUM U.S., male vocalist

2 May 70	SPIRIT IN THE SKY	Reprise RS 20885	2 wks

Bill HALEY and his COMETS U.S., male vocalist with male vocal/instrumental group

25 Nov 55	ROCK AROUND THE CLOCK	Brunswick 05317	3 wks
6 Jan 56	ROCK AROUND THE CLOCK	Brunswick 05317	2 wks

Steve HARLEY and COCKNEY REBEL U.K., male vocal/instrumental group

22 Feb 75	MAKE ME SMILE (COME UP AND SEE ME)	EMI 2263	2 wks

Jet HARRIS and Tony MEEHAN U.K., male instrumental duo, bass guitar and drums

31 Jan 63	DIAMONDS	Decca F 11563	3 wks

See also SHADOWS

Rolf HARRIS Australia, male vocalist

20 Dec 69	TWO LITTLE BOYS	Columbia DB 8630	6 wks

George HARRISON U.K., male vocalist

30 Jan 71	MY SWEET LORD	Apple R 5884	5 wks

See also BEATLES

Jimi HENDRIX EXPERIENCE U.S./U.K., male vocal/instrumental group

21 Nov 70	VOODOO CHILE	Track 2095 001	1 wk

HERMAN'S HERMITS U.K., male vocal/instrumental group

24 Sep 64	I'M INTO SOMETHING GOOD	Columbia DB 7338	2 wks

HIGHWAYMEN U.S., male vocal group

12 Oct 61	MICHAEL	HMV POP 910	1 wk

Benny HILL U.K., male vocalist

11 Dec 71	ERNIE (THE FASTEST MILKMAN IN THE WEST)	Columbia DB 8833	4 wks

Ronnie HILTON U.K., male vocalist

4 May 56	NO OTHER LOVE	HMV POP 198	6 wks

Michael HOLLIDAY U.K., male vocalist

14 Feb 58	THE STORY OF MY LIFE	Columbia DB 4058	2 wks
29 Jan 60	STARRY EYED	Columbia DB 4378	1 wk

HOLLIES U.K., male vocal/instrumental group

24 Jun 65	I'M ALIVE	Parlophone R 5287	1 wk
8 Jul 65	I'M ALIVE	Parlophone R 5287	2 wks

Buddy HOLLY U.S., male vocalist

24 Apr 59	IT DOESN'T MATTER ANY MORE	Coral Q 72360	3 wks

See also CRICKETS

HONEYCOMBS U.K., male/female vocal/instrumental group

27 Aug 64	HAVE I THE RIGHT	Pye 7N 15664	2 wks

Mary HOPKIN U.K., female vocalist

25 Sep 68	THOSE WERE THE DAYS	Apple 2	6 wks

HOT CHOCOLATE U.K., male vocal/instrumental group

2 Jul 77	SO YOU WIN AGAIN	RAK 259	3 wks

HUMAN LEAGUE U.K., male/female vocal/instrumental group

12 Dec 81	DON'T YOU WANT ME?	Virgin VS 466	5 wks

Engelbert HUMPERDINCK U.K., male vocalist

2 Mar 67	RELEASE ME	Decca F 12541	6 wks
6 Sep 67	THE LAST WALTZ	Decca F 12655	5 wks

Tab HUNTER U.S., male vocalist

22 Feb 57	YOUNG LOVE	London HLD 8380	7 wks

IAN and the BLOCKHEADS U.K., male vocal/instrumental group

27 Jan 79	HIT ME WITH YOUR RHYTHM STICK	Stiff BUY 38	1 wk

Frank IFIELD U.K., male vocalist

26 Jul 62	I REMEMBER YOU	Columbia DB 4856	7 wks
8 Nov 62	LOVESICK BLUES	Columbia DB 4913	5 wks
21 Feb 63	WAYWARD WIND	Columbia DB 4960	3 wks
18 Jul 63	CONFESSIN'	Columbia DB 7062	2 wks

Julio IGLESIAS Spain, male vocalist

5 Dec 81	BEGIN THE BEGUINE (VOLVER A EMPEZAR)	CBS A 1612	1 wk

Terry JACKS Canada, male vocalist

6 Apr 74	SEASONS IN THE SUN	Bell 1344	4 wks

Michael JACKSON U.S., male vocalist

27 Jun 81	ONE DAY IN YOUR LIFE	Motown TMG 976	2 wks

See also JACKSONS

JACKSONS U.S., male vocal group

25 Jun 77	SHOW YOU THE WAY TO GO	Epic EPC 5266	1 wk

See also Michael JACKSON

JAM U.K., male vocal/instrumental group

22 Mar 80	GOING UNDERGROUND/ DREAMS OF CHILDREN	Polydor POSP 113	3 wks
6 Sep 80	START	Polydor 2059 266	1 wk
13 Feb 82	A TOWN CALLED MALICE/PRECIOUS	Polydor POSP 400	3 wks

Tommy JAMES and The SHONDELLS U.S., male vocal/instrumental group

31 Jul 68	MONY MONY	Major Minor MM 567	2 wks
21 Aug 68	MONY MONY	Major Minor MM 567	1 wk

Elton JOHN and Kiki DEE U.K., male/female vocal duo

24 Jul 76	DON'T GO BREAKING MY HEART	Rocket ROKN 512	6 wks

JOHNSTON BROTHERS U.K., male vocal group

11 Nov 55	HERNANDO'S HIDEAWAY	Decca F 10608	2 wks

Jimmy JONES U.S., male vocalist

7 Jul 60	GOOD TIMIN'	MGM 1078	3 wks

Tom JONES U.K., male vocalist

11 Mar 65	IT'S NOT UNUSUAL	Decca F 12062	1 wk
1 Dec 66	GREEN GREEN GRASS OF HOME	Decca F 22511	7 wks

KALIN TWINS U.S., male vocal duo

22 Aug 58	WHEN	Brunswick 05751	5 wks

Kitty KALLEN U.S., female vocalist

10 Sep 54	LITTLE THINGS MEAN A LOT	Brunswick 05287	1 wk

Eden KANE U.K., male vocalist

3 Aug 61	WELL I ASK YOU	Decca F 11353	1 wk

Jerry KELLER U.S., male vocalist

9 Oct 59	HERE COMES SUMMER	London HLR 8890	1 wk

KELLY MARIE U.K., female vocalist

13 Sep 80	FEELS LIKE I'M IN LOVE	Calibre PLUS 1	2 wks

Johnny KIDD and the PIRATES U.K., male vocal/instrumental group

4 Aug 60	SHAKIN' ALL OVER	HMV POP 753	1 wk

KINKS U.K., male vocal/instrumental group

10 Sep 64	YOU REALLY GOT ME	Pye 7N 15673	2 wks
18 Feb 65	TIRED OF WAITING FOR YOU	Pye 7N 15759	1 wk
7 Jul 66	SUNNY AFTERNOON	Pye 7N 17125	2 wks

Fern KINNEY U.S., female vocalist

15 Mar 80	TOGETHER WE ARE BEAUTIFUL	WEA K 79111	1 wk

KRAFTWERK German, male vocal/instrumental group

6 Feb 82	THE MODEL/COMPUTER LOVE	EMI 5207	1 wk

Billy J KRAMER and the DAKOTAS U.K., male vocal/instrumental group

22 Aug 63	BAD TO ME	Parlophone R 5049	3 wks
19 Mar 64	LITTLE CHILDREN	Parlophone R 5105	2 wks

Frankie LAINE U.S., male vocalist

24 Apr 53	I BELIEVE	Philips PB 117	9 wks
3 Jul 53	I BELIEVE	Philips PB 117	6 wks
21 Aug 53	I BELIEVE	Philips PB 117	3 wks
23 Oct 53	HEY JOE	Philips PB 172	2 wks
13 Nov 53	ANSWER ME	Philips PB 196	8 wks
19 Oct 56	A WOMAN IN LOVE	Philips PB 617	4 wks

LEE – *See* PETERS and LEE

John LENNON U.K., male vocalist

20 Dec 80	(JUST LIKE) STARTING OVER	WEA/Geffen K 79186	1 wk
10 Jan 81	IMAGINE	Parlophone R 6009	4 wks
7 Feb 81	WOMAN	Geffen K 79195	2 wks

See also BEATLES

Jerry Lee LEWIS U.S., male vocalist/instrumentalist – piano

10 Jan 58	GREAT BALLS OF FIRE	London HLS 8529	2 wks

John LEYTON U.K., male vocalist

31 Aug 61	JOHNNY REMEMBER ME	Top Rank JAR 577	3 wks
28 Sep 61	JOHNNY REMEMBER ME	Top Rank JAR 577	1 wk

LIEUTENANT PIGEON U.K., male/female instrumental group

14 Oct 72	MOULDY OLD DOUGH	Decca F 13278	4 wks

Johnny LOGAN Australia, male vocalist

17 May 80	WHAT'S ANOTHER YEAR	Epic EPC 8572	2 wks

LOVE AFFAIR U.K., male vocal/instrumental group

31 Jan 68	EVERLASTING LOVE	CBS 3125	2 wks

Frankie LYMON – *See* Teenagers featuring Frankie LYMON

Vera LYNN U.K., female vocalist

5 Nov 54	MY SON MY SON	Decca F 10372	2 wks

Paul McCARTNEY with Stevie WONDER U.K./U.S. male vocal duo

24 Apr 82	EBONY AND IVORY	Parlophone R 6054	3 wks

See also BEATLES, WINGS

George McCRAE U.S., male vocalist

27 Jul 74	ROCK YOUR BABY	Jayboy BOY 85	3 wks

Scott McKENZIE U.S., male vocalist

9 Aug 67	SAN FRANCISCO (BE SURE TO WEAR SOME FLOWERS IN YOUR HAIR)	CBS 2816	4 wks

Don McLEAN U.S., male vocalist

17 Jun 72	VINCENT	United Artists UP 35359	2 wks
21 Jun 80	CRYING	EMI 5051	3 wks

MANHATTAN TRANSFER U.S., male/female vocal group

12 Mar 77	CHANSON D'AMOUR	Atlantic K 10886	3 wks

MANFRED MANN South Africa/U.K., male vocal/instrumental group

13 Aug 64	DO WAH DIDDY DIDDY	HMV POP 1320	2 wks
5 May 66	PRETTY FLAMINGO	HMV POP 1523	3 wks
14 Feb 68	MIGHTY QUINN	Fontana TF 897	2 wks

MANTOVANI U.K., orchestra

14 Aug 53 MOULIN ROUGE Decca F 10094 1 wk

See also David WHITFIELD.

MARCELS U.S., male vocal group

4 May 61 BLUE MOON Pye International 7N 25073 2 wks

MARMALADE U.K., male vocal/instrumental group

1 Jan 69 OB-LA-DI OB-LA-DA CBS 3892 1 wk
15 Jan 69 OB-LA-DI OB-LA-DA CBS 3892 2 wks

Lena MARTELL U.K., female vocalist

27 Oct 79 ONE DAY AT A TIME Pye 7N 46021 3 wks

Dean MARTIN U.S., male vocalist

17 Feb 56 MEMORIES ARE MADE OF THIS Capitol CL 14523 4 wks

Al MARTINO U.S., male vocalist

14 Nov 52 HERE IN MY HEART Capitol CL 13779 9 wks

Lee MARVIN U.S., male vocalist

7 Mar 70 WAND'RIN' STAR Paramount PARA 3004 3 wks

MASH U.S., male vocal/instrumental group

31 May 80 THEME FROM M*A*S*H* (SUICIDE IS PAINLESS) CBS 8536 3 wks

Johnny MATHIS U.S., male vocalist

25 Dec 76 WHEN A CHILD IS BORN (SOLEADO) CBS 4599 3 wks

MATTHEWS' SOUTHERN COMFORT U.K./U.S., male vocal/instrumental group

31 Oct 70 WOODSTOCK Uni UNS 526 3 wks

Tony MEEHAN – *See* Jet HARRIS and Tony MEEHAN

MICK – *See* Dave DEE, DOZY, BEAKY, MICK and TICH

MIDDLE OF THE ROAD U.K., male/female vocal/instrumental group

19 Jun 71 CHIRPY CHIRPY CHEEP CHEEP RCA 2047 5 wks

Roger MILLER U.S., male vocalist

13 May 65 KING OF THE ROAD Philips BF 1397 1 wk

MIRACLES – *See* Smokey ROBINSON and the MIRACLES

Guy MITCHELL U.S., male vocalist

13 Mar 53 SHE WEARS RED FEATHERS Columbia DB 3238 4 wks
11 Sep 53 LOOK AT THAT GIRL Philips PB 162 6 wks
4 Jan 57 SINGING THE BLUES Philips PB 650 1 wk
18 Jan 57 SINGING THE BLUES Philips PB 650 1 wk
1 Feb 57 SINGING THE BLUES Philips PB 650 1 wk
17 May 57 ROCK-A-BILLY Philips PB 685 1 wk

MONKEES U.S./U.K., male vocal/instrumental group

19 Jan 67 I'M A BELIEVER RCA 1560 4 wks

Hugo MONTENEGRO U.S., orchestra

13 Nov 68 THE GOOD THE BAD AND THE UGLY RCA 1727 4 wks

MOODY BLUES U.K., male vocal/instrumental group

28 Jan 65 GO NOW Decca F 12022 1 wk

Jane MORGAN U.S., female vocalist

23 Jan 59 THE DAY THE RAINS CAME London HLR 8751 1 wk

MOVE U.K., male vocal/instrumental group

5 Feb 69 BLACKBERRY WAY Regal Zonophone RZ 3015 1 wk

MUD U.K., male vocal/instrumental group

26 Jan 74 TIGER FEET RAK 166 4 wks
21 Dec 74 LONELY THIS CHRISTMAS RAK 187 4 wks
3 May 75 OH BOY RAK 201 2 wks

MUNGO JERRY U.K., male vocal/instrumental group

13 Jun 70	IN THE SUMMERTIME	Dawn DNX 2502	7 wks
6 Mar 71	BABY JUMP	Dawn DNX 2505	2 wks

Ruby MURRAY Ireland, female vocalist

18 Feb 55	SOFTLY SOFTLY	Columbia DB 3558	3 wks

Johnny NASH U.S., male vocalist

12 Jul 75	TEARS ON MY PILLOW	CBS 3220	1 wk

NEW SEEKERS U.K., male/female vocal/instrumental group

8 Jan 72	I'D LIKE TO TEACH THE WORLD TO SING	Polydor 2058 184	4 wks
19 Jan 74	YOU WON'T FIND ANOTHER FOOL LIKE ME	Polydor 2058 421	1 wk

Anthony NEWLEY U.K., male vocalist

5 Feb 60	WHY	Decca F 11194	4 wks
28 Apr 60	DO YOU MIND	Decca F 11220	1 wk

Olivia NEWTON-JOHN and ELECTRIC LIGHT ORCHESTRA U.K., female vocalist, male vocal/instrumental group

12 Jul 80	XANADU	Jet 185	2 wks

See also John TRAVOLTA and Olivia NEWTON-JOHN.

NICOLE Germany, female vocalist

15 May 82	A LITTLE PEACE	CBS A 2365	2 wks

NILSSON U.S., male vocalist

11 Mar 72	WITHOUT YOU	RCA 2165	5 wks

Gary NUMAN U.K., male vocalist

30 Jun 79	ARE 'FRIENDS' ELECTRIC?	Beggars Banquet BEG 18	4 wks
22 Sep 79	CARS	Beggars Banquet BEG 23	1 wk

"Are 'Friends' Electric?" by Gary Numan under the group name Tubeway Army

Des O'CONNOR U.K., male vocalist

24 Jul 68	I PRETEND	Columbia DB 8397	1 wk

ODYSSEY U.S., male/female vocal group

26 Jul 80	USE IT UP AND WEAR IT OUT	RCA PB 1962	2 wks

Esther and Abi OFARIM Israel, female/male vocal duo

28 Feb 68	CINDERELLA ROCKEFELLA	Philips BF 1640	3 wks

Roy ORBISON U.S., male vocalist

20 Oct 60	ONLY THE LONELY	London HLU 9149	2 wks
25 Jun 64	IT'S OVER	London HLU 9882	2 wks
8 Oct 64	OH PRETTY WOMAN	London HLU 9919	2 wks
12 Nov 64	OH PRETTY WOMAN	London HLU 9919	1 wk

Tony ORLANDO – *See* DAWN

Donny OSMOND U.S., male vocalist

8 Jul 72	PUPPY LOVE	MGM 2006 104	5 wks
31 Mar 73	THE TWELFTH OF NEVER	MGM 2006 199	1 wk
25 Aug 73	YOUNG LOVE	MGM 2006 300	4 wks

See also OSMONDS.

Little Jimmy OSMOND U.S., male vocalist

23 Dec 72	LONG HAIRED LOVER FROM LIVERPOOL	MGM 2006 109	5 wks

OSMONDS U.S., male vocal/instrumental group

31 Aug 74	LOVE ME FOR A REASON	MGM 2006 458	3 wks

Gilbert O'SULLIVAN U.K., male vocalist

11 Nov 72	CLAIR	MAM 84	2 wks
7 Apr 73	GET DOWN	MAM 96	2 wks

OVERLANDERS U.K., male vocal/instrumental group

27 Jan 66	MICHELLE	Pye 7N 17034	3 wks

PACEMAKERS – *See* GERRY and the PACEMAKERS

PAPER LACE U.K., male vocal/instrumental group

16 Mar 74	BILLY DON'T BE A HERO	Bus Stop BUS 1014	3 wks

Simon PARK ORCHESTRA U.K., orchestra

29 Sep 73 EYE LEVEL Columbia DB 8946 4 wks

Freda PAYNE U.S., female vocalist

19 Sep 70 BAND OF GOLD Invictus INV 502 6 wks

PETER and GORDON U.K., male vocal duo

23 Apr 64 A WORLD WITHOUT LOVE Columbia DB 7225 2 wks

PETERS and LEE U.K., male/female vocal duo

21 Jul 73 WELCOME HOME Philips 6006 307 1 wk

PILOT U.K., male vocal/instrumental group

1 Feb 75 JANUARY EMI 2255 3 wks

PINK FLOYD U.K., male vocal/instrumental group

15 Dec 79 ANOTHER BRICK IN THE WALL (PART II) Harvest HAR 5194 5 wks

PIRATES – *See* Johnny KIDD and the PIRATES

PLATTERS U.S., male/female vocal group

20 Mar 59 SMOKE GETS IN YOUR EYES Mercury AMT 1016 1 wk

POLICE U.K./U.S., male vocal/instrumental group

29 Sep 79 MESSAGE IN A BOTTLE A & M AMS 7474 3 wks
8 Dec 79 WALKING ON THE MOON A & M AMS 7494 1 wk
27 Sep 80 DON'T STAND SO CLOSE TO ME A&M AMS 7564 4 wks
14 Nov 81 EVERY LITTLE THING SHE DOES IS MAGIC A&M AMS 8174 1 wk

Brian POOLE and the TREMELOES U.K., male vocal/instrumental group

10 Oct 63 DO YOU LOVE ME Decca F 11739 3 wks

See also TREMELOES.

Perez PRADO U.S., orchestra with Cuban bandleader

29 Apr 55 CHERRY PINK AND APPLE BLOSSOM WHITE HMV B 10833 2 wks

Elvis PRESLEY U.S., male vocalist

12 Jul 57 ALL SHOOK UP HMV POP 359 7 wks
24 Jan 58 JAILHOUSE ROCK RCA 1028 3 wks
30 Jan 59 ONE NIGHT/I GOT STUNG RCA 1100 3 wks
15 May 59 A FOOL SUCH AS I/I NEED YOUR LOVE TONIGHT RCA 1113 5 wks
3 Nov 60 IT'S NOW OR NEVER RCA 1207 8 wks
26 Jan 61 ARE YOU LONESOME TONIGHT? RCA 1216 4 wks
23 Mar 61 WOODEN HEART RCA 1226 6 wks
1 Jun 61 SURRENDER RCA 1227 4 wks
9 Nov 61 HIS LATEST FLAME/LITTLE SISTER RCA 1258 4 wks
22 Feb 62 ROCK-A-HULA BABY/CAN'T HELP FALLING IN LOVE RCA 1270 4 wks
24 May 62 GOOD LUCK CHARM RCA 1280 5 wks
13 Sep 62 SHE'S NOT YOU RCA 1303 3 wks
13 Dec 62 RETURN TO SENDER RCA 1320 3 wks
1 Aug 63 (YOU'RE THE) DEVIL IN DISGUISE RCA 1355 1 wk
17 Jun 65 CRYING IN THE CHAPEL RCA 1455 1 wk
1 Jul 65 CRYING IN THE CHAPEL RCA 1455 1 wk
1 Aug 70 THE WONDER OF YOU RCA 1974 6 wks
3 Sep 77 WAY DOWN RCA PB 0998 5 wks

Billy PRESTON – *See* the BEATLES

Johnny PRESTON U.S., male vocalist

17 Mar 60 RUNNING BEAR Mercury AMT 1079 2 wks

PRETENDERS U.K./U.S., male/female vocal/instrumental group

19 Jan 80 BRASS IN POCKET Real ARE 11 2 wks

PROCOL HARUM U.K., male vocal/instrumental group

8 Jun 67 A WHITER SHADE OF PALE Deram DM 126 6 wks

Gary PUCKETT – *See* UNION GAP featuring Gary PUCKETT

PUSSYCAT Holland, male/female vocal/instrumental group

4 Sep 76	MISSISSIPPI	Sonet SON 2077	4 wks

Suzi QUATRO U.S., female vocalist/instrumentalist – guitar

16 Jun 73	CAN THE CAN	RAK 150	1 wk
23 Feb 74	DEVIL GATE DRIVE	RAK 167	2 wks

QUEEN U.K., male vocal/instrumental group

29 Nov 75	BOHEMIAN RHAPSODY	EMI 2375	9 wks

See also QUEEN and David BOWIE

QUEEN and David BOWIE UK, male vocal/instrumental group with guest vocalist

21 Nov 81	UNDER PRESSURE	EMI 5250	2 wks

See also QUEEN, David BOWIE.

Marvin RAINWATER U.S., male vocalist

25 Apr 58	WHOLE LOTTA WOMAN	MGM 974	3 wks

Johnnie RAY U.S., male vocalist

30 Apr 54	SUCH A NIGHT	Philips PB 244	1 wk
16 Nov 56	JUST WALKIN' IN THE RAIN	Philips PB 624	7 wks
7 Jun 57	YES TONIGHT JOSEPHINE	Philips PB 686	3 wks

REAL THING U.K., male vocal/instrumental group

26 Jun 76	YOU TO ME ARE EVERYTHING	Pye International 7N 25709	3 wks

Jim REEVES U.S., male vocalist

22 Sep 66	DISTANT DRUMS	RCA 1537	5 wks

Cliff RICHARD U.K., male vocalist

31 Jul 59	LIVING DOLL	Columbia DB 4306	6 wks
30 Oct 59	TRAVELLIN' LIGHT	Columbia DB 4351	5 wks
28 Jul 60	PLEASE DON'T TEASE	Columbia DB 4479	1 wk
11 Aug 60	PLEASE DON'T TEASE	Columbia DB 4479	2 wks
29 Dec 60	I LOVE YOU	Columbia DB 4547	2 wks
11 Jan 62	THE YOUNG ONES	Columbia DB 4761	6 wks
3 Jan 63	THE NEXT TIME/BACHELOR BOY	Columbia DB 4950	3 wks
14 Mar 63	SUMMER HOLIDAY	Columbia DB 4977	2 wks
4 Apr 63	SUMMER HOLIDAY	Columbia DB 4977	1 wk
15 Apr 65	THE MINUTE YOU'RE GONE	Columbia DB 7496	1 wk
10 Apr 68	CONGRATULATIONS	Columbia DB 8376	2 wks
25 Aug 79	WE DON'T TALK ANYMORE	EMI 2975	4 wks

The SHADOWS appear on all Cliff's number ones up to and including 'Summer Holiday'. See also SHADOWS.

Wendy RICHARD – *See* Mike SARNE with Wendy RICHARD

RIGHTEOUS BROTHERS U.S., male vocal duo

4 Feb 65	YOU'VE LOST THAT LOVIN' FEELIN'	London HLU 9943	2 wks

Smokey ROBINSON U.S., male vocalist

13 Jun 81	BEING WITH YOU	Motown TMG 1223	2 wks

See also Smokey ROBINSON and the MIRACLES.

Smokey ROBINSON and the MIRACLES U.S., male vocal group

12 Sep 70	TEARS OF A CLOWN	Tamla Motown TMG 745	1 wk

Lord ROCKINGHAM'S XI U.K., orchestra

28 Nov 58	HOOTS MON	Decca F 11059	3 wks

Tommy ROE U.S., male vocalist

4 Jun 69	DIZZY	Stateside SS 2143	1 wk

Kenny ROGERS U.S., male vocalist

18 Jun 77	LUCILLE	United Artists UP 36242	1 wk
16 Feb 80	COWARD OF THE COUNTY	United Artists UP 614	2 wks

The ROLLING STONES U.K., male vocal/instrumental group

16 Jul 64	IT'S ALL OVER NOW	Decca F 11934	1 wk
3 Dec 64	LITTLE RED ROOSTER	Decca F 12014	1 wk
18 Mar 65	THE LAST TIME	Decca F 12104	3 wks

9 Sep 65	(I CAN'T GET NO) SATISFACTION	Decca F 12220	2 wks
4 Nov 65	GET OFF MY CLOUD	Decca F 12263	3 wks
26 May 66	PAINT IT, BLACK	Decca F 12395	1 wk
19 Jun 68	JUMPING JACK FLASH	Decca F 12782	2 wks
23 Jul 69	HONKY TONK WOMEN	Decca F 12952	5 wks

Diana ROSS U.S., female vocalist

21 Aug 71	I'M STILL WAITING	Tamla Motown TMG 781	4 wks

See also SUPREMES.

Demis ROUSSOS Greece, male vocalist

17 Jul 76	THE ROUSSOS PHENOMENON (EP)	Philips DEMIS 001	1 wk

Tracks on The Roussos Phenomenon EP: Forever and Ever/Sing An Ode To Love/So Dreamy/My Friend The Wind.

ROXY MUSIC U.K., male vocal/instrumental group

14 Mar 81	JEALOUS GUY	Polydor ROXY 2	2 wks

The Pipes and Drums and Military Band of the ROYAL SCOTS DRAGOON GUARDS U.K., military band

15 Apr 72	AMAZING GRACE	RCA 2191	5 wks

Lita ROZA U.K., female vocalist

17 Apr 53	(HOW MUCH IS) THAT DOGGIE IN THE WINDOW	Decca F 10070	1 wk

RUBETTES U.K., male vocal/instrumental group

18 May 74	SUGAR BABY LOVE	Polydor 2058 442	4 wks

ST. WINIFRED'S SCHOOL CHOIR U.K., girls school choir

27 Dec 80	THERE'S NO-ONE QUITE LIKE GRANDMA	MFP FP 900	2 wks

Mike SARNE with Wendy RICHARD U.K., male vocalist with female vocal interruptions

28 Jun 62	COME OUTSIDE	Parlophone R 4902	2 wks

Peter SARSTEDT U.K., male vocalist

26 Feb 69	WHERE DO YOU GO TO, MY LOVELY?	United Artists UP2262	4 wks

Telly SAVALAS U.S., male vocalist

8 Mar 75	IF	MCA 174	2 wks

Leo SAYER U.K., male vocalist

19 Feb 77	WHEN I NEED YOU	Chrysalis CHS 2127	3 wks

SCAFFOLD U.K., male vocal group

11 Dec 68	LILY THE PINK	Parlophone R 5734	3 wks
8 Jan 69	LILY THE PINK	Parlophone R 5734	1 wk

SEARCHERS U.K., male vocal/instrumental group

8 Aug 63	SWEETS FOR MY SWEET	Pye 7N 15533	2 wks
30 Jan 64	NEEDLES AND PINS	Pye 7N 15594	3 wks
7 May 64	DON'T THROW YOUR LOVE AWAY	Pye 7N 15630	2 wks

SEEKERS Australia male/female vocal group

25 Feb 65	I'LL NEVER FIND ANOTHER YOU	Columbia DB 7431	2 wks
25 Nov 65	THE CARNIVAL IS OVER	Columbia DB 7711	3 wks

SHADOWS U.K., male instrumental group

25 Aug 60	APACHE	Columbia DB 4484	5 wks
5 Oct 61	KON-TIKI	Columbia DB 4698	1 wk
22 Mar 62	WONDERFUL LAND	Columbia DB 4790	8 wks
24 Jan 63	DANCE ON!	Columbia DB 4948	1 wk
28 Mar 63	FOOT TAPPER	Columbia DB 4984	1 wk

See also Cliff RICHARD.

Del SHANNON U.S., male vocalist

29 Jun 61	RUNAWAY	London HLX 9317	3 wks

Helen SHAPIRO U.K., female vocalist

10 Aug 61	YOU DON'T KNOW	Columbia DB 4670	3 wks
19 Oct 61	WALKIN' BACK TO HAPPINESS	Columbia DB 4715	3 wks

Sandie SHAW U.K., female vocalist

22 Oct 64	(THERE'S) ALWAYS SOMETHING THERE TO REMIND ME	Pye 7N 15704	3 wks
27 May 65	LONG LIVE LOVE	Pye 7N 15841	3 wks
27 Apr 67	PUPPET ON A STRING	Pye 7N 17272	3 wks

Anne SHELTON U.K., female vocalist

21 Sep 56	LAY DOWN YOUR ARMS	Philips PB 616	4 wks

SHONDELLS – *See* Tommy JAMES and the SHONDELLS

SHOWADDYWADDY U.K., male vocal/instrumental group

4 Dec 76	UNDER THE MOON OF LOVE	Bell 1495	3 wks

SIMON and GARFUNKEL U.S., male vocal duo

28 Mar 70	BRIDGE OVER TROUBLED WATER	CBS 4790	3 wks

Frank SINATRA U.S., male vocalist

17 Sep 54	THREE COINS IN THE FOUNTAIN	Capitol CL 14120	3 wks
2 Jun 66	STRANGERS IN THE NIGHT	Reprise RS 23052	3 wks

See also Nancy SINATRA and Frank SINATRA.

Nancy SINATRA U.S., female vocalist

17 Feb 66	THESE BOOTS ARE MADE FOR WALKIN'	Reprise R 20432	4 wks

See also Nancy SINATRA and Frank SINATRA.

Nancy SINATRA and Frank SINATRA U.S., male/female vocal duo

13 Apr 67	SOMETHING STUPID	Reprise RS 23166	2 wks

See also Nancy SINATRA, Frank SINATRA.

SLADE U.K., male vocal/instrumental group

13 Nov 71	COZ I LUV YOU	Polydor 2058 155	4 wks
1 Jul 72	TAKE ME BAK 'OME	Polydor 2058 231	1 wk
9 Sep 72	MAMA WEER ALL CRAZEE NOW	Polydor 2058 274	3 wks
3 Mar 73	CUM ON FEEL THE NOIZE	Polydor 2058 339	4 wks
30 Jun 73	SKWEEZE ME PLEEZE ME	Polydor 2058 377	3 wks
15 Dec 73	MERRY XMAS EVERYBODY	Polydor 2058 422	5 wks

SLIK U.K., male vocal/instrumental group

14 Feb 76	FOREVER AND EVER	Bell 1464	1 wk

SMALL FACES U.K., male vocal/instrumental group

15 Sep 66	ALL OR NOTHING	Decca F 12470	1 wk

SOFT CELL U.K., male vocal/instrumental duo

5 Sep 81	TAINTED LOVE	Bizarre BZS 2	2 wks

SONNY and CHER U.S., male/female vocal duo

26 Aug 65	I GOT YOU, BABE	Atlantic AT 4035	2 wks

David SOUL U.S., male vocalist

15 Jan 77	DON'T GIVE UP ON US	Private Stock PVT 84	4 wks
8 Oct 77	SILVER LADY	Private Stock PVT 115	3 wks

SPECIALS, The U.K., male vocal/instrumental group

2 Feb 80	THE SPECIAL A.K.A. LIVE (EP)	2 Tone CHS TT 7	2 wks
11 Jul 81	GHOST TOWN	2 Tone CHS TT 17	3 wks

Tracks on The Special A.K.A. Live (EP): Too Much Too Young, Guns of Navarone, Long Shot Kick The Bucket, The Liquidator, Skinhead Moonstop.

SPINNERS – *See* DETROIT SPINNERS

Dusty SPRINGFIELD U.K., female vocalist

28 Apr 66	YOU DON'T HAVE TO SAY YOU LOVE ME	Philips BF 1482	1 wk

Jo STAFFORD U.S., female vocalist

16 Jan 53	YOU BELONG TO ME	Columbia DB 3152	1 wk

Alvin STARDUST U.K., male vocalist

9 Mar 74	JEALOUS MIND	Magnet MAG 5	1 wk

STARGAZERS U.K., male/female vocal group

10 Apr 53	BROKEN WINGS	Decca F 10047	1 wk
12 Mar 54	I SEE THE MOON	Decca F 10213	5 wks
23 Apr 54	I SEE THE MOON	Decca F10213	1 wk

Kay STARR U.S., female vocalist

23 Jan 53	COMES A-LONG A-LOVE	Capitol CL 13876	1 wk
30 Mar 56	ROCK AND ROLL WALTZ	HMV POP 168	1 wk

STATUS QUO U.K., male vocal/instrumental group

18 Jan 75	DOWN DOWN	Vertigo 6059 114	1 wk

Tommy STEELE U.K., male vocalist

11 Jan 57	SINGING THE BLUES	Decca F 10819	1 wk

Ray STEVENS U.S., male vocalist

15 Jun 74	THE STREAK	Janus 6146 201	1 wk

Shakin' STEVENS U.K., male vocalist

28 Mar 81	THIS OLE HOUSE	Epic EPC 9555	3 wks
1 Aug 81	GREEN DOOR	Epic EPCA 1354	4 wks
30 Jan 82	OH JULIE	Epic EPCA 1742	1 wk

Dave STEWART with Barbara GASKIN U.K., male instrumentalist – keyboards with female vocalist

17 Oct 81	IT'S MY PARTY	Stiff/Broken BROKEN 2	4 wks

Rod STEWART U.K., male vocalist

9 Oct 71	MAGGIE MAY	Mercury 6052 097	5 wks
2 Sep 72	YOU WEAR IT WELL	Mercury 6052 171	1 wk
6 Sep 75	SAILING	Warner Brothers K 16600	4 wks
21 May 77	I DON'T WANT TO TALK ABOUT IT/FIRST CUT IS THE DEEPEST	Riva 7	4 wks
2 Dec 78	DA YA THINK I'M SEXY	Riva 17	1 wk

STINGERS – *See* B.BUMBLE and the STINGERS

Barbra STREISAND U.S., female vocalist

25 Oct 80	WOMAN IN LOVE	CBS 8966	3 wks

STYLISTICS U.S., male vocal group

16 Aug 75	CAN'T GIVE YOU ANYTHING (BUT MY LOVE)	AVCO 6105 039	3 wks

Donna SUMMER U.S., female vocalist

23 Jul 77	I FEEL LOVE	GTO GT 100	4 wks

SUPREMES U.S., female vocal group

19 Nov 64	BABY LOVE	Stateside SS 350	2 wks

Uncredited lead singer is Diana ROSS
See Diana ROSS.

SWEET U.K., male vocal/instrumental group

27 Jan 73	BLOCKBUSTER	RCA 2305	5 wks

SWEET SENSATION U.K., male vocal group

19 Oct 74	SAD SWEET DREAMER	Pye 7N 45385	1 wk

T REX U.K., male vocal/instrumental group

20 Mar 71	HOT LOVE	Fly BUG 6	6 wks
24 Jul 71	GET IT ON	Fly BUG 10	4 wks
5 Feb 72	TELEGRAM SAM	T Rex 101	2 wks
20 May 72	METAL GURU	EMI MARC 1	4 wks

TAMS U.S., male vocal group

18 Sep 71	HEY GIRL DON'T BOTHER ME	Probe PRO 532	3 wks

TEENAGERS featuring Frankie LYMON U.S., male vocal group

20 Jul 56	WHY DO FOOLS FALL IN LOVE	Columbia DB 3772	3 wks

TEMPERANCE SEVEN U.K., male vocal/instrumental jazz band

25 May 61	YOU'RE DRIVING ME CRAZY	Parlophone R 4757	1 wk

10 CC U.K., male vocal/instrumental group

23 Jun 73	RUBBER BULLETS	UK 36	1 wk
28 Jun 75	I'M NOT IN LOVE	Mercury 6008 014	2 wks
23 Sep 78	DREADLOCK HOLIDAY	Mercury 6008 035	1 wk

On 'Dreadlock Holiday', 10 CC were a vocal/instrumental duo.

THREE DEGREES U.S., female vocal group

17 Aug 74	WHEN WILL I SEE YOU AGAIN	Philadelphia International PIR 2155	2 wks

THUNDERBIRDS – *See* Chris FARLOWE

THUNDERCLAP NEWMAN U.K., male vocal/instrumental group

2 Jul 69	SOMETHING IN THE AIR	Track 604-031	3 wks

TICH – *See* Dave DEE, DOZY, BEAKY, MICK and TICH

TIGHT FIT U.K., male/female vocal group

6 Mar 82	THE LION SLEEPS TONIGHT	Jive 9	3 wks

Johnny **TILLOTSON** U.S., male vocalist

12 Jan 61	POETRY IN MOTION	London HLA 9231	2 wks

TORNADOS U.K., male instrumental group

4 Oct 62	TELSTAR	Decca F 11494	5 wks

John **TRAVOLTA AND OLIVIA NEWTON-JOHN** U.S./U.K., male/female vocal duo

17 Jun 78	YOU'RE THE ONE THAT I WANT	RSO 006	9 wks
30 Sep 78	SUMMER NIGHTS	RSO 18	7 wks

See also Olivia NEWTON-JOHN and ELECTRIC LIGHT ORCHESTRA.

TREMELOES U.K., male instrumental group

18 May 67	SILENCE IS GOLDEN	CBS 2723	3 wks

See also Brian POOLE and The TREMELOES.

Jackie **TRENT** U.K., female vocalist

20 May 65	WHERE ARE YOU NOW (MY LOVE)	Pye 7N 15776	1 wk

TROGGS U.K., male vocal/instrumental group

4 Aug 66	WITH A GIRL LIKE YOU	Fontana TF 717	2 wks

TUBEWAY ARMY – *See* Gary NUMAN

Conway **TWITTY** U.S., male vocalist

19 Dec 58	IT'S ONLY MAKE BELIEVE	MGM 992	5 wks

TYMES U.S., male vocal group

25 Jan 75	MS. GRACE	RCA 2493	1 wk

TYPICALLY TROPICAL U.K., male vocal/instrumental duo

9 Aug 75	BARBADOS	Gull GULS 14	1 wk

UNION GAP featuring GARY PUCKETT U.S./Canada, male vocal/instrumental group

22 May 68	YOUNG GIRL	CBS 3365	4 wks

UNIT FOUR PLUS TWO U.K., male vocal/instrumental group

8 Apr 65	CONCRETE AND CLAY	Decca F 12071	1 wk

Ricky **VALANCE** U.K., male vocalist

29 Sep 60	TELL LAURA I LOVE HER	Columbia DB 4493	3 wks

Dickie **VALENTINE** U.K., male vocalist

7 Jan 55	FINGER OF SUSPICION	Decca F 10394	1 wk
21 Jan 55	FINGER OF SUSPICION	Decca F 10394	2 wks
16 Dec 55	CHRISTMAS ALPHABET	Decca F 10628	3 wks

Frankie **VAUGHAN** U.K., male vocalist

25 Jan 57	GARDEN OF EDEN	Philips PB 660	4 wks
7 Dec 61	TOWER OF STRENGTH	Philips PB 1195	3 wks

VILLAGE PEOPLE U.S., male vocal/instrumental group

6 Jan 79	YMCA	Mercury 6007 192	3 wks

WALKER BROTHERS U.S., male vocal group

23 Sep 65	MAKE IT EASY ON YOURSELF	Philips BF 1428	1 wk
17 Mar 66	THE SUN AIN'T GONNA SHINE ANYMORE	Philips BF 1473	4 wks

Anita WARD U.S., female vocalist

16 Jun 79	RING MY BELL	TK TKR 7543	2 wks

Barry WHITE U.S., male vocalist

7 Dec 74	YOU'RE THE FIRST THE LAST MY EVERYTHING	20th Century BTC 2133	2 wks

David WHITFIELD U.K., male vocalist

6 Nov 53	ANSWER ME	Decca F 10192	1 wk
11 Dec 53	ANSWER ME	Decca F 10192	1 wk
2 Jul 54	CARA MIA	Decca F 10327	10 wks

"Cara Mia" credited David Whitfield and the Mantovani Orchestra. See also Mantovani.

Slim WHITMAN U.S., male vocalist

29 Jul 55	ROSE MARIE	London HL 8061	11 wks

Andy WILLIAMS U.S., male vocalist

24 May 57	BUTTERFLY	London HLA 8399	2 wks

Danny WILLIAMS U.K., male vocalist

28 Dec 61	MOON RIVER	HMV POP 932	2 wks

Deniece WILLIAMS U.S., female vocalist

7 May 77	FREE	CBS 4978	2 wks

WINGS U.K./U.S., male/female vocal/instrumental group

3 Dec 77	MULL OF KINTYRE/GIRLS' SCHOOL	Capitol R 6018	9 wks

See also BEATLES, Paul McCARTNEY with Stevie WONDER.

WIZZARD U.K., male vocal/instrument group

19 May 73	SEE MY BABY JIVE	Harvest HAR 5070	4 wks
22 Sep 73	ANGEL FINGERS	Harvest HAR 5076	1 wk

Stevie WONDER – *See* Paul McCARTNEY with Stevie WONDER

WURZELS U.K., male vocal/instrumental group

12 Jun 76	COMBINE HARVESTER (BRAND NEW KEY)	EMI 2450	2 wks

Tammy WYNETTE U.S., female vocalist

17 May 75	STAND BY YOUR MAN	Epic EPC 7137	3 wks

Jimmy YOUNG U.K., male vocalist

24 Jun 55	UNCHAINED MELODY	Decca F 10502	3 wks
14 Oct 55	THE MAN FROM LARAMIE	Decca F 10597	4 wks

ZAGER and EVANS U.S., male vocal duo

30 Aug 69	IN THE YEAR 2525 (EXORDIUM AND TERMINUS)	RCA 1860	3 wks

PART 3

The Five Hundred Number Ones: Listed Alphabetically by Title

Different songs with the same title (e.g. **Forever And Ever** which has been a number one title for both Slik and Demis Roussos) are indicated by (A), (B) etc. Where there is no letter in brackets after the title, all recordings are of just one number. Individual titles of songs or tunes on the two EPs which reached number one are also included, as are the titles of the EPs.

The recording act named alongside each song title is not necessarily exactly the same act that is billed on the record, but is the act under whose name all the information about the title can be found in Part 2 of this book.

ALBATROSS
Fleetwood Mac 264
ALL I HAVE TO DO IS DREAM
Everly Brothers 73
ALL KINDS OF EVERYTHING
Dana 284
ALL OR NOTHING
Small Faces 223
ALL SHOOK UP
Elvis Presley 62
ALL YOU NEED IS LOVE
Beatles 235
ALWAYS YOURS
Gary Glitter 351
AMAZING GRACE
Royal Scots Dragoon Guards 312
ANGEL FINGERS
Wizzard 337
ANGELO
Brotherhood of Man 410
ANNIE'S SONG
John Denver 357
ANOTHER BRICK IN THE WALL (PART II)
Pink Floyd 448
ANSWER ME
David Whitfield 14
ANSWER ME
Frankie Laine 15
ANYONE WHO HAD A HEART
Cilla Black 164
APACHE
Shadows 106
ARE 'FRIENDS' ELECTRIC?
Gary Numan 439
ARE YOU LONESOME TONIGHT?
Elvis Presley 112
ASHES TO ASHES
David Bowie 464
AS I LOVE YOU
Shirley Bassey 81
ATOMIC
Blondie 452
BABY COME BACK
Equals 252
BABY JUMP
Mungo Jerry 297
BABY LOVE
Supremes 181
BABY NOW THAT I'VE FOUND YOU
Foundations 239
BATCHELOR BOY
Cliff Richard 144
BACK HOME
England World Cup Squad 286
BAD MOON RISING
Creedence Clearwater Revival 276
BAD TO ME
Billy J Kramer and the Dakotas 156
BALLAD OF BONNIE AND CLYDE, THE
Georgie Fame 242
BALLAD OF JOHN AND YOKO, THE
Beatles 272
BAND OF GOLD
Freda Payne 291
BARBADOS
Typically Tropical 375
BEGIN THE BEGUINE (VOLVER A EMPEZAR)
Julio Iglesias 490
BEING WITH YOU
Smokey Robinson 480
BILLY DON'T BE A HERO
Paper Lace 346
BLACKBERRY WAY
Move 265
BLOCKBUSTER
Sweet 325
BLUE MOON
Marcels 116
BOHEMIAN RHAPSODY
Queen 382
BRASS IN POCKET
Pretenders 449
BRIDGE OVER TROUBLED WATER
Simon and Garfunkel 283
BRIGHT EYES
Art Garfunkel 436
BROKEN WINGS
Stargazers 7
BUTTERFLY
Andy Williams 59
BYE BYE BABY
Bay City Rollers 368
CABARET
Louis Armstrong 249
CALL ME
Blondie 456
CAN THE CAN
Suzi Quatro 331
CAN'T BUY ME LOVE
Beatles 166
CAN'T GIVE YOU ANYTHING (BUT MY LOVE)
Stylistics 376
CAN'T HELP FALLING IN LOVE
Elvis Presley 133
CARA MIA
David Whitfield 20
CARNIVAL IS OVER, THE
Seekers 206
CAROLINA MOON
Connie Francis 75

CARS
Gary Numan 442
CATHY'S CLOWN
Everly Brothers 101
CHANSON D'AMOUR
Manhattan Transfer 402
CHERRY PINK AND APPLE BLOSSOM WHITE
Perez Prado 31
CHERRY PINK AND APPLE BLOSSOM WHITE
Eddie Calvert 33
CHIRPY CHIRPY CHEEP CHEEP
Middle of the Road 301
CHRISTMAS ALPHABET
Dickie Valentine 40
CINDERELLA ROCKEFELLA
Esther and Abi Ofarim 245
CLAIR
Gilbert O'Sullivan 322
CLAUDETTE
Everly Brothers 73
CLIMB EVERY MOUNTAIN
Shirley Bassey 125
COMBINE HARVESTER (BRAND NEW KEY)
Wurzels 390
COME OUTSIDE
Mike Sarne with Wendy Richard 137
COMES A-LONG A-LOVE
Kay Starr 3
COMPUTER LOVE
Kraftwerk 494
CONCRETE AND CLAY
Unit Four Plus Two 191
CONFESSIN'
Frank Ifield 153
CONGRATULATIONS
Cliff Richard 248
COWARD OF THE COUNTY
Kenny Rogers 451
COZ I LUV YOU
Slade 306
CRYING
Don McLean 460
CRYING IN THE CHAPEL
Elvis Presley 197
CUMBERLAND GAP
Lonnie Donegan 57
CUM ON FEEL THE NOIZE
Slade 326
DANCE ON!
Shadows 145
DANCING QUEEN
Abba 394
DA YA THINK I'M SEXY
Rod Stewart 429
DAYDREAMER
David Cassidy 339
DAY THE RAINS CAME, THE
Jane Morgan 79
DAY TRIPPER
Beatles 207
DECEMBER '63 (OH WHAT A NIGHT)
Four Seasons 385
DEVIL GATE DRIVE
Suzi Quatro 344
DIAMONDS
Jet Harris and Tony Meehan 146
DIANA
Paul Anka 63
DIANE
Bachelors 163
DISTANT DRUMS
Jim Reeves 224
D.I.V.O.R.C.E.
Billy Connolly 381
DIZZY
Tommy Roe 271
DO IT AGAIN
Beach Boys 256
DON'T CRY FOR ME ARGENTINA
Julie Covington 400
DON'T GIVE UP ON US
David Soul 399
DON'T GO BREAKING MY HEART
Elton John and Kiki Dee 393
DON'T LET THE STARS GET IN YOUR EYES
Perry Como 5
DON'T STAND SO CLOSE TO ME
Police 467
DON'T THROW YOUR LOVE AWAY
Searchers 168
DON'T YOU WANT ME?
Human League 491
DOUBLE BARREL
Dave and Ansil Collins 299
DO WAH DIDDY DIDDY
Manfred Mann 175
DOWN DOWN
Status Quo 363
DO YOU LOVE ME
Brian Poole and the Tremeloes 158
DO YOU MIND
Anthony Newley 100
DREADLOCK HOLIDAY
10 CC 426
DREAMBOAT
Alma Cogan 35
DREAM LOVER
Bobby Darin 87
DREAMS OF CHILDREN
Jam 454
EBONY AND IVORY
Paul McCartney with Stevie Wonder 499
ELEANOR RIGBY
Beatles 222
ERNIE (THE FASTEST MILKMAN IN THE WEST)
Benny Hill 307
EVERLASTING LOVE
Love Affair 243
EVERY LITTLE THING SHE DOES IS MAGIC
Police 488
EVERYTHING I OWN
Ken Boothe 359
EYE LEVEL
Simon Park Orchestra 338
FEELS LIKE I'M IN LOVE
Kelly Marie 466
FERNANDO
Abba 388
FIGARO
Brotherhood of Man 418
FINGER OF SUSPICION
Dickie Valentine 27
FIRE
Crazy World of Arthur Brown 255
FIRST CUT IS THE DEEPEST
Rod Stewart 405
FLOAT ON
Floaters 411
FOOL SUCH AS I, A
Elvis Presley 85
FOOT TAPPER
Shadows 149
FOREVER AND EVER (A)
Slik 384
FOREVER AND EVER (B)
Demis Roussos 392
FREE
Deniece Williams 404
FROM ME TO YOU
Beatles 151
GAMBLIN' MAN
Lonnie Donegan 61
GARDEN OF EDEN
Frankie Vaughan 55
GENO
Dexy's Midnight Runners 457
GET AWAY
Georgie Fame 219
GET BACK
Beatles 270
GET DOWN
Gilbert O'Sullivan 328
GET IT ON
T Rex 302
GET OFF MY CLOUD
Rolling Stones 205
GHOST TOWN
Specials 482
GIRLS SCHOOL
Wings 416
GIVE A LITTLE LOVE
Bay City Rollers 374
GIVE ME YOUR WORD
Tennessee Ernie Ford 30
GLAD ALL OVER
Dave Clark Five 161
GOING UNDERGROUND
Jam 454
GONNA MAKE YOU A STAR
David Essex 360
GO NOW
Moody Blues 185
GOOD THE BAD AND THE UGLY, THE
Hugo Montenegro and his Orchestra and Chorus 261
GOOD LUCK CHARM
Elvis Presley 136
GOOD TIMIN'
Jimmy Jones 103
GOOD VIBRATIONS
Beach Boys 226
GRANDAD
Clive Dunn 295
GREAT BALLS OF FIRE
Jerry Lee Lewis 66
GREEN DOOR
Shakin' Stevens 483
GREEN GREEN GRASS OF HOME
Tom Jones 227
GUNS OF NAVARONE
Specials 450
HARD DAY'S NIGHT, A
Beatles 174
HAVE I THE RIGHT
Honeycombs 176
HEART OF GLASS
Blondie 433
HELLO GOODBYE
Beatles 241
HELP!
Beatles 200
HERE COMES SUMMER
Jerry Keller 90
HERE IN MY HEART
Al Martino 1

HERNANDO'S HIDEAWAY
Johnston Brothers 38
HEY GIRL DON'T BOTHER ME
Tams 304
HEY JOE
Frankie Laine 13
HEY JUDE
Beatles 258
HIS LATEST FLAME
Elvis Presley 129
HIT ME WITH YOUR RHYTHM STICK
Ian and the Blockheads 432
HOLD ME CLOSE
David Essex 378
HOLD MY HAND
Don Cornell 23
HONKY TONK WOMEN
Rolling Stones 274
HOOTS MON
Lord Rockingham's XI 77
HOT LOVE
T Rex 298
HOUSE OF THE RISING SUN, THE
Animals 172
HOW CAN I BE SURE
David Cassidy 320
HOW DO YOU DO IT?
Gerry and the Pacemakers 150
(HOW MUCH IS) THAT DOGGIE IN THE WINDOW
Lita Roza 8
I BELIEVE
Frankie Laine 9
(I CAN'T GET NO) SATISFACTION
Rolling Stones 202
I CAN'T STOP LOVING YOU
Ray Charles 138
I'D LIKE TO TEACH THE WORLD TO SING
New Seekers 308
I DON'T LIKE MONDAYS
Boomtown Rats 440
I DON'T WANT TO TALK ABOUT IT
Rod Stewart 405
IF
Telly Savalas 367
(IF PARADISE IS) HALF AS NICE
Amen Corner 266
I FEEL FINE
Beatles 183
I FEEL LOVE
Donna Summer 409
IF YOU LEAVE ME NOW
Chicago 396
I GOT STUNG
Elvis Presley 80
I GOT YOU, BABE
Sonny and Cher 201
I HEARD IT THROUGH THE GRAPEVINE
Marvin Gaye 268
I HEAR YOU KNOCKIN'
Dave Edmunds 294
I LIKE IT
Gerry and the Pacemakers 152
I'LL BE HOME
Pat Boone 47
I'LL NEVER FALL IN LOVE AGAIN
Bobby Gentry 278
I'LL NEVER FIND ANOTHER YOU
Seekers 188
I LOVE TO LOVE(BUT MY BABY LOVES TO DANCE)
Tina Charles 386
I LOVE YOU
Cliff Richard 110
I LOVE YOU LOVE ME LOVE
Gary Glitter 340
I'M A BELIEVER
Monkees 228
IMAGINE
John Lennon 473
I'M ALIVE
Hollies 198
I'M INTO SOMETHING GOOD
Herman's Hermits 178
I'M THE LEADER OF THE GANG (I AM)
Gary Glitter 335
I'M NOT IN LOVE
10 CC 372
I'M STILL WAITING
Diana Ross 303
I'M WALKING BEHIND YOU
Eddie Fisher 10
I NEED YOUR LOVE TONIGHT
Elvis Presley 85
IN THE SUMMERTIME
Mungo Jerry 288
IN THE YEAR 2525 (EXORDIUM AND TERMINUS)
Zager and Evans 275
I ONLY HAVE EYES FOR YOU
Art Garfunkel 379
I PRETEND
Des O'Connor 253
I REMEMBER YOU
Frank Ifield 139
I SEE THE MOON
Stargazers 17
ISRAELITES, THE
Desmond Dekker and the Aces 269
IT DOESN'T MATTER ANY MORE
Buddy Holly 84
IT'S ALL IN THE GAME
Tommy Edwards 76
IT'S ALL OVER NOW
Rolling Stones 173
IT'S ALMOST TOMORROW
Dreamweavers 43
IT'S MY PARTY
Dave Stewart with Barbara Gaskin 487
IT'S NOT UNUSUAL
Tom Jones 189
IT'S NOW OR NEVER
Elvis Presley 109
IT'S ONLY MAKE BELIEVE
Conway Twitty 78
IT'S OVER
Roy Orbison 171
I'VE GOTTA GET A MESSAGE TO YOU
Bee Gees 257
I WANT TO HOLD YOUR HAND
Beatles 160
I WILL SURVIVE
Gloria Gaynor 435
JAILHOUSE ROCK
Elvis Presley 67
JANUARY
Pilot 365
JAPANESE BOY
Aneka 484
JEALOUS GUY
Roxy Music 476
JEALOUS MIND
Alvin Stardust 345
JE T'AIME...MOI NON PLUS
Jane Birkin and Serge Gainsbourg 277
JOHNNY REMEMBER ME
John Leyton 124
JULIET
Four Pennies 169
JUMPING JACK FLASH
Rolling Stones 251
(JUST LIKE) STARTING OVER
John Lennon 471
JUST WALKIN' IN THE RAIN
Johnnie Ray 52
KEEP ON RUNNING
The Spencer Davis Group 208
KING OF THE ROAD
Roger Miller 194
KNOCK THREE TIMES
Dawn 300
KNOWING ME KNOWING YOU
Abba 403
KON-TIKI
Shadows 126
KUNG FU FIGHTING
Carl Douglas 356
LADY MADONNA
Beatles 247
LAND OF MAKE BELIEVE
Buck's Fizz 492
LAST TIME, THE
Rolling Stones 190
LAST WALTZ, THE
Engelbert Humperdinck 237
LAY DOWN YOUR ARMS
Anne Shelton 50
LEGEND OF XANADU, THE
Dave Dee, Dozy, Beaky, Mick and Tich 246
LET THE HEARTACHES BEGIN
Long John Baldry 240
LET'S HAVE ANOTHER PARTY
Winifred Atwell 26
LILY THE PINK
Scaffold 262
LION SLEEPS TONIGHT, THE
Tight Fit 496
LIQUIDATOR
Specials 450
LITTLE CHILDREN
Billy J Kramer & the Dakotas 165
LITTLE PEACE, A
Nicole 500
LITTLE RED ROOSTER
Rolling Stones 182
LITTLE SISTER
Elvis Presley 129
LITTLE THINGS MEAN A LOT
Kitty Kallen 21
LIVING DOLL
Cliff Richard 88
LONELY THIS CHRISTMAS
Mud 362
LONG HAIRED LOVER FROM LIVERPOOL
Little Jimmy Osmond 324
LONG LIVE LOVE
Sandie Shaw 196
LONG SHOT KICK DE BUCKET
Specials 450
LOOK AT THAT GIRL
Guy Mitchell 12
LOVE GROWS (WHERE MY ROSEMARY GOES)
Edison Lighthouse 281
LOVE ME FOR A REASON
Osmonds 355
LOVESICK BLUES
Frank Ifield 142

LUCILLE
Kenny Rogers 406
MACK THE KNIFE
Bobby Darin 91
MAGGIE MAY
Rod Stewart 305
MAGIC MOMENTS
Perry Como 69
MAKE IT EASY ON YOURSELF
Walker Brothers 203
MAKE ME SMILE (COME UP AND SEE ME)
Steve Harley and Cockney Rebel 366
MAKING YOUR MIND UP
Buck's Fizz 478
MAMA WEER ALL CRAZEE NOW
Slade 319
MAMBO ITALIANO
Rosemary Clooney 28
MAMMA MIA
Abba 383
MAN FROM LARAMIE, THE
Jimmy Young 37
MARY'S BOY CHILD
Harry Belafonte 65
MARY'S BOY CHILD – OH MY LORD
Boney M 430
MASSACHUSETTS
Bee Gees 238
MATCHSTALK MEN AND MATCHSTALK CATS AND DOGS
Brian and Michael 421
MEMORIES ARE MADE OF THIS
Dean Martin 42
MERRY XMAS EVERYBODY
Slade 341
MESSAGE IN A BOTTLE
Police 443
METAL GURU
T Rex 313
MICHAEL
Highwaymen 127
MICHELLE
Overlanders 209
MIGHTY QUINN
Manfred Mann 244
MINUTE YOU'RE GONE, THE
Cliff Richard 192
MISSISSIPPI
Pussycat 395
MODEL, THE
Kraftwerk 494
MONY MONY
Tommy James and The Shondells 254
MOON RIVER
Danny Williams 131
MOULDY OLD DOUGH
Lieutenant Pigeon 321
MOULIN ROUGE
Mantovani 11
MR TAMBOURINE MAN
Byrds 199
MS. GRACE
Tymes 364
MULL OF KINTYRE
Wings 416
MY CAMERA NEVER LIES
Buck's Fizz 498
MY DING-A-LING
Chuck Berry 323
MY FRIEND THE WIND
Demis Roussos 392
MY OLD MAN'S A DUSTMAN
Lonnie Donegan 99
MY SON MY SON
Vera Lynn 24
MY SWEET LORD
George Harrison 296
NAME OF THE GAME
Abba 415
NEEDLES AND PINS
Searchers 162
NEXT TIME, THE
Cliff Richard 144
NIGHT FEVER
Bee Gees 422
NO CHARGE
J J Barrie 389
NO OTHER LOVE
Ronnie Hilton 46
NUT ROCKER
B Bumble and The Stingers 135
OB-LA-DI OB-LA-DA
Marmalade 263
OH BOY
Mud 369
OH JULIE
Shakin' Stevens 493
OH MEIN PAPA
Eddie Calvert 16
OH PRETTY WOMAN
Roy Orbison 179
ONE DAY AT A TIME
Lena Martell 445
ONE DAY IN YOUR LIFE
Michael Jackson 481
ONE NIGHT
Elvis Presley 80
ONLY THE LONELY
Roy Orbison 108
ONLY SIXTEEN
Craig Douglas 89
ON THE REBOUND
Floyd Cramer 117
ON THE STREET WHERE YOU LIVE
Vic Damone 72
OUT OF TIME
Chris Farlowe and the Thunderbirds 220
OUTSIDE OF HEAVEN
Eddie Fisher 4
PAINT IT, BLACK
Rolling Stones 215
PAPERBACK WRITER
Beatles 217
PLEASE DON'T TEASE
Cliff Richard 104
POETRY IN MOTION
Johnny Tillotson 111
POOR ME
Adam Faith 97
POOR PEOPLE OF PARIS
Winifred Atwell 45
PRECIOUS
Jam 495
PRETTY FLAMINGO
Manfred Mann 214
PRINCE CHARMING
Adam and the Ants 486
PUPPET ON A STRING
Sandie Shaw 232
PUPPY LOVE
Donny Osmond 316
PUPPY SONG, THE
David Cassidy 339
PUTTING ON THE STYLE
Lonnie Donegan 61
RAT TRAP
Boomtown Rats 428
REACH FOR THE STARS
Shirley Bassey 125
REACH OUT I'LL BE THERE
Four Tops 225
RELEASE ME
Engelbert Humperdinck 230
RETURN TO SENDER
Elvis Presley 143
RING MY BELL
Anita Ward 438
RIVERS OF BABYLON
Boney M 423
ROCK-A-BILLY
Guy Mitchell 58
ROCK-A-HULA BABY
Elvis Presley 133
ROCK AND ROLL WALTZ
Kay Starr 44
ROCK AROUND THE CLOCK
Bill Haley and his Comets 39
ROCK YOUR BABY
George McCrae 353
ROSE MARIE
Slim Whitman 36
ROULETTE
Russ Conway 86
ROUSSOS PHENOMENON (EP), THE
Demis Roussos 392
RUBBER BULLETS
10 CC 332
RUNAWAY
Del Shannon 120
RUNNING BEAR
Johhny Preston 98
SAD SWEET DREAMER
Sweet Sensation 358
SAILING
Rod Stewart 377
SAILOR
Petula Clark 113
SAN FRANCISCO (BE SURE TO WEAR SOME FLOWERS IN YOUR HAIR)
Scott McKenzie 236
SAVE YOUR KISSES FOR ME
Brotherhood of Man 387
SCHOOL'S OUT
Alice Cooper 317
SEASONS IN THE SUN
Terry Jacks 347
SECRET LOVE
Doris Day 18
SEE MY BABY JIVE
Wizzard 330
SEVEN TEARS
Goombay Dance Band 497
SHADDUP YOU FACE
Joe Dolce 475
SHAKIN' ALL OVER
Johnny Kidd and the Pirates 105
SHE
Charles Aznavour 352
SHE LOVES YOU
Beatles 157
SHE'S NOT YOU
Elvis Presley 140
SHE WEARS RED FEATHERS
Guy Mitchell 6
SHOW YOU THE WAY TO GO
Jacksons 407
SIDE SADDLE
Russ Conway 83

SILENCE IS GOLDEN
Tremeloes 233
SILVER LADY
David Soul 413
SING AN ODE TO LOVE
Demis Roussos 392
SINGING THE BLUES
Guy Mitchell 53
SINGING THE BLUES
Tommy Steele 54
SIXTEEN TONS
Tennessee Ernie Ford 41
SKINHEAD MOONSTOMP
Specials 450
SKWEEZE ME PLEEZE ME
Slade 333
SMOKE GETS IN YOUR EYES
Platters 82
SO DREAMY
Demis Roussos 392
SOFTLY SOFTLY
Ruby Murray 29
SOMEBODY HELP ME
Spencer Davis Group 212
SOMETHING IN THE AIR
Thunderclap Newman 273
SOMETHING STUPID
Nancy Sinatra and Frank Sinatra 231
SON OF MY FATHER
Chicory Tip 310
SO YOU WIN AGAIN
Hot Chocolate 408
SPACE ODDITY
David Bowie 380
SPECIAL A.K.A. LIVE (EP), THE
Specials 450
SPIRIT IN THE SKY
Norman Greenbaum 285
STAND AND DELIVER
Adam and the Ants 479
STAND BY YOUR MAN
Tammy Wynette 370
STARRY EYED
Michael Holliday 95
START
Jam 465
STORY OF MY LIFE, THE
Michael Holliday 68
STRANGER IN PARADISE
Tony Bennett 32
STRANGERS IN THE NIGHT
Frank Sinatra 216
STREAK, THE
Ray Stevens 350
STUPID CUPID
Connie Francis 75
SUCH A NIGHT
Johnnie Ray 19
SUGAR BABY LOVE
Rubettes 349
SUGAR SUGAR
Archies 279
SUMMER HOLIDAY
Cliff Richard 148
SUMMER NIGHTS
John Travolta and Olivia Newton-John 427
SUN AIN'T GONNA SHINE ANYMORE, THE
Walker Brothers 211
SUNDAY GIRL
Blondie 437
SUNNY AFTERNOON
Kinks 218
SUPER TROUPER
Abba 470
SURRENDER
Elvis Presley 119
SWEETS FOR MY SWEET
Searchers 155
TAINTED LOVE
Soft Cell 485
TAKE A CHANCE ON ME
Abba 419
TAKE ME BAK 'OME
Slade 315
TEARS
Ken Dodd 204
TEARS OF A CLOWN
Smokey Robinson and the Miracles 290
TEARS ON MY PILLOW
Johnny Nash 373
TELEGRAM SAM
T Rex 309
TELL LAURA I LOVE HER
Ricky Valance 107
TELSTAR
Tornados 141
TEMPTATION
Everly Brothers 121
THAT'LL BE THE DAY
Crickets 64
THEME FROM M*A*S*H (SUICIDE IS PAINLESS)
Mash 459
(THERE'S) ALWAYS SOMETHING THERE TO REMIND ME
Sandie Shaw 180
THERE'S NO-ONE QUITE LIKE GRANDMA
St Winifred's School Choir 472
THESE BOOTS ARE MADE FOR WALKIN'
Nancy Sinatra 210
THIS IS MY SONG
Petula Clark 229
THIS OLE HOUSE
Rosemary Clooney 25
THIS OLE HOUSE
Shakin Stevens' 477
THOSE WERE THE DAYS
Mary Hopkin 259
THREE COINS IN THE FOUNTAIN
Frank Sinatra 22
THREE STEPS TO HEAVEN
Eddie Cochran 102
THREE TIMES A LADY
Commodores 425
TICKET TO RIDE
Beatles 193
TIDE IS HIGH, THE
Blondie 469
TIE A YELLOW RIBBON ROUND THE OLD OAK TREE
Dawn featuring Tony Orlando 329
TIGER FEET
Mud 343
TIRED OF WAITING FOR YOU
Kinks 187
TOGETHER WE ARE BEAUTIFUL
Fern Kinney 453
TOO MUCH TOO YOUNG
Specials 450
TOWER OF STRENGTH
Frankie Vaughan 130
TOWN CALLED MALICE, A
Jam 495
TRAGEDY
Bee Gees 434
TRAVELLIN' LIGHT
Cliff Richard 92
TWELFTH OF NEVER, THE
Donny Osmond 327
TWO LITTLE BOYS
Rolf Harris 280
UNCHAINED MELODY
Jimmy Young 34
UNDER THE MOON OF LOVE
Showaddywaddy 397
UNDER PRESSURE
Queen and David Bowie 489
UP TOWN TOP RANKING
Althia and Donna 417
USE IT UP AND WEAR IT OUT
Odyssey 462
VIDEO KILLED THE RADIO STAR
Buggles 444
VINCENT
Don McLean 314
VOODOO CHILE
Jimi Hendrix Experience 293
WALKIN' BACK TO HAPPINESS
Helen Shapiro 128
WALKING ON THE MOON
Police 447
WALK RIGHT BACK
Everly Brothers 114
WAND'RIN STAR
Lee Marvin 282
WATERLOO
Abba 348
WAY DOWN
Elvis Presley 412
WAYWARD WIND
Frank Ifield 147
WE CAN WORK IT OUT
Beatles 207
WE DON'T TALK ANYMORE
Cliff Richard 441
WELCOME HOME
Peters and Lee 334
WELL I ASK YOU
Eden Kane 122
WHAT A WONDERFUL WORLD
Louis Armstrong 249
WHAT DO YOU WANT
Adam Faith 93
WHAT DO YOU WANT TO MAKE THOSE EYES AT ME FOR?
Emile Ford and the Checkmates 94
WHATEVER WILL BE WILL BE
Doris Day 49
WHAT'S ANOTHER YEAR
Johnny Logan 458
WHEN
Kalin Twins 74
WHEN A CHILD IS BORN (SOLEADO)
Johnny Mathis 398
WHEN I NEED YOU
Leo Sayer 401
WHEN WILL I SEE YOU AGAIN
Three Degrees 354
WHEN YOU'RE IN LOVE WITH A BEAUTIFUL WOMAN
Dr Hook 446
WHERE ARE YOU NOW (MY LOVE)
Jackie Trent 195
WHERE DO YOU GO TO, MY LOVELY?
Peter Sarstedt 267
WHISPERING GRASS
Windsor Davies and Don Estelle 371

WHITER SHADE OF PALE, A
Procol Harum 234
WHOLE LOTTA WOMAN
Marvin Rainwater 70
WHO'S SORRY NOW
Connie Francis 71
WHY
Anthony Newley 96
WHY DO FOOLS FALL IN LOVE
Teenagers featuring Frankie Lymon 48
WINNER TAKES IT ALL, THE
Abba 463
WITH A GIRL LIKE YOU
Troggs 221
WITH A LITTLE HELP FROM MY FRIENDS
Joe Cocker 260
WITHOUT YOU
Nilsson 311
WOMAN
John Lennon 474
A WOMAN IN LOVE (A)
Frankie Laine 51
WOMAN IN LOVE (B)
Barbra Streisand 468
WONDERFUL LAND
Shadows 134
WONDER OF YOU, THE
Elvis Presley 289
WOODEN HEART
Elvis Presley 115
WOODSTOCK
Matthews' Southern Comfort 292
WORKING MY WAY BACK TO YOU
Detroit Spinners 455
WORLD WITHOUT LOVE, A
Peter and Gordon 167
WUTHERING HEIGHTS
Kate Bush 420
XANADU
Olivia Newton-John and the Electric Light Orchestra 461
YEH YEH
Georgie Fame 184
YELLOW RIVER
Christie 287
YELLOW SUBMARINE
Beatles 222
YES SIR I CAN BOOGIE
Baccara 414
YES TONIGHT JOSEPHINE
Johnnie Ray 60
YMCA
Village People 431
YOU BELONG TO ME
Jo Strafford 2
YOU DON'T HAVE TO SAY YOU LOVE ME
Dusty Springfield 213
YOU DON'T KNOW
Helen Shapiro 123
YOU'LL NEVER WALK ALONE
Gerry and the Pacemakers 159
YOUNG GIRL
Union Gap featuring Gary Puckett 250
YOUNG LOVE
Tab Hunter 56
YOUNG LOVE
Donny Osmond 336
YOUNG ONES, THE
Cliff Richard 132
YOU REALLY GOT ME
Kinks 177
YOU'RE DRIVING ME CRAZY
Temperance Seven 118
YOU'RE THE FIRST THE LAST MY EVERYTHING
Barry White 361
YOU'RE MY WORLD
Cilla Black 170
(YOU'RE THE) DEVIL IN DISGUISE
Elvis Presley 154
YOU'RE THE ONE THAT I WANT
John Travolta and Olivia Newton-John 424
YOU TO ME ARE EVERYTHING
Real Thing 391
YOU'VE LOST THAT LOVIN' FEELIN'
Righteous Brothers 186
YOU WEAR IT WELL
Rod Stewart 318
YOU WON'T FIND ANOTHER FOOL LIKE ME
New Seekers 342

PART 4

The Five Hundred Number Ones: Facts and Feats

This section of the book should not be used as proof that Abba are a greater group than the Rolling Stones, nor that Burt Bacharach writes better songs than Carl Sigman. Statistics and information given in this part are subdivided as follows: **The Hits, The Record Labels, The Writers and The Producers**

Photo Brian Aris/Scope Features

One of three girls to have sung on at least five number ones, but the only girl to have written as many as three — Debbie Harry of Blondie

MOST NUMBER ONE HITS

17 Elvis Presley
Beatles (one 'with Billy Preston')
10 Cliff Richard (7 with the Shadows)
9 Abba
8 Rolling Stones
6 Slade
5 Blondie
Shadows (plus 7 with Cliff Richard)
Rod Stewart
4 Bee Gees
Everly Brothers
Frank Ifield
Frankie Laine
Guy Mitchell
Police
T.Rex
3 Brotherhood of Man
Buck's Fizz
Lonnie Donegan
Georgie Fame
Gerry and the Pacemakers
Gary Glitter
Jam
Kinks
John Lennon (plus 17 with Beatles)
Manfred Mann
Mud
Roy Orbison
Donny Osmond (plus 1 with Osmonds)
Johnnie Ray
Sandie Shaw
Searchers
Shakin' Stevens
10 cc

Olivia Newton-John has had two number one hits with John Travolta and one with Electric Light Orchestra. Frank Sinatra has had two solo number ones and one with Nancy Sinatra. Art Garfunkel has had two solo number ones and one with Paul Simon. David Bowie has had two solo number ones and one with Queen.

MOST WEEKS AT NUMBER ONE

73 Elvis Presley
65 Beatles (Paul McCartney 9 more with Wings and 3 more with Stevie Wonder, John Lennon 7 more solo, George Harrison 5 more solo)
35 Cliff Richard
32 Frankie Laine (one week top equal)
31 Abba
20 Slade
19 Everly Brothers (one week top equal)
18 Rolling Stones
17 Frank Ifield
16 Shadows (plus 28 weeks backing Cliff Richard)
T. Rex
John Travolta and Olivia Newton-John (Olivia Newton-John 2 more with Electric Light Orchestra)
15 Doris Day
Rod Stewart
14 Guy Mitchell (one week top equal)
13 Eddie Calvert
Perry Como

MOST CONSECUTIVE NUMBER ONES:

11 in a row	**Beatles** (FROM ME TO YOU through to YELLOW SUBMARINE/ELEANOR RIGBY, 1963 to 1966)
6 in a row	**Beatles** (ALL YOU NEED IS LOVE through to BALLAD OF JOHN AND YOKO, 1967 to 1969)
5 in a row	**Elvis Presley** (HIS LATEST FLAME through to RETURN TO SENDER, 1961 to 1962)
5 in a row	**Rolling Stones** (IT'S ALL OVER NOW through to GET OFF MY CLOUD, 1964 to 1965)
4 in a row	**Elvis Presley** (IT'S NOW OR NEVER through to SURRENDER, 1960 to 1961). The first number one hat-trick.
4 in a row	**T Rex** (HOT LOVE through to METAL GURU, 1971 to 1972)
3 in a row	**Frank Ifield** (I REMEMBER YOU, LOVESICK BLUES and WAYWARD WIND, 1962 to 1963). The first number one hat trick by a British act.
3 in a row	**Gerry and the Pacemakers** (HOW DO YOU DO IT, I LIKE IT and YOU'LL NEVER WALK ALONE, 1963). The first and only instance of an act hitting number one with each of their first three releases.
3 in a row	**Abba** (MAMMA MIA, FERNANDO and DANCING QUEEN, 1975 to 1976)
3 in a row	**Abba** (KNOWING ME KNOWING YOU, NAME OF THE GAME and TAKE A CHANCE ON ME, 1977 to 1978)

12 Blondie
Connie Francis
11 Lonnie Donegan
Tennessee Ernie Ford
Gerry and the Pacemakers
Engelbert Humperdinck
Johnnie Ray
David Whitfield (one week top equal)
Slim Whitman
10 Mud
Donny Osmond (plus 3 weeks with Osmonds)

Queen have been top for 9 weeks, plus 2 weeks with David Bowie. Art Garfunkel has been top for 8 weeks, plus 3 weeks with Simon and Garfunkel. Mantovani has been top for one week, plus 10 weeks backing David Whitfield

MOST WEEKS AT NUMBER ONE IN ONE CALENDAR YEAR

27 Frankie Laine 1953 (one week top equal)
18 Elvis Presley 1961
16 Beatles 1963
John Travolta & Olivia Newton-John 1978
15 Elvis Presley 1962
12 Connie Francis 1958
Frank Ifield 1962
Beatles 1964

LONGEST STAY AT NUMBER ONE BY ONE RECORD

Total Weeks
18 I BELIEVE Frankie Laine
11 ROSE MARIE Slim Whitman
10 CARA MIA David Whitfield

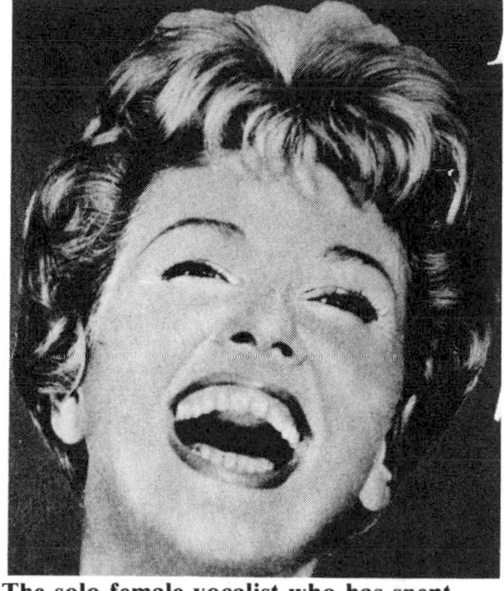

The solo female vocalist who has spent more weeks at number one than any other, Doris Day

9 HERE IN MY HEART Al Martino
OH MEIN PAPA Eddie Calvert
SECRET LOVE Doris Day
DIANA Paul Anka
BOHEMIAN RHAPSODY Queen
MULL OF KINTYRE/GIRLS SCHOOL Wings
YOU'RE THE ONE THAT I WANT John Travolta and Olivia Newton-John

Consecutive Weeks
11 ROSE MARIE Slim Whitman
10 CARA MIA David Whitfield
9 HERE IN MY HEART Al Martino
I BELIEVE Frankie Laine
OH MEIN PAPA Eddie Calvert
DIANA Paul Anka
BOHEMIAN RHAPSODY Queen
MULL OF KINTYRE/GIRLS SCHOOL Wings
YOU'RE THE ONE THAT I WANT John Travolta & Olivia Newton-John

3 in a row **Police** (MESSAGE IN A BOTTLE, WALKING ON THE MOON and DON'T STAND SO CLOSE TO ME, 1979 to 1980). The only instance of the third record of the hat trick coming on to the chart at number one.
3 in a row **Blondie** (ATOMIC, CALL ME and THE TIDE IS HIGH, 1980)
3 in a row **John Lennon** (IMAGINE, (JUST LIKE) STARTING OVER and WOMAN 1980 to 1981). Both the fastest and the slowest hat-trick, depending whether it started when IMAGINE first entered the chart or when (JUST LIKE) STARTING OVER came in late in 1980.

Successive releases for the purposes of this table are successive official single releases. The Beatles' two runs of number ones were each interrupted by irregular releases – an old single with Tony Sheridan reached number 29 in the middle of their 11 number ones spell, and their double EP Magical Mystery Tour made number two while Hello Goodbye was becoming the second of their six number ones on the trot. An LP track, Jeepster, and an old recording, Debora/One Inch Rock were released during T Rex's run of number ones, while the group were changing labels. An EP by Elvis, Follow That Dream pottered about the lower reaches of the charts durng Elvis' run of five consecutive number ones. During Police's hat-trick, one single on another label, one old single re-issued and one six-pack hit the charts in an attempt to confuse the compilers of this table. John Lennon's Imagine was the first of the three singles of his hat-trick to be released (his last single for five years), but the second of the three to reach the top.

8 ANSWER ME Frankie Laine (one week top equal)
SECRET LOVE Doris Day
MAGIC MOMENTS Perry Como
IT'S NOW OR NEVER Elvis Presley
WONDERFUL LAND Shadows
SUGAR SUGAR Archies

FIRST TWO HITS AT NUMBER ONE

Almost half the acts who have hit the top did so with their first chart hit. Only ten acts have started off with two number ones. They are:

Eddie Calvert (not consecutive releases), Adam Faith, Tennessee Ernie Ford (not consecutive releases), Art Garfunkel (not consecutive releases), Gerry and the Pacemakers, Mungo Jerry, Gary Numan/Tubeway Army, Stargazers (not consecutive releases), Rod Stewart, John Travolta and Olivia Newton-John.

Cliff was the first British performer to enter the charts at number one; he is the only act to have two records that returned to number one, and is the co-holder of the record for most number two hits

Of these acts, only Gerry and the Pacemakers, Mungo Jerry and John Travolta & Olivia Newton-John hit the top with their first two releases.

FIRST THREE HITS AT NUMBER ONE

Only Gerry and the Pacemakers have achieved this feat, and it is difficult to imagine it ever being equalled. These were their first three releases, and the group never had another number one hit.

ONE HIT WONDERS

Qualification: one number one hit and nothing else – ever.

1954 Kitty Kallen LITTLE THINGS MEAN A LOT
1956 Dreamweavers IT'S ALMOST TOMORROW
1958 Kalin Twins WHEN
1959 Jerry Keller HERE COMES SUMMER
1960 Ricky Valance TELL LAURA I LOVE HER
1962 B Bumble and the Stingers NUT ROCKER
1966 Overlanders MICHELLE
1967 Nancy Sinatra and Frank Sinatra SOMETHIN' STUPID
1968 Crazy World of Arthur Brown FIRE
1969 Zager and Evans IN THE YEAR 2525
Jane Birkin and Serge Gainsbourg JE T'AIME . . . MOI NON PLUS
Archies SUGAR SUGAR
1970 Lee Marvin WAND'RIN' STAR
Norman Greenbaum SPIRIT IN THE SKY

STRAIGHT IN AT NUMBER ONE

Only 13 records have gone straight into the chart at number one:

14 Nov 52	HERE IN MY HEART	Al Martino
24 Jan 58	JAILHOUSE ROCK	Elvis Presley
3 Nov 60	IT'S NOW OR NEVER	Elvis Presley
11 Jan 62	THE YOUNG ONES	Cliff Richard & The Shadows
23 Apr 69	GET BACK	Beatles with Billy Preston
3 Mar 73	CUM ON FEEL THE NOIZE	Slade
30 Jun 73	SKWEEZE ME PLEEZE ME	Slade
17 Nov 73	I LOVE YOU LOVE ME LOVE	Gary Glitter
15 Dec 73	MERRY XMAS EVERYBODY	Slade
22 Mar 80	GOING UNDERGROUND/DREAMS OF CHILDREN	Jam
27 Sep 80	DON'T STAND SO CLOSE TO ME	Police
9 May 81	STAND AND DELIVER	Adam & The Ants
13 Feb 82	A TOWN LIKE MALICE/PRECIOUS	Jam

Slade are the only act to go straight in at number one with consecutive releases. Jam, Adam and The Ants and Al Martino went straight in at number one with their first number one hit.

Matthews Southern Comfort WOODSTOCK
1971 Clive Dunn GRANDAD
1973 Simon Park Orchestra EYE LEVEL
1974 John Denver ANNIE'S SONG
1975 Typically Tropical BARBADOS
1976 J J Barrie NO CHARGE
Elton John and Kiki Dee DON'T GO BREAKING MY HEART
1977 Floaters FLOAT ON
1978 Althia and Donna UP TOWN TOP RANKING
Brian and Michael MATCHSTALK MEN AND MATCHSTALK CATS AND DOGS
1979 Anita Ward RING MY BELL
Lena Martell ONE DAY AT A TIME
1980 Fern Kinney TOGETHER WE ARE BEAUTIFUL
Johnny Logan WHAT'S ANOTHER YEAR
Mash THEME FROM M*A*S*H*
Olivia Newton-John and Electric Light Orchestra XANADU
St Winifred's School Choir THERE'S NO-ONE QUITE LIKE GRANDMA
1981 Joe Dolce SHADDUP YOU FACE
Dave Stewart with Barbara Gaskin IT'S MY PARTY
Queen and David Bowie UNDER PRESSURE
1982 Paul McCartney with Stevie Wonder EBONY AND IVORY
Nicole A LITTLE PEACE

***Yellow Submarine* was the Beatles' eleventh consecutive number one hit, and their ninth consecutive single to hit the top in its second week on the chart**

Of these performers, David Bowie, Kiki Dee, Electric Light Orchestra, Elton John, Paul McCartney, Olivia Newton-John, Queen, Frank Sinatra, Nancy Sinatra and Stevie Wonder have all had hits as solo acts. John Denver has also had a hit with Placido Domingo, and Dave Stewart has had a hit with Colin Blunstone.

The least successful of all these one hit wonders is Johnny Logan, whose Eurovision Song Contest winner stayed on the charts for only 8 weeks, two of which were at number one. The longest stay at number one by any one hit wonder is 8 weeks by the Archies. The longest stay in the chart by any one hit wonder is 34 weeks by Jane Birkin and Serge Gainsbourg.

Of the 36 one-hit wonders, (over 10 per cent of all number one acts), 4 were in the 1950's, 8 in the 1960's, 14 in the 1970's and already 10 in the 1980's. In recent years, the only acts to remove themselves from the list of one hit wonders after more than a year on the list are Art Garfunkel and the England World Cup Squad.

FASTEST NUMBER ONE HIT.

The period of time between an artist's first chart appearance and his first number one.

0 days	**Al Martino**	(14 Nov 52) *This was the first chart of all*
7 days	**Edison Lighthouse**	(24 to 31 Jan 1970)
	Mungo Jerry	(6 to 13 Jun 1970)
	Dave Edmunds	(21 to 28 Nov 1970)
	George Harrison	(23 to 30 Jan 1971)
	Queen & David Bowie	(14 to 21 Nov 1981)
	Nicole	(8 to 15 May 1982)
14 days	**20 different acts.**	

SLOWEST NUMBER ONE HIT: ARTIST

If an artist is going to have a number one hit, it usually happens within a year or two of the artist's first chart hit. About half of all number one acts have hit the top with their very first hit. The acts listed below are the only ones who took more than 10 years after their chart début to record their first number one hit.

18 years 216 days	**Johnny Mathis**	(23 May 1958 to 25 Dec 1976)
15 years 164 days	**Chuck Berry**	(21 Jun 1957 to 25 Nov 1972)
15 years 127 days	**Louis Armstrong**	(19 Dec 1952 to 24 Apr 1968)
14 years 279 days	**Barbra Streisand**	(20 Jan 1966 to 25 Oct 1980)
13 years 140 days	**Four Seasons**	(4 Oct 1962 to 21 Feb 1976)
12 years 260 days	**Pink Floyd**	(30 Mar 1967 to 15 Dec 1979)
11 years 183 days	**Tymes**	(25 Jul 1963 to 25 Jan 1975)
11 years 164 days	**John Lennon**	(9 Jul 1969 to 20 Dec 1980)
10 years 298 days	**Benny Hill**	(16 Feb 1961 to 11 Dec 1971)

It is interesting (slightly) to note that only John Lennon of these acts has had more than one number one hit and that four of the nine acts had the number one Christmas hit of their year. Chuck Berry missed this distinction by only 2 days, being displaced by Little Jimmy Osmond (who was not born when Berry's first hit entered the British charts) on 23 December 1972.

SLOWEST NUMBER ONE HIT: DISC

Only five records have taken longer than 200 days to reach the top after their first appearance on the chart.

6 years 63 days	SPACE ODDITY
David Bowie	(6 Sep 1969 to 8 Nov 1975)
5 years 70 days	IMAGINE
John Lennon	(1 Nov 1975 to 10 Jan 1981)
322 days	ROCK AROUND THE CLOCK
Bill Haley	(7 Jan 1955 to 25 Nov 1955)
307 days	EYE LEVEL
Simon Park	(25 Nov 1972 to 29 Sep 1973)
210 days	THE MODEL/COMPUTER LOVE
Kraftwerk	(11 Jul 1981 to 6 Feb 1982)

Apart from these discs, all of which reached number one in a second distinct run on the charts, the slowest climber to the top is ONLY THE LONELY by Roy Orbison. This hit the top 84 days after its initial entry on 28 July 1960, but it had spent 7 of those 84 days off the chart. The longest continual climb to number one is by four records which all reached the top in their twelfth week on the charts, as follows:

MOULIN ROUGE	Mantovani	(29 May 1953 to 14 Aug 1953)
WHAT A WONDERFUL WORLD/CABARET	Louis Armstrong	(7 Feb 1968 to 24 Apr 1968)
I PRETEND	Des O'Connor	(8 May 1968 to 24 Jul 1968)
JE T'AIME . . . MOI NON PLUS	Jane Birkin & Serge Gainsbourg	(30 Jul 1969 to 11 Oct 1969)

JE T'AIME changed labels after 10 weeks of chart action, by which time it had climbed to number two. The Major Minor version hit number one in its second week.

GAP BETWEEN NUMBER ONE HITS

Of all the acts who have had two or more number one hits, only four acts have suffered through a gap of more than 7 years between consecutive number ones. The Beatles crammed all 17 of their number ones into a period of 6 years and 54 days.

11 years 239 days	FRANK SINATRA	(7 Oct 1954 to 2 Jun 1966)
11 years 124 days	CLIFF RICHARD	(23 Apr 1968 to 25 Aug 1979)
9 years 231 days	BEE GEES	(10 Sep 1968 to 29 Apr 1978)
7 years 357 days	DON MCLEAN	(30 Jun 1972 to 21 Jun 1980)

There was a gap of 10 years 268 days between Smokey Robinson and the Miracles' TEARS OF A CLOWN and Smokey Robinson's BEING WITH YOU at number one.

LAST HIT AT NUMBER ONE

Excluding the one hit wonders (listed earlier) few of the 319 number one acts have failed to follow up a number one hit. Excluding those number one hitmakers who at the time of going to press had not issued a follow up to their latest hit, the list is very short, as follows. Charles Aznavour, Rolf Harris, Benny Hill, Tommy James and The Shondells, Pink Floyd, Specials, Kay Starr, Tams, 10 CC, John Travolta and Olivia Newton-John.

To add to their long list of original achievements, John Travolta and Olivia Newton-John share with Kay Starr the record of being the only acts to hit number one with both their first and their last chart hits. It should be noted that in the case of the Specials and John Travolta and Olivia Newton-John, their final hit was also their final release.

MOST WEEKS ON CHART BY A NUMBER ONE DISC

57 weeks	ROCK AROUND THE CLOCK	Bill Haley and his Comets
56 weeks	RELEASE ME	Engelbert Humperdinck
40 weeks	RIVERS OF BABYLON	Boney M
40 weeks	TIE A YELLOW RIBBON ROUND THE OLD OAK TREE	Dawn
36 weeks	I BELIEVE	Frankie Laine
36 weeks	I PRETEND	Des O'Connor
35 weeks	ALBATROSS	Fleetwood Mac
34 weeks	CHIRPY CHIRPY CHEEP CHEEP	Middle Of the Road
34 weeks	JE T'AIME . . . MOI NON PLUS	Jane Birkin and Serge Gainsbourg
33 weeks	SHE LOVES YOU	Beatles
31 weeks	SAILING	Rod Stewart
30 weeks	SIDE SADDLE	Russ Conway
30 weeks	YOUNG GIRL	Union Gap featuring Gary Puckett

RELEASE ME has the longest unbroken chart run of any record in the history of British pop music. ALBATROSS is the longest lasting instrumental of all, although SIDE SADDLE has the longest unbroken chart run of all the number one instrumentals.

Part of ROCK AROUND THE CLOCK also featured in HALEY'S GOLDEN MEDLEY which enjoyed a five week chart run in 1981.

FEWEST WEEKS ON CHART BY A NUMBER ONE DISC

7 weeks	CHRISTMAS ALPHABET	Dickie Valentine
8 weeks	LET'S HAVE ANOTHER PARTY	Winifred Atwell
8 weeks	LADY MADONNA	Beatles
8 weeks	MARY'S BOY CHILD – OH MY LORD	Boney M
8 weeks	MY CAMERA NEVER LIES	Buck's Fizz
8 weeks	START	Jam
8 weeks	A TOWN CALLED MALICE/PRECIOUS	Jam
8 weeks	HEY JOE	Frankie Laine
8 weeks	WHAT'S ANOTHER YEAR	Johnny Logan
9 weeks	GIVE A LITTLE LOVE	Bay City Rollers
9 weeks	ATOMIC	Blondie
9 weeks	CALL ME	Blondie
9 weeks	ALWAYS YOURS	Gary Glitter
9 weeks	MAKE ME SMILE (COME UP AND SEE ME)	Steve Harley and Cockney Rebel
9 weeks	GOING UNDERGROUND/ DREAMS OF CHILDREN	Jam
9 weeks	OH BOY	Mud
9 weeks	A LITTLE PEACE	Nicole
9 weeks	LOVE ME FOR A REASON	Osmonds
9 weeks	IF	Telly Savalas
9 weeks	FOREVER AND EVER	Slik

The Beatles, Boney M and Frankie Laine all feature in the long-running and the short-running number ones lists. For Boney M and Frankie Laine, their long-running number ones were followed fairly quickly by their short-running number ones. Frankie Laine's I BELIEVE came on the chart almost 7 months before HEY JOE, and dropped off only 2 weeks before it. Boney M's RIVERS OF BABYLON entered the charts over 7 months before MARY'S BOY CHILD – OH MY LORD, but outlasted it by 1 week.

DOUBLE SIDED NUMBER ONE HITS

The following are the only songs that were listed as double sided hits when the record was at number one. Some discs, while in reality double sided hits, were never listed as such (eg. WALK RIGHT BACK/EBONY EYES by the Everly Brothers). Some discs were double-

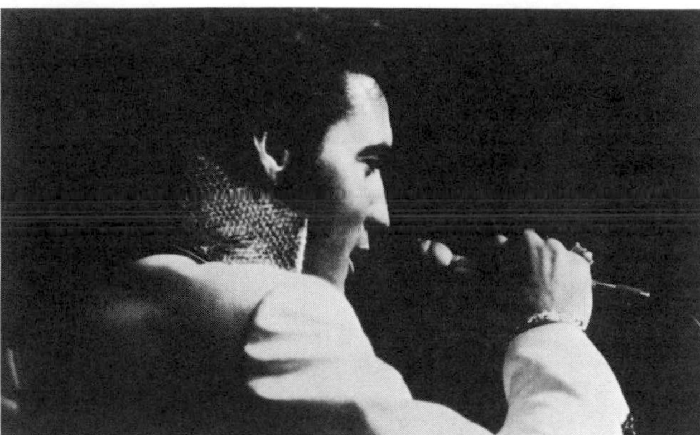

Among Elvis' more obscure chart records are Longest Span of Number One Hits (20 years and 88 days) and Most Double-Sided Number Ones (3)

sided hits only when the record was not at the top of the chart (eg. RIVERS OF BABYLON/BROWN GIRL IN THE RING). Sometimes in the early days of the chart, the two sides of the same record were given different chart placings (eg. MAGIC MOMENTS and CATCH A FALLING STAR by Perry Como). One disc, listed as a triple sided hit in the published chart, has been listed as THE SPECIAL AKA LIVE (EP) for our books.
The double sided number ones, in chronological order, are:

GAMBLIN' MAN/PUTTING ON THE STYLE Lonnie Donegan
ALL I HAVE TO DO IS DREAM/CLAUDETTE Everly Brothers
CAROLINA MOON/STUPID CUPID Connie Francis
ONE NIGHT/I GOT STUNG Elvis Presley
A FOOL SUCH AS I/I NEED YOUR LOVE TONIGHT Elvis Presley
REACH FOR THE STARS/CLIMB EV'RY MOUNTAIN Shirley Bassey
LITTLE SISTER/HIS LATEST FLAME Elvis Presley
ROCK-A-HULA BABY/CAN'T HELP FALLING IN LOVE Elvis Presley
NEXT TIME/BACHELOR BOY Cliff Richard
DAY TRIPPER/WE CAN WORK IT OUT Beatles
YELLOW SUBMARINE/ELEANOR RIGBY Beatles
WHAT A WONDERFUL WORLD/CABARET Louis Armstrong
DAYDREAMER/THE PUPPY SONG David Cassidy
I DON'T WANT TO TALK ABOUT IT/FIRST CUT IS THE DEEPEST Rod Stewart
MULL OF KINTYRE/GIRLS SCHOOL Wings
GOING UNDERGROUND/DREAMS OF CHILDREN Jam
THE MODEL/COMPUTER LOVE Kraftwerk
A TOWN CALLED MALICE/PRECIOUS Jam

RECORDS THAT RETURNED TO NUMBER ONE

after slipping for at least one week from the top

Date of return to number one		
3 Jul 53	I BELIEVE	Frankie Laine
21 Aug 53	I BELIEVE	Frankie Laine
11 Dec 53	ANSWER ME	David Whitfield (1=)
23 Apr 54	I SEE THE MOON	Stargazers
7 May 54	SECRET LOVE	Doris Day
19 Nov 54	HOLD MY HAND	Don Cornell
21 Jan 55	FINGER OF SUSPICION	Dickie Valentine
4 Feb 55	MAMBO ITALIANO	Rosemary Clooney
6 Jan 56	ROCK AROUND THE CLOCK	Bill Haley and his Comets
6 Apr 56	IT'S ALMOST TOMORROW	Dreamweavers

Like the Beatles, the Hollies derived their name from Buddy Holly and the Crickets, and recorded on Parlophone. Unlike the Beatles, they only hit the top with one record, but that one record had two spells at the top

18 Jan 57	SINGING THE BLUES	Guy Mitchell
1 Feb 57	SINGING THE BLUES	Guy Mitchell (1=)
11 Aug 60	PLEASE DON'T TEASE	Cliff Richard and the Shadows
28 Sep 61	JOHNNY REMEMBER ME	John Leyton
4 Apr 63	SUMMER HOLIDAY	Cliff Richard and the Shadows
28 Nov 63	SHE LOVES YOU	Beatles
12 Nov 64	OH PRETTY WOMAN	Roy Orbison
1 Jul 65	CRYING IN THE CHAPEL	Elvis Presley
8 Jul 65	I'M ALIVE	Hollies
21 Aug 68	MONY MONY	Tommy James and the Shondells
8 Jan 69	LILY THE PINK	Scaffold
15 Jan 69	OB-LA-DI OB-LA-DA	Marmalade

I BELIEVE and SINGING THE BLUES both had three stints at the top. What is more, a cover version of SINGING THE BLUES also topped the charts, giving the song four separate goes on top. The Dreamweavers are the only one-hit wonders to return to the top spot, and the Beatles fell off the top for the longest period before getting back – SHE LOVES YOU was in the top 10 for 7 weeks between its two spells at the very top.

Adam Faith shared the top spot with Emile Ford on 4 Dec 1959, but was on his own at the top of the first Record Retailer chart on 10 March 1960

Emile Ford's first week on top was the last time that two records shared the number one position

RECORDS THAT HAVE BEEN TOP EQUAL

11 Dec 53	ANSWER ME/Frankie Laine and ANSWER ME/David Whitfield
1 Feb 57	GARDEN OF EDEN/Frankie Vaughan and SINGING THE BLUES/Guy Mitchell
4 Jul 58	ON THE STREET WHERE YOU LIVE/Vic Damone and ALL I HAVE TO DO IS DREAM/CLAUDETTE/Everly Brothers
4 Dec 59	WHAT DO YOU WANT/Adam Faith and WHAT DO YOU WANT TO MAKE THOSE EYES AT ME FOR/Emile Ford

Since the introduction of the Record Retailer/Music Week chart in March 1960, there has never been a top equal.

LONGEST TITLES OF NUMBER ONE HITS

45 letters	SAN FRANCISCO (BE SURE TO WEAR SOME FLOWERS IN YOUR HAIR)
37 letters	MATCHSTALK MEN AND MATCHSTALK CATS AND DOGS
36 letters	(THERE'S) ALWAYS SOMETHING THERE TO REMIND ME
35 letters	WHAT DO YOU WANT TO MAKE THOSE EYES AT ME FOR?
34 letters	TIE A YELLOW RIBBON ROUND THE OLD OAK TREE
	WHEN YOU'RE IN LOVE WITH A BEAUTIFUL WOMAN
32 letters	YOU'RE THE FIRST THE LAST MY EVERYTHING
	I LOVE TO LOVE (BUT MY BABY LOVES TO DANCE)
31 letters	ERNIE (THE FASTEST MILKMAN IN THE WEST)
30 letters	CHERRY PINK AND APPLE BLOSSOM WHITE
	(HOW MUCH IS) THAT DOGGIE IN THE WINDOW
	THEME FROM M*A*S*H* (SUICIDE IS PAINLESS)
	EVERY LITTLE THING SHE DOES IS MAGIC

SHORTEST TITLES OF NUMBER ONE HITS

2 letters	IF
3 letters	SHE
	WHY
4 letters	CARS
	FIRE
	FREE
	GENO
	HELP
	WHEN
	YMCA

MOST NUMBER ONE HITS

Columbia	50
Decca	38
RCA	37
Pye/Pye International	30
Philips	29
Parlophone	27
CBS	25
London American	17
Polydor	17
Epic	17
HMV	15
Bell	13
Capitol	11
EMI	11
MGM	11

These are the big fifteen labels.
Next come:

Warner Brothers, Tamla Motown, Mercury	7
Rak, Chrysalis	6
Apple, Atlantic/Hansa, Fontana	5
Brunswick, Reprise, A & M, United Artists, RSO	4
Vogue/Coral, MAM, Harvest, Top Rank, Track	3
14 labels	2
41 labels	1

A total of 88 labels have been represented at the top of the charts.

MOST WEEKS AT NUMBER ONE

Columbia	165 weeks
RCA	141 weeks
Philips	109 weeks
Decca	107 weeks
Parlophone	92 weeks
Pye/Pye International	77 weeks
CBS	70 weeks
London-American	58 weeks

No other labels have spent more than one year at the top of the charts.

CONSECUTIVE LABEL CATALOGUE NUMBERS AT NUMBER ONE

Philips PB 616	LAY DOWN YOUR ARMS	Anne Shelton
Philips PB 617	A WOMAN IN LOVE	Frankie Laine
Philips PB 685	ROCK-A-BILLY	Guy Mitchell
Philips PB 686	YES TONIGHT JOSEPHINE	Johnnie Ray
MGM 974	WHOLE LOTTA WOMAN	Marvin Rainwater
MGM 975	WHO'S SORRY NOW	Connie Francis
RCA 1226	WOODEN HEART	Elvis Presley
RCA 1227	SURRENDER	Elvis Presley
CBS 3124	BALLAD OF BONNIE AND CLYDE	Georgie Fame
CBS 3125	EVERLASTING LOVE	Love Affair
Polydor 2058 421	YOU WON'T FIND ANOTHER FOOL LIKE ME	The New Seekers
Polydor 2058 422	MERRY XMAS EVERYBODY	Slade
RAK 166	TIGER FEET	Mud
RAK 167	DEVIL GATE DRIVE	Suzi Quatro

Catalogue numbers have become so personalised in the late 1970's and early 1980's (eg. Vertigo QUO 1, RCA BOW 1 etc) that consecutive releases now often do not have consecutive catalogue numbers.

Only two artists have had number one hits on three different labels:
T Rex, on Fly, T Rex and EMI
Rod Stewart, on Mercury, Warner Brothers and Riva.

Paul McCartney had hits on Parlophone and Apple while with the Beatles, and on Capitol with Wings. The catalogue numbers on all three labels were in the same sequence (eg. Parlophone R 5675, Apple R5722 and Capitol R 6018)

Anne Shelton's *Lay Down Your Arms* and Frankie Laine's *A Woman In Love* gave Philips two number ones with consecutive releases

The Writers

MOST SUCCESSFUL WRITERS

Most number one hits written or co-written. Double-sided hits count as one hit only for all writers concerned.

26 John Lennon
24 Paul McCartney
9 Benny Andersson
Bjorn Ulvaeus
7 Burt Bacharach
Mick Jagger
Keith Richard
6 Hal David
Noddy Holder
Jim Lea
Tony Macaulay
5 Stig Anderson
Mike Chapman
Nicky Chinn
Barry Gibb
Robin Gibb
Roy Orbison
Carl Sigman
Bruce Welch
4 Marc Bolan
Phil Coulter
Bob Gaudio
Maurice Gibb
Wally Gold
Oscar Hammerstein II
Bill Martin
Bob Merrill
Mitch Murray
Richard Rodgers
Mort Shuman
Sting
George David Weiss
3 Paul Anka, Jeff Barry, Otis Blackwell, David Bowie, L.Russell Brown, Luigi Creatore, Bob Crewe, Ray Davies, Ray Dorset, Gary Glitter, Graham Gouldman, Debbie Harry, Andy Hill, Tony Hiller, Mike Leander, Martin Lee, Jay Livingston, Jerry Lordan, Barry Mason, Giorgio Moroder, Hugo Peretti, Doc Pomus, Les Reed, Aaron Schroeder, Lee Sheriden, Chris Stein, Rod Stewart, Les Vandyke, Paul Francis Webster, Paul Weller, Roy Wood

After his erstwhile partner John Lennon, Paul McCartney is the most successful songwriter in British chart history

WRITERS OF CONSECUTIVE NUMBER ONE HITS

Gerhard Winkler, Fred Rauch and Carl Sigman	14	ANSWER ME David Whitfield
	15	ANSWER ME Frankie Laine
Melvin Endsley	53	SINGING THE BLUES Guy Mitchell
	54	SINGING THE BLUES Tommy Steele
Burt Bacharach and Hal David	68	STORY OF MY LIFE Michael Holliday
	69	MAGIC MOMENTS Perry Como
Bruce Welch	148	SUMMER HOLIDAY Cliff Richard (with Brian Bennett)
	149	FOOT TAPPER The Shadows (with Hank Marvin)
John Lennon and Paul McCartney	156	BAD TO ME Billy J Kramer & Dakotas
	157	SHE LOVES YOU The Beatles
John Lennon and Paul McCartney	157	SHE LOVES YOU The Beatles
	160	I WANT TO HOLD YOUR HAND The Beatles
John Lennon and Paul McCartney	166	CAN'T BUY ME LOVE The Beatles
	167	WORLD WITHOUT LOVE Peter and Gordon
Tony Macaulay and John McLeod	239	BABY NOW THAT I'VE FOUND YOU Foundations
	240	LET THE HEARTACHES BEGIN Long John Baldry
Mike Chapman and Nicky Chinn	343	TIGER FEET Mud
	344	DEVIL GATE DRIVE Suzi Quatro
John Lennon	473	IMAGINE John Lennon
	474	WOMAN John Lennon

The most successful writing partnerships are:

22	Lennon/McCartney
9	Andersson/Ulvaeus
7	Jagger/Richard
6	Bacharach/David
	Holder/Lea
5	Chapman/Chinn
4	Martin/Coulter
	Barry, Maurice and Robin Gibb
3	Crewe/Gaudio
	Glitter/Leander
	Hiller/Lee/Sheriden
	Pomus/Shuman
	Rodgers/Hammerstein

Debbie Harry is the only woman to have written as many as three number ones. She has written three for Blondie, two with Chris Stein and one with Giorgio Moroder. Jerry Lordan is the only person to have written three instrumental number ones.

MOST VERSATILE WRITERS

The only writers who have written number one hits for at least five different acts are:

John Lennon	8
Paul McCartney	8
Burt Bacharach	7
Hal David	6
Tony Macaulay	5
Carl Sigman	5

Paul McCartney holds the unique distinction of having performed on a total of 19 number ones with three acts (Beatles, Wings and Paul McCartney with Stevie Wonder): he has also written for these three acts and five other acts who made number one with his songs: he has produced Wings and the Beatles number one hits, and he has produced a number one for Mary Hopkin. Nobody else can match his versatility in the making of number one hits.

The Producers

MOST NUMBER ONES

Full or joint productions. Double-sided hits count as only one production for each producer.

27	Norrie Paramor
26	George Martin
17	Mitch Miller
15	Steve Sholes
11	Chet Atkins
10	Johnny Franz
9	Benny Andersson
	Mike Chapman
	Bjorn Ulvaeus
8	Dick Rowe
7	Tony Hatch
	Norman Newell
6	Chas Chandler
	Andrew Loog Oldham
	Mike Smith
5	Nicky Chinn
	Mike Curb
	Walter Ridley
	Wesley Rose
	Tony Visconti
4	Michael Barclay
	John Burgess
	Alan Freeman
	Barry Gibb
	Bunny Lewis
	Tony Macaulay
	Richard Perry
	Police (Sting, Andy Summers and Stewart Copeland)
	Shel Talmy
	Phil Wainman
3	Archie Bleyer, Larry Butler, Stuart Colman, Denny Cordell, Don Costa, Phil Coulter, Tom Dowd, Milt Gabler, Albhy Galuten, Maurice Gibb, Robin Gibb, Graham Gouldman, Nigel Gray, Andy Hill, Tony Hiller, Roy Horricks, Mike Leander, John Lennon, Joe Meek, Hugh Mendl, Jimmy Miller, Mickie Most, Yoko Ono, Karl Richardson, Phil Spector, Eric Stewart, Peter Sullivan and Hugo Winterhalter

MOST NUMBER ONES WITH DIFFERENT ACTS

This table is designed to distinguish the professional producer from the performer who also produces (eg. Andersson and Ulvaeus). Of the acts who have produced number one hits for three or more acts, only Mitch Miller has had a Top 10 hit in UK, and only Mickie Most ever had a career as a pop singer. Orchestras conducted by Norrie Paramor, Tony Hatch and Mike Curb have had hits, as well as Mitch Miller, and Chet Atkins has had one hit single in UK. But basically the only way to be a versatile producer is not to be a performer too.

Norrie Paramor	9
Mitch Miller	8
Johnny Franz	8
George Martin	6
Mike Smith	6
Norman Newell	6
Tony Hatch	5
Walter Ridley	5
Dick Rowe	5
Richard Perry	4
Chet Atkins	3
Michael Barclay	3
Archie Bleyer	3
Mike Chapman	3
Denny Cordell	3
Phil Coulter	3
Mike Curb	3
Milt Gabler	3
Bunny Lewis	3
Tony Macaulay	3
Joe Meek	3
Hugh Mendl	3

Mickie Most	3
Phil Spector	3
Phil Wainman	3

Mike Smith, with 6 number ones by six different acts, has produced the most number ones without ever producing two for any one act.

The most prolific producer of chart-toppers. No less than seven of Norrie Paramor's 27 number one productions were instrumentals

Producer of seven number ones, but writer of only one, his wife's only big smash *Where Are You Now (My Love)* — Tony Hatch

CONSECUTIVE NUMBER ONES

The producer's hat trick has been performed seven times as follows.

Mitch Miller	9	I BELIEVE	Frankie Laine
	12	LOOK AT THAT GIRL	Guy Mitchell
	13	HEY JOE	Frankie Laine
Mitch Miller	51	A WOMAN IN LOVE	Frankie Laine
	52	JUST WALKIN' IN THE RAIN	Johnnie Ray
	53	SINGING THE BLUES	Guy Mitchell
Norrie Paramor	104	PLEASE DON'T TEASE	Cliff Richard & The Shadows
	106	APACHE	Shadows
	107	TELL LAURA I LOVE HER	Ricky Valance
Norrie Paramor	147	WAYWARD WIND	Frank Ifield
	148	SUMMER HOLIDAY	Cliff Richard & The Shadows
	149	FOOT TAPPER	Shadows
George Martin	150	HOW DO YOU DO IT	Gerry & The Pacemakers
	151	FROM ME TO YOU	Beatles
	152	I LIKE IT	Gerry & The Pacemakers
George Martin	157	SHE LOVES YOU	Beatles
	159	YOU'LL NEVER WALK ALONE	Gerry & The Pacemakers
	160	I WANT TO HOLD YOUR HAND	Beatles
George Martin	164	ANYONE WHO HAD A HEART	Cilla Black
	165	LITTLE CHILDREN	Billy J Kramer & The Dakotas
	166	CAN'T BUY ME LOVE	Beatles

After FOOT TAPPER became the third of Norrie Paramor's second hat-trick, SUMMER HOLIDAY climbed back to number one, giving Norrie Paramor a 'fourth' consecutive number one.

Two number ones in a row has been achieved by eight production teams, most recently by John Lennon and Yoko Ono (IMAGINE and WOMAN).